CW01095846

The History of the Great Irish Famine of 1847

TO

MY FELLOW COUNTRYMEN

THIS NARRATIVE

OF ONE OF THE MOST TERRIBLE EPISODES

IN THE CHEQUERED HISTORY

OF

OUR NATIVE LAND,

IS

RESPECTFULLY AND AFFECTIONATELY

DEDICATED.

* * * * *

PREFACE.

The Author of this volume has, for a considerable time, been of opinion, that the leading facts of the Great Irish Famine of 1847 ought to be put together without unnecessary delay. Several reasons occurred to him why such a work should be done: the magnitude of the Famine itself; the peculiarity of its immediate cause; its influence on the destiny of the Irish Race. That there should be no unnecessary delay in performing the task was sufficiently proved, he thought, by the fact, that testimony of the most valuable kind, namely, contemporary testimony, was silently but rapidly passing away with the generation that had witnessed the Scourge.

Having made up his mind to undertake such a work, the Author's first preparation for it was, to send query sheets to such persons as were supposed to be in possession of information on the subject. And he has here to express his gratitude and thanks to his numerous correspondents, for the kindness and promptness with which his queries were answered. He cannot recall even one case in which this was not done. But there is a dark side to the picture too. In looking over the query sheets now, it is sad to find how many of those whose signatures they bear have already passed from amongst us.

Other materials of great importance lay scattered over the Public Journals of the period; were buried and stowed away in Parliamentary Blue Books, and Parliamentary debates;—were to be sought for in pamphlets, in periodicals, and more especially in the Reports of the various Societies and Associations, which were appointed for dispensing the alms given with such free hand, to aid in saving the lives of the famishing people.

Those Records will be found quoted and referred to in the course of the work.

Amongst them, it is but just to acknowledge, how much the Author owes to the Report of the Census Commissioners for 1851; to the "Transactions" of the Society of Friends; and to the *Irish Crisis*, by Sir Charles E. Trevelyan, Bart.; which originally appeared as an article in the *Edinburgh Review* for January, 1848, but was reprinted in a small volume of two hundred pages. Although far from agreeing with many of Sir Charles's conclusions (he was Secretary to the Treasury during the Famine), still the Author cheerfully acknowledges, that the statistical information in the *Irish Crisis* is very valuable to a student of the history of the Famine period.

It was to be expected, that the alarm about the Potato Blight and the Famine would be first raised through the public Press. This was done by letters from various localities, and by Special Reporters and Commissioners, who travelled through the country to examine the state of the people, as well as that of the potato crop. There was a Commissioner from the London *Times* in Ireland at this period. His letters written to that Journal were afterwards collected, and they made an octavo volume of nearly eight hundred pages.

The English people, and many in Ireland, long adhered to the opinion, that there was much exaggeration in the Irish Newspapers regarding both the Blight and the Famine; but subsequent investigation showed, that there was very little, if any, exaggeration; nay, that the real facts were often understated. As to the Famine, several of the gentlemen sent by the Charitable Societies to make Reports, wrote back, that there was no exaggeration whatever, and, for a very sufficient reason, namely, that, in their opinion, it was impossible to exaggerate the dreadful condition in which they found the people.

Another mode of acquiring information adopted by the Author was, to visit those parts of the country in which the Famine had raged with the greatest severity. On such occasions he not only had the advantage of examining the localities, but of conversing with persons whose knowledge of that awful Calamity made them valuable and interesting guides.

As to the rest, it is left to the kindness of the Reader.
ST. MARY'S, MAYNOOTH,
1st December, 1874.

* * * * *

CONTENTS

the frauds of tenants"—This Bill the basis of legislation on the Land Question up to 1870—Land thrown into Grazing—State of the Catholics—Renewal of the Penal Statutes—Fever and bloody flux—Deaths—State of Prisoners—Galway Physicians refuse to attend Patients—The Races of Galway changed to Tuam on account of the Fever in Galway—Balls and Plays!— Rt. Rev. Dr. Berkeley's account of the Famine—The "Groans of Ireland"—Ireland a land of Famine—Dublin Bay—The Coast—The Wicklow Hills—Killiney—Obelisk Hill—What the Obelisk was built for—The Potato more cultivated than ever after 1741—Agricultural literature of the time—Apathy of the Gentry denounced—Comparative yield of Potatoes a hundred years ago and at present—Arthur Young on the Potato—Great increase of its culture in twenty years—The disease called "curl" in the Potato (*Note*)—Failure of the Potato in 1821—Consequent Famine in 1822—Government grants—Charitable collections—High price of Potatoes—Skibbereen in 1822—Half of the superficies of the Island visited by this Famine—Strange apathy of Statesmen and Landowners with regard to the ever-increasing culture of the Potato—Supposed conquest of Ireland—Ireland kept poor lest she should rebel—The English colony always regarded as the Irish nation—The natives ignored—They lived in the bogs and mountains, and cultivated the Potato, the only food that would grow in such places—No recorded Potato blight before 1729— The probable reason—Poverty of the English colony—Jealousy of England of its progress and prosperity—Commercial jealousy— Destruction of the Woollen manufacture—Its immediate effect— William the Third's Declaration—Absenteeism—Mr. M'Culloch's arguments (Note A.)—Apparently low rents—Not really so—No capital—Little skill—No good Agricultural Implements—Swift's opinion—Arthur Young's opinion—Acts of Parliament—The Catholics permitted to be loyal—Act for reclaiming Bogs—Pension

Peel—Appointments of Drs. Lindley and Playfair to investigate the Blight—Sir R. Peel announces that he is a convert to the repeal of the Corn Laws—States his views, but does not reason on them—The Quarterly Review—Special Commissioners—Mr. Buller's letter—Sir James Graham and the Premier—Proceeding by Proclamation instead of by Order in Council—Sir James's sharp reply—Agitation to stop distillation—County Meetings proposed by the Lord Lieutenant—Cabinet Council—The Premier puts his views before it in a memorandum—The Corn Laws—Some of the Cabinet displeased with his views—On the 6th November he submits another memorandum to the Cabinet—Lord Stanley dissents from the Premier's views—The Cabinet meet again next day and he concludes the memorandum—On the 29th November he sends to each of his colleagues a more detailed exposition of his views—Several reply—Another mem. brought before them on the 2nd December—The Cabinet in permanent session—On the 5th of December Sir Robert resigns—Lord John Russell fails to form a Government—The old Cabinet again in power—Mr. Gladstone replaces Lord Stanley

Meeting of Parliament—Queen's Speech—The Premier's speech on the Address—Goes into the whole question of Free Trade—The protectionists—Lord Brougham's views (*Note*)—The twelve nights' debate on the Corn Laws—No connection between it and the Famine—Stafford O'Brien's speech—Sir James Graham's reply—Smith O'Brien's speech—His imprisonment (Note B.)—O'Connell's motion—His speech—Sir Robert Peel replies—Substantially agrees with O'Connell—Bill for the protection of life in Ireland—Its first reading opposed by the Irish members—O'Connell leads the Opposition in a speech of two hours—Mr. D'Israeli mistaken in calling it his last speech—His account of it—He misrepresents it—The opinions expressed in it were those O'Connell always held. Break up of the Tory party—Lord George Bentinck becomes leader of the Protectionists—Their difficulty in opposing the Coercion Bill—Ingenious plan of Lord George—Strange combination against the Government—Close of Debate on Coercion Bill—Government defeated by a majority of 73—Measures to meet the Famine—Delay—Accounts from various parts of the country—Great distress—"Are the Landlords making any efforts?"—Notice for rent—The bailiff's reply—Number of Workhouses open—Number of persons in them—Sir Robert Peel's speech on his resignation—Accident to him—His death—The Peels—Sir Robert's qualities and character—His manner of dealing with the Famine—His real object the repeal of the Corn Laws

John Russell Prime Minister—He confers important offices on some Irish Catholics—His address to the electors of London—Its vagueness—Addresses of some of the other new Ministers—The Irish difficulty greater than ever—Young and Old Ireland—The *Times* on O'Connell and English rule in Ireland—Overtures of the Whig Government—O'Connell listens to them—The eleven measures—Views of the advanced Repealers—Lord Miltown's letter to O'Connell—Dissensions in the Repeal Association—The "Peace Resolutions"—O'Connell's letters—He censures the *Nation* newspaper—Debate in the Repeal Association—Thomas Francis Meagher's "Sword speech"—The Young Ireland party leave Conciliation Hall in a body—Description of the scene (*Note*)—Reflections—Sir Robert Peel's speech after his resignation—Lord John Russell's speech at Glasgow—His speech on the Irish Coercion Bill—His speech after becoming Prime Minister—The Potato Blight reappears—Accounts from the

Provinces—Father Mathew's letter—Value of the Potato Crop of 1846—Various remedies, theories, and speculations—State of the weather—Mr. Cooper's observations at Markree Castle—Lord Monteagle's motion in the House of Lords for employing the people—Profitable employment the right thing—The Marquis of Lansdowne replies—It is hard to relieve a poor country like Ireland—Lord Devon's opinion—The Premier's statement about relief—The wonderful cargo of Indian meal—Sir R. Peel's fallacies—Bill for Baronial Sessions—Cessation of Government Works—The Mallow Relief Committee—Beds of stone!—High rents on the poor—The Social Condition of the Hottentot as compared with that of Mick Sullivan—Rev. Mr. Gibson's views—Mr. Tuke's account of Erris (*Note*)—Close of the Session of Parliament

The Labour-rate Act passed without opposition: entitled, An Act to Facilitate the Employment of the Labouring Poor—Its provisions—Government *Minute* explaining them—Heads of Minute—Rate of wages—Dissatisfaction with it—Commissary-General Hewetson's letter—Exorbitant prices—Opinion expressed on this head by an American Captain—The Government will not order food as Sir R. Peel did—Partial and unjust taxation—Opposition to the Labour-rate Act—Reproductive employment called for—Lord Devon's opinion—Former works not to be completed under the Act—Minute of 31st of August—Modified by Mr. Labouchere's letter of 5th of September—People taxed who paid a rent of £4 a year—In many cases a hardship—Barren works the great blot of the Labour-rate Act—Arguments against the Act—Resources of the country should have been developed—Panic among landowners—Rev. Mr. Moore's letters—Level roads a good thing—Food better—A cry of excessive population raised—

landlord and tenant—Discontent at rate of wages on public works being 2d. per day under the average wages of the district—Founded on error—Taskwork—Great dissatisfaction at it—Combination—Attempt on the Life of Mr. W.M. Hennessy—True way to manage the people (*Note*)—Stoppage of Works—Captain Wynne—Dreadful destitution—Christmas eve—Opposition to Taskwork continues—Causes—Treasury Minute on the subject—Colonel Jones on Committees—Insulting his officers—Insult to Mr. Cornelius O'Brien, M.P.—Captain Wynne at Ennistymon—A real Irish Committee—Major M'Namara—His version of the Ennistymon affair (*Note*)—Charges against the Gentry of Clare by Captain Wynne—Mr. Millet on Ennistymon—Selling Tickets for the Public Works—Feeling of the Officials founded often on ignorance and prejudice—The Increase of Deposits in the Savings' Banks a Proof of Irish Prosperity—How explained by Mr. Twistleton, an official—Scarcity of silver—The Bank of Ireland authorized to issue it—The Public Works of 1845-6 brought to a close in August, 1846—The Labour-rate Act—Difficulty of getting good Officials—The Baronies—Issues to them—Loans—Grants—Total—Sudden and enormous Increase of Labourers on the Works under the Labour-rate Act—How distributed over the Provinces—Number of Officials superintending the Public Works—Correspondence—Number of Letters received at Central Office—Progress of the Famine—Number employed—Number seeking employment who could not get it—The Death-roll

Operations of the Commissariat Relief Department—Not to interfere with Mealmongers or Corn Merchants—Effects of this Rule—Deputation from Achill (*Note*)—Organization of the Commissariat Relief Department—Reports on the Potato Crop—The Blight in Clare—Commissary-General Hewetson's opinion—

Commissary-General Dobree's Report—Depôts—Universality of the Blight—Rules with regard to Food Depôts—Fault of the Treasury—Scarcity of Food—Depôts besieged for it in the midst of harvest—Depôts to be only on the West Coast—What was meant by the West Coast—Coroner's Inquests at Mallow—Rev. Mr. Daly—Lord Mountcashel—Famine Demonstration at Westport—Sessions at Kilmacthomas—Riot at Dungarvan—Captain Sibthorpe's Order—Mr. Howley's Advice—Attempt to rescue Prisoners—Captain Sibthorpe asks leave to fire—Refused by Mr. Howley—Riot Act read—Leave to fire given—People retire from the town—Two men wounded—The carter's reason for fighting—Lame Pat Power—Death of Michael Fleming, the carter—Formidable bands traverse the country—Advice of the Clergy—Carrigtuohill—Macroom—Killarney—Skibbereen—March on that town by the workmen of Caheragh—Dr. Donovan's account of the movement—The military, seventy-five in number, posted behind a schoolhouse—Firmness and prudence of Mr. Galwey, J.P.—Biscuits ordered from the Government Store—Peace preserved—Demonstration at Mallow—Lord Stuart de Decies—Deputation from Clonakilty to the Lord Lieutenant—Ships prevented from sailing at Youghal—Sir David Roche—Demonstrations simultaneous—Proclamation against food riots—Want of mill-power—No mill-power in parts of the West where most required—Sir Randolph Routh's opinion—Overruled by the Treasury—Mr. Lister's Account of the mill-power in parts of Connaught—Meal ground at Deptford, Portsmouth, Plymouth, and Rotherhithe; also in Essex and the Channel Islands—Mill-power at Malta—Quantity of wheat there—Five hundred quarters purchased—The French—The Irish handmill, or quern, revived—Samples of it got—Steel-mills—Mill-power useless from failure of water-supply—Attempt to introduce whole corn boiled as food

Letter"—Quotes Smith O'Brien approvingly—Mr. O'Brien's
letters to the Landlords of Ireland (*Note*)—Confounding the
questions of temporary relief and permanent improvement—
Fallacy—Demoralization of labour—The Premier's "group
of measures"—Soup kitchens—Taskwork—Break down of
the Public Works—Food for nothing—Mode of payment of
loans—£50,000 for seed—Impossibility of meeting the Famine
completely—The permanent measures for Ireland—Drainage
Act—Reclamation of waste lands—Sir Robert Kane's "Industrial
Resources" of Ireland—Emigration again—Ireland not overpeopled—Description of England and Scotland in former times by
Lord John Russell—His fine exposition of "the Irish question"—
Mr. P. Scrope's Resolution—A count out—Bernal Osborne—
Smith O'Brien—The good absentee landlords—The bad resident
landlords—Sir C. Napier's view—Mr. Labouchere's kind words—
Confounds two important questions—Mr. Gregory's quarter-acre
clause—Met with some opposition—Irish liberals vote for it—The
opponents of the quarter-acre clause—Lord George Bentinck's
attack on the Government (*Note*)

Lord George Bentinck's Railway Scheme; he thought the finishing
of the railways would be useful; he was a practical man, and
wished to use the labour of the people on useful and profitable
work—The state of England in 1841-2—The remedy that relieved
England ought to have the same effect in Ireland—Under certain
arrangements, there could have been no Irish Famine—Tons
of Blue books—No new Acts necessary for Railways—1,500
miles of Railway were passed—Only 123 miles made—Lord
George Bentinck's speech—Waste of power—Traffic—Great
Southern and Western Railway—Principles of the Railway Bill—
Shareholders—What employment would the Railway Bill give?—

Mode of raising the money—£20,000,000 paid to slave-owners—
Why not do the same thing for Ireland?—Foreign Securities in
which English money has been expended—Assurances of support
to Lord George—The Irish Members in a dilemma—The Irish
Party continue to meet—Meeting at the Premier's in Chesham
Place—Smith O'Brien waits on Lord George—The Government
stake their existence on postponing the second reading of Lord
Bentinck's Bill—Why? No good reason—Desertion of the Irish
Members—Sir John Gray on the question—The Prime Minister's
speech—The Chancellor of the Exchequer's speech a mockery—
Loans to Ireland (falsely) asserted not to have been repaid—Mr.
Hudson's speech—The Chancellor going on no authority—Mr.
Hudson's Railway Statistics—The Chancellor of the Exchequer
hard on Irish Landlords—His way of giving relief—Sir Robert
Peel on the Railway Bill—The Railway Bill a doomed measure—
Peel's eulogium on industry in general, and on Mr. Bianconi in
particular—Lord G. Bentinck's reply—His arguments skipped by
his opponents—Money spent on making Railways—The Irish vote
on the Bill—Names

State of the Country during the Winter of 1847—State of Clare—
Capt. Wynne's Letter—Patience of the suffering people—Ennis
without food—The North—Belfast—great distress in it—Letter
to the *Northern Whig*—Cork—rush of country people to it—
Soup—Society of Friends—The sliding coffin—Deaths in the
streets—One hundred bodies buried together!—More than one
death every hour in the Workhouse—Limerick—Experience
of a Priest of St. John's—Dublin—Dysentery more fatal than
cholera—Meetings—"General Central Relief Committee for all
Ireland"—Committee of the Society of Friends—The British
Association for the Relief of Extreme Distress in Ireland and

number of deaths—Verdict of "Wilful murder" against Lord John Russell—The Workhouse at Bantry—Estimated deaths—The hinged coffin—Shafto Adair's idea of the Famine of the dismissals in various parts of the country—Soup kitchens attacked—Third Report of the Relief Commissioners—Questions from Inspectors—O'Connell's last illness—His attempt to reach Rome—His death—His character—Remaining Reports of the Relief Commissioners—The Accountant's department—Number of rations—Money spent

The Fever Act—Central Board of Health—Fever Hospitals—Changes in the Act—Outdoor Attendance—Interment of the Dead—The Fever in 1846—Cork Workhouse—Clonmel—Tyrone—Newry—Sligo—Leitrim—Roscommon—Galway—Fever in 1847—Belfast—Death-rate in the Workhouses—Swinford—Cork—Dropsy—Carrick-on-Shannon—Macroom—Bantry Abbey—Dublin—Cork Street Hospital—Applications for Temporary Hospital accommodation—Relapse a remarkable feature—Number of cases received—Percentage of Mortality—Weekly Cost of Patients—Imperfect Returns—Scurvy—The cause of it—Emigration—Earlier Schemes of Emigration—Mr. Wilmot Horton—Present Stats of Peterborough (Note)—Various Parliamentary Committees on Emigration—Their Views—The Devon Commission—Its Views of Emigration—A Parliamentary Committee opposed to Emigration—Statistics of Emigration—Gigantic Emigration Scheme—Mr. Godley—Statement to the Premier—The Joint Stock Company for Emigration—£9,000,000 required—How to be applied—It was to be a Catholic Emigration—Mr. Godley's Scheme—Not accepted by the Government—Who signed it—Names (Note)—Dr. Maginn on the Emigration Scheme—Emigration to be left to itself—Statistics of Population—The Census of 1841—Deaths from the Famine—

Deaths amongst Emigrants—Deaths amongst those who went to Canada—Emigration to the United States—Commission to protect Emigrants—Revelations—Mortality on board Emigrant Ships—Plunder of Emigrants—Committee of Inquiry—Its Report—Frauds about Passage Tickets—Evidence—How did any survive?—Remittances from Emigrants—Unprecedented—A proof of their industry and perseverance.

* * * * *

CHAPTER I.

The Potato—Its introduction into Europe—Sir Walter Raleigh—The Potato of Virginia—The Battata, or sweet Potato—Sir John Hawkins—Sir Francis Drake—Raleigh's numerous exploring expeditions—Story of his distributing Potatoes on the Irish coast on his way from Virginia groundless—Sir Joseph Banks—His history of the introduction of the Potato—Thomas Heriot—His description of the Opanawk a correct description of the Potato—That root in Europe before Raleigh's time—Raleigh an "Undertaker"—The Grants made to him—The Famine after the War with the Desmonds—Introduction of the Potato into Ireland—Did not come rapidly into cultivation—Food of the poorest—Grazing—Graziers—Destruction of Irish Manufactures—Causes of the increasing culture of the Potato—Improvement of Agriculture—Rotation of Crops—Primate Boulter's charity—Buys Corn in the South to sell it cheaply in the North—Years of scarcity from 1720 to 1740—The Famine of 1740-41—The Great Frost—No combined effort to meet this Famine—Vast number of Deaths—The Obelisk at Castletown (*Note*)—Price of Wheat—Bread Riots—Gangs of Robbers—"The Kellymount Gang"—Severe punishment—Shooting down Food-rioters—The Lord Lieutenant's Address to Parliament—Bill "for the more effectual securing the payments of rents and preventing the frauds of tenants"—This Bill the basis of legislation on the Land Question up to 1870—Land thrown into Grazing—State of the Catholics—Renewal of the Penal Statutes—Fever and bloody flux—Deaths—State of Prisoners—Galway Physicians refuse to attend Patients—The Races of Galway changed to

Tuam on account of the Fever in Galway—Balls and Plays!—Rt. Rev. Dr. Berkeley's account of the Famine—The "Groans of Ireland"—Ireland a land of Famines—Dublin Bay—The Coast—The Wicklow Hills—Killiney—Obelisk Hill—What the Obelisk was built for—The Potato more cultivated than ever after 1741—Agricultural literature of the time—Apathy of the Gentry denounced—Comparative yield of Potatoes a hundred years ago and at present—Arthur Young on the Potato—Great increase of its culture in twenty years—The disease called "curl" in the Potato (*Note*)—Failure of the Potato in 1821—Consequent Famine in 1822—Government grants—Charitable collections—High price of Potatoes—Skibbereen in 1822—Half of the superficies of the Island visited by this Famine—Strange apathy of Statesmen and Landowners with regard to the ever-increasing culture of the Potato—Supposed conquest of Ireland—Ireland kept poor lest she should rebel—The English colony always regarded as the Irish nation—The Natives ignored—They lived in the bogs and mountains, and cultivated the Potato, the only food that would grow in such places—No recorded Potato blight before 1729—The probable reason—Poverty of the English colony—jealousy of England of its progress and prosperity—Commercial jealousy—Destruction of the Woollen manufacture—Its immediate effect—"William the Third's Declaration—Absenteeism—Mr. M'Cullagh's arguments—See *Note* in Appendix—Apparently low rents—Not really so—No capital—Little skill—No good Agricultural Implements—Swift's opinion—Arthur Young's opinion—Acts of Parliament—The Catholics permitted to be loyal—Act for reclaiming Bogs—Pension to Apostate Priests increased—Catholic Petition in 1792—The Belief Act of 1793—Population of Ireland at this time—The Forty-shilling Freeholders—Why they were created—Why they were abolished—The cry of over-population.

The great Irish Famine, which reached its height in 1847, was, in many of its features, the most striking and most deplorable known to history. The deaths resulting from it, and the emigration which it caused, were so vast, that, at one time, it seemed as if America and the grave were about to absorb the whole population of this country between them. The cause of the calamity was almost as wonderful as the result. It arose from the failure of a root which, by degrees, had become the staple food of the whole working population: a root which, on its first introduction, was received by philanthropists and economists with joy, as a certain protection against that scarcity which sometimes resulted from short harvests. Mr. Buckland, a Somersetshire gentleman, sent in 1662 a letter to the Royal Society, recommending the planting of potatoes in all parts of the kingdom, *to prevent famine*, for which he received the thanks of that learned body; and Evelyn, the well-known author of "The Sylva," was requested to mention the proposal at the end of that work.

The potato was first brought into this country about three centuries ago. Tradition and, to some extent, history attributes its introduction to Sir Walter Raleigh. Whether this was actually the case or not, there seems to be no doubt about his having cultivated it on that estate in Munster which was bestowed upon him by his royal mistress, after the overthrow of the Desmonds.[1] Some confusion has arisen about the period at which the potato of Virginia, as I shall for the present call the potato, was brought to our shores, from the fact that another root, the *batatas*, or sweet potato, came into these islands, and was used as a delicacy before the potato of Virginia was known; and what adds to the confusion is, that the name potato, applied to the Virginian root, is derived from *batatas*, it not bearing in Virginia any name in the least resembling the word potato. Up to 1640 it was called in England the potato of Virginia, to distinguish it from the sweet potato, which is another evidence that it derived the name potato from *batatas*.[2] The latter root was extensively cultivated for food in parts of America, but it never got into anything like general cultivation here, perhaps because our climate was too cold for it. It is now only found in our hot-houses, where it produces tubers from one to two pounds in weight.

It has been asserted that Sir John Hawkins brought the potato to Ireland in 1565, and his kinsman Sir Francis Drake to England in 1585. Although this is not improbable, writers generally assume that it was the sweet potato which was introduced by those navigators.

Whether or not Raleigh's third expedition, which sailed from England in 1584, was the *first* to bring into these countries the potato of Virginia, there can be no reasonable doubt of its having been brought home by that expedition. The story of Raleigh having stopped on some part of the Irish coast on his way from Virginia, when he distributed potatoes to the natives, is quite groundless. Raleigh was never in Virginia; for although by his money and influence, and perhaps yet more by his untiring energy, he organized nine exploring expeditions, he did not sail with any of them except the first, which was commanded by his half-brother, Sir Humphrey Gilbert. But this had to return disabled to England without touching land.[3]

Sir Joseph Banks, the well-known naturalist, and President of the Royal Society from 1777 till his death in 1820, was at great pains to collect the history of the introduction of the potato into these countries. His account is, that Raleigh's expedition, granted to him under patent "to discover such remote heathen and barbarous lands, not yet actually possessed by any Christian prince, nor inhabited by Christian people, as to him shall seem good," brought home the potato of Virginia. This Charter bears date 25th March, 1584, and was a new and more extensive one than the first granted to him, which was in June, 1578. With this expedition sailed one Thomas Heriot, called the Mathematician, who was probably sent out to examine and report upon the natural history of such countries as they might discover. He wrote an account of Virginia, and of the products of its soil, which is printed in the first volume of De Bry's collection of Voyages. Under the article "Roots," he describes a plant which he calls Opanawk. "These roots," he says, "are round, some as large as a walnut, others much larger; they grow in damp soil, many hanging together as if fixed with ropes. They are good food either boiled or roasted." This must strike anyone as a very accurate description of the potato. Gerarde, in his Herbal, published in 1597, gives a figure of the potato under the name of the potato of Virginia. He asserts that he received the roots from that country, and that they were denominated Naremberga.

Raleigh's expedition, which seems to have been already prepared, sailed in April, and having taken possession of that portion of America which was afterwards named Virginia, in honour of Queen Elizabeth, and by her own express desire, returned to England about the middle of September of the same year. Although, as already stated, in all likelihood the potato of Virginia was introduced into England and Ireland by that expedition, Sir Joseph Banks was of opinion that the root had come to Europe earlier. His reasons for thinking so are: 1. Clusius, otherwise L'Ecluse, the great botanist, when residing in Vienna, in 1598, received the potato from the Governor of Mons, in Hainault, who had obtained it the year before from one of the attendants of the Pope's Legate under the name of Taratouflè,[4] and learned from him that in Italy, where it was then in use, no person knew whether it came from Spain or America. From this we may conclude that the root was in Italy before it was brought to England; for this conversation happened only three years after the sailing of the expedition of 1584. It is further very probable that the root found its way from Spain into Italy, as those parts of America, where the potato was indigenous, were then subject to Spain. 2. Peter Cicca, in his Chronicle of 1553, says, the inhabitants of Quito and its vicinity have, besides mays (maize), a tuberous root which they eat and call *papas*; which Clusius with much probability guesses to be the same sort of plant that he received from the Governor of Mons.

There is one obvious difficulty in this reasoning: we are not at all sure that it was the potato of Virginia that Clusius obtained from the Governor of Mons, it may have been the sweet potato. However, the conclusion which Sir Joseph Banks draws from these details is, that potatoes were brought from the mountainous parts of South America in the neighbourhood of Quito, and that, as the Spaniards were the sole possessors of that country, there can be little doubt of their having been first carried into Spain. Further, that as it would take a considerable time to introduce them into Italy, and make the Italians acquainted with them to the extent of giving them a name, there is good reason to believe, that they had been several years in Europe before they had been sent to Clusius.

About 600,000 acres of land in Munster were declared forfeited to the Crown on the fall of the Desmonds. This was parceled out to "Gentlemen undertakers" on certain conditions; one being that they were bound, within a limited time, to people their estates with "Well-affected Englishmen." Raleigh became an undertaker, and by a legal instrument, bearing the Queen's name, dated from Greenwich, last of February, 1586, he had given to him 42,000 acres of this land, and by a further grant the year after, the Monastery of Molanassa and the Priory of Black Friars, near Youghal.[5]

Famine followed close upon the war with the Desmonds. "At length," says Hooker, "the curse of God was so great, and the land so barren both of man and beast, that whatsoever did travel from one end to the other of all Munster, even from Waterford to Smerwick, about six score miles, he should not meet man, woman, or child, saving in cities or towns, nor yet see any beast, save foxes, wolves, or other ravening beasts."[6] Such was Munster when the great colonizer planted the potato there, in the hope, perhaps, of averting future famines!

It is generally assumed by writers on Ireland that, soon after the introduction of the potato, it became a general favourite, and was cultivated in most parts of the country as an important crop. This seems to be far from correct. Supposing the potato which we now grow, the *Solanum tuberosum* of botanists, to have come to Ireland in 1586, the usually accepted date, it does not seem to have been in anything like general favour or cultivation one hundred and forty years later, at least in the richer and more important districts of the country. In a pamphlet printed in 1723, one hundred and thirty-seven years after the introduction of the potato, speaking of the fluctuation of the markets, the writer says: "We have always either a glut or a dearth; very often there are not ten days distance between the extremity of the one and the other; such a want of policy is there (in Dublin especially) on the most important affair of bread, without a plenty of which *the poor must starve*." If potatoes were at this time looked upon as an important food-crop, the author would scarcely omit noticing the fact, especially in speaking of the food of the poor. At page 25 of the same pamphlet, after exposing and denouncing the corruptions of those who farmed tithes, the writer adds: "Therefore an Act of Parliament to ascertain the tithe of hops, now in the infancy of their great growing improvement, flax, hemp, turnip-fields, grass-seeds, and dyeing roots or herbs, of all mines, coals, minerals, commons to be taken in, etc., seems necessary towards the encouragement of them."[7] No mention of the potato.

In the next year, 1724, this pamphleteer was answered by an anonymous M.P., who mentions potatoes twice. Arguing against what he calls "extravagant stocks," he says: "Formerly (even since Popery) it was thought no ill policy to be well with the parson, but now the case is quite altered, for if he gives him [*sic*] the least provocation, I'll immediately stock one part of my land with bullocks and the other with potatoes . . . so farewell tithes."[8] The fact of potatoes not being titheable at this period seems to have encouraged their cultivation. The next passage goes to show that they were becoming the food of those who could afford no better. Speaking of high rents, and what he calls "canting of land" by landlords, he says: "Again, I saw the same farm, at the expiration of the lease, canted over the improving tenant's head, and set to another at a rack-rent, who, though coming in to the fine improvements of his predecessor, (and himself no bad improver,) yet can scarce afford his family butter to their potatoes, and is daily sinking into arrears besides."[9] From the tone of this passage, and from the context, the writer seems to regard the potato as food to be used only by the very poorest; for he adduces its use to show to what a state rack-renting can bring even an industrious farmer.

The burthen of all the pamphlets of this period dealing with the land question, was an attack on landowners for their excessive desire to throw land into grass. One published in 1727 has this passage: "By running into the fancy of grazing after the manner of the Scythians, they [the landowners] are every day depopulating the country."[10] In another, printed in the same type, and apparently by the same hand, we read: "To bestow the whole kingdom on beef and mutton, and thereby drive out half the people, who should eat their share, and force the rest to send sometimes as far as Ægypt for bread to eat with it, is a most peculiar and distinguished piece of public economy of which I have no comprehension."[11] At this time there was extreme want in the country, on account, it was thought, of the great quantity of land which, within a short period, had been put out of tillage; graziers (whom the writer calls "that abominable race of graziers") being mad after land then as they are now. But there were other causes. William the Third, at the bidding of the English Parliament, annihilated the flourishing woollen manufacture of Ireland; her trade with the Colonies was not only cramped, but ruined, by the navigation laws in force; which, amongst other things, enacted that no colonial produce could come to Ireland until it had at first entered an English port, *and had been landed there*. Thus, whilst the fact that vast tracts of the soil had been put out of cultivation compelled the country to buy food abroad, the unjust and selfish destruction of her trade and commerce by England left her without the money to do so.

The people being in a state of great destitution, the author of the "Memorial" quoted above, said, there should be raised by taxes on a few commodities, such as tea, coffee, etc., £110,000. £100,000 to buy 100,000 barrels of wheat, and £10,000 premium to those who would import it. To this the Author of the Answer replies:—"By talking so familiarly of £110,000 by a tax upon a few commodities, it is plain you are either naturally or affectedly ignorant of our present condition, or else you would know and allow, that such a sum is not to be raised here without a general excise; since, in proportion to our wealth, we pay already in taxes more than England ever did in the height of the war. And when you have brought over your corn, who who will be the buyers? Most certainly, not the poor, who will not be able to purchase the twentieth part of it . . . If you will propose a general contribution in supporting the poor on potatoes and buttermilk till the new corn comes in, perhaps you may succeed better, because the thing at least is possible."

Potato culture was clearly on the increase; the corn crop, however, was still looked to as the food of the nation. But if the growing of potatoes was on the increase, it seems to have partly arisen from the very necessity of the case. There was not land enough under tillage to give food to the people, it was laid down for grazing. Mountains, poor lands, and bogs were unsuitable to graziers, nor yet would they yield wheat, nor, in many instances, oats, or any white crop whatever; but the potato was found to succeed very well in such places, and to give a larger quantity of sustenance than such land would otherwise yield. Its cultivation was therefore spreading, but spreading, it would seem, chiefly amongst the poor Celtic natives, who had to betake themselves to the despised wastes and barren mountains. In the rich lowlands, and therefore amongst the English colony (for whom alone all the publications of those times were intended), the potato was still a despised article of food. And to this the latter part of the above-cited passage points. The proposal to sustain the people on potatoes and buttermilk until the new corn should come in, is evidently an ironical one, really meant to convey the degradation to which grazing had brought the country. Seventy or eighty years later the irony became a sad and terrible reality.

Meantime increased attention was given to the improvement of agriculture, arising, in a great measure, from the widespread panic which the passion for grazing had caused. Good and patriotic men saw but one result from it, a dangerous and unwise depopulation, and they called aloud for remedies against so terrible a calamity. The Author of the "Answer to the Memorial" quoted above, says, with bitter sarcasm:—"You are concerned how strange and surprising it would be in foreign parts to hear that the poor were starving in a rich country . . . But why all this concern of the poor? We want them not as the country is now managed; they may follow thousands of their leaders, and seek their bread abroad. Where the plough has no work, one family can do the business of fifty, and you may send away the other forty-nine. An admirable piece of husbandry never known or practised by the wisest nations, who erroneously thought people to be the riches of a country."

This anxious desire to prevent the country from "running into grazing," called forth many treatises and pamphlets on the improvement of agriculture. Some writers undertook to show that agriculture was more profitable than grazing; others turned their attention to improve the implements of husbandry, and to lay down better rules for the rotation of crops. Potatoes must have been pretty extensively grown at this time, and yet they do not get a place in any of the rotations given. We have fallow, wheat, oats, rye, turnips, saintfoin, lucerne, barley, peas, beans, clover, rye-grass, and even buck-wheat, tares and lentils rotated in various ways, but the potato is never mentioned. The growth of turnips is treated with special importance. Hops, too, receive much consideration, and the Royal Dublin Society published in 1733 careful and elaborate instructions for their growth and management. The reason the growing of potatoes gets no place in any of the rotations of this period seems to be, that their culture was chiefly confined to the poor Celtic population in the mountainous and neglected districts; or, as the author whose pamphlet has a short introduction from Swift[12] says, "to the Popish parts of the kingdom." Those who wrote in favour of tillage instead of grazing, set great importance on the increase of population, and bewailed emigration as the effect of bad harvests and want of tillage. All such observations made at this period must be taken as referring to the English colony, or Protestant population, exclusively, for there was no desire to keep the Catholics from emigrating; quite the contrary; but they were utterly ignored in the periodical literature of the time, except when some zealot called for a more strict enforcing of the laws "to prevent the growth of Popery." And this view is supported by the writer quoted above, who says it would be for the "Protestant interest" to encourage tillage. Primate Boulter, bewailing the emigration which resulted from the famine of 1728, "the result of three bad harvests together," adds, "the worst is that it affects only the Protestants, and reigns chiefly in the North."[13] He, in his tender anxiety for the Protestant colony, purchased corn in the South to sell it cheaply in the North, which caused serious food riots in Cork, Limerick, Waterford, Clonmel, and other places. These riots were of course quelled, and the rioters severely punished. The broad rich acres of the lowlands were in the hands of the Protestants; and these being specially suited to grazing were accordingly thrown into grass, whilst the Catholic Celts planted the potato in the despised half-barren wilds, and were increasing far more rapidly than those who were possessed of the choicest lands of the kingdom.

But a terrible visitation was at the threshold of Celt and Saxon in Ireland; the Famine of 1740 and '41. There were several years of dearth, more or less severe between 1720 and 1740. "The years 1725, 1726, 1727, and 1728 presented scenes of wretchedness unparalleled in the annals of any civilized nation," says a writer in the *Gentleman's Magazine*.[14] A pamphlet published in 1740 deplores the emigration which was going forward as the joint effect of bad harvests and want of tillage: "We have had," says the author, "twelve bad harvests with slight intermission." To find a parallel for the dreadful famine which commenced in 1740, we must go back to the close of the war with the Desmonds.[15] Previous to 1740 the custom of placing potatoes in pits dug in the earth, was unknown in Ireland. When the stems were withered, the farmer put additional earth on the potatoes in the beds where they grew, in which condition they remained till towards Christmas, when they were dug out and stored.[16] An intensely severe frost set in about the middle of December, 1739, whilst the potatoes were yet in this condition, or probably before they had got additional covering. There is a tradition in some parts of the South that this frost penetrated nine inches into the earth the first night it made its appearance. It was preceded by very severe weather. "In the beginning of November, 1739, the weather," says O'Halloran, "was very cold, the wind blowing from the north east, and this was succeeded by the severest frost known in the memory of man, which entirely destroyed the potatoes, the chief support of the poor."[17] It is known to tradition as the "great frost," the "hard frost," the "black frost," etc. Besides the destruction of the potato crop it produced other surprising effects; all the great rivers of the country were so frozen over that they became so many highways for traffic; tents were erected upon the ice, and large assemblies congregated upon it for various purposes. The turnips were destroyed in most places, but the parsnips survived. The destruction of shrubs and trees was immense, the frost making havoc equally of the hardy furze and the lordly oak; it killed birds of almost every kind, it even killed the shrimps of Irishtown Strand, near Dublin, so that there was no supply of them at market for many years from that famous shrimp ground.[18] Towards the end of the frost the wool fell off the sheep, and they died in great numbers.[19]

On Saturday, the 29th of December, there was a violent storm in Dublin, which did much damage to the shipping in the river; and the cruiser, "Man of War," which was at the North Bull, being in great danger, "cut her cables, and ran up between the walls as far as Sir John's *Key*,[20] where," adds the chronicler, "she now lies frozen up."[21] Another curious incident is recorded which proves the intensity of the frost at this time: the pressgang was very busy on the river catching sailors to man the navy for the war with Spain, and under the above date we are informed that more than one hundred pressed men walked on shore on the ice with several of the crews; but, it is added, "they gave their honour they would return."[22]

The frost continued about eight or nine weeks, during which all employment ceased; the potato crop was destroyed, and the mills being frozen up no corn could be ground. The effect on the population was general and immediate. In the middle of January the destitution was so great, that subscriptions to relieve the people were set on foot in Dublin, Cork, Limerick, Waterford, Clonmel, Wexford, and other places. Some landlords distributed money and food to their starving tenants; but, I am sorry to have to say, that the number of such cases on record is very limited.[23] There was no general combined effort to meet the calamity, the Government taking no action whatever, except that the Lord Lieutenant (the Duke of Devonshire) gave to the starving citizens of Dublin £150 in two donations, and forbade, by proclamation, the exportation of grain, meal, bread, etc., *except to England*, "apprehending," says his Excellency, "that the exportation of corn will be bad for the kingdom during this extreme season." Later on in the Famine, and when about two hundred thousand of the people had died of hunger and pestilence, there was another proclamation ordering a *general fast* for the success of his Majesty's arms against the King of Spain! But the fasting does not seem to have had much effect; Admiral Vernon, commander of the fleet at the seat of war in the West Indies, took Portobello, but had to give it up again; he attacked Carthagena with all his forces, was repulsed, and so the war ended.

To add to the miseries of the people there was a great drought all the winter and spring.[24] A person writing from the West on the 15th of April, says: "There has not been one day's rain in Connaught these two months." The price of provisions continued to rise. Wheat, quoted towards the end of January in the Dublin market at £2 1s. 6d. the quarter, reached £2 15s. 6d. in April, £3 14s. in June, and £3 16s. 6d. in August. About the end of May there was a very formidable bread riot in the city. Several hundred persons banded themselves together, and, proceeding to the bakers' shops and meal stores, took the bread and meal into the streets, and sold them to the poor at low prices. Some gave the proceeds to the owners, but others did not. They were evidently not thieves, and at least a portion of them seem to have been even respectable, yet they were punished with much severity, several having been whipped, and one transported for seven years. Some days after the riot the Lord Mayor issued a proclamation giving permission to "foreign bakers and others" to bake bread in Dublin; he also sent to all the churchwardens of the city to furnish him with information of any persons who had concealed corn on their premises; he denounced "forestallers," who met in the suburbs the people coming in with provisions, in order to buy them up before they reached the market; thus in a great measure justifying the rioters who were whipped and transported. The bakers began to bake household bread, which for some time they had ceased to do, and prices fell.[25]

Throughout the country there were numerous gangs of robbers, most of them undoubtedly having sprung into existence through sheer starvation; some, probably taking advantage of the Famine, pursued with more profit and boldness a course of life to which they had been previously addicted. The most noted of these was "the Kellymount gang." Their head-quarters seem to have been Coolcullen Wood, about seven miles from Kilkenny, but they extended their operations into the King and Queen's Counties, and even to Galway. They were so formidable that a strong military force had to be sent against them. This gang committed no murders, disdained to take anything but money, horses, and sheep; sometimes divided their plunder with the starving people; and had in the outset pledged their honour not to rob any of the gentlemen of the County Kilkenny. They were dispersed, after giving much trouble to the military; many were taken prisoners, tried by a Special Commission, and of course hanged; for, while the Government did nothing to alleviate the horrors of the Famine, it put the law in force with a bloody severity. The number of persons condemned to death at the Spring Assizes of 1741 was really appalling. There was a sort of small food riot at Carrick-on-Suir, where a boat laden with oats was about sailing for Waterford, when the starving people assembled to prevent the food they so much needed from being taken away. Their conduct was clearly illegal, but they were at death's door with hunger, and ought to have been treated with some consideration and patience. A justice of the peace, with eighteen foot soldiers and a troop of horse, came out and ordered them to disperse; they would not, or at least they did not do so with sufficient alacrity. One account, published a fortnight or so after the occurrence, asserts with a feeble timidity akin to falsehood, that stones were thrown by the people. Be that as it may, they were fired upon; five starving wretches were shot dead on the spot, and eleven badly wounded. To give the finishing touch to this wicked slaughter, the Lords Justices, Primate Boulter and Lord Chancellor Jocelyn, in the absence of the Lord Lieutenant, came out with a proclamation, offering a handsome reward for the apprehension of any of those who had escaped the well-directed fire of the soldiery.

The Famine continued through the year 1741 and even deepened in severity, provisions still keeping at starvation prices. The Duke of Devonshire met the Parliament on the 6th of October, and in the course of his address said: "The sickness which hath proved so mortal in several parts of the kingdom, and is thought to have been principally owing to the scarcity of wholesome food, must very sensibly affect His Majesty, who hath a most tender concern for all his subjects, and cannot but engage your serious attention to consider of proper measures to prevent the like calamity for the future, and to this desirable end the increase of tillage, which would at the same time usefully employ the industrious poor, may greatly contribute." In answer to this portion of the speech, they promise to "prepare such laws as, by encouraging tillage, and employing the industrious poor, may be the means for the future to prevent the like calamity." A Committee was appointed to inquire into "the late great scarcity," and some matters connected with tillage. They met many times; now and then reported to the House that they had made some progress, and at last the heads of a bill were presented by Mr. Le Hunte, the Chairman, which were ordered to be sent to England. Nothing, as far as I can discover, resulted from this proceeding, unless indeed it was a bill passed in 1743 "to prevent the pernicious practice of burning land," which is probable enough, as the heads of this bill were presented to the House by the same Mr. Le Hunte. During the time this Committee was sitting and reporting, and sitting again, Mr. Thos. Cuffe, seconded by Mr. George M'Cartney, presented the heads of a bill "for the more effectual securing the payment of rents and preventing the frauds of tenants," which was received and read and committed by a Committee of the whole House on presentation, and was hurried through its other stages, apparently without discussion, but certainly without opposition; and this in the second year of a Famine, now combined with pestilence, which slaughtered one-eighth of the whole population.[26] The Act was a temporary one, but was never afterwards allowed to die out. It was renewed in various reigns, and is the foundation of the Acts which were in force up to 1870 "for the more effectual securing the payment of rents."

The land had been thrown into grazing to an alarming extent for years, so that the acreage for producing grain and other such food was very limited; the people fell into listless despair from what they had endured in 1740, and did not cultivate the ground that was still left for tillage. The Catholics were paralyzed and rendered unfit for industrious pursuits, by an active renewal of the worst penal statutes. The prospect of a war with Spain, which was actually declared in October, 1739, was made the pretext for this new persecution, and all the severities recommended by Primate Boulter were put into rigid execution. These measures plunged the people into the deepest distress: horror and despair pervaded every mind.[27]

Such was the state of Ireland in 1741, when bloody flux and malignant fever came to finish what the Famine had left undone. These scourges, unlike the Famine, fell upon the castle as well as on the hovel, many persons in the higher ranks of life having died of them during the year; amongst whom we find several physicians; the son of Alderman Tew; Mr. John Smith, High Sheriff of Wicklow; Mr. Whelan, Sub-Sheriff of Meath; the Rev. Mr. Heartlib, Castle Chaplain; Mr. Kavanagh, of Borris House, and his brother; the son of the Lord Mayor-Elect; two judges, namely, Baron Wainright and the Right Hon. John Rogerson, Chief Justice of the King's Bench. The prisoners died in thousands in the jails, especially poor debtors, who had been long incarcerated. In November, 1741, the prisoners in Cork jail sent a petition to Parliament, in which they say, that "above seven hundred persons died there during the late severe seasons, and that the jail is now so full that there is scarce room for their lying on the floors." The fever was so general in Limerick that there was hardly one family in the whole city who had not some member ill of it. Galway was cruelly scourged by the Famine, to meet which little or nothing seems to have been done by those whose bounden duty it was to come to the relief of their starving brethren. When fever appeared on the terrible scene, the town became one great lazaretto. Under date of July the 8th, the following intelligence comes from that unhappy place: "The fever so rages here that the physicians say it is more like a plague than a fever, and refuse to visit patients for any fee whatever."[28] "The gentlemen of the county" met, in a way peculiar to themselves, this twofold calamity which threatened utter annihilation to their historic capital. To counteract the inevitable results of famine, they announced that they would give the reward of £30 for the first, and £10 for every other robber that would be prosecuted to conviction, and this in addition to whatever the Government would allow. What excessive liberality! They must have had plenty of money. The plague, which no physician would attend, they dealt with by a proclamation also, of which they seemed proud, for they published it repeatedly in the journals of the time. Here is an extract: "The town of Galway being at this time very sickly, the gentlemen of the county *think proper* to remove the races that were to be *run for* at Park, near the said town of Galway, to Terlogh Gurranes, near the town of Tuam, in the said county." What humane, *proper-thinking* "gentlemen" they were, to be sure; and such precise legal phraseology! But their enticing bill of fare contained more than the "races that were to be run for;" it announced balls and plays every night for the entertainment of the ladies.

The learned and kind-hearted Dr. Berkeley, Protestant Bishop of Cloyne, under date 21st May, 1741, writes to a a friend in Dublin:—"The distresses of the sick and poor are endless. The havoc of mankind in the counties of Cork, Limerick, and some adjacent places, hath been incredible. The nation probably will not recover this loss in a century. The other day I heard one from the county of Limerick say, that whole villages were entirely dispeopled. About two months since I heard Sir Richard Cox say, that five hundred were dead in the parish, though in a county I believe not very populous. It were to be wished people of condition were at their seats in the country during these calamitous times, which might provide relief and employment for the poor. Certainly if these perish the rich must be sufferers in the end." The author of a letter entitled "The Groans of Ireland," addressed to an Irish. Member of Parliament, thus opens his subject:—"I have been absent from this country for some years, and on my return to it, last summer, found it the most miserable scene of universal distress that I have ever read of in history: want and misery in every face; the rich unable almost as they were willing to relieve the poor; the roads spread with dead and dying bodies; mankind of the colour of the docks and nettles they fed on; two or three, sometimes more, going on a car to the grave for want of bearers to carry them, and many buried only in the fields and ditches where they perished. This universal scarcity was ensued by fluxes and malignant fevers, which swept off multitudes of all sorts: whole villages were left waste by want, and sickness, and death in various shapes; and scarcely a house in the whole island escaped from tears and mourning. The loss must be upwards of 400,000, but supposing it 200,000, (it was certainly more) it was too great for this ill-peopled country, and the more grievous as they were mostly of the grown-up part of the working people." "Whence can this proceed?" he asks; and he answers, "From the want of proper tillage laws to guide and to protect the husbandman in the pursuit of his business." [29]

This writer further says, the terrible visitation of 1740 and '41 was the third famine within twenty years; so that in view of these and other famines, since and before, Ireland might be not inaptly described as the land of Famines. Almost the first object one sees on sailing into Dublin Bay is a monument to Famine. This beautiful bay, as far-famed as the Bay of Naples itself, has often been put in comparison with it. More than once has it been my lot to witness the tourist on board the Holyhead packet, coming to Ireland for the first time, straining his eyes towards the coast, when the rising sun gave a faint blue outline of the Wicklow mountains, and assured him that he had actually and really before him, "The Holy Hills of Ireland." Nearer and nearer he comes, and Howth at one side and Wicklow Head at the other define what he, not unjustly, regards as the Bay. And surely on a bright clear morning, with just enough of sunlight, it is as fair a scene as mortal eye can rest on. The Dublin and Wicklow hills, which at first seemed to rise from the shore, recede by degrees, and with their undulating graceful outlines, become a charming background. Wicklow Head drops quietly out of the landscape, and Howth to the north, and Bray Head to the south, now become the bold gigantic flanking towers of what is more strictly regarded as Dublin Bay. The traveller's eyes, beaming with enjoyment, survey the fine perpendicular rock of Bray Head, with the railway marking a thin line upon its side nearly midway above the sea, and almost suspended over it. And then there is that beautiful cone, the Sugarloaf mountain; further still away, the loftier Djous, overhanging a dark, misty valley, which marks the spot where the waters of Powerscourt tumble down the rock a height of three hundred feet; on, on across the Dublin range to Montpelier, the valley of the Liffey, the city—notable to the north-west by its dusky-brown atmosphere; then the historic plains of Clontarf; Howth once again, and the panorama is complete. But he nears the shore rapidly, and the harbour grows more distinct, Kingstown, rising from it with its terraces, and spires, and towers, looking important and aristocratic. The rich and varied fringe of gardens, and lawns, and villas from Dalkey to Seapoint, mark at once the fashionable watering-place; whilst Dalkey Castle, standing over the great precipitous quarry from which Kingstown harbour was built, and the Obelisk on Killiney Hill indicate points from which commanding views can be obtained.

The morrow, and let us suppose the tourist ascends to the massive but friendly gate which admits to that same Obelisk hill. Was ever such an ascent open to him before? The broad, winding avenue, literally carpeted with its firm green satin sward, defined by a belt of graceful planting at either side, whilst in nooks and cozy places are inviting seats for the weak and weary to rest awhile, and gain breath to enable them to pursue their journey upwards. The Obelisk, as it is called, stands on the highest point; the view from it on every side is unrivalled for beauty—the sublime it has not—but the beautiful is perfect. The mountains, which yesterday morning at sea, gave the first glimmering indication of the Irish coast, assume new shapes, and are thrown into new combinations. Inland, the landscape stretches on till it touches the sky in all directions except where the mountains intervene. Looking north, over the flat plain of Clontarf, he beholds the lofty Mourne range, relieved against the sky; glancing along the Dublin mountains he has that wooded and villaed slope, far as the eye can reach, which forms the southern suburb, a rival for which no city in Europe can boast: to the east are the deep clear waters of the sea, four hundred feet beneath; and he gazes with delight on the tranquil and gracefully curved strand, stretching three or four miles on to Bray, which fringes that charming inlet known as Killiney Bay; its waves sending upwards, in measured cadence, their soft, distinct, suggestive murmurs, whilst they spend themselves on the shore of the ever new, ever delightful, ever enchanting Vale of Shangannah, immortalized by our Irish poet, Denis Florence M'Carthy. But this old Obelisk itself, what is it?—What brought it here? The tourist reads: "Last year being hard with the POOR, the walls about these HILLS, and THIS, etc., erected by JOHN MALPAS, Esq., June, 1742." The story of Ireland is before him; it is told in the landscape, and the inscription, it may be expressed in two words—Beauty and Starvation.

The famine of 1741 did not deter farmers from the culture of the potato; on the contrary, it increased rapidly after that period, and we now find it, for the first time, recognised as a rotation crop. They preferred to turn their attention to improve its quality and productiveness, and to take measures for its protection from frost, rather than to abandon its culture. And, indeed, it was as much a matter of necessity as choice that they did so. The potato, on a given area, supplied about four times as much food as any other crop; and, from the limited breadth of land then available for tillage, the population would be in continual danger of falling short of food, unless the potato were cultivated to a large extent. The agricultural literature of the country from 1741 until the arrival of the celebrated traveller, Arthur Young, in Ireland, consisted chiefly of fierce attacks upon graziers—of a continual demand for the breaking up of grass lands into tillage—of plans for the establishment of public granaries to sustain the people in years of bad harvests, and of the results of experiments undertaken to improve the culture of the potato. The writers on these subjects also frequently denounced the rich for the wretchedness and misery to which they allowed the labouring poor to be reduced. The author of a pamphlet, which went through several editions, thus attacks them, in the edition of 1755:—"The want of trade and industry causes such inequality in the distribution of their (the people's) property, that while a few of the richer sort can wantonly pamper appetites of every kind, and indulge with the affluence of so many monarchs, the poor, alas! who make at least ninety-nine of every hundred among them, are under the necessity of going clad after the fashion of the old Irish, whose manners and customs they retain to this day, and of feeding on potatoes, the most generally embraced advantage of the inhabitants, which the great Sir Walter Raleigh left behind him."[30] This writer's remarks apply chiefly to Cork, Waterford, Kerry, and Limerick. He proceeds: "The feeding of cattle on large dairies of several hundred acres together, may be managed by the inhabitants of one or two cabins, whose wretched subsistence, for the most part, depends upon an acre or two of potatoes and a little skimmed milk."[31]

Many think that the yield per acre of potatoes has greatly increased with time in Ireland. This opinion, although true, is not true to the extent generally supposed; for, when Arthur Young travelled in this country, and even before it, the yield, as far as recorded, seems nearly equal to the quantity produced at present, except in some peculiar cases. A well-known agriculturist, John Wynne Baker, writing in 1765, says, in a note to his "Agriculture Epitomized," that he had in the past year (1764) of apple potatoes (not a prolific kind) in the proportion of more than one hundred and nine barrels an acre.

Arthur Young came to Ireland in 1776, and he brings his account of the country down to 1779. Thirty-six years had elapsed since the great Famine, only one generation, and he found the famous root of Virginia a greater favourite than ever. From Slane, in Meath, he writes that potatoes are a great article of culture at Kilcock, where he found them grown for cattle; store bullocks were fed upon them, and they were even deemed good food for horses when mixed with bran. In Slane itself, the old custom, which was the chief cause of the famine of 1740, still prevailed; for he says, the people there were not done taking up their potatoes till Christmas. The potato culture, he elsewhere remarks, has increased twenty-fold within the last twenty years, all the hogs in the country being fattened on them. They were usually given to them half-boiled. Wherever he went he almost invariably found the food of the people, at least for nine months of the year, to be potatoes and milk, excepting parts of Ulster, where they had oatbread, and sometimes flesh meat. In the South, for the labourers of Sir Lucius O'Brien and their families, consisting of two hundred and sixty-seven souls, the quantity of potatoes planted, as appears from a paper given to him, was forty-five acres and a quarter, ranging from a quarter of an acre to four acres for each family. As to yield, the lowest he gives is forty barrels per acre, Irish of course; and the highest reported to him was at Castle Oliver, near Bruff, namely, one hundred and fifty barrels (Bristol).[32] The average produce of the entire country he gives at three hundred and twenty-eight bushels per acre—about sixty-six barrels. "Yet, to gain this miserable produce," he says, "much old hay, and nineteen-twentieths of all the dung in the kingdom is employed." Potatoes grown on the coast were frequently sent to Dublin by sea; and Lord Tyrone told Arthur Young at Curraghmore, that much of the potatoes grown about Dungarvan were sent thither, together with birch-brooms. The boats were said to be freighted with *fruit* and *timber*!

Amongst the endless varieties of the potato which appeared from time to time, that known as the "apple" was the best in quality, and stood its ground the longest, having been a favourite for at least seventy or eighty years. The produce recorded above as raised by Mr. Wynne Baker was as we have seen from this species, what kind gave the still greater yield at Castle Oliver is not recorded. Thus it is perfectly clear that in 1780, and even before that time, the staple food of the Irish nation was once again the potato. In fact, it was cultivated to a far greater extent than before 1740, which caused the population to increase with wonderful rapidity.[33]

The prolific but uncertain root on which the Irish people became, year after year, more dependent for existence, once again dashed their hopes in 1821, and threw a great part of the South and West into a state of decided famine. The spring of that year was wet and stormy, retarding the necessary work, especially the planting of potatoes. The summer was also unfavourable, May was cold and ungenial; in June there was frost, with a north wind, and sometimes a scorching sun. The autumn, like the spring, was wet and severe, rain falling to a very unusual extent. The consequent floods did extensive injury; not merely were crops of hay floated off the lowland meadows, but in various places fields of potatoes were completely washed out of the ground and carried away. The crops were deficient, especially the potato crop, much of which was left undug until the ensuing spring, partly on account of the inclement weather, partly because it was not worth the labour. The low grounds were, in many instances, inundated to such a depth that even the potatoes in pits could not be reached. About the middle of December "the Shannon at Athlone," says an eye-witness, "looked like a boundless ocean," covering for weeks the potato fields, souring the crop, and preventing all access to the pits. The loss of the potato in this year, and its cause, are thus epitomised in the following extract from the Report of the London Tavern Committee:—"From the most authentic communications, it appeared that the bad quality and partial failure of the potato crop of the preceding year (1821)—the consequence of the excessive and protracted humidity of the season—had been a principal cause of the distress, and that it had been greatly aggravated by the rotting of the potatoes in the pits in which they were stored. This discovery was made at so late a period that the peasantry were not able to provide against the consequences of that evil."[34] From the letters published in their own Report, the Committee would have been abundantly justified in adding, that the distress was greatly increased by the almost total want of employment for the labouring classes, arising from the fact, that very many of the landlords in the districts that suffered most were absentees. A writer on this Famine, who, in general, is inclined to be severe in his strictures upon the people, thus opens the subject:—"The distress which has almost universally prevailed in Ireland has not been occasioned so much by an excessive population as by a culpable remissness on the part of persons possessing property, and neglecting to take advantage of those great resources, and of those ample means of providing for an increasing population, which Nature has so liberally bestowed on this country."[35]

The winter and spring of 1822 continued very wet, and it was extremely difficult to perform any agricultural work. Seed potatoes were excessively scarce, and the first relief that reached the country was a prudent and timely one; it consisted of fourteen hundred tons of seed potatoes, bought by the Government in England and Scotland. Charitable persons at home also gave seed potatoes, cut into *sets*, to prevent their being used for food; yet, in many instances, those sets were taken out of the ground by the starving people and eaten. Cork, Limerick, Kerry, Clare, Mayo, and Galway were the counties most severely visited. These, according to the accounts given in the public journals of the time, were in a state of actual famine. Potatoes were eight pence a stone in districts where they usually sold from one penny to two pence. But although the potato had failed, food from the cereal crops was abundant and cheap enough if the people had money to buy it. "There was no want of food of another description for the support of human life; on the contrary, the crops of grain had been far from deficient, and the prices of corn and oatmeal were very moderate. The calamities of 1822 may, therefore, be said to have proceeded less from the want of food itself, than from the want of adequate means of purchasing it; or, in other words, from the want of profitable employment."[36] Poor Skibbereen, that got such a melancholy notoriety in the later and far more terrible Famine of '47, was reported, in May, 1822, to be in a state of distress "horrible beyond description." Potatoes were not merely dear, they were inferior, not having ripened for want of sufficient heat; and, furthermore, they soured in the pits. The use of such unwholesome food soon brought typhus fever and dysentery upon the scene, which slaughtered their thousands. In parts of the West the living were unable to bury the dead, more especially in Achill, where, in many cases, the famine-stricken people were found dead on the roadside. A Committee appointed by the House of Commons to investigate this calamity reported, amongst other things, that the Famine was spread over districts representing half the superficies of the country, and containing a population of 2,907,000 souls.

There are no statistics to give an accurate knowledge of the numbers that died of want in this Famine, and of the dysentery and fever which followed. If the Census of 1821 can be relied on, which I much doubt, the famine and pestilence of the succeeding year did not in the least check the growth of the population, as it increased in the ten years from 1821 to 1831, fifteen per cent.; an increase above the average, even in the absence of any disturbing cause.

This famine was met by Government grants; by the contributions from the London Tavern Committee; the Dublin Mansion House Committee, and, to a limited extent, by private charity.[37] In June, 1822, Parliament voted £100,000 "for the employment of the poor in Ireland, and other purposes relating thereto, as the exigency of affairs may require." And in July, £200,000, "to enable His Majesty to take such measures as the exigency of affairs may require." The London Tavern Committee, with the aid of a King's letter, received subscriptions amounting to £304,180 17s. 6d., of which £44,177 9s. was raised in Ireland. The Dublin Mansion House Committee collected £30,406 11s. 4-1/2d. Thus, the whole sum from charitable collections was £334,587 8s. 10-1/2d., of which £74,584, 0s. 4-1/2d. was raised in Ireland. This, with the grant of £300,000 from Government, makes a grand total of £634,587 8s. 10-1/2d. The sum appears to have been quite sufficient, as the London Tavern Committee closed its labours whilst it had yet in hands £60,000, which sum was partly distributed and partly invested in ways considered beneficial to this country.[38]

Every two or three years from 1821 to the great blight of '45 and '46, a failure of some kind, more or less extensive, occurred to the potato crop, not merely in Ireland, but in almost every country in which it was cultivated to any considerable extent. Reviewing, then, the history of this famous root for over a period of one hundred years, we find, that although it produces from a given acreage more human food than any other crop, it is yet a most treacherous and perishable one; and it may, perhaps, surprise future generations, that the statesmen and landed proprietors of that lengthened period did nothing whatever to regulate the husbandry of the country, in such a way as to prevent the lives of a whole people from being dependant on a crop liable to so many casualties. Perhaps the social and political condition of Ireland, during these times, will be found to have had something to do with this culpable apathy.

It is commonly assumed that the subjugation of Ireland was effected by Elizabeth, but the submission to English rule was only a forced one;

the spirit of the nation was one of determined opposition, which was abundantly shown at Aughrim and Limerick, and on many a foreign field besides. Great Britain knowing this, and being determined to hold the country at all risks, was continually in fear that some war or complication with foreign powers would afford the Irish people an opportunity of putting an end to English rule in Ireland, and of declaring the country an independent nation. As progress in wealth and prosperity would add to the probabilities of success in such an event, it was the all but avowed— nay, truth compels me to say, the *frequently avowed* policy of England to keep Ireland poor, and therefore feeble, that she might be held the more securely. For that reason she was not treated as a portion of a united kingdom, but as an enemy who had become England's slave by conquest, who was her rival in manufactures of various kinds, who might undersell her in foreign markets, and, in fact, who might grow rich and powerful enough to assert her independence.

The descendants of the Norman adventurers who got a footing here in the twelfth century; English and Scotch planters; officials and undertakers who, from time to time, had been induced to settle in Ireland by grants of land and sinecures, were, by a legal fiction, styled The Nation, although they were never more than a small fraction of it. For a great number of years every writer, every public man, every Act of Parliament, assumed that the English colony in Ireland was the Irish nation. Denunciations of Papists, the "common enemy"—gross falsehoods about their principles and acts—fears real or pretended, of their wicked, bloodthirsty plots, thickly strewn in our path as we journey through this dismal period of our history—reveal to us, as it were by accident, that there was another people in this island, besides those whom the law regarded as the nation; but they had no rights, they were outlaws—"the Irish enemy." One hundred and fifty years ago Primate Boulter expressed his belief that those outlaws made four-fifths of the population, and the English colony only one-fifth; but the colonists held the rich lands; the bulk of the people, who formed the real nation, were in the bogs, the lonely glens, and on the sterile mountains, where agriculture was all but impossible, except to the great capitalist. Capital they had none, and they were forced to subsist, as best they could, on little patches of tillage among the rocks, whose *debris* made the land around them in some sort susceptible of cultivation. By degrees those outlaws discovered that the potato, coming from the high moist soil of Quito, found in the half-barren wilds of Ireland, if not a climate, a soil at least congenial to its nature. It was palatable food, as it became acclimatized; it grew where no other plant fit for human food would grow; it was a great fertilizer; it was prolific: no wonder the poor Celt of our bogs and mountains, in time, made the potato more associated with the name of Ireland than it ever was with its native country, Virginia.

Before 1729 we have no record of the potato having suffered from blight or frost, or anything else. But this is not to be wondered at; even though such things occurred, the outlaws, who were its chief cultivators, excited neither interest nor pity in the hearts of the ruling minority. They were watched and feared; they were known to be numerous; and many were the plans set on foot to reduce their numbers, and cause them to become extinct, like the red deer of their native hills. Surely, then, a potato blight, followed by a famine, would not be regarded as a calamity, unless it affected the English colony. The Celtic nation in Ireland could have no record of such a visitation, unless in the fugitive ballad of some hedge schoolmaster.[39] Anyhow, the Celt, forced to live for the most part, in barren wilds, where it was all but impossible to raise sufficient food, found the potato his best friend, and his race increased and multiplied upon it, in spite of that bloody code which ignored his existence, and with regard to which Lord Clare, no friend to Ireland, thus expresses his views in his speech on the Union: "The Parliament of England seem to have considered the permanent debility of Ireland as the best security of the British crown, and the Irish Parliament to have rested the security of the colony upon maintaining a perpetual and impossible barrier against the ancient inhabitants of the country."[40]

Another cause for the increased cultivation of the potato may be found in the poverty of the English colony itself. Whilst the people of whom that colony was composed, through the Parliament that represented them, pursued the Catholic natives with unmitigated persecution, they were themselves the object of jealous surveillance, both by the Parliament and the commercial classes of England. Long before the times of which I am writing, the English always showed uneasiness at the least appearance of amalgamation between the descendants of the Norman invaders and the natives, although their fears on this head were to a great extent set at rest by the change of religion in England, which change extended in a very considerable degree to the English colony in Ireland. After the Reformation there was not much danger of a union between the Catholic Celt and the Protestant Norman. Still another jealousy remained—a commercial jealousy. The colonization of Ireland meant, in the English mind, the complete extirpation of the natives, and the peopling of this island by the adventurers and their descendants; but it is a strange fact, that even had this actually happened, we can, from what we know of the history of the period, assert with truth, that still their commercial prosperity and progress would be watched, and checked, and legislated against, whenever they would even seem to clash, or when there was a possibility of their clashing, with the commercial supremacy of Great Britain. Not to go into all the commercial restraints imposed on Irish manufactures by the English Parliament, let us take what, perhaps, was the most important one—that imposed on the woollen manufacture. For a long period this branch of industry had flourished in Ireland. We not only manufactured what we required for ourselves, but our exports of woollens were very considerable. This manufacture existed in England also, and the Englishmen engaged in it were determined to have the foreign markets to themselves. After many previous efforts, they at length induced both Houses of the English Parliament to address William the Third on what they were pleased to consider a grievance—the grievance of having foreign markets open to Irish woollens equally with their own.

To those addresses the King replied that he would do all in his power to "discourage" the woollen trade in Ireland, to encourage the linen trade, and *to promote the trade of England*.[41] Accordingly, a duty equal to a prohibition was imposed upon the exportation of Irish woollens, except, indeed, to England and Wales, where they were not required—England at the time manufacturing more woollens than were necessary for her home consumption. About forty thousand people in Ireland were thrown out of bread by this law, nearly every one of whom were Protestants; for that trade was almost entirely in their hands, so that neither Palesman nor Protestant was spared when their interests seemed opposed to those of England. William's declaration on this occasion about encouraging the linen manufacture in Ireland was regarded as a compact, yet it was violated at a later period by the imposition of duties.[42] The jealousy and unkindness of the prohibitory duty on the export of woollens is exposed by the able author of the "Groans of Ireland," who says: "It is certain that on the coasts of Spain, and Portugal, and the Mediterranean, in the stuffs, etc., which we send them, we, under all the difficulties of a clandestine trade, undersell the French eight per cent., and it is as certain that the French undersell the English as much—it has been said—*eleven per cent.*"[43] So that although the English manufacturer was unable to compete with the Frenchman abroad, his narrow selfishness would not permit Ireland to do so, although she was in a position to do it with advantage to herself.

Impoverished by such legislation, the English colony itself, Protestant and all as it was, had to lower its dietary standard and cultivate the potato, or, at least, promote its cultivation by the use of it.

Another of the alleged causes for the poverty of the country, and the consequent increase of potato culture, was absenteeism. In 1729 a list of absentees was published by Mr. Thomas Prior, which ran through several editions. The list includes the Viceroy himself, then an absentee, which he well might be, at that time and for long afterwards, as Primate Boulter was the ruler of Ireland. Mr. Prior sets down in his pamphlet the incomes of the absentees, and the total amounts to the enormous annual sum of £627,769 sterling, a sum in excess of the entire revenue of the country, which, though increasing year after year, even twenty-nine years afterwards was only £650,763.

Besides the exhausting drain by absentee proprietors, there was another kind of absenteeism, namely, that of Englishmen who, through Court or other influence, obtained places in Ireland, but discharged the duties of them, such as they were, by deputy. Mr. Prior cites the following instance as an example:—"One of those Englishmen who got an appointment in Ireland landed in Dublin on a Saturday evening, went next day to a parish church, received the Sacrament there, went to the Courts on Monday, took the necessary oaths, and sailed for England that very evening! This was certainly expedition, but still coming over at all was troublesome: so those who had obtained appointments in Ireland got an Act quietly passed in the English Parliament dispensing them from visiting Ireland at all, even to take possession of those offices to which they were promoted."[44]

That a large proportion of the owners of the soil of a country should reside out of it, has been always regarded as a great evil, as well as a real loss to that country. Mr. M'Cullagh's elaborate attempt to prove there is no real pecuniary loss inflicted by mere absenteeism convinces no impartial man, least of all does it convince those who experience, daily in their own persons, the evils which inevitably result from absenteeism. It is fallacious with regard to any country, but especially so as regards Ireland, which, in his argument, he assumes to have her proportion of the profit from the manufactured exports of the United Kingdom, whereas she is not a manufacturing country at all, having as exports, only some linen and the food that should be kept at home to be consumed by her people. When taxes are to be levied and battles to be fought, we are always an integral part of the United Kingdom; but when there is a question of encouraging or extending manufactures, we are treated as the rival and the enemy of England.[45]

The avarice and tyranny of landlords, is usually set down as a principal cause of the great poverty and misery of the Irish people, during a long period. If we examine the rents paid one hundred and fifty, or even one hundred years ago, they will appear trifling when compared with the rents of the present day; so that, at first, one is inclined to question the accuracy of those writers who denounce the avarice and rack-renting propensities of the landlords of their time. But when we examine the question more closely, we find so many circumstances to modify and even to change our first views, that by degrees we arrive at the belief, that the complaints made were substantially true. If the rents of those times seem to us very low, we must remember that the land, for the most part, was in a wretched condition; that the majority of farms had much waste upon them, and that the portions tilled were not half tilled; so that whilst the acreage was large, the productive portion of the land was only a percentage of it. Then, agricultural skill was wanting; good implements were wanting; capital was wanting; everything that could improve the soft and make it productive, was wanting. These and many other causes made rents that seem trifling to us, rack-rents to the farmers who paid them. Swift had no doubt at all upon the matter, for he says: "Another great calamity is the exorbitant raising of the rents of lands. Upon the determination of all leases made before the year 1690, a gentleman thinks that he has but indifferently improved his estate if he has only doubled his rent-roll. Farms are screwed up to a rack-rent; leases granted but for a small term of years; tenants tied down to hard conditions, and discouraged from cultivating the lands they occupy to the best advantage by the certainty they have of the rent being raised on the expiration of their lease, proportionably to the improvements they shall make."[46] As to the unlimited power of landlords, and its tyrannical use, Arthur Young, writing in 1779, less than one hundred years ago, says: "The age has improved so much in humanity, that even the poor Irish have experienced its influence, and are every day treated better and better; but still the remnant of the old manners, the abominable distinction of religion, united with the oppressive conduct of the little country gentlemen, or rather vermin, of the kingdom, who were never out of it, altogether bear still very heavy on the poor people, and subject them to situations more mortifying than we ever behold in England. The landlord of an Irish estate, inhabited by Roman Catholics, is a sort of despot, who yields obedience in whatever concerns the poor to no law but that of his will . . . A long series of oppressions, aided by very many ill-judged laws, have brought landlords into a habit of exerting a very lofty superiority, and their vassals into that of an almost unlimited submission. Speaking a language that is despised, professing a religion that is abhorred, and being disarmed, the poor find themselves in many cases slaves even in the bosom of *written* liberty." And again, this enlightened Protestant English gentleman says of the Irish landlord, that "nothing satisfies him but an unlimited submission."[47]

Forty years later, some of their more obvious, not to say essential duties, were brought under the notice of Irish landlords, but in vain. The writer quoted above on the Famine of 1822 says: "It is therefore a duty incumbent on all those who possess property, and consequently have an interest in the prosperity of this country, to prevent a recurrence of this awful calamity [the Famine], and to provide for those persons over whom fortune has placed them, and whom they should consider as entrusted to their care, and entitled to their protection; and this can only be successfully carried into execution by their procuring and substituting other articles of food, so as to leave the poor only partially dependant on the potato crop, for their support."[48]

Some Acts of Parliament, without perhaps intending it, gave a further impulse to potato cultivation in Ireland. As if the violation of the treaty of Limerick by William the Third; the exterminating code of Anne; its continuance and intensification, under the first and second George were not a sufficient persecution of the native race, statutes continued to be enacted against them, during the first twenty-five years of George the Third's reign—that is, up to 1785, But although this was the case, the necessity of making some concessions to them began to be felt by their rulers, from the time the revolt of the American colonies assumed a dangerous aspect. So that, whilst, on the one hand, the enactment of persecuting laws was not wholly abandoned, on the other, there sprang up a spirit, if not of kindness, at least of recognition, and perhaps of fear. "It was in the year 1744," says Sir Henry Parnell, "that the Irish Legislature passed the first Act towards conciliating the Catholics."[49] And a very curious concession it was. It was entitled—"An Act to enable His Majesty's subjects, of whatever persuasion, to testify their allegiance to him."[50] Previously, the Catholics dared not to approach the foot of the throne even to swear, that they were ready to die in defence of it. But, two years before this an Act was passed of no apparent political significance, which was of much more practical value to the Catholics. It was "An Act to encourage the reclaiming of unprofitable bogs."[51] This Act made it lawful "for every Papist, or person professing the Popish religion," to lease fifty acres, plantation measure, of such bog, and one half acre of arable land thereunto adjoining, "as a site for a house, or for the purpose of delving for gravel or limestone for manure." Certain immunities were granted, and certain restrictions imposed. The immunities were, that, for the first seven years after the bog was reclaimed, the tenant should be free from all tithes, cesses, or applotment; the restrictions were: (1) that no bog should be deemed unprofitable, unless it were at least four feet from the surface to the bottom of it, when reclaimed—the Act having been especially passed for the reclaiming of *unprofitable* bogs; (2) that no person should be entitled to the benefit of the Act, unless he reclaimed ten plantation acres; (3) that half whatever quantity was leased, should be reclaimed in twenty-one years; (4) that such bog should be at least one mile from any city or market-town. Alas, how utterly prostrate the Catholics must have been, when this was regarded as a concession to them! Yet it was, and one of such importance, that "in times of less liberality it had been repeatedly thrown out of Parliament, as tending to encourage Popery, to the detriment of the Protestant religion;" and to counter-balance it, the pension allotted to apostate priests in Anne's reign was, in the very same Session of Parliament, raised from £30 to £40 per annum, by the Viceroy, Lord Townsend.[52] The wretched serfs were of course glad to get any hold upon the soil, even though it was unprofitable bog, and largely availed themselves of the provisions of the Act. Ten or twelve years later, we find Arthur Young speaking with much approval of the many efforts that were being made, in various parts of Ireland, to reclaim the bogs—efforts resulting, no doubt, in a great measure, from this Bill. In the process of reclaiming the bogs, the potato was an essential auxiliary.

But of all the means of increasing the growth of that renowned esculent in Ireland, the Catholic Relief Act of 1793 must, at least in more recent times, be accorded the first place. That Act, it is said, was the result of the fears excited in England by the French Revolution. Whether this was so or not, the concessions it made were large for the time; and its effect upon potato culture in Ireland is unquestionable. Dr. Beaufort, in his Ecclesiastical Map, gives our whole population in 1789 as 4,088,226. Sir Henry Parnell says the Catholics were, at this time, at least three-fourths of the population.[53] And this agrees with the estimate which the Catholics themselves made of their numbers at the period; for, in a long and remarkable petition, presented to the House of Commons in January, 1792, they say: "Behold us then before you, three millions of the people of Ireland." These three millions became, by the Bill of '93, entitled to the elective franchise; or, as the Bill itself more correctly expressed it, "such parts of all existing oaths," as put it out of their power to exercise the elective franchise, were repealed. The Catholics were not slow in availing themselves of this important privilege, which they had not enjoyed since the first year of George the Second's reign—a period of sixty-six years.[54] They soon began to influence the elections in at least three out of the four provinces; but they influenced them only through their landlords, not daring, for a full generation after, to give independent votes. A landlord had political influence in proportion to the number of voters he brought, or rather drove, to the poll. To secure and extend this influence, the manufacture of forty-shilling freeholders went on rapidly, and to an enormous extent. The Catholics were poor, numerous, subservient, and doubtless grateful for recent concessions; so bits of land, merely sufficient to qualify them for voting, were freely leased to them, which they as freely accepted.[55] On these they built cabins, relying on the potato for food, and on a little patch of oats or wheat, to pay their rent and taxes. By the influence of O'Connell and the Catholic Association, the forty-shilling freeholders broke away from landlord influence in the great General Election of 1826, and supported the candidates who promised to vote for Catholic Emancipation, in spite of every threat. From that day their doom was sealed; the landlords began to call loudly for their disfranchisement, and accordingly they were disfranchised by the Relief Bill of 1829, but of course they still retained their little holdings. Immediately the landlords began to utter bitter complaints of surplus population; they began to ventilate their grievances through the English and Irish press, saying that their land was overrun by cottiers and squatters—the main cause of all this being kept in the background, namely, the immense and continuous increase of forty-shilling freeholders, by themselves, and for their own purposes. But the moment those poor men presumed to vote according to the letter and the spirit of the Constitution, they were sacrificed to landlord indignation; they were declared to be an incumbrance on the soil that ought to be removed. Landlords began to act upon this view: they began to evict, to exterminate, to consolidate; and in this fearful work the awful Famine of '47 became a powerful, and I fear in many cases even a welcome, auxiliary to the Crowbar Brigade.[56]

Thus was the cultivation of the potato extended in various ways, until it had become the principal food of nineteen-twentieths of the population long before the Famine of '47.

FOOTNOTES:

1.   Raleigh earned this property by some terrible services. He was an officer in the expedition of the Lord Deputy Gray, when he attacked the Italian camp on *Dun-an-oir*, at Smerwick harbour in Kerry. After some time the Italians yielded, but on what precise terms it is now impossible to say, the accounts of the transaction are so various and conflicting. Indeed, O'Daly says the English were the first to send a flag of truce. Anyhow, the Italian garrison, which had come to aid the Irish, fell into the power of the English, and here is Dr. Leland's account of what followed:—"Wingfield was commissioned to disarm them, and when this service was performed an English company was sent into the fort. The Irish rebels found they were reserved for execution by martial law. The Italian general and some of the officers were made prisoners of war, but the garrison was butchered in cold blood; *nor is it without pain that we find a service so horrid and detestable committed to Sir Walter Raleigh.*"

2.   The people of Quito said *papas*. The Spaniards corrupted this to *battata*, and the Portuguese to the softer *batata*.

3.   Edwards (Life of Sir W. Raleigh. M'Millan, 1868), says Hooker is the only contemporary writer who asserts that Raleigh sailed with this expedition, and Edwards adds, "It is by no means certain that he did so." But from the following entry in the State Papers of Elizabeth's reign it appears quite certain that he did sail with it:—"The names of all the ships, officers, and gentlemen, with the pieces of ordnance, etc., *gone* in the voyage with Sir Humfrey Gylberte,—Capt. Walter Rauley, commanding the Falcon," etc.— *State Papers (Domestic)*, Vol. 126, No. 149, Nov. 18 & 19, 1578.

        Mr. Edwards may not have met this entry, as he does not refer to it.

        In spite of his many failures, Raleigh was, to the last, confident in the final success of his scheme for colonizing America. After the failure of nine expeditions, and on the ere of his fall, he said: "I shall yet live to see it (America) an English nation." (Edwards.)

4.   Perhaps *Kartoffel*, one of the German names for potato, is a corruption of this.

5.   Mr. Edwards says, I know not on what authority, that the land given to Raleigh was about 12,000 acres. The grants are set forth plainly enough in the following entries:—"The Queen, desirous to have the Province of Munster, in the realm of Ireland, re-peopled and inhabited with civil, loyal,

and dutiful subjects, in consideration of the great charge and trouble which Sir Walter Raleghe sustained in transporting and planting English people into the province, and in recompense of his good service rendered in Ireland, pursuant to her royal letters dated the last of February, 1586 to the Lord Deputy and Lord Chancellor directed, and intending to bestow upon him three seignories and a-half of land, . . . 'lying as near to the town of Youghall as they may be conveniently,' *each seignory containing* 12,000 *acres of tenanted land, not accounting mountains, bogs, or barren heath.*" And again: "And as Sir Walter made humble suit, to enable him the better to perform the enterprize for the habitation and repeopling of the land, to grant him and his heirs, in fee-farm for ever, the *possessions* of the late dissolved abbey or monastery called Molanassa, otherwise Molana, and the late dissolved priory of the Observant Friars, or the Black Friars, near Youghall, . . . and, as they lie adjoining the lands already granted to him, her Majesty is pleased to comply with his request, and by her letters, dated at Greenwich the 2nd of July, 1587, directed to the Lord Deputy, expressed her intention to that effect." *Patent and Close Rolls, Chancery, Ireland, reg. Elizabeth*, Mem. 5, 41, 1595, p. 323.

As the lands at first granted did not measure the 42,000 acres, the Lord Deputy is instructed to issue a commission to measure off so much of other escheated lands adjoining "as shall be requisite to make up the full number and quantity of three seignories and a-half of tenantable land, without mountains, bogs, or barren heath; To hold for ever in fee-farm, as of the Castle of Carregroghan, in the Co. of Cork, in free soccage and not in capite."—*Ibid.* p. 327.

Alas! how soon he tired of the great and coveted prize.

6. Hooker, Suppl. to Holinshed's Chronicle, p. 183.
7. Some Considerations for the Promoting of Agriculture and Employing the Poor, addressed to Members of the House of Commons, by R.L. V.M. Haliday Collection of pamphlets in the Library of the Royal Irish Academy, Vol. 54.
8. Page 18.
9. Page 35.
10. Short View of the State of Ireland. Haliday Pamphlets, Vol. 74.
11. An answer to a paper called "A Memorial of the Poor Inhabitants of the Kingdom of Ireland." *Same Vol.*
12. "Answer to Memorial," signed A.B., March 25, 1728.

13.   "Letter to the Duke of Newcastle."

14.   Vol. I., p. 166.

15.   "The famine of 1741 was not regarded with any active interest in England or in any foreign country, and the subject is scarcely alluded to in the literature of the day. No measures were adopted, either by the Executive or the Legislature, for the purpose of relieving the distress caused by this famine."—*Irish Crisis*, by Sir C.E. Trevelyan, Bart., p. 13.

16.   Probably the origin of the potato pit, as we now have it, in Ireland was the following advice given in *Pue's Occurrences* of Nov. 29th, 1740:—

"Method of securing potatoes from the severest frost.

"Dig up your potatoes in the beginning of December, or sooner, and, in proportion to your quantity of potatoes, dig a large hole about ten foot deep in such place as your garden or near your house where the ground is sandy or dry, and not subject to water; then put your potatoes into the hole, with all their dirt about them, to within three feet of the surface of the ground. If you have sand near you, throw some of it among the potatoes and on top of them. When you have thus lodged your potatoes, then fill up the rest of the hole with the earth first thrown out, and, with some stuff, raise upon the hole a large heap of earth in the form of a large haycock, which you may cover with some litter or heath. By the covering of earth of five or six feet deep, your potatoes will be secured against the severest frosts, which are not known to enter over two feet into the ground. The same pit will serve you year after year, and when the frosts are over you may take out your potatoes."

17.   "O'Halloran on the Air."

18.   *Exshaw's Magazine*.

19.   *Pue's Occurrences*, March 11, 1740.

20.   Sir John Rogerson's Quay, of course.

21.   *Pue's Occurrences*, Jan 1, 1740.

22.   This storm visited other parts of the coast. The news from Dundalk under the same date is, that the *Jane* and *Andrew* of Nantz was wrecked there, "the weather continuing very stormy, with a very great frost." Accounts from Nenagh under date of Jan. 5th say:—"The Shannon is frozen over, and a hurling match has taken place upon it; and Mr. Parker had a sheep roast whole on the ice, with which he regaled the company who had assembled to witness the hurling match." Under January 29th we have a ludicrous accident

recorded, namely, "that the Drogheda postboy's horse fell at Santry, near Dublin, and broke his neck. One of the postboy's legs being caught under the horse *got so frozen that he could not pull it out!*" At length some gentlemen who were passing released him.—*Ibid.*

23. I find by the newspapers of the time that Primate Boulter acted with much generosity, especially in the second year of the famine, feeding many thousands at the workhouse at his own expense. He also appealed to his friends to subscribe for the same purpose. The Right Honourable William Conolly, then living at Leixlip Castle, distributed £20 worth of meal in Leixlip, and ordered his steward to attend to the wants of the people there during the frost. Lords Mountjoy and Tullamore, Sir Thomas Prendergast, and other influential persons commenced a general collection in Dublin, but it was only for the starving artizans of Dublin. The co-heirs of Lord Ranelagh ordered £110 to be distributed in Roscommon; Lady Betty Brownlow, then abroad, sent home £440 for her tenants in the North; Chief Justice Singleton gave twenty tons of meal to be sold in Drogheda at one shilling and a penny a stone; the Rt. Hon. Wm. Graham did the same—it was then selling from one shilling and sixpence to one shilling and eightpence a stone; Lord Blundell gave £50 to his tenants; Dean Swift gave £10 to the weavers of the Liberty.

An obelisk 140 feet in height, supported upon open arches, and surrounded by a grove of full-grown trees, stands on a hill near Maynooth, and can be seen to advantage both from the Midland and the Great Southern Railway. It is usually known as "Lady Conolly's Monument." From its being built without any apparent utility, illnatured people sometimes call it "Lady Conolly's Folly." It is said to have been designed by Castelli (Anglicised "Castells"), the architect of Carton, Castletown House, and Leinster House, Kildare Street, now the Royal Dublin Society House. It bears on the keystones of its three principal arches the suggestive date, "1740." It was erected to give employment to the starving people in that year, not by Lady Louisa Conolly, as is generally supposed, but by a Mrs. Conolly, as the following information, kindly supplied by the Marquis of Kildare, will show:—

"I find in my notes," says the Marquis, "that the obelisk was built by Mrs. Conolly, widow of the Rt. Hon. Wm. Conolly, Speaker of the Irish House of Commons. She had Castletown for her life, and died in 1752, in her ninetieth year. Mrs. Delany, in her Autobiography, vol. iii, p. 158, mentions that her table was open to her friends of all ranks, and her purse to the poor . . . She dined at three o'clock, and generally had two tables of eight or ten people each . . . She was clever at business . . . A plain and vulgar woman in her manners, but had very valuable qualities. 1740 was a year of great scarcity, and farmers were ploughing their wheat in May to sow summer barley. In March Mrs. Conolly's sister, Mrs. Jones, wrote to another sister, Mrs. Bound, that Mrs. Conolly was building an obelisk opposite a vista at the back of Castletown House, and that it would cost £300 or £400 at least, and she wondered how she could afford it. The nephew of the Speaker, also the Rt. Hon. Wm. Conolly, lived at Leixlip Castle till he succeeded to Castletown in 1752. He married Lady Anne Wentworth, daughter of an Earl of Strafford. His son was the Right Hon. Thos. Conolly, who married Lady Louisa Lennox, daughter of the Duke of Richmond. From her Castletown passed to the father of the present Mr. Conolly, after the death of Lady Louisa."

Mrs. Jones must have made a very erroneous guess at the expense of building the obelisk, even at that time; now, instead of three or four hundred pounds, double as many thousands would scarcely build it. Although erected by Mrs. Conolly, it stands on the Duke of Leinster's property. The site is the finest in the neighbourhood, and she obtained it from the Earl of Kildare, by giving him a portion of the Castletown estate instead. Lately those two pieces of ground have been re-exchanged, and when they came to be measured, they were found to be of exactly the same extent.

24. The coming of the thaw was indicated by some accidents on the ice. Under date 10th Feb. it was reported from Derry that the ice gave way there, and several persons were drowned. In Dublin, at the same date, a man was also drowned who attempted to cross the river on the ice near the Old Bridge. But a boy was more fortunate. He, too, was on the ice on the Liffey, and the part on which he stood becoming detached was driven by the current through Ormond and Essex Bridges; he kept his position, however, on the floating ice till he was taken off in a boat.

25. The following story is told in *Pue's Occurrences*, in May, 1740:—A broguemaker had been committed to Dungannon jail for some offence, but managed to make his escape. He was pursued and searched for in vain. The jailer gave him up as lost when, one day, after being at large during five weeks, he presented himself at the jail to the astonishment of the jailer, who questioned him as to the cause of his return. He replied, that he had travelled to Dublin, and

had gone through a great part of Munster, but finding nowhere such good quarters as he had in Dungannon jail, he came back.

26.   On the passing of this bill Sir Charles E. Trevelyan remarks with quiet severity:—"There is no mention of grants or loans; but an Act was passed by the Irish Parliament, 1741 (15 George II, cap. 8), for the more effectual securing the payment of rents and preventing frauds by tenants."—*Irish Crisis*, p. 13.

27.   Matthew O'Connor's *History of the Irish Catholics*, p. 222.

28.   The Judges held the assizes in Tuam instead of Galway this year, on account of the fever in the latter place.—*Dutton's Galway*.

29.   *The Groans of Ireland, in a letter to an M.P.*, 1741. The estimated population in 1731 was 2,010,221. Rutty says it was computed, perhaps, with some exaggeration, that one-fifth of the people died of famine and pestilence. This agrees with the higher estimate above.

30.   *Philo-Ierne*, London, May 20, 1755. Reprinted in Cork with the author's name, Richard Bocklesly, Esq., M.D. It is hardly necessary to say that the "people" referred to in the above extract mean merely the English colony in Ireland.

31.   *Ibid.*, pp. 5 & 6—He seems to use the word "dairy" here in a sense somewhat different from its present application.

32.   The Bristol barrel contained 22 stones—one stone more than the Irish barrel.

33.   A disease called the *Curl* appeared in the potato in Lancashire in 1764. It was in that Shire the potato was first planted in England; and we are told the Curl appeared in those districts of it in which it was first planted. The nature of the disease is indicated by its name. The stalk became discoloured and stunted almost from the beginning of its growth; it changed its natural healthy green for a sickly greenish brown, the leaves literally curling like those of that species of ornamental holly known as the "screw-leaved." The plant continued to grow, and even to produce tubers, but they never attained any considerable size, and from their inferior quality could not be used for food. The Curl appeared in Ireland about the year 1770, where it caused much loss, as we find a large quantity of grain was imported for food about that period. Isolated cases of the Curl were not unfrequent in this country long after it ceased to cause alarm to the farmer. I have seen many such cases, especially where potatoes were planted on lea. On examining the *set* beneath a plant affected with Curl, I invariably found it had not rotted away

as was usual with those sets that produced healthy plants. There were as many remedies propounded for the Curl as for the blight of 1846-7 with a like result—none of them were of any use.

34.   Report of the Committee for the "Relief of the Distressed Districts in Ireland," appointed at a general meeting, held at the City of London Tavern, on the 7th May, 1822.

35.   *Impartial Review*. Miliken, Dublin, 1822.

36.   Report of Parliamentary Committee.

37.   Amongst the means resorted to at this time to raise funds for the starving Irish was a ball at the Opera House in London, at which the King was present, and which realized the large sum of £6,000. This piece of information the Irish Census Commissioners for 1851, curiously enough, insert in that column of their Report set apart for "*Contemporaneous Epidemics.*"

38.   The chief part of this £60,000 is still under the management of the "Society for Bettering the Condition of the Poor of Ireland."

39.   The following extract from a letter of Mr. Secretary Legge, dated London, May 4, 1740, and addressed to Dublin Castle, expresses very *naively* an English official's feelings about the terrible frost and famine of that year:—"I hope the weather, which seems mending at last, will be of service to Ireland, *and comfort our Treasury, which, I am afraid, has been greatly chilled with the long frost and embargo.*"—*Records, Birmingham Tower, Chief Sec.'s Department, Box 10.*

40.   Speech, p. 26; quoted by Plowden, vol. i., p. 253. Note.

41.   Answer to Address of Commons, 2nd July, 1698.

42.   *Arthur Young's Tour in Ireland*, App., p. 149.

43.   *Groans of Ireland*, p. 20.

44.   Mr. Prior's Pamphlet was dedicated to the Viceroy, Lord Carteret, and both Houses of Parliament, which proves how certain he was of his facts and statements.

45.   See Note A in Appendix, for a fuller discussion of the question of Absenteeism.

46.   "The present miserable state of Ireland." How like the Ireland of the other day!

47.   *Arthur Young's Tour in Ireland*, App., p. 40.

48.   *Impartial Review*, p. 3.

49.   *History of the Penal Laws.*

50.   13 & 14 Geo. II, cap. 35.

51. 11th & 12th Geo. II, cap. 21.

52. Plowden.

53. *History of the Penal Laws.*

54. By the 1st Geo. II, cap. 9, sec. 7, it was enacted that no Papist could vote at an election, without taking the oath of supremacy—an oath which no Catholic could take. Primate Boulter thought he saw a disposition on the part of the English colony to make common cause with the natives in favour of Irish, interests, and taking alarm at the prospect of such a dreadful calamity, he got the Ministers to pass this law. It is said it was carried through Parliament under a false title, being called a Bill for Regulating, etc.; but it would have passed under any title.

55. The feelings of the Irish Catholics for these concessions are curiously illustrated, by an inscription on the Carmelite Church in Clarendon Street, Dublin, in which the year 1793 is called, "the first year of restored liberty," and George the Third is proclaimed as the "best of kings." Here is the full inscription:—

> D. O. M.
> Sub invocatione B.V. Mariæ.
> C.
> Primum hujus Ecclesiæ lapidem
>   posuit Johannes Sweetman, Armiger.
> Memoriale hoc grati animi restitutæ
>   Catholicæ Libertatis Georgio
> tertio Regum optimo, annuente Parlia-
>   mento ac toto populo
> acclamante, Dedicat Patriæ Pietas. Anno
>   supradictæ Libertatis primo.
> Regni vigesimo tertio, ab Incarnatione
>   1793, die Octobris tertio.
>   T. BEAHAN,
>   Arch

56. Forty-shilling freeholders in Ireland and forty-shilling freeholders in England were quite different classes. The latter, by the statute, 8 Henry VI, cap. 7, passed in 1429, must be "people dwelling and resident in the counties, who should have *free land* or *tenement* to the value of forty shillings by the year at

least, above all charges;" whilst in Ireland, every tenant having a lease for a life was entitled to a Parliamentary vote, provided he swore that his farm was worth forty shillings annual rent, more than the rent reserved in his lease.

Mr. Pim writes:—"A numerous tenantry having the right to vote, and practically obliged to exercise that right at the dictation of their landlord, was highly prized . . . When the Emancipation Act was passed in 1829, the forty-shilling freeholders were disfranchised, and, being no longer of use to their landlords, every means has since been employed to get rid of them."—*The Condition and Prospects of Ireland, by Jonathan Pim*, late M.P. for Dublin City.

"It is in vain to deny or to conceal the truth in respect to that franchise the forty-shilling franchise.   . It was, until a late period, the instrument through which the landed aristocracy—the resident and the absentee proprietor, maintained their local influence—through which property had its weight, its legitimate weight, in the national representation. The landlord has been disarmed by the priest . . . that weapon which the landlord.
has forged with so much care, and has heretofore wielded with such success, has broken short in his hand."—*Mr. Peel's Speech in the House of Commons, 5th March, 1829, introducing the Catholic Relief Bill.*

Leaving out the *"legitimate weight"* of landed proprietors, as exercised through the forty-shilling freeholders, the above statement, besides being a remarkable one from such a cautious Minister, is not far from being correct.

* * * * *

CHAPTER II.

The Potato Blight of 1845—Its appearance in England—In Ireland—
Weather—Scotland—Names given to the Blight—First appearance
of the Blight in Ireland—Accounts of its progress—The Royal
Agricultural Improvement Society of Ireland—Its action—The Dublin
Corporation—O'Connell—His plan for meeting the Crisis—Deputation
to the Lord Lieutenant—How it was received—Lord Heytesbury's
Reply—It displeases the Government—The *Times'* Commissioner—
His suggestions—Mr. Gregory's Letter—Mr. Crichton's—Sir James
Murray on the Blight—Action of the Clergy—The Mansion House
Committee—Resolutions—Analysis of five hundred letters on the
Blight—Partial cessation of the Rot caused by the Blight—Report of
Professors Lindley and Playfair—Estimated loss—Query Sheets sent
out—Corporation Address to the Queen—Her Reply—Address of the
London Corporation asking for Free Trade—The Potato Blight made a
party question—Dean Hoare's Letter—Failure of remedies.

The disease which cut off at least one-half of the potato crop of Ireland
in 1845, and completely destroyed that of 1846, had made its appearance
several years before, in other countries. It is said to have existed for a
long time in the western parts of America, before it appeared in Europe;
but as it was at first confounded with dry rot and wet rot, the American
may have been a different disease from ours. What seems certain is, that
the potato disease, as known to us, made its first appearance in Germany;
and in the year 1842, travelling thence into Belgium, it manifested itself in

a very destructive form in the neighbourhood of Liege. It visited Canada in 1844, and in 1845 it appeared in almost every part of the United Kingdom, being observed first of all in the Isle of Wight, where it was most virulent on wheat lands which had been manured with guano.

In the first week of September, the potatoes in the London market were, to a very considerable extent, found to be unfit for human food. To the eye they did not show any sign of disease, but when boiled and cut its presence was but too evident, by the black, or rather brownish-black mass they presented. The potato fields began to be examined, and the provincial journals soon teemed with accounts of the destructive visitation, with speculations concerning its cause, and suggestions as to probable remedies. The descriptions of the disease given by the English newspapers do not quite agree with the symptoms observed somewhat later in Ireland. "Whatever may have been the cause," says one account, "it is certain that, externally, the disease indicates itself by a fungus or moss producing decomposition of the farinaceous interior."[57] "The disease is very general in this locality," says another, "beginning with a damp spot on some part of the potato."[58] A third observer writes: "The commencement of the attack is generally dated here from Tuesday, the 19th ultimo. A day of the heaviest rain almost ever known. It first appears a bluish speck on the potato, and then spreads rapidly."[59]

Whether it was that, in England, in their anxiety about the tuber, people paid little or no attention to the stems or leaves of the potato; or, that the earlier symptoms differed from the later, matters but little, the disease was certainly the same throughout the United Kingdom. In Ireland it was first observed on the leaves of the plant as brown spots of various shapes and sizes, pretty much as if a dilution of acid had fallen upon them like drops of rain. Sometimes the blight made its appearance near high hedges, or under trees; sometimes portions of a field would be greatly affected with it before other parts were touched at all; and I have sometimes observed the very first symptoms of the disease opposite an open gateway, as if a blighting wind had rushed in, making for some distance a sort of avenue of discoloured leaves and stalks, about the width of the gateway at first, but becoming wider onwards. When the decomposition produced by the blight was in a somewhat advanced stage, the odour from the potato field, which was very offensive, was perceptible at a considerable distance. There may have been cases in this country in which the disease was first observed in the tubers, but they must have been rare. It appeared in Scotland with the same symptoms as in Ireland. A contemporary account says: "In various parts of Scotland the potatoes have suffered fearfully from the blight. The leaves of the plant have, generally speaking, first been affected, and then the root." From this mode of manifesting itself, the potato disease was commonly called in Ireland, as in Scotland, the Potato Blight. It had other names given to it; potato murrain, cholera in the potato, and so on; but Potato Blight in Ireland, at least, was and is its all but universal name. The whole stem soon became affected after the blight had appeared on the leaves, more especially if the weather was damp; and for some time before the period for digging out the crop had arrived, the potato fields showed nothing but rank weeds, with here and there the remains of withered-up stems—bleached skeletons of the green healthy plants of some weeks before.

I have a vivid recollection of the blight as it appeared in the southern portion of Kildare in 1850. The fifteenth of July in that year—St. Swithin's day—was a day of clouds and lightning, of thunder and terrific rain. It was one of those days that strike the timid with alarm and terror: sometimes it was dark as twilight; sometimes a sudden ghastly brightness was produced by the lightning. That the air was charged with electricity to a most unusual extent was felt by everybody. Those who had an intimate knowledge of the various potato blights from '45 said, "This is the beginning of the blight." So it was. It is well known that after the blight of '45 the potatoes in Ireland had scarcely shown any blossom for some years, even those unaffected by the blight, or affected by it only to a small extent; and the few exceptional blossoms which appeared produced no seed. This feebleness of the plant was gradually disappearing, and in 1850 it was remarked as a very hopeful sign that the potatoes blossomed almost as of old. The crop having been sown much earlier than was customary before '45, most of the fields, on this memorable fifteenth of July, were rich with that beautiful and striking sheet of blossom, which they show when the plant is in vigorous health. Next day—a still, oppressive, sultry, electric sort of day—I, in company with some others, visited various potato fields. There was but one symptom that the blight had come; all the blossoms were closed, even at mid-day: this was enough to the experienced eye—the blight had come. Heat, noontide sun, nothing ever opened them again. In some days they began to fall off the stems; in eight or ten days other symptoms appeared, and so began the Potato Blight of 1850, a mild one, but still the true blight. How like this fifteenth of July must have been to the nineteenth of August, 1845, described above by the *Cambridge Chronicle*.

The blight of 1845 was noticed in Ireland about the middle of September. Like the passage birds, it first appeared on the coast, and, it would seem, first of all on the coast of Wexford. It soon travelled inland, and accounts of its alarming progress began to be published in almost every part of the country. Letters in the daily press from Cork, Tyrone, Meath, Roscommon, and various other places, gave despairing accounts of its extent and rapidity. A Meath peasant writes:—"Awful is our story; I do be striving to *blindfold them* (the potatoes) in the boiling. I trust in God's mercy no harm will come from them." The Very Rev. Dr. M'Evoy, P.P., writing from Kells, October the 24th, says:—"On my most minute personal inspection of the state of the potato crop in this most fertile potato-growing *locale*, is founded my inexpressibly painful conviction, that one family in twenty of the people will not have a single potato left on Christmas Day next . . . With starvation at our doors, grimly staring us, vessels laden with our whole hopes of existence, our provisions, are hourly wafted from our every port. From one milling establishment I have last night seen no less than fifty dray-loads of meal moving on to

Drogheda, thence to go to feed the foreigner, leaving starvation and death the soon and certain fate of the toil and sweat that raised this food."

From other places the accounts were more favourable. "I have found no field without the disease," writes Mr. Horace Townsend to the *Southern Reporter*, "but in great variety of degree; in some at least one-third of the crop is tainted, in others not a tenth, and all the remainder seems sound as ever." From Athy, Kilkenny, Mayo, Carlow, and Newry, the accounts were that the disease was partial, and seemed in some cases arrested. But these hopeful accounts had, almost in every instance, to be contradicted later on. The blight did not appear in all places at once; it travelled mysteriously but steadily, and from districts where the crop was safe a few days before, the gloomiest accounts were unexpectedly received. The special correspondent of a Dublin newspaper, writing from the West, explains this when he says: "The disease appeared suddenly, and the tubers are sometimes rotten in twenty-four hours afterwards."[60]

On the 18th of October, "*The Royal Agricultural Improvement Society of Ireland*" held a special meeting relative to the disease in the potatoes. They had, some short time before, appointed a sub-committee on the subject, Professor (now Sir Robert) Kane being its Chairman. He stated to the meeting that the sub-committee had sat the two previous days, but were not as yet prepared with anything definite on the subject. They, however, communicated some advice to farmers, under eight heads, founded on experiments. This advice, whether useful or not, was, for the most part, not within the power of small farmers to put in practice; but the sub-committee made one observation that should have aroused all the energies of those who had the lives of the people in their hands. They said that, "on mature consideration of the evidence now before them, it was advisable that the Council should direct the attention of the Irish Government to the now undoubted fact, that a great portion of the potato crop in this country was seriously affected by the disease in question." A cautious, well-weighed sentence, which, coming from such a responsible quarter, was full of portentous meaning for the future.

The Dublin Corporation took up the question of the Potato Blight with much and praiseworthy earnestness. They appointed a committee to enquire and report on the subject. A meeting of this committee was held in the City Assembly House on the 28th of October; the Lord Mayor, John L. Arabin, presided, who, from the accounts which had reached him, gave a gloomy picture of the progress of the disease. The late Mr. William Forde, then Town Clerk, in a letter to the committee, said he had recently inspected the produce of eight or ten acres dug and housed in an apparently sound state three weeks before, and that now it was difficult to find a sound potato amongst them. That all might not, however, be gloom, he added that he never saw so much corn safe and thatched in the haggards as he had seen this year.

It was at this meeting O'Connell first brought forward his plan for dealing with the impending famine, a plan which met with no favour from those in power, there not having been a single suggestion put forward in it which was taken up by them. The crisis, he said, was one of terrible importance; the lives of the people were at stake; the calamity was all but universal; something must be done, and done immediately, to meet it. Private subscriptions would not be sufficient; they might meet a local, but not a national calamity like the present. By a merciful dispensation of Providence there was one of the best oat crops that we ever have had in the country, but that crop was passing out of Ireland day by day. Then, quoting from the *Mark Lane Express*, he said, sixteen thousand quarters of oats were imported from Ireland to London alone in one week. His proposal was, that a deputation should be appointed to wait on the Lord Lieutenant (Lord Heytesbury) to urge certain measures on the Government, in order to mitigate the calamitous state of the country. 1. The first measure he proposed was the immediate stoppage of distillation and brewing, 2. Next, that the export of provisions of every kind to foreign countries should be immediately prohibited, and our own ports open to receive provisions from all countries. From this prohibition he, strangely enough, excepted England, although he had just

81

shown that it was England which was carrying away our provisions with the most alarming rapidity. He probably made this exception to induce the Government to lend a more willing ear to his other propositions. He adduced the example of Belgium, Holland, and even of Russia and Turkey, in support of this view; all these countries having closed their ports against the exportation of provisions, under analagous circumstances. 3. But all this, he said, was not enough; the Government must be called on to assist the country in buying provisions—called on, not in a spirit of begging or alms-seeking—but called on to supply from the resources of Ireland itself money for this purpose. Let our own money be applied to it. The proceeds of the Woods and Forests in this country are, he said, £74,000 a year; money, which instead of being applied to Irish purposes, had gone to improve Windsor and Trafalgar Square—two millions of Irish money having been already expended in this manner. This is no time to be bungling at trivial remedies; let a loan of a million and a half be raised on this £74,000 a year, which, at four per cent., would leave a portion of it for a sinking fund; let absentees be taxed fifty per cent., and every resident ten per cent. By these means abundant funds would be found to keep the people alive. Let there be got up in each county machinery for carrying out the relief: let the projected railways be commenced, and let the people be put to work from one end of the country to the other, and let them be paid in food. He concluded, amidst the applause of the gentlemen present, by moving, that a deputation do wait on His Excellency to lay this plan before him, and to explain to him the pressing necessity which existed for its adoption.

To the Tory Government of the day, especially to a politician like Lord Heytesbury, the scheme, in all likelihood, appeared very extravagant, and yet at this distance of time, and with the history of that terrible period before us, it was, on the whole, sound, statesmanlike, and practical.

In accordance with O'Connell's suggestion, a deputation was appointed to wait on the Lord Lieutenant. He received them at the Phoenix Park, on Wednesday, the 3rd of November. They were coldly received. This may be in part accounted for by the fact, that the two or three previous years were remarkable for the great Repeal agitation; O'Connell himself having baptized the year 1843, the Repeal year. Then the State trials came, in which the Repeal leaders fought the Government, inch by inch, putting it to enormous cost, trouble, and anxiety. To be sure it succeeded, at last, in securing a verdict, and in sending O'Connell and some four or five others to Richmond prison; but their imprisonment there, like their journey to it, was a continuous triumph. Besides, the Government were in the end defeated by an appeal to the House of Lords, and the State prisoners set free in the fall of 1844. O'Connell, it was known through the Press, had propounded a scheme to meet the impending famine, which was, in substance, the one laid before the Viceroy. It is not much to be wondered at, that a small politician and narrow party-man, as Lord Heytesbury was, should think it a victory to make the deputation feel his high displeasure at the manner in which agitators had been, for so long a period, bearding the Government to which he belonged.

The deputation was highly respectable, and ought to have been influential, consisting, as it did, of the Duke of Leinster, Lord Cloncurry, the Lord Mayor, O'Connell, Henry Grattan, Sir James Murray, John Augustus O'Neill, and some twenty other gentlemen of position. The journals of the next morning informed the public that the deputation was "most formally" received. The Lord Mayor read to His Excellency the resolutions drawn up by the committee by which the deputation was appointed. They stated—(1), That famine and pestilence were immediately imminent, unless the Government took prompt measures against them; (2), That this could be best done by employing the people in works of national utility; (3), That the ports ought to be closed against the exportation of corn; (4), That public granaries ought to be established in various parts of the country, the corn to be sold to the people at moderate prices; and (5), That the use of grain for distillation ought to be stopped.

The Lord Lieutenant read the following reply:—

"My Lord Mayor and Gentlemen,—It can scarcely be necessary for me to assure you that the state of the potato crop has for some time occupied, and still occupies, the most anxious attention of the Government.

"Scientific men have been sent over from England to co-operate with those of this country, in endeavouring to investigate the nature of the disease, and, if possible, to devise means to arrest its progress. They have not yet terminated their enquiries; but two reports have already been received from them, which have been communicated to the public.

"The Government is also furnished with constant reports from the stipendiary magistrates and inspectors of constabulary, who are charged to watch the state of the potato disease, and the progress of the harvest. These vary from day to day, and are often contradictory; it will, therefore, be impossible to form an accurate opinion on the whole extent of the evil till the digging of the potatoes shall be further advanced. To decide, under such circumstances, upon the most proper measures to be adopted, would be premature; particularly as there is reason to hope that, though the evil exists to a very great extent in some localities, in others it has but partially manifested itself.

"There is no immediate pressure in the market. I will, however, lose no time in submitting your suggestions to the consideration of the Cabinet. The greater part of them can only be enforced by legislative enactment, and all require to be maturely weighed before they can be adopted. It must be clear to you, that in a case of such great national importance, no decision can be taken without a previous reference to the responsible advisers of the Crown."

When the Lord Lieutenant had concluded reading the above answer, he immediately commenced bowing the deputation out. As they were about to withdraw, O'Connell made an observation about distilleries. Lord Heytesbury, not condescending to mention him by name, said, that the observation *of the gentleman who had spoken* was one deserving of much consideration, and one which had not been overlooked by the Government, when it had the matter under discussion; and again began bowing them out, "which," writes one of those present, "was *distinctly* understood, and the deputation forthwith retired."

Although there is clear evidence in Sir Robert Peel's memoirs of himself, that Lord Heytesbury immediately submitted the views of the deputation to the Cabinet, His Excellency's letter, which no doubt accompanied them, is not given, neither is the address itself; nor does the Premier or Home Secretary discuss these views, or in any way allude to them in subsequent communications. The evidence we have, that they were in the hands of the Cabinet without delay, is contained in a letter of Lord Heytesbury himself, dated 8th of November, given in the Peel Memoirs, the name of its recipient, contrary to his usual practice, being suppressed by Sir Robert Peel. The Lord Lieutenant's address to the deputation was evidently found fault with, at least in one particular, at head quarters—and he is on his defence in this letter. "It is perfectly true" writes His Excellency, "that I did, in my answer to the Lord Mayor, say there was no immediate pressure on the market; but you must not give too wide a meaning to that observation, which had reference merely to his demand that the exportation of grain should be prohibited and the ports immediately thrown open. My meaning was that there was nothing so pressing as to require us to act without waiting for the decision of the responsible advisers of the Crown. But the danger may be upon us before we are aware of its being near; for, as I said in a former letter, the sudden decay of potatoes dug up in an apparently sound state sets all calculation at defiance. Some precautionary measures must be adopted, and adopted promptly, for there is danger in delay."

It is worthy of remark, that the only part of the Viceroy's answer to the deputation, that could weaken the arguments in favour of Free

Trade, was his saying, "there was no immediate pressure on the market;" and this was the only part found fault with by the un-named minister to whom the above defence was addressed.

The reception accorded to the deputation was soon known through, the city, and the chief liberal daily journal opened its leader on the subject next morning in this indignant fashion:—"They may starve! Such in spirit, if not in words, was the reply given yesterday by the English Viceroy, to the memorial of the deputation, which, in the name of the Lords and Commons of Ireland, prayed that the food of this kingdom be preserved, lest the people thereof perish."[61]

Meantime the newspapers were filled with accounts of the progress of the disease, with remedies to arrest it, and with suggestions of various kinds for warding off the impending famine. Mr. Campbell Foster, then travelling in Ireland as "Times' Commissioner," made some very sensible suggestions, which, he says, he had obtained during his journeys through the country. (1). He says it was generally agreed, that the potato crop of 1845 was about one-fifth more than the average of other years. This arose partly from the greater breadth of land that had been placed under potato culture, and partly from the unusually abundant produce of the crop. Although he admits the general opinion that, at the time[62] about one-third of the crop was lost, still, if even then the disease could be arrested, his opinion was, that there would be food enough in the country for the wants of the people. "Various plans," he writes, "such as quick lime, layers of ashes, kiln drying, exposure to the air, and ventilation have been suggested, to obtain dryness. Most of these are utterly futile, as beyond the general means and comprehension of the people." He then gives a simple plan of ventilation which was within the reach of every peasant. It was, to make an air passage under the whole length of the potato pit, and to have one or two vent holes, or chimnies, on the surface of it. The next thing to guard against was frost, which always descends perpendicularly. This being the fact, the only thing required was simply a sod to place over the chimney, or vent hole, every night, or when it might be raining hard, to keep the potatoes dry and free from frosting. His second important suggestion was, to save seed for the coming year—a point, strange to say, that was never sufficiently attended to throughout the whole of this calamitous time, though occasionally spoken of. He says truly, that the vitality of the potato being at the top, where the eyes cluster, in preparing to boil the meal of potatoes each day, the tops ought to be cut off and preserved for seed. In doing this, carefully and sufficiently, the quantity of the edible portion of the potato lost would be the merest trifle. He might have added, that the top is usually the least nutritious, or "mealy" part of the potato, which would make the loss still less. His third suggestion, he says, he received from a Sligo miller. It was a plan to prevent extortion and high prices, should a famine really come. It consisted in this, that a "nominal subscription" should be entered into by each county, and that a committee of the leading men of each county should be formed, having at their disposal this subscription, should it be found necessary to call it in: that these committees should, each, purchase, as they might deem it expedient, say one thousand tons of oatmeal at the lowest present price, holding this oatmeal over in stores till the next spring or summer, and that then it should be retailed, under proper superintendence by a storekeeper *for cash*, at a moderate profit, merely sufficient to cover the storeage and salary of the storekeeper: that the committee should raise money for the purchase of the oatmeal by their *joint notes*, which the banks would at once discount; all sales of the meal to be lodged each day in the bank to the account of the promissory notes outstanding. On winding up the transaction the oatmeal would be at least worth its present value; and if sold at a small profit, enough to cover the expenses, there would be no necessity for calling in any portion of the subscriptions; but should there be a loss on the sale, the proportion to each subscriber, according to the amount of his subscription, would be trifling. One good effect of this plan would be, that these stores would regulate the prices of oatmeal in the market, and would prevent the ruin of the farmers by extortioners and meal-mongers, and insure to them, if they must unfortunately buy food, *that* food at a reasonable rate. Mr. Foster adds: "These three plans will, if carried out, I feel assured by all that I have seen and heard, insure, first, *the arrest of the disease in the potatoes*, and the preservation of food for the *people*; secondly, *seed for next year*; and lastly, if there should occur the calamity of a famine, *there will be a substituted food secured for the people at a reasonable price."*

All these suggestions were well worthy of serious and immediate attention when they were written, and although every mode of saving the tuber was, to a great extent, a failure, the mode suggested above was at least as good as any other, and far simpler than most of them. But the third suggestion, about a county organization to keep the food in the country was admirable, practicable, effective; but as the poorer classes, from various causes, could not, and, in some instances, would not carry out any organized plan, the *Times'* Commissioner warns the Government to look to it. He says: "I am as firmly convinced as that I am now writing to you, such is the general apathy, want of exertion, and feeling of fatality among the people—such their general distrust of everybody, and suspicion of every project—such the disunion among the higher classes, with similar apathetic indifference, that unless the Government steps forward to carry out, to order, to enforce these or similar plans for the national welfare, *not any of them will be generally adopted, and nothing will be done.* Christmas is approaching, when the potato pits, most of them, will be opened; the poor people will clasp their hands in helpless despair, on seeing their six months' provisions a mass of rottenness; there will be no potatoes for seed next season; a general panic will seize all, and oatmeal for food will be scarcely purchasable by the people at *any price*. The Goverment, however, have been *warned*—let them act promptly, decisively, and *at once*, and not depend on the people helping themselves; for such is the character of the people that *they will do nothing till starvation faces them.*"[63]

Mr. Foster collected his letters on Ireland into a volume in March, 1846, and says, with justice, in a note to the above passage, "the truth of this prediction, in every particular, is now unhappily being verified."

Although Mr. Foster is here, as in several other places throughout his letters on Ireland, unjustly severe upon the people—poor, helpless, unaided, uncared for as they were by those whose sacred duty it was to come to their assistance—still many of his views, as in the present instance, are full of practical good sense. He gave many valuable hints for the amelioration of Irish grievances, and several of his recommendations have been since embodied in Acts of Parliament; but when he says the people will do nothing, are apathetic, and so on, he ought to remember that in such a fearful crisis, combined effort alone is of value. This must come from the leaders of the people. The best army cannot fight without generals, and in this battle against famine the Irish people had no leaders: their natural leaders, the proprietors of the soil, did next to nothing—the Government of the country did next to nothing. The Government alone had the power to combine, to direct, to command; it was called upon from all parts of the country to do so—the Viceroy was waited on—Mr. Foster himself, in the passage quoted above, warned the Government to act, and to act at once, and yet what had it done up to the time he closed his Irish tour? Where was the real, the culpable, the unpardonable apathy?

Mr. Gregory, writing from Coole Park on the 12th of November, says, he cannot get the people to take precautions against the disease. By putting drains under his own pits, and holes in them for ventilation, and throwing turf mould and lime upon them, he says they are still safe. His opinion is, that half the potatoes in his neighbourhood are tainted. The police-sergeant of the Kinvara district makes a return, the result of an examination of fifty-two acres of potatoes in eighteen fields of from one and a-half to seven acres. The least diseased field, one of four acres, had twelve tubers in the hundred diseased. In a field of seven acres, ninety-six in every hundred were diseased, and the average losses in all the fields was seventy per cent. Charles K. O'Hara, Chairman of the Sligo Board of Guardians, writes to the Mansion House Committee: "In many instances the conacre tenants have refused to dig the crops, and are already suffering from want of food." Mr. Crichton, of Somerton, Ballymote, says, the disease in his locality is not so bad as it is elsewhere, but still it is his opinion that many families about him cannot count on having a potato left in January. Mr. Christopher Hamilton, Land Agent, of Leeson Street, writing to the Marquis of Lansdowne, says, he "ascertained by personal inspection that a great proportion of the ordinary food of the people had become useless, and that from the nature of the blight it is impossible to depend on any adequate proportion being saved." Mr. Hamilton praises the submission of the people under the trial.

On the 24th of November, Sir James Murray, M.D., published a remarkable letter, headed "Surgery *versus* Medicine," in which, I believe, he came as near the immediate cause of the disease as any writer who has dealt with the subject. He attributes it to electrical agency. "During the last season," he writes, "the clouds were charged with excessive electricity, and yet there was little or no thunder to draw off that excess from the atmosphere. In the damp and variable autumn this surcharge of electrical matter was attracted by the moist, succulent, and pointed leaves of the potato." As medicine is found to be useless for the disease, he recommends the use of the knife to cut away the diseased parts, and to keep the sound portions on shelves.

The clergy of every denomination came forward with a zeal and charity worthy of their sacred calling. Out of hundreds of letters written by them, I cannot deny myself the pleasure of making a few extracts. The Rev. Mr. Killen, Rector of Tyrrilla, Co. Down, writes: "This is the famous potato-growing district. One-third of the crop is already affected, both in the pits and those in the ground." The Rev. Mr. M'Keon, of Drumlish, in his letter to the Mansion House Committee, says: "The people must starve in summer, *having paid their rents by selling their oats*; their rents being rigorously exacted on the Granard and Lorton estates." The Rev. James M'Hall, of Hollymount, Mayo, mentions the startling fact, that a poor man in his neighbourhood having opened a pit, where he had stored six barrels of potatoes, of sixty-four stone each, *found he had not one stone of sound potatoes*! The Rev. John Stuart, Presbyterian minister in Antrim, declares that fully one-half of the crop is lost in his district. He adds: "Some have tried lime dust, and pits aired with tiles, and in a few days have found a mass of rottenness." The Rev. Mr. Waldron, Parish Priest of Cong, writes, that he had examined the crop in every village in his parish, and reports that more than one-half of it is lost on sound lands, above three-fourths on others. "The panic," he continues, "which at first took the people has lately subsided into *silent despair and hopelessness.*" A Protestant clergyman in Mayo, who had thirty men digging his potatoes, of the species called Peelers, "thinks they did not dig as much sound potatoes as two men would do in a sound year." The Rev. Mr. Cantwell, of Kilfeacle, makes the suggestive announcement that "parents are already *counting* the potatoes they give their children." The good Rector of Skull, Dr. Robert Traill, writes to Lord Bernard with prophetic grief. "Am I to cry peace, peace, where there is no peace? But what did I find in the islands? *the pits, without one single exception in a state of serious decay, and many of the islanders apprehending famine in consequence.* Oh, my heart trembles when I think of all that may be before us."

Meantime the accounts of the progress of the disease were every day more disheartening; the Government appeared to do nothing except publish a few reports from those "Scientific men sent over from England," alluded to by the Viceroy in his reply to the deputation of the 3rd of November. The Mansion House Committee met on the 19th of that month and unanimously passed the following resolutions, Lord Cloncurry being in the chair:—

1. "That we feel it an imperative duty to discharge our consciences of all responsibility regarding the undoubtedly approaching calamities, famine and pestilence, throughout Ireland, an approach which is imminent, and almost immediate, and can be obviated only by the most prompt, universal and efficacious measures for procuring food and employment for the people.
2. "That we have ascertained beyond the shadow of doubt, that considerably more than one-third of the entire of the potato crop in Ireland has been already destroyed by the potato disease;

and that such disease has not, by any means, ceased its ravages, but, on the contrary, it is daily extending more and more; and that no reasonable conjecture can be formed with respect to the limits of its effects, short of the destruction of the entire remaining potato crop.

3. "That our information upon the subject is positive and precise and is derived from persons living in all the counties of Ireland. From persons also of all political opinions and from clergymen of all religious persuasions.

4. "We are thus unfortunately able to proclaim to all the inhabitants of the British Empire, and in the presence of an all-seeing Providence, that in Ireland famine of a most hideous description must be immediate and pressing, and that pestilence of the most frightful kind is certain, and not remote, unless immediately prevented.

5. "That we arraign in the strongest terms, consistent with personal respect to ourselves, the culpable conduct of the present administration, as well in refusing to take any efficacious measure for alleviating the existing calamity with all its approaching hideous and necessary consequences; as also for the positive and unequivocal crime of keeping the ports closed against the importation of foreign provisions, thus either abdicating their duty to the people or their sovereign, whose servants they are, or involving themselves in the enormous guilt of aggravating starvation and famine, by unnaturally keeping up the price of provisions, and doing this for the benefit of a selfish class who derive at the present awful crisis pecuniary advantages to themselves by the maintenance of the oppressive Corn Laws.

6. "That the people of Ireland, in their bitter hours of misfortune, have the strongest right to impeach the criminality of the ministers of the crown, inasmuch as it has pleased a merciful Providence to favour Ireland in the present season with a most

abundant crop of oats. Yet, whilst the Irish harbours are closed against the importation of foreign food, they are left open for the exportation of Irish grain, an exportation which has already amounted in the present season to a quantity nearly adequate to feed the entire people of Ireland, and to avert the now certain famine; thus inflicting upon the Irish people the abject misery of having their own provisions carried away to feed others, whilst they themselves are left contemptuously to starve.

7. "That the people of Ireland should particularly arraign the conduct of the ministry in shrinking from their duty, to open the ports for the introduction of provisions by royal proclamation, whilst they have had the inhumanity to postpone the meeting of Parliament to next year.

8. "That we behold in the conduct of the ministry the contemptuous disregard of the lives of the people of Ireland, and that we, therefore, do prepare an address to her Majesty, most humbly praying her Majesty to direct her ministers to adopt without any kind of delay the most extensive and efficacious measures to arrest the progress of famine and pestilence in Ireland.

> "Signed,
> "JOHN L. ARABIN,
> "Lord Mayor of Dublin."

It does not appear that the address to the Queen agreed to by the last resolution was ever presented, which omission is sufficiently accounted for by the resignation of the Peel Cabinet, which occurred a few days afterwards, on the 8th of December.

Not to prolong those extracts, I will here quote an analysis of five hundred letters received by the Mansion House Committee, which was given by the Earl of Mountcashel at a meeting of farmers held in Fermoy, in the county Cork. "I have seen," says his Lordship, "an analysis of five hundred letters received by the Mansion House Committee, made by Mr. Sinnott, the Secretary. Of those, one hundred and ninety-seven have come from clergymen of the Established Church; one hundred and forty-three from Roman Catholic clergymen; thirty from Presbyterian clergymen; one hundred and seven from deputy-lieutenants and magistrates; and the remainder from poor-law guardians and so forth. Taking all these communications together, one hundred and fifty eight calculated upon a loss of less than one-third of the potato crop; one hundred and thirty-five upon the loss of a full third; one hundred and thirty-four, that one-half of the crop was destroyed, and forty apprehended a destruction of more than one-half. With respect to the residue of the crops, there are two hundred and sixteen letters in which no opinion is given, whilst the writers of one hundred and one think that the remainder of the crop may be saved, and one hundred and eighteen are of a contrary opinion. Thus, we have all classes and parties in the country—Protestant and Presbyterian clergymen more numerous than Roman Catholic clergymen—peers, deputy-lieutenants, magistrates, poor-law guardians—all concurring in the main fact, that a vast portion of the food of millions of the people has been destroyed whilst all is uncertainty as to the remainder."

With this information before them and a vast deal more besides, it is not to be wondered at that the Mansion House Committee passed the resolutions given above. A strong protest, indeed, but it came from a body of men who had laboured with energy and diligence from the very first day the Committee was formed. One of the earliest acts of that Committee was to prepare a set of queries, that, through them, they might put themselves in communication with persons of position and intelligence throughout the entire country. The result was that they felt themselves compelled to pass a deliberate censure upon the apathy of the Government; and it will be found, in the course of this narrative, that the want of prompt vigorous action on the part of the Government, more especially at this early stage of the famine, had quite as much to do with that famine as the failure of the potato crop itself.

In November a cessation of the rot was observed in some districts, but in that month the assertion made in the first resolution of the Mansion House Committee, that more than one-third of the potato crop was lost, was not only vouched for by hundreds of most respectable and most trustworthy witnesses, as we have seen, but it was accepted as a truth by every party. Moreover, the Government, whose culpable apathy and delay was denounced on all sides, except by its partizans, was in possession of information on the subject, which made the loss of the potato crop at least *one-half* instead of *one-third*. Professors Lindley and Playfair made a report to Sir Robert Peel, bearing date the 15th of November, from which he quoted the following startling passage in his speech on the address, on the 22nd of January, 1846:—"We can come to no other conclusion," they write, "than that *one-half* of the actual potato crop of Ireland is either destroyed, or remains in a state unfit for the food of man. We, moreover, feel it our duty to apprize you that we fear this to be a low estimate."[64]

Estimating the value of the potato crop of 1845 in Ireland at £18,000,000, not a high estimate, it was now certain that food to the value of £9,000,000 was already lost, yet no answer could be had from the Viceroy or the Premier but the stereotyped one, that the matter was receiving the most serious consideration of the Government. And on they went enquiring when they should have been acting. With the information given by Professors Lindley and Playfair in their hands, they appointed another Commission about this time, which sat in Dublin Castle and was presided over by Mr. Lucas, then Under-Secretary. Its Secretary, Captain Kennedy, applied to the Mansion House Committee for information. That body at once placed its whole correspondence at the disposal of the Commissioners; the Lord Mayor had an interview with Sir Thomas Freemantle, one of them, by whom he was assured that the Government was fully prepared to take such steps as might be found necessary for the protection of the people, when the emergency should arise.

Most people thought it had arisen already.

On the 8th of December, a full fortnight after this interview, a set of queries, similar to those issued months before by the Mansion House Committee, were printed and circulated by the new Commissioners, asking for information that had already come in from every part of the country—even to superabundance.

On the 10th of December the Corporation of Dublin agreed to an address to the Queen, calling her Majesty's attention to the potato blight, and the impending famine consequent upon it. In their address they respectfully bring before her two facts then lately elicited, or rather confirmed, by the Devon Commission—namely, that four millions of the labouring population of Ireland "are more wretched than any people in Europe—their only food the potato, their only drink water." They add, that even these facts do not convey to her Majesty an adequate idea of the destitution by which the Irish people are threatened, or of the numbers who shall suffer by the failure of the potato crop; facts related of the inhabitants of a country which, of late years, may be justly styled the granary of England, exporting annually from the midst of a starving people food of the best kind in sufficient abundance for treble its own inhabitants. They assure her Majesty that fully one-third of their only support for one year is destroyed by the potato blight, which involves a state of destitution for four months of a great majority of her Majesty's Irish subjects. They say, with respectful dignity, that they ask no alms; they only ask for public works of utility; they ask that the national treasury should be "poured out to give employment to the people at remunerative wages." Finally they pray her Majesty to summon Parliament for an early day.

The Corporation did not get an opportunity of presenting their address to the Queen until the 3rd of January following—four-and-twenty days after it was agreed to. This delay, no doubt chiefly arose from the resignation of the Peel ministry on the 5th of December; the failure of Lord John Russell to form a Government, and the consequent return of Sir Robert Peel to office on the 20th of the same month, after a fortnight's interregnum.

In the Queen's reply to the Dublin address she deplores the poverty of a portion of her Irish subjects, their welfare and prosperity being objects of her constant care; she has, she says, ordered precautions to be taken; she has summoned Parliament for an early day, and looks with confidence to the advice she shall receive from the united council of the realm.

The Corporation of London addressed her Majesty on the same occasion, deploring the sufferings and privations of a large portion of her subjects in England, Ireland, and Scotland, which they attributed to "erroneous legislation, which, by excluding the importation of food, and restricting commerce, shuts out from the nation the bounty of Providence." They, therefore prayed that the ports of the kingdom might be opened for the free importation of food. While the Corporation of London did not, we may presume, exclude the peculiar distress of Ireland from their sympathies, their real object in going to Windsor was to make an anti-Corn Law demonstration. So much was this the case, that the deputation consisted of the enormous number of two hundred gentlemen. The Queen's reply to them was hopeful. She said she would "gladly sanction any measure which the legislature might suggest as conducive to the alleviation of this temporary distress, and to the permanent welfare of all classes of her people."

It is a noticeable fact, and one to be deplored, that even the potato blight was made a party question in Ireland. If we except the Protestant and dissenting clergy, and a few philanthropic laymen, the upper classes, especially the Conservatives, remained aloof from the public meetings held to call attention to it, and its threatened consequences. The Mansion House Committee, which did so much good, was composed almost exclusively of Catholics and Liberals; and the same is substantially true of the meetings held throughout the country—in short, the Conservatives regarded, or pretended to regard, those meetings as a new phase of the Repeal agitation. Then, as the distress must chiefly occur amongst the poor Catholics, who were repealers, it was, they assumed, the business

97

of repealers and agitators to look to them and relieve them. The Premier himself was not free from these feelings. In the memorandum which he read to the Cabinet on the 1st of November, amongst many other things, he says: "There will be no hope of contributions from England for the mitigation of this calamity. Monster meetings, the ungrateful return for past kindness, the subscriptions in Ireland to Repeal rent and O'Connell tribute, will have disinclined the charitable here to make any great exertions for Irish relief."[65] There was even, I fear, something behind all this—the old feeling of the English colony in Ireland, that it was no business of theirs to sustain the native race, whose numerical strength they regarded, now as ever, to be a standing threat and danger to themselves.

The sentiments of the leading journals of the Tory party quite coincided with this view. They kept constantly asserting that the ravages of the potato blight were greatly exaggerated; and they eagerly seized on any accidental circumstance that could give them a pretext for supporting this assertion. The chief Dublin Conservative journal, the *Evening Mail*, on the 3rd of November, writing about the murder of Mr. Clarke, "inclines to believe that the agrarian outrage had its origin in a design to intimidate landlords from demanding their rents, at a season when corn of all kinds is superabundant, and the partial failure of the potato crop gives a pretence for not selling it. And if we recollect," it continues, "that the potato crop of this year far exceeded an average one, and that corn of all kinds is so far abundant, it will be seen that the apprehensions of a famine in that quarter are unfounded, and are merely made the pretence for withholding the payment of rent." Such was the language of a newspaper supposed largely to express landlord feeling in Ireland, and supposed, too, to be the chief organ of the existing Government, represented by Lord Heytesbury.

Later on in the month, a Protestant dignitary, Dean Hoare of Achonry, wrote a letter to the Mansion House Committee, in which, whilst he gave substantially the same views of the potato failure as hundreds of others, he complained in a mild spirit of the people in his locality as being "very slow" to adopt the methods recommended for preserving the potatoes from decay. Another Tory journal of the time, since amalgamated with the former, made this letter the pretence of an attack on the Mansion House Committee, accusing it of withholding Dean Hoare's letter, because it gave a favourable account of the state of the potato crop, and an unfavourable one of the peasantry—charging it with "fraud, trickery and misrepresention," and its members with "associating for factious purposes alone." In reply, it was clearly shown that the Committee did not withhold the Dean's letter, even for an hour, and as clearly shown that the *Evening Packet*, the journal in question, antedated his letter by a day, in order to sustain its charge of suppression.

The *Packet* also omitted those portions of the letter which represented the loss of the potato crop as extensive, and which called on the Government to employ the people.[66]

The *Freeman's Journal* of the 24th of November, in commenting on the way in which its Tory contemporary dealt with Dean Hoare's letter, says: "The *Packet*, in its last issue, has returned to its appointed task of denying that the failure of the potato crop is so extensive as to demand extraordinary measures on the part of the Government." Although, at the time, this could be nothing more than a bold guess, it is highly probable that the writer of it hit the mark, for in his memoirs, published by his literary executors, Earl Stanhope and Lord Cardwell, we find the Premier, in the middle of October giving this caution to the Lord Lieutenant: "I need not recommend to you the utmost reserve as to the future, *I mean as to the possibility of Government interference.*"[67]

A few days after the *Packet* had published the above sentiment, the *Evening Mail* said, "there was a sufficiency—an abundance of sound potatoes in the country for the wants of the people." And it goes on to stimulate farmers to sell their corn, by threats of being forestalled by Dutch and Hanoverian merchants. In the beginning of December, a Tory provincial print, not probably so high as its metropolitan brethren in the confidence of its party, writes: "It may be fairly presumed the losses have been enormous . . . We repeat it, *and we care not whom it displeases*, that there are not now half as many sound potatoes in the country as there were last December." The Editor seemed to feel he was doing a perilous thing in stating a fact which he knew would be displeasing to many of his readers.

FOOTNOTES:

57.   *Morning Post*, 11th September.
58.   *Ipswich Gazette*, 9th September.
59.   *Cambridge Chronicle* for September.
60.   But the disease was not so rapid as this in all cases.
61.   *Freeman's Journal*, Nov. 4.
62.   The letter is dated Cork, 22nd Nov., 1845
63.   All the italics in the above quotations are Mr. Foster's own.
64.   The last short sentence about the "low estimate" was not quoted by Sir Robert, although it immediately follows the previous one in the portion of the communication given in the Memoirs. Part 3, page 171.
65.   Memoirs, part 3, page 143.
66.   The remedies which Dean Hoare said the people were "slow" to adopt, were proved to be worthless, and in some instances even pernicious. The steward on Mr. Leslie's estate in Monaghan writes that, "The potatoes dug and arranged according to the advice of the Government Commissioners had become diseased and useless." On the very day the Dean's letter was written, there was a meeting of the landlords of Cavan held; and in a Report emanating from that meeting, signed by Lord Farnham, the following passage occurs: "With reference to the potatoes stored with solid substance, or packing stuff, intervening in any form, in pit, on floors, or lofts, the use of packing stuff appears to be highly prejudicial. In the words of an extensive contractor the heap becomes 'a mass of mortar.'" The report adds: "*This description includes the plan of pitting recommended by her Majesty's Commissioners, which we strongly deprecate.*"
67.   Memoirs, part 3, page 123.

* * * * *

CHAPTER III.

Lord Heytesbury and Sir Robert Peel—The Potatoes of last year!—Is there a stock of them?—Sir R. Peel and Free Trade—Strength of his Cabinet—Mr. Cobden proposes a Committee of Inquiry—His speech—Its effect—Committee refused—D'Israeli's attack on Sir R. Peel (*note.*)—Sir Robert puts forward the Potato Blight as the cause for repealing the Corn Laws—The extent of the Failure not exaggerated—Sir James Graham and Sir R. Peel—Appointment of Drs. Lindley and Playfair to investigate the Blight—Sir R. Peel announces that he is a convert to the repeal of the Corn Laws—States his views, but does not reason on them—The Quarterly Review—Special Commissioners—Mr. Butler's letter—Sir James Graham and the Premier—Proceeding by Proclamation instead of by Order in Council—Sir James's sharp reply—Agitation to stop distillation—County Meetings proposed by the Lord Lieutenant—Cabinet Council—The Premier puts his views before it in a memorandum—The Corn Laws—Some of the Cabinet displeased with his views—On the 6th November he submits another memorandum to the Cabinet—Lord Stanley dissents from the Premier's views—The Cabinet meet again next day and he concludes the memorandum—On the 29th November he sends to each of his colleagues a more detailed exposition of his views—Several reply—Another Mem. brought before them on the 2nd December—The Cabinet in permanent session—On the 5th of December Sir Robert resigns—Lord John Russell fails to form a Government—The old Cabinet again in power—Mr. Gladstone replaces Lord Stanley.

As stated in the last chapter, the deputation that waited on the Lord Lieutenant was superciliously bowed out, the moment his Excellency had finished the reading of his reply; so that the usual courtesy extended to such bodies, of having some conversation and friendly discussion on the subject of the address, was denied to the noblemen and gentlemen who presented themselves at the Viceregal Lodge on the 3rd of November. Yet, more than a fortnight previously, Lord Heytesbury had written to the Premier, expressing great concern at the accounts daily received of the blight. "The reports," he writes, "continue to be of a very alarming nature, and leave no doubt upon the mind but that the potato crops have failed almost everywhere."[68] This admission he took care not to make to the deputation, although its truth had not only been verified but strengthened by the accounts which he continued to receive between the date of the letter and the 3rd of November. In the Premier's communication, to which Lord Heytesbury was replying, are, amongst others, the following queries:—"At what period would the pressure be felt? Would it be immediate, if the reports of the full extent of the evil are confirmed, or, *is there a stock of* old potatoes sufficient to last for a certain time?" The Viceroy replies, that he is assured, "*there is no stock* whatever of *last year's* potatoes in the country." That is, in the middle of October, 1845, no stock of the potatoes grown in 1844 had remained! Such was the knowledge which the Premier of England (once an Irish Secretary), and the Lord Lieutenant of Ireland possessed of the nature and constitution of the potato!

One of Sir Robert Peel's biographers, evidently a great admirer of his, says of him that he was a freetrader in principle long before 1845[69]; whilst his enemies assert, that having been placed by the Tory party at the head of a Protectionist Government, he betrayed that party and suddenly threw himself into the arms of the Corn Law League. Neither of these views appears to be quite correct. The common, and it would seem, the more accurate opinion about him is, that he was a politician by profession—a man of expediency—and that on the question of the

Corn Laws he did no more than he had previously done with regard to Catholic emancipation,—followed the current of public opinion, which he always watched with the most anxious care,—and turning round, carried through Parliament a measure which he had long and strenuously opposed. There was, to be sure, this difference in his conduct with regard to those two great measures, that, whilst up to the time he undertook, in conjunction with the Duke of Wellington, to free the Catholics, he never advocated their claims, on the other hand, he had been twice a party to modifications of the Corn Laws, first in 1828, and secondly in 1842. In the latter year he, cautiously indeed, but not unsubstantially, legislated in the direction of free trade.

He became First Lord of the Treasury in August, 1841, and soon afterwards brought before the Cabinet the question of the duties on the importation of food, more especially of corn. He recommended his colleagues to make the revision of those duties a Cabinet question; and he further submitted "a proposal in respect to the extent to which such revision should be carried, and to the details of the new law."[70] A bill founded on his views was passed in the Parliament of 1842, "providing for a material diminution in the amount of the import duties on the several kinds of foreign grain." But these changes did not satisfy the Corn Law Leaguers, who sought complete repeal; but they had the effect of alarming the Premier's Tory supporters, and led to the resignation of one Cabinet Minister—the Duke of Buckingham. His partizans endeavoured to obtain from him a guarantee that this Corn Law of 1842 should, as far as he was concerned, be a final measure; but, although he tells us, that he did not then contemplate the necessity for further change, he uniformly refused to fetter either the Government or himself by such an assurance. Yet, in proposing the introduction of the tariff in 1842, he seems to have foreshadowed future and still more liberal legislation on the subject. "I know that many gentlemen," he said, "who are strong advocates for free trade may consider that I have not gone far enough. I know that. I believe that on the general principle of freetrade there is *now no great difference of opinion; and that all agree* in the general rule, that we should purchase in the cheapest market, and sell in the dearest."

The opposition, more especially the freetraders, received this sentiment with rapturous applause, so the adroit statesman added: "I know the meaning of those cheers. I do not now wish to raise a discussion on the Corn Laws or the Sugar duties, which (I contend) are exceptions from the general rule."[71] His exceptions were futile, because they were illogical, which of course he must have known; they were therefore only meant to reassure, to some extent, the affrighted Protectionist gentlemen behind him.

The anti-Corn Law League, not accepting the concessions made in 1842 as final, continued to agitate and insist upon total repeal. They held meetings, made able speeches, published pamphlets, delivered lectures, and continued to keep before the English public the iniquity, as they said, of those laws which compelled the English artizan to eat dear bread. Sir Robert, as a politician and statesman, watched the progress of this agitation, as also the effect of the changes made in 1842; and he tells us he was gradually weakened in his views as to the protection of British grown corn. "The progress of discussion," he says, "had made a material change in the opinions of many persons with regard to the policy of protection to domestic agriculture, and the extent to which that policy should be carried;"[72] while the success of the changes made in 1842, falsifying, as they did, all the prophecies of the Protectionists, tended further to shake his confidence in the necessity of maintaining those laws.

Since its formation in August, 1841, Sir Robert Peel's Government had continued to carry its measures through Parliament with overwhelming majorities; still the question of free trade was making rapid progress throughout the country, especially in the great towns, the anti-Corn Law League had become a power, and thoughtful men began to see that the principle it embodied could not be long resisted in a commercial nation like England. The Parliamentary Session of 1845 opened with an attempt, on the part of Lord John Russell, the leader of the Opposition, to compel the Government to declare its policy on free trade. Sir Robert Peel was silent, probably because, at the moment, he had no fixed policy about it; or, if he had, he was not the man to declare it at an inconvenient time. Great agricultural distress prevailed, a fact admitted by both sides of the House: the Protectionist members maintained that it was caused by the concessions already made to free trade, the free traders, on the contrary, held it to be the result of the continuance of absurd protective duties. Meantime, Mr. Cobden came forward with a proposal, which, unless agreed to must necessarily put the Protectionists in the wrong. He asked for a Committee of Inquiry into the causes of this distress, before which he undertook to prove that it was caused by the Corn Laws. For some time it had been whispered abroad that Sir Robert Peel was fast inclining to freetrade, and only looked to the country for sufficient support to justify him in declaring his views openly: the leading members of the League were not slow to make use of those rumours: and, in his strikingly able speech, calling for the Committee, Mr. Cobden more than hinted that the Premier, although not yet a free trader before the country, was one at least in heart. "There are politicians in the House," said he, "men who look with an ambition—probably a justifiable one—to the honors of office; there may be men who—with thirty years continuous service, having been pressed into a groove from which they can neither escape nor retreat—*may be holding office, and high office*: maintained there probably at the expense of their present convictions which do not harmonize very well with their early opinions. I make allowances for them; but the great body of honorable gentlemen opposite came up to this House, not as politicians, but as the farmer's friends, and protectors of the agricultural interests. Well! what do you propose to do? You have heard the Prime Minister declare that, if he could restore all the protection which you have had, that protection would not benefit the agriculturists. Is that your belief? If so, why not proclaim it; but if it is not your conviction, you will have falsified your mission in this House by following the right hon.

baronet into the lobby, and opposing inquiry into the condition of the very men who sent you here. I have no hesitation in telling you, that if you give me a Committee of this House I will explode the delusion of agricultural protection. I will bring forward such a mass of evidence, and give you such a preponderance of talent and of authority, that when the Blue Book is published and sent forth to the world your system of protection shall not live in the public opinion for two years afterwards." And again he said with irresistible logic: "I ask you to go into this Committee with me. I will give you a majority of county members. I ask you only to go into a fair inquiry as to the causes of the distress of your own population. Whether you establish my principle or your own, good will come out of the inquiry; and I do therefore beg and entreat you not to refuse it."

The effect of this speech in the House and throughout the country was very great. The anti-Corn Law League printed it by the million and scattered it broad-cast over the land; it was even said that it had no inconsiderable effect on Sir Robert Peel himself, and many of his friends believed that Mr. Cobden exercised, on the occasion, "a real influence over him." The Premier refused the Committee, but remained silent; Sidney Herbert it was whom his chief entrusted with the arduous duty of replying to the great Leaguer. In the course of his speech he said, "it would be distasteful to the agriculturists to come whining to Parliament at every period of temporary distress; but in adverse circumstances they would meet them manfully, and put their shoulder to the wheel."[73]

On the 9th of August the Parliamentary Session of 1845 closed, leaving Sir Robert Peel still at the head of that imposing majority which had sustained him since 1841. Not long after commenced those gloomy reports of potato blight which continued to increase, until the fact was placed beyond the possibility of doubt.

It was not originally Sir Robert Peel's desire to propose a repeal of the Corn Laws in the session of 1846; he would have much preferred the postponement of the question for a year or so, in order to prepare the public mind for his altered opinions; besides, he not unreasonably hoped that the success of the changes of 1842 would have so enlightened his party as to induce them to accept further and greater changes in the commercial tariff. Meantime, he could be feeling his way with them by the aid of trusted friends, and be making them, in various ways, familiar with the new sacrifices he was about to require at their hands. Hence, the potato blight was, in more senses than one, an untoward event for himself and his Cabinet, since it hurried him into the doing of that, which he hoped to have done without giving any very violent shock to the opinions or prejudices of his Tory supporters.

Sir Robert, if not a man of great forecast or intuition, was certainly one to make the most of circumstances as they arose, provided he had time for reflection. When the news of the potato failure in Ireland became an alarming fact, he recast his plan, and put that failure foremost amongst his reasons for repealing the Corn Laws; in fact, in his own adroit way he left it to be understood, that this was the immediate and urgent cause for dealing with the question—nay more, that the real, the *only* question he was dealing with was the potato blight, and the threatened famine in Ireland; and that, in anxiously seeking for an adequate remedy for such terrible evils, he could find but one—the total repeal of the Corn Laws. Some in his own Cabinet, and numbers of thoughtful people throughout the country, saw a variety of plans for meeting the failure distinct from such repeal; very many even, so far from regarding it as a remedy against Irish famine, considered it would be a positive injury to this country, under existing circumstances; but Sir Robert Peel, with that charming frankness and simplicity, the assumption of which had become a second nature to him, could see but one remedy for poor Ireland—a repeal of the Corn Laws. Others, which were hinted to him by some of his colleagues, he dexterously avoids discussing, and only repeats his own great conviction—repeal the Corn Laws and save poor, famine-threatened Ireland.

From the end of August to the beginning of October several communications passed between the Premier and Sir James Graham, relative to the failure of the potato. During that period the accounts were very varied, partly from the disease not having made very much progress, and partly because there was not as yet sufficient time to examine the crop with care; but a perusal of the correspondence which reached the Government, so far as it is given in Sir Robert Peel's Memoirs, and his speeches in Parliament, prove that the accounts in newspapers, and above all in letters received and published by the Mansion House Committee, did not overstate the failure, but rather the reverse—this fact is more especially evident from the joint letter of Professors Lindley and Playfair already quoted.

Of all the ministers, Sir James Graham seems to have had the greatest share of the Premier's confidence; Sir Robert thus writes to him from Whitehall on the 13th of October:—"The accounts of the state of the potato crop in Ireland are becoming very alarming. I enclose letters which have very recently reached me. Lord Heytesbury says that the reports which reach the Irish Government are very unsatisfactory. I presume that if the worst should happen which is predicted, the pressure would not be *immediate*. There is such a tendency to exaggeration and inaccuracy in Irish reports, that delay in acting upon them is always desirable; but I foresee the necessity that may be imposed upon us at an early period of considering whether there is not that well grounded apprehension of actual scarcity that justifies and compels the adoption of every means of relief which the exercise of the prerogative or legislation might afford. *I have no confidence in such remedies as the prohibition of exports or the stoppage of distilleries. The removal of the impediments to import is the only effectual remedy.*"

Sir James Graham wrote to the Premier from Netherby on the same day enclosing a communication from the Lord Lieutenant of Ireland, *which is not given* in the Peel Memoirs, but which Sir James says, "conveys information of the most serious kind, which requires immediate attention." He goes on to give it as his opinion that the time had come when speculation was reduced to certainty, as the potatoes were being taken out of the ground; it was therefore the duty of the Government to apply their attention without delay to measures for the mitigation of this national calamity. He refers to Belgium and Holland, and says it is desirable to know, without loss of time, what has been done by our Continental neighbours in similar circumstances. Indian corn might, of course, he says, be obtained on cheap terms, "*if the people would eat it*," but unfortunately it is an acquired taste. He thinks the summoning of Parliament in November a better course than the opening of the ports by an Order in Council.[74] On receipt of the above Sir Robert again wrote to the Home Secretary: "My letter on the awful question of the potato crop will have crossed yours to me. Interference with the due course of the law respecting the supply of food is so momentous and so lasting in its consequences, that we must not act without the most accurate information. I fear the worst. I have written to the Duke also."

It was about this time that the Premier appointed Drs. Lindley and Playfair to come to Ireland for the purpose of investigating the causes of the blight, and if possible to apply remedies. He summoned the latter to Drayton Manor before leaving, and both were struck by the very short time in which the blight rendered the potato worthless for food. Sir Robert says to Sir James Graham on the 18th of October: "We have examined here various potatoes that have been affected; and witnessing the rapidity of decay, and the necessity of immediate action, I have not hesitated to interrupt Playfair's present occupation, and to direct his attention to this still more pressing matter."[75] Two days later Sir James sends his chief a desponding letter in reply, and, with much good sense, says he is not sanguine about any chemical process, *within the reach of the peasantry*, arresting the decay in tubers already affected; besides the rainfall continues so great that, independently of disease, he feels the potatoes must rot in the ground from the wet, unless on very dry lands. He then mentions a matter of the utmost consequence which had not been alluded to before. "There are many points," he says, on which a scientific inquiry may be most useful, "particularly the vital one with respect to the seed for next year."[76]

In his letter of the 13th of October, given above, the Premier opened his mind to his friend, the Home Secretary, that he was a convert to the repeal of the Corn Laws, but even to him he put forward the potato blight in Ireland as the cause. Some days afterwards, in a very carefully worded letter to Lord Heytesbury, he introduces the same business. "The accounts from Ireland of the potato crop, confirmed as they are by your high authority," says Sir Robert, "are very alarming, and it is the duty of the Government to seek a remedy for the 'great evil.'" Of course it was, and he had made up his mind to apply one which he knew was distasteful to most of his colleagues; but time was pressing, and he must bring it forward, so making a clean breast of it, he states his remedy in a bold clear sentence to the Protectionist Lord Lieutenant of Ireland. "The remedy," he writes, "is the removal *of all impediments* to the import of all kinds of human food—that is the total and absolute repeal for ever of all duties on all articles of subsistence."[77] Sir Robert Peel seldom penned so clear a sentence, but its very clearness had an object, for he seems to desire to shut out discussion on any of the other remedies which were put forward in Ireland. He then goes on to join the *temporary* relief of Irish distress with the *permanent* arrangement of the Corn Law question. "You might," he says, "remit nominally for one year; but who will re-establish the Corn Laws once abrogated, though from a casual and temporary pressure? I have good ground therefore for stating that the application of a temporary remedy to a temporary evil does in this particular case involve considerations of the utmost and most lasting importance."

These passages were indited by a minister who, coolly, and without any sufficient authority whatever, assumed that there was no other remedy for the failure of the potato crop in Ireland but a repeal of the Corn Laws, and that it was the remedy the Irish public were calling for, to meet the threatened danger. And yet so far from this being the case, it was never propounded by any one as a principal remedy at all. What the Irish public thought about the impending famine, and what they said about it was, that the oat crop was unusually fine and more than sufficient to feed the whole population, and that it should be kept in the country for that purpose. A most obvious remedy; but the Premier had other plans in his head, and could not see this one, because he would not. Like Nelson on a memorable occasion, he persisted in keeping his telescope to the eye that suited his own purpose. He does not condescend to give a reason for his views, he only expresses them. He had no confidence in the old-fashioned remedy of keeping the food in the country, but he did put his trust in the remedy of sending 3,000 miles for Indian corn—a food which, he elsewhere admits he fears the Irish cannot be induced to use. He thought it quite right, and in accordance with political science, to allow, or rather to compel Ireland, threatened with famine, to sell her last loaf and then go to America to buy maize, the preparation of which, she did not understand. Political economists will hardly deny that people ought not to sell what they require for themselves—that they should only part with *surplus* food. But to sell wheat and oats, and oatmeal and flour with one hand and buy Indian corn with the other to avoid starvation could be hardly regarded as the act of a sane man. "There had been— it was hinted, and we believe truly, in Lord John Russell's letter from Edinburgh—some talk in the Cabinet, and there was some discussion in the press, about opening the Irish ports by proclamation. *Opening the Irish ports!* Why the real remedy, had any interference with the law been necessary, would have been to *close* them—the torrent of food was running *outwards*."[78] So did the leading Tory periodical put this obvious truth some months later.

The Viceroy, replying to the Premier's letter on the 17th of October, says he is deeply impressed with the extent and alarming nature of the failure of the potato crop, and has no doubt on his mind that it is general. The Premier had, sometime before, suggested Special Commissioners to collect information, but the Lord Lieutenant does not think they would be able to collect more accurate information than that *already* furnished by the county inspectors. He suggests that when the potato digging is more advanced it would be well to move the Lieutenants of counties to call meetings of the resident landholders, with a view of ascertaining the amount of the evil, and their opinion of the measures most proper to be adopted. He sees no objection to such a course, though he dutifully adds that the Premier may.

There could be no objection whatever to such a course. It was, so far as it went, the right course, because it would have called upon the proprietors of the soil to discharge the duties of their position, and to take counsel as to the best mode of doing it. In his after correspondence with Lord Heytesbury the Premier *never alluded to this suggestion in any way!* Of course it fell to the ground.

On the 19th of October, Mr. Buller, Secretary to the Royal Agricultural Society of Ireland, wrote to Sir Robert Peel that he was after making the tour of several of the counties of the Province of Connaught, and the result was, that he found the potato crop affected in localities where people thought the blight had not reached. Mr. Buller's was a private letter to the Premier in anticipation of a more formal report from the Society, because, as he says, he "did not wish a moment to elapse" before informing him of the extent of the fearful malady, in order that no time should be lost, in adopting the necessary measures of precaution and relief for Ireland. He concludes by announcing, that a panic had seized all parties to a greater extent than he ever remembers since the cholera; which panic, he thinks, will go on increasing as the extent of the failure becomes better known.

Subordinates like Lord Heytesbury and Sir James Graham, writing to their chief can only hint their views. Both did so more than once with regard to the immediate action to be taken in securing food for the Irish people, to replace the potatoes destroyed by the blight. In one of the Viceroy's letters to the Premier, he quotes some precedents of what had been done in former years by proclamation in Ireland, especially referring to proclamations issued by Lord Cornwallis in 1800-1. He also refers to some Acts of Parliament, no longer, however, in force. Sir James Graham writing some days later to the Premier, says: "The precedents for proceeding by proclamation from the Lord Lieutenant of Ireland, and not by Order in Council, *are directly in point;*" adding of course that such proclamations should be followed by an Act of Indemnity. Surely, anybody can see, that for a Government to meet an extraordinary evil by an extraordinary remedy, would not only be sanctioned by an Act of Indemnity, but would be certain to receive the warm approval of Parliament.

Sir Robert Peel wanted neither county meetings nor proclamations; so, writing to Sir James Graham on the 22nd of October, he says,— all but misstating Lord Heytesbury's views on proclamations:—"Lord Heytesbury, from his occasional remarks on proclamations, seems to labour under an impression that there is a constitutional right to issue them. Now there is absolutely none. There is no more abstract right to prohibit the export of a potato than to command any other violation of law. Governments have assumed, and will assume, in extreme cases, unconstitutional power, and will trust to the good sense of the people, convinced by the necessity to obey the proclamation, and to Parliament to indemnify the issuers. The proclamations to which Lord Heytesbury refers may be useful as precedents, but they leave the matter where they found it in point of law; they give no sort of authority. I have a strong impression that we shall do more harm than good by controlling the free action of the people in respect to the legal *export* of these commodities, or the legal use of them."[79]

The above passage naturally drew from Sir James Graham the following remarks: "I enclose another letter from the Lord Lieutenant, giving a worse account of the potato crop as the digging advances, but stating that we are as yet unacquainted with the full extent of the mischief. *I think* that Lord Heytesbury is aware that the issue of proclamations is the exercise of a power beyond the law, which requires subsequent indemnity, and has not the force of law. *The precedents which he cites illustrate this known truth*; yet proclamations remitting duties, backed by an order of the Custom-house not to levy, are very effective measures, though the responsibility which attaches to their adoption is most onerous, especially when Parliament may be readily called together."[80]

Some days later the Lord Lieutenant announced to the Premier that Professors Lindley and Playfair had arrived in Dublin, and also gave a set of queries which he had placed in their hands—all very useful, but one of special importance—"What means can be adopted for securing seed potatoes for next year?" This communication contained the following passage:—"There is a great cry for the prohibition of exportation, particularly of oats. With regard to potatoes, it seems to be pretty generally admitted that to prohibit the exportation of so perishable a produce would be a very doubtful advantage. Towards the end of next week we shall know, I presume, the result of the deliberations of her Majesty's Government; and as by that time the digging will be sufficiently advanced to enable us to guess at the probable result of the harvest, I shall then intimate to the several Lieutenants the propriety of calling county meetings, unless I should hear from you that you disapprove of such proceedings. The danger of such meetings is in the remedies they may suggest, and the various subjects they may embrace in their discussions, wholly foreign to the question before them."[81] Three days later (Oct. 27) he again writes to the Premier: "Everything is rising rapidly in price, and the people begin to show symptoms of discontent which may ripen into something worse. Should I be authorized in issuing a proclamation prohibiting distillation from grain? This is demanded on all sides." There is no reply to this letter given by Sir Robert Peel in his Memoirs, and yet he must have written one. He certainly wrote to the Lord Lieutenant between the 3rd and the 8th of November; for the Mansion House deputation was received at the Viceregal Lodge on the 3rd, and we find the Viceroy in a letter to the Premier on the 8th explaining what he had said to the deputation on the 3rd; so that the Premier must, in the meantime, have put him on his defence; "it is perfectly true," writes Lord Heytesbury, "that I did, in my answer to the Lord Mayor, say there was no immediate pressure in the market; but you must not give too wide a meaning to that observation, which had reference merely to his demand that the exportation of grain should be prohibited and the ports immediately thrown open." But neither this passage, nor anything in the subsequent part of the letter, sufficiently explains what he had written eleven days before, namely, that everything was rising rapidly in price.

During the last days of October two very desponding reports were made to the Premier by Dr. Playfair, in the latter of which he says that Dr. Lindley was after making a tour of the potato shops of the city; that he had examined the potatoes, "carefully picked as good," and warranted to be sound, and that he had found "nineteen bad for fourteen good."

The first Cabinet Council assembled at the Premier's house on the 31st of October, on which occasion he read for his colleagues all the information received either by himself or the Home Secretary, after which the sitting was adjourned until next day, November the 1st, when he put his views before them in the shape of an elaborate memorandum. He begins by calling their attention to the great probability of a famine in Ireland consequent upon the potato blight. The evil, he thinks, may be much greater than the reports would lead them to anticipate, but whether it is or is not, the Cabinet cannot exclude from its consideration "the contingency of a great calamity." He tells them that he has sent eminent men of science to Ireland to examine and report on the question; that they are proceeding cautiously, but will suggest at the earliest period the simplest and most practical remedies which their inquiries and scientific knowledge may enable them to offer. Inquiries have also been addressed to the consular agents in different parts of Europe as to the available supply of potatoes for the purpose of seed. The noticeable fact in this, the first portion of the memorandum, is, that the Premier keeps his Cabinet in ignorance of the private reports made to himself by the "scientific men," assuring him that half the potato crop in Ireland had ceased to be fit for the food of man. Sir Robert next proceeds to discuss measures of relief to meet the danger. His first suggestion is a commission to be appointed by the Lord Lieutenant to inquire into the mode of giving relief, the head of the Board of Works to be a member of the Commission. The Commissioners are to see how money can be advanced, and employment given, and also how remote outlying districts can be relieved, where no employment exists; the power of calling this Commission into existence to be immediately given to the Lord Lieutenant, who could nominate its members after consulting with others, or immediately if he thought it necessary. In the third and last part of his memorandum the Premier comes to the really delicate and dangerous question—the repeal of the Corn Laws. He thinks the potato blight and the measures he proposes to meet its probable consequences would necessitate the calling of Parliament before Christmas—a very important step, as "it compels," he says, "an immediate decision on these questions—'Shall we maintain unaltered—shall we modify—shall we suspend—the operation of the Corn Laws?'" The first vote the Cabinet proposes, say a vote of £100,000, to be placed at the disposal of the Lord Lieutenant for the supply of food, opens the whole question. Can the Government, then, vote public money for the sustenance of the people and maintain existing restrictions on the free importation of grain? He thinks not, and he goes on to give the example of other countries threatened with scarcity, which are opening their ports for foreign grain, and prohibiting their own to be exported, thereby closing some of our ordinary sources of supply. If, he asks, the Corn Laws are suspended, is it to be done by an act of prerogative, or by legislation at the instance of the Government?

Such were the leading points placed before his Cabinet by Sir Robert Peel in his memorandum of the 1st of November. "In the course of the conversation which followed the reading of the above memorandum, it became evident," he says, "that very serious differences of opinion existed as to the necessity of adopting any extraordinary measures, and as to the character of the measures which it might be advisable to adopt."

The Cabinet broke up to meet again on the 6th of November, on which day the Premier submitted to his colleagues the following memorandum: "To issue forth an Order in Council remitting the duty on grain in bond to one shilling, and opening the ports for the admission of all species of grain at a smaller rate of duty until a day named in the Order. To call Parliament together on the 27th instant, to ask for indemnity and a sanction of the Order by law. To propose to Parliament no other measure than that during the sitting before Christmas. To declare an intention of submitting to Parliament immediately after the recess, a modification of the existing law, but to decline entering into any details in Parliament with regard to such modification. Such modification to include the admission at a nominal duty of Indian corn and of British Colonial corn—to proceed with regard to other descriptions of grain upon the principle of the existing law, after a careful consideration of the practical working of the present machinery for taking the averages."[82] These proposals were rejected by a very decided majority of the Cabinet, only three ministers, Lord Aberdeen, Sir James Graham and Mr. Sidney Herbert, supporting them. Sir Robert tells us that he would, at this juncture, have felt himself justified in resigning office, but that on weighing all the circumstances of his position, he resolved to retain it until the end of November, when the Cabinet would meet again, as he thought by that time new information would be forthcoming, and in all likelihood new phases of the crisis would have arisen, to induce his colleagues to change or modify their views. He also thought his immediate resignation, if not a cowardly, would be an undignified course, as it would be sure to create excitement and even panic in the country.

The most decided opponent of the Premier's views was Lord Stanley. After the Cabinet Council of the 1st of November, he wrote a memorandum detailing his objections to those views, and sent it to his chief, who says "it contained a very detailed, clear, and able exposition of the grounds on which Lord Stanley dissented from the proposals he had submitted to the Cabinet."[83]

The Cabinet re-assembled on the 25th of November, and agreed to the instructions which were to be issued to the Lord Lieutenant, and by him given to the Commission which had been appointed, to consider and adopt such measures as they deemed useful to mitigate the apprehended scarcity. In these instructions the opinion of Drs. Lindley and Playfair, that half the potato crop was destroyed, is not only given, but emphatically put forward. Apprehension is expressed at the difficulty of substituting a dearer for a cheaper food, the probability of fever closely succeeding famine, and the formidable danger of not having a sufficiency of sound seed for the ensuing crop. "The proportion," say the instructions, "which seed bears to an average crop of potatoes is very large; it has been estimated at not less than one-eighth; and when we remember that a considerable portion of this year's crop in Ireland is already destroyed, and that the remaining portion, if it be saved, must supply food for nine months as well as seed for next year, it is obvious that no ordinary care is required, to husband a sufficient quantity of sound potatoes for planting in the spring. Unless this be done, the calamity of the present year is but the commencement of a more fatal series."[84] No prophecy was ever more accurately and terribly verified.

The Cabinet met again next day, and the Premier read to them a memorandum, which opened thus: "I cannot consent to the issue of these instructions, and undertake at the same time to maintain the existing Corn Law." And again he says, towards the close, "I am prepared, for one, to take the responsibility of suspending the law by an Order in Council, or of calling Parliament at a very early period, and advising in the Speech from the Throne the suspension of the law." On the 29th of November, the Premier sent to each of his colleagues a more detailed and elaborate exposition of his views, in order that they might be prepared to discuss them at the next Cabinet Council.

According to the course he had evidently laid down for himself, he made the whole question of the repeal of the Corn Laws turn on the impending Irish famine. He begins with the question he intends to discuss in this manner:—"What is the course most consistent with the public interests under the present circumstances, in reference to the future supply of food?" His answer to his own question is, "that the proper precaution, though it may turn out to be a superfluous one, is the permission, for a limited time, to import foreign grain free of duty." He repeats that several of the countries of Europe have taken precautions to secure a sufficiency of food for their people. He goes into a history of what the English Government had done on former occasions, when a scarcity of food was imminent, admitting that, while, in 1793, it opened the ports for food supplies, it also prohibited their exportation. He goes on to show the advantages to be derived from the opening of the ports. He touches the repeal of the Corn Laws but slightly, knowing full well that the other points treated in the memorandum must raise a discussion on that question in the Cabinet. However he does say enough to show it must be treated. He asks, "is the Corn Law in all its provisions adapted to this unforeseen and very special case?" He sums up his views in these words: "Time presses, and on some definite course we must decide. Shall we undertake without suspension to modify the existing Corn Law? Shall we resolve to maintain the existing Corn Law? Shall we advise the suspension of that law for a limited period? My opinion is for the last course, admitting as I do that it involves the necessity for the immediate consideration of the alterations to be made in the existing Corn Law, such alterations to take effect after the period of suspension. I should rather say it involves the question of the principle and degree of protection to agriculture."[85]

Several of the Cabinet Ministers sent replies to the Premier's memorandum before the day for their next meeting, which replies he thought might lead to long discussions without any practical result, so on the 2nd of December he brought before them, in another memorandum, what he calls a specific measure—the announcement, in fact, that if the ports were once opened the Corn duties could not be re-imposed; and whether the ports were or were not opened, he said the state of those laws must be re-considered—nay more, that they must gradually, but, "at no distant day," be repealed. He finally stated in this paper the principles on which he was ready to undertake that repeal.

119

When this last memorandum was prepared, the Cabinet was in a sort of permanent session: Sir Robert Peel tells us its discussions continued from the 25th of November to the 5th of December. With the exception of the Duke of Buccleugh and Lord Stanley, his colleagues gave their consent to his proposal; in some instances, however, he felt it was a reluctant consent. Under such circumstances, he considered he could not succeed in a complete and final adjustment of the Corn Law; so, on the 5th of December, he repaired to Osborne and placed his resignation in the hands of the Queen.

Lord John Russell was summoned by the Queen on the 8th of December; he was still at Edinburgh and was unable to present himself before her Majesty until the 11th. He was in the unfortunate position of being in a minority in the House of Commons. However, being empowered to form an administration, he asked for time to consult his political friends; besides which he also opened a communication with the late First Lord, to see how far he could reckon on his support, at least with respect to the question of the Corn Laws. He received from Sir Robert Peel what seemed a kind and re-assuring answer; but although Sir Robert, in his letter to the Queen of the 8th of December, told her Majesty he would support the new Government in carrying out the principles, to carry out which a majority of the members of his own Cabinet refused to aid him; still he did not, when interrogated on the subject, pledge himself to support Lord John who then saw the promised aid could not be relied on; for any change in the programme might be regarded as a change of principle, and no minister takes up the precise programme of his predecessor. Still, on the 18th Lord John undertook to form a Government; on the 20th, he writes to the Queen to say he found it impossible to do so. It was no secret, that Lord Grey's objection to *one* appointment was the immediate cause of this failure, nor was it a secret, that the person objected to was Lord Palmerston.[86] Some, however, thought that this incident was cleverly laid hold of by Lord John, to free himself from an untenable position. On the same day Sir

Robert Peel found himself again in the Queen's presence, who at once announced to him, that instead of taking leave of him, she must request him to continue in her service. On his return to town he immediately summoned his late colleagues to meet him. All but two agreed to enter the Cabinet again. These were Lord Stanley and the Duke of Buccleugh; the former stood firm to his principles of protection, the latter asked time for consideration, which resulted in his re-accepting his former place; the rapid changes and events since the 6th of December giving, he said, such a new character to things, that he was now of opinion that a measure for the absolute repeal of the Corn Laws, at an early period, was the true policy. Thus, after an interregnum of fifteen days, the old Government, Lord Stanley excepted, was back in power. Mr. Gladstone replaced Lord Stanley at the Colonial Office, giving "the new administration the weight of his high character, and great abilities and acquirements."[87]

FOOTNOTES:

68.   Letter of 17th October: Peel Memoirs, part 3.

69.   Writer of the article Sir R. Peel, in Encycl. Brit.

70.   Memoirs, part 3, page 100.

71.   Ibid.

72.   Memoirs, part 3, page 98.

73.   A short time after this speech was delivered, Mr. D'Israeli commented upon it with great severity, and made it the ground work of one of his most bitter attacks on Sir Robert Peel, in the course of which he made use of the celebrated phrase, "organized hypocrisy." "Dissolve if you please," said Mr. D'Israeli, "the Parliament you have betrayed, and appeal to the people, who, I believe, mistrust you. For me there remains this at least—the opportunity of expressing thus publicly my belief, that a Conservative Government is an organised hypocrisy." It was Sir Robert Peel who had set aside the word "Tory" for that of "Conservative,"—hence the point. Sir Robert, who was neither quick nor brilliant at repartee, rose and replied with dignity, yet with the style and manner of one who felt keenly the arrows of his adversary, steeped, as they were, in gall. His closing observations were telling:—"When

I proposed the Tariff of 1842, and when the charge which the honorable member now repeats was made against me, I find the honorable gentleman got up in his place, and stated, that 'that charge had been made without due examination of the facts of the case, and that the conduct pursued by the right honourable baronet was in exact, permanent, and perfect consistency with the principles of free trade as laid down by Mr. Pitt. His Sir R. Peel's.

reason for saying this much was to refute the accusation brought against the Government, that they had put forward their present views in order to get into power.' These sentiments I find attributed to Mr. D'Israeli. I do not know whether they are of sufficient importance to mention them in the House; but this I know, that I then held in the same estimation the panegyric with which I now regard the attack."

74.   Memoirs by Sir Robert Peel, part 3, page 113.
75.   Sir Robert Peel's Memoirs, part 3, page 119.
76.   Ibid.
77.   Memoirs, part 3, page 121.
78.   Quarterly Review, Sept. 1846
79.   Memoirs, part 3, page 131.
80.   Sir R. Peel's Memoirs, part 3, page 132.
81.   *Ib.* 134.
82.   Memoirs, part 3, page 158.
83.   It is a great pity we have not this Mem. before us. It was returned to Lord Stanley at his request, and Sir Robert says he kept no copy of it.
84.   Memoirs, part iii, p. 181.
85.   Memoirs, part 3, page 185.
86.   "You will have heard the termination, of our attempt to form, a government. All our plans were frustrated by Lord Grey." T.B. (Lord) Macaulay's letter to J.F. M'Farlane, 22nd Dec., 1845.
87.   Sir R. Peel, in his Memoirs, part 3, p. 259.

* * * * *

CHAPTER IV.

MEETING OF PARLIAMENT—Queen's Speech—The Premier's speech on the Address—Goes into the whole question of Free Trade—The Protectionists—Lord Brougham's views (*note*)—The twelve night's debate on the Corn Laws—No connection between it and the Famine—Stafford O'Brien's speech—Sir James Graham's reply—Smith O'Brien's speech—His imprisonment (*note B Appendix*)—O'Connell's motion—His speech—Sir Robert Peel replies—Substantially agrees with O'Connell—Bill for the protection of life in Ireland—Its first reading opposed by the Irish members—O'Connell leads the Opposition in a speech of two hours—Mr. D'Israeli mistaken in calling it his last speech—His account of it—He misrepresents it—The opinions expressed in it were those O'Connell always held. Break up of the Tory party—Lord George Bentinck becomes leader of the Protectionists—Their difficulty in opposing the Coercion Bill—Ingenious plan of Lord George—Strange combination against the Government—Close of Debate on Coercion Bill—Government defeated by a majority of 73—Measures to meet the Famine—Delay—Accounts from various parts of the country—Great distress—"Are the landlords making any efforts?"—Notice for rent—The bailiff's reply—Number of workhouses open—Number of persons in them—Sir Robert Peel's speech on his resignation—Accident to him—His death—The Peels—Sir Robert's qualities and character—His manner of dealing with the Famine—His real object the repeal of the Corn Laws.

Sir Robert Peel, thus reinstated as Prime Minister of England for the third time, met Parliament on the 22nd of January with a Queen's speech, in which her Majesty's first allusion to Ireland was one of deep regret at the deliberate assassinations so frequent in that country. The speech then goes on to deplore the failure of the potato in the United Kingdom—the failure being greatest in Ireland—assuring Parliament that "all precautions that could be adopted were adopted for the purpose of alleviating the calamity." An eulogium is next passed on previous legislation in the direction of Free Trade, and upon the benefits conferred by it, with a recommendation that Parliament should take into early consideration the principles which guided that legislation, with a view of having them more extensively applied.

And her Majesty is finally made to say, that she thinks further reductions in the existing duties "upon many articles, the produce of other countries, will tend to ensure the continuance of these great benefits." The wily Premier did not allow the word "Corn" or "Corn Laws" to have a place in the speech of his Royal Mistress.

Anxious to explain, at the very earliest moment, the causes which led to the dissolution of his Ministry and their return to office, he spoke upon the Address, and went into the whole question. He put the potato blight in the foreground; for, with the instinct of the caddice worm, he felt that this was the piece of bulrush by which he could best float his Free Trade policy, his Government and himself. And, indeed, from the first night of the session until the resolutions on the Corn Laws were carried, the members of the Government showed the greatest anxiety to keep the terrible consequences of the potato failure before Parliament. They did not exaggerate the failure, nor its then probable effects; they gave to both that importance which they really demanded, but which, only the admission helped the repeal of the Corn Laws, they would hardly be so ready to concede. The Protectionists, on the contrary, took up the cry of "exaggeration," against the most undoubted evidence, supplied from every part of the country, by persons in every rank of life, and of every

124

shade of political opinion. "We have," said one of them,[88] "famine in the newspapers, we have famine in the speeches of Cabinet Ministers, but we find abundance in the markets; the cry of famine is a pretext, but it is not the reason for the changes." There is some truth in the latter part of this sentence—famine was not all a pretext, but it was certainly used by ministers as a cry to strengthen their Corn Law policy. "It was," said Sir Robert Peel, "that great and mysterious calamity, the potato failure, that was the immediate and proximate cause which led to the dissolution of the Government on the 6th of December, 1845." Two most important points, he said, they had now before them; (1) the measures to be immediately adopted in consequence of the potato blight; (2) and the ultimate course to be pursued in relation to the importation of grain. His opinions, he goes on to say, on the subject of Protection had undergone a change, and chiefly because the prophecies of the protectionists, when the tariff was altered in '42, were falsified by experience. Now, if the Free Traders had a watchword which they used more frequently than any other, it was the cry of "cheap bread;" and yet in the face of this, the Premier said:—"I want, at the same time, to show that concurrently with the increase of importation, there has been an increase in the prices of the articles." He then quotes several of the Government contracts to prove this assertion, which was quite correct.[89] Once again, he puts prominently forward the advice he gave his Government in the beginning of November, 1845, which was, either to open the ports by an Order in Council, or to call Parliament together as soon as possible, to meet the "great and pressing danger of the potato failure;" but what he does *not* put forward is, that he grounded both these proposals on the condition that the Corn Laws should be repealed. To be sure he stated this condition mildly, when he told his colleagues that once the ports were opened, he would not undertake to close them—yet what was this but saying to a protectionist Cabinet,—there is great danger of a famine in Ireland—we ought to open the ports or assemble Parliament, but I will not agree to one or the other unless you all become Free-traders; thus making the feeding or the starving of the Irish people depend on the condition, that the members of his Government were to change their views, and preach Free Trade from those benches, to which they had been triumphantly carried on the shoulders of Protection. In truth, Sir Robert, more than most politicians, was in the habit of suppressing those portions of a question which he found inconvenient; limiting his statement to such parts of it, as suited his present purpose. In his communications with his colleagues, he was very fond of such phrases as, "to lay aside all reserve," "to speak in the most unreserved manner," etc.; thus forcibly impressing one with his habitual love of reserve, even with his greatest intimates. And in his speech of the 22nd of January, on the Address, he said, with suspicious indignation, that "nothing could be more base or dishonest" than to use the potato blight as a means of repealing the Corn Laws.

The great twelve nights' debate on the repeal of these laws, commenced five days after the speech above referred to, was made. The Premier, at great length and very ably, repeated the arguments he had been putting forward since the previous November, in favour of taking the duty off everything that could be called human food; he even proposed to repeal the duty on the importation of potatoes, by which, he said, he hoped to obtain sound seed from abroad. Sir Robert, in this speech, may be said to have been in his best vein,—full, explanatory, clear, assumptive, persuasive,—often appealing to the kindness and forbearance of his hearers,—always calculating a good deal on his power of bending people to his views by a plausible, diplomatic treatment of the whole question. Addressing Mr. Greene, the chairman of the Committee, he said, with solemn gravity: "Sir, I wish it were possible to take advantage of this calamity, for introducing among the people of Ireland the taste for a better and more certain provision for their support than that which they have heretofore cultivated." Surely, the Indian meal, which he so often boasted of having ordered on his own responsibility, was not a step in that direction. To have purchased and stored for their use the wheat and oats of their own soil, would have been, one should suppose, the direct way of achieving this philanthropic desire.

On the fifth night of the debate, Sir Robert rose again, and, in his speech, applied himself almost exclusively to the famine part of the question. He read many letters from persons in high position in Ireland, to prove to the House what was unfortunately but too well known in that country for many months, that the greater portion of the only food of four millions of the people was destroyed. Reading from an official report, substantially embracing the whole kingdom, he said: "In four electoral divisions, nearly nine-tenths of the potato crop are gone; in ninety three, between seven-tenths and eight-tenths; and in one hundred and twenty-five, the loss approaches to seven-tenths of the whole crop; in sixteen divisions, to six-tenths; in five hundred and ninety-six divisions, nearly one-half; and in five hundred and eighty-two, nearly four-tenths are destroyed." Appealing to the House, he says it has but two courses,— "to maintain the existing law, or make some proposal for increasing the facilities of procuring foreign articles of food." "Will you not, then," he concludes, in an elaborate peroration, "will you not then cherish with delight the reflection, that, in this, the present hour of *comparative prosperity*, yielding to no clamour—impelled by no fear—except, indeed, that provident fear which is the mother of safety—you had anticipated the evil day, and, long before its advent, had trampled on every impediment to the free circulation of the Creator's bounty."

The old Tory party had, in the beginning, admitted, to a great extent, the failure of the potato crop in Ireland; but seeing the use the Peel Government were making of it, they seem to have agreed to maintain that the reports—Government as well as others—were greatly exaggerated,—and for a purpose. Lord George Bentinck, the coming leader of the Protectionists, said, that "in his opinion, which every day's experience confirmed, the potato famine in Ireland was a gross delusion— a more gross delusion had never been practised upon the country by any Government." Mr. Shaw, the member for the University of Dublin, maintained that "great exaggeration existed." "The case," he said, "was not extraordinary—*fever, dysentery,* and *death* being a kind of normal state" in Ireland!

Members on both sides of the House soon began to see, that there was no necessary connection between the potato failure in Ireland, and the repeal of the Corn Laws, although, in all his speeches on the subject, Sir Robert Peel assumed it as a matter of course. The only member of the Government who attempted to prove this connection, was Sir James Graham. Mr. Stafford O'Brien, the member for North Northamptonshire, but connected by marriage with the county Clare, and one of the ablest men in the Tory ranks, said he had just returned from Ireland; that there was no exaggeration about the failure of the potato crop there, but that it had nothing to do with the question of the Corn Laws. He accused the Government of introducing a new principle for a disaster which he hoped would be casual, and of announcing that new principle without, in the least, tracing out how the Corn Laws had contributed to the famine in Ireland; or how the total abrogation of those laws was likely to alleviate that country's distress. The Irish members, he said, all asked for employment; they wished the railways to be made; they expressed their fears about the want of seed for the ground;—but they said, "if you wish to complete our ruin destroy our agriculture." Whilst he expressed the opinion, that there never was a country which called for more urgent attention on the part of the Government than Ireland did at the moment, he did not believe, he said, that if they passed the Government Bill to-morrow, that one more quarter of corn, or one more hundred weight of meal, would be placed within the reach of the poor of Ireland, unless it was accompanied by other measures. Sir James Graham replied, that "it did appear to him, that this matter of the coming scarcity, if not of famine, in Ireland, had an immediate and indissoluble connection with the question of the Corn Laws; and that he, for one, would not propose to the people of Great Britain, to take out of the taxes of Great Britain public money, to aid in the sustenance of their fellow-countrymen in

Ireland, while, artificially, by the laws, the price of the food of the people of Great Britain is enhanced." With regard to this logic of Sir James, it may be remarked, (1) that the immediate effect produced, *and sought to be produced*, by a repeal of the Corn Laws, was to cheapen in the market the only thing Ireland had to sell—corn; (2) that the Irish members did not ask any portion of the taxes of Great Britain, to feed their countrymen,—they proclaimed and proved, that the resources of their own country were sufficient for this purpose; and this view was frequently put forward by O'Connell, and other leading Irish representatives.

William Smith O'Brien, the member for Limerick county, spoke but little during the session. He, and that advanced party in the Repeal Association which acknowledged him as leader, had made up their minds, that Irish Parliamentary business should be transacted in Ireland; and that St. Stephen's was not the place, where patriotic Irish members could best serve their country. Agreeably to this view, he remained in Ireland for nearly two months after the meeting of Parliament, in regular attendance at the Repeal Association, throwing out suggestions for the formation of an Irish party, on a basis wide enough to admit Liberals, Conservatives, and all others with national aspirations. He also paid much attention to the measures brought forward by the Government for the relief of his famishing countrymen; he prepared and brought up reports in the Association on those measures, and reviewed and criticised them in his speeches. At length, he entered an appearance in the House of Commons on the 13th of March. There was a motion before the House, brought forward by the Home Secretary, Sir James Graham, that provision should be made to meet the impending fever and famine in Ireland. Sir James, in his speech, boasted of the sums of money already advanced, with such liberality, for the relief of Ireland. Smith O'Brien made a brief reply, in which he said that the moneys advanced were badly expended, having found their way into other channels than those intended. "He would," he further observed, "tell them frankly—and it was a feeling participated in by the majority of Irishmen—that he was not disposed to appeal to their generosity. There was no generosity in the matter. They had taken, and they had tied the purse-strings of the Irish purse." "They should compel the landlords," he again urged, "to do their duty to the people, and if they did, there would be neither disturbance nor starvation." In making these observations he must have spoken with unwonted energy, and with a boldness unusual in Parliament, as he apologised for his tone and manner, which, he said, he knew could not be acceptable to the House. When he sat down, Lord Claud Hamilton rose and replied to him, by one of those fierce invectives which, after the lapse of a quarter of a century he still, on occasion, can summon up vigour enough to deliver. He taunted the hon. member for Limerick with having then, for the first time during the Session, made his appearance in the House. He told him that, having neglected his own duties both as a representative and a landlord, an attack upon the landlords of Ireland came from him with a bad grace. He further accused him with lending himself to a baneful system of agitation, by which Ireland was convulsed, and prosperity rendered unattainable in that country. Lord Claud having resumed his seat, Smith O'Brien again rose, and said he would not take up their time in replying to him, but he wished to tell the House, that the tone, not so much of the House as of the English press, "about those miserable grants had exasperated him, and a large number of his fellow-countrymen." "If Parliament met in November," be continued, "to enact good laws, instead of now coming forward with a Coercion Bill, they would not be under the necessity of making those painful appeals to Parliament." On the 18th of March he spoke again, calling for a tax of ten per cent, on absentees, which would at once, he said, produce £400,000. But it was on the 17th of April he made his longest and most effective speech. On that occasion, he began by reading extracts from the provincial press of Ireland, giving accounts of "Fearful destitution," "Deaths from Famine," and so forth. He then said, "the circumstance which appeared most aggravating was, that the people were starving in the midst of plenty, and that every tide carried from the Irish ports corn sufficient for the maintenance of thousands of the Irish people." He put forward the sound, but then unpopular view of the repeal of the Corn Laws, which was, that its immediate effect would be injurious to Ireland. "He could not," he told the House, "refrain from expressing his regret, that Government should think it necessary to couple the question of Ireland with the question of the Corn Laws. These laws did not affect the description of food available for the people of Ireland . . . he was one of those who differed from the great majority of the hon. members at his side of the House—he meant with respect to measures to alter the Corn Law, which he had no doubt would be of service to this country, but would for some time be injurious to Ireland." He closed his speech by the declaration, that "he felt it his duty to throw the responsibility upon Government; and in his conscience he believed that, for whatever loss of life might arise from want of food, or from outbreaks, the result of want, ministers would be answerable."[90]

Meantime, the Irish liberal members grew heart-sick of the endless debate upon the Corn Laws, out of which they expected nothing would come to relieve their starving countrymen. During its progress, O'Connell made a motion that the House would resolve itself into a committee, to take into consideration the state of Ireland, with a view to devise means to relieve the distress of the Irish people. He called attention to the vast exports of food from Ireland; showed that while Poor Laws might mitigate distress in ordinary seasons, they were not capable of meeting a famine; and, speaking from the depths of his conviction, he declared that, in his conscience he believed, the result of neglect on the part of the House, in the present instance, would be deaths to an enormous amount. "It may be said," the Liberator continued, with a dignity worthy of him, "that I am here to ask money to succour Ireland in her distress: *No such thing, I scorn the thought*; I am here to say, Ireland has resources of her own." The Home Secretary replied; admitted O'Connell's facts, but begged of him "to leave the matter in the hands of the responsible advisers of the Crown." Lord John Russell counselled the withdrawal of the motion, as he considered the measures of the Government judicious.

It was accordingly withdrawn, and so the matter ended for that time. But again, on the 9th of March, O'Connell asked the First Lord of the Treasury if he were prepared to lay before the House a statement of the measures taken by the Government, to obviate the impending famine and disease in Ireland. Delay, he said, would be fatal, and the sums of money already voted would not be of the least avail. He repeated, that the Irish people were not suing *in forma pauperis*; there were resources in the country, and some further measures should be adopted, to meet the exigencies of their case. Sir Robert Peel replied, that "the statement did not fall much short of the impression *first formed in his mind* in October and November last," and concluded thus: "I again assure the honorable and learned member that *every precaution that can be taken by Government has been taken, not within the last week, or fortnight, but long ago.*"

In the Speech from the throne, her Majesty was made to say, that she observed with deep regret the very frequent instances, in which the crime of deliberate assassination had been, of late, committed in Ireland; and that it would be the duty of Parliament to consider, whether any measure could be devised, to give increased protection to life in that country. In accordance with this striking passage in the Royal Message, Lord St. Germans, Chief Secretary for Ireland, introduced in the House of Lords, on the 23rd of February, a bill for the protection of life in Ireland, better known by the title of Coercion Bill, given to it by the liberal Irish members, and by the Irish people. Of course it passed without difficulty, Lord Bingham, as became one of his name and blood, making a furious speech in its favour.

Strong as the Peel Cabinet had been for years, the Premier's newly announced policy on the Corn Law question led to such a disruption of party ties, that the progress of the Coercion Bill through the Commons could not be regarded by the Government without apprehension. When it went down from the Lords, the unusual, though not unprecedented proceeding of opposing its first reading, was had recourse to by O'Connell and his supporters. O'Connell led the opposition in a speech of two hours, which Mr. D'Israeli calls his last speech in the House of Commons; but this is a mistake. He spoke on the 8th of February, 1847, nearly a year after, on the famine. It is quite possible, that Mr. D'Israeli confounds the two occasions, for the account he gives of O'Connell on the 3rd of April, 1846, was far more applicable to him in February, 1847. Of the speech delivered on the former occasion, against the first reading of the Coercion Bill, Mr D'Israeli says: "It was understood that the House would adjourn for the Easter recess on the 8th instant. There were, therefore, only two nights remaining for Government business, before the holidays. On the first of these, (Friday, April the 3rd), Mr. O'Connell had announced, that he should state his views at length on the condition of Ireland, and the causes of these agrarian outrages. Accordingly, when the order of the day for resuming the adjourned debate was read, he rose at once, to propose an amendment to the motion. He sate in an unusual place—in that generally occupied by the leader of the opposition, and spoke from the red box, convenient to him, from the number of documents to which he had to refer. His appearance was of great debility, and the tones of his voice were very still. His words, indeed, only reached those who were immediately around him, and the ministers sitting on the other side of the green table, and listening with that interest, and respectful attention which became the occasion. It was a strange and touching spectacle, to those who remembered the form of colossal energy, and the clear and thrilling tones, that had once startled, disturbed, and controlled senates. Mr. O'Connell was on his legs for nearly two hours, assisted occasionally, in the management of his documents, by some devoted aide-de-camp. To the house generally, it was a performance of dumb show, a feeble old man muttering before a table; but respect for the great parliamentary personage kept all as orderly as if the fortunes of a party hung upon his rhetoric; and though not an accent reached the gallery, means were taken that, next morning, the country should not lose the last, and not the least interesting of the speeches of one, who had so long occupied and agitated the mind of nations. This remarkable address was an abnegation of the whole policy of Mr. O'Connell's career. It proved, by a mass of authentic evidence, ranging over a long term of years, that Irish outrage was the consequence of physical misery, and that the social evils of that country, could not be successfully encountered by political remedies. To complete the picture, it concluded with a panegyric of Ulster and a patriotic quotation from Lord Clare."[91]

That the rich and splendid voice, which had so often sounded in the ears of his countrymen, like the varied and touching music of their native land, and led them where he would, had lost its finest tones, was true enough; but it had not so utterly failed as Mr. D'Israeli asserts. I heard O'Connell speak in public after this time, and although the marks of age and feebleness were in his whole manner, he managed his voice so as to be heard and understood at a considerable distance. "Respect for the great parliamentary personage kept all as orderly as if the fortunes of a party hung upon his rhetoric," Mr. D'Israeli says. He ought to have recollected, that the fortunes of a party did really hang upon his rhetoric on this very occasion; for, to the uncompromising opposition of O'Connell and his friends, may be fairly attributed the ultimate defeat of this Coercion Bill, which defeat drove Sir Robert Peel from power, and brought in Lord John Russell. As to some means or other having been taken to publish a speech that had not been heard, there can be little doubt but the reporters took it down substantially, with the exception of the documents read. It was not O'Connell's habit to write his speeches; where then could the means of publishing this one come from, except from the reporters? He made several short speeches during the progress of the bill, which were printed in the newspapers in the usual way, surely they must have been reported in the usual way.

But this is a trifle: the most unkind and groundless assertion the author of the letters of Runnymede makes, with regard to the man who called him the lineal descendant of the impenitent thief, is, when he says, that "this remarkable address was an abnegation of the whole policy of Mr. O'Connell's career." This is strangely inexact: nay more, if Mr. D'Israeli heard the speech, as is to be inferred, or if he read it, it is disingenuous. The speech was a bold denunciation of the system of evictions, carried out by Irish landlords, to which O'Connell attributed the murders the Government relied on, to justify them in bringing forward the Coercion Bill. Speaking of the murder of Mr. Carrick, he said: "here again let me solemnly protest—I am sure I need not—that I do not consider any of these acts as an excuse, or a reason, or even as the slightest palliation of his murder (hear, hear); no, they are not, it was a horrible murder; it was an atrocious murder; it was a crime that was deserving of the severest punishment which man can inflict, and which causes the red arm of God's vengeance to be suspended over the murderer (hear, hear)." But he adds: "I want the House to prevent the recurrence of such murders. You are going to enact a Coercion Bill against the peasantry and the tenantry, and my object is, that you should turn to the landlords, and enact a Coercion Bill against them." Who but Mr. D'Israeli can perceive any abnegation of O'Connell's principles in these sentiments? He quoted Parliamentary reports to prove what tyrannical use had been made of the powers conferred by Coercion Acts, and he enumerated those passed since 1801, under some of which trial by jury was abolished. He cited blue books to show the misery and destitution to which ejected tenants were sometimes reduced, closing his proofs with this sentence: "such is the effect of the ejectment of tenantry in Ireland." He next dwelt on the physical wretchedness of the people in general, relying chiefly for his facts on the Devon Commission. He reminded Sir James Graham of a statement of his, that the murders in Ireland were a blot upon Christianity. "Is not," said O'Connell, "the state of things I have described a blot upon Christianity? (hear, hear). This, be it recollected," he continued, "is forty-five years after the Union, during which time Ireland has been under the government of this country, which has reduced the population of that country to a worse condition than that of any other country in Europe" (hear, hear).

His great object was to prove that the state of the Land Laws was the cause of agrarian murders, and that Coercion Acts were not a remedy. In the County Tipperary, where there were most ejectments, there were also most murders, and he called the particular attention of the house to this fact. He referred to the Land Commission report with regard to ejectments, and showed from it, that in the year 1843 there were issued from the Civil Bill Courts 5,244 ejectments, comprising 14,816 defendants, and from the Superior Courts 1,784 ejectments, comprising 16,503 defendants, making a total of 7,028 ejectments, and 31,319 defendants; or within the period of five years—1839 to 1843—comprised in the return, upwards of 150,000 persons had been subjected to ejectment process in Ireland.

He complained of the administration of justice in that country. The government had, he said, appointed partizan judges (he named several of them) and partizan magistrates, in whom the people had no confidence, whilst they took away the commission of the peace from seventy-four gentlemen, simply because they advocated a repeal of the Legislative Union.

He came to remedies. His opinion was that the great cause of the existing state of Ireland was the land question. The fact is, he said, the House has done too much for the landlord and too little for the tenant. He enumerated the principal laws conferring power on the landlords, adding that he did not believe there was a more fertile source of murder and outrage than those powers. *"Thus,"* said he, *"the source of crime is directly traceable to the legislation of this House."* The repeal of those Land Laws was one of the remedies which he called for, but not the only one. He wanted the House to determine at once to do justice to Ireland politically as well as in relation to the law of landlord and tenant. In the first place, he said Ireland had not an adequate number of members to represent her in the House, next she wanted an extension of the franchise, thirdly, corporate reform, and, lastly, a satisfactory arrangement of the temporalities of the church. These four general remedies he demanded from the House, as a mode of coercing the people of Ireland, by their affections and their interests, into a desire to continue the Union with England. "I want," he said, "the House to determine at once to do justice to Ireland politically as well as in relation to the law of landlord and tenant."

He maintained that the Land Laws passed since the Union should be repealed, and above all he called for full compensation for every improvement made by the tenant. "Labour," he said, "is the property of the tenant, and if the tenant by his labour and skill improved the land, and made it more valuable, let him have the benefit of those improvements, before the landlord turns him out of possession." In Lord Devon's report he found the superior tranquillity of Ulster was traced to the security given to the tenant by tenant right, in proof of which he quoted the evidence of Mr. Handcock, Lord Lurgan's agent, and other Northern witnesses who were examined before the Devon Commission. "This then," he continued, "is the evidence of the North of Ireland as to the value of tenant right. How often have I heard all the boast of the superior tranquillity of the North? It was because they were better treated by their landlords, and, generally speaking, there was a better feeling there towards the landlords, and because the tenants were allowed to sell their tenant right. In the County Tipperary there is an agrarian law, which is the law of ejectment; in the province of Ulster there is a general law giving the tenants valuable rights. He (Mr. O'Connell) called upon the House to make their choice between the two. Now was the time for the choice. The country had arrived at a state when something must be done."

This is what Mr. D'Israeli calls "a panegyric of Ulster."

"Are you," he concluded, "desirous of putting an end to these murders? Then it must be by removing the cause of the murder. You could not destroy the effect without taking away the cause. I repeat, the tranquillity of Ulster is owing to the enjoyment of tenant right; when that right was taken away, the people were trodden under foot, and, in the words of Lord Clare, 'ground to powder.'"

This is what Mr. D'Israeli calls "a patriotic quotation from Lord Clare."

It would seem to me that any impartial reader of the Liberator's speech on this occasion would regard it as an iteration of the whole policy of his career, rather than an abnegation of it; but smooth and kind as Mr. D'Israeli's words appear, it is manifest he did not forget their ancient feud, and he therefore adroitly tries to give a parting stab, ungenerous as it was false, to the expiring lion.

That portion of the Tory party which remained faithful to Protection, being deserted by their leaders, rallied round Lord George Bentinck, and in some sense forced him to become their champion against their late chief, the Premier, and his policy. Thus was formed the Protectionist party, strictly so called. This party being of opinion that there was sufficient necessity for the Government Coercion Bill were in "great difficulty to find a plausible pretext for opposing it." Lord George himself hit upon one. The party held a meeting at the house of Mr. Bankes, and after anxious discussion on the part of many members present, Lord George at last spoke. He said "he was for giving the Government a hearty support, provided they proved they were in earnest in their determination to put down murder and outrage in Ireland, by giving priority in the conduct of public business to the measure in question,"—the Coercion Bill.[92] This was ingenious. The party supported what was called public order in Ireland, but with a proviso that might eventually defeat free trade by postponement. After some finessing, the Government showed a determination to go on with both bills. Lord John Russell and the Whigs saw their opportunity, and to the dismay of the First Lord, he found the strange, incongruous, unprecedented combination of Irish Repealers, Tory Protectionists, Whigs, and Manchester League-men prepared to vote against him on his Irish Coercion Act. The debate on it occupied six nights. It was closed on the 25th of June by Mr. Cobden; the division was taken, and the Government was left in a minority of SEVENTY THREE. It was a memorable night in the life of Sir Robert Peel. Although a night of defeat, it was also a night of triumph for him; for, two hours before the division, and whilst the debate was going on, Commissioners from the House of Lords announced to the Commons that their lordships had finally passed the bill for the repeal of the Corn Laws. It was the law of the land! Writing to Lord Harding, Governor-General of India, ten days afterwards, Sir Robert says: "You will see that we are out—defeated by a combination of Whigs and Protectionists. A much less emphatic hint would have sufficed for me. I would not have held office by sufferance for a week . . . There are no secrets. We have fallen in the face of day, and with our front to to our enemies. There is nothing I would not have done to ensure the carrying of the measure I had proposed this session. I pique myself on never having proposed anything which I have not carried. But the moment their success was ensured, and I had the satisfaction of seeing two drowsy Masters in Chancery mumble out, at the table of the House of Commons that the Lords had passed the Corn and Customs Bills, I was satisfied."[93] Sir Robert expresses himself satisfied, but the coincidence which caused this satisfaction was not, in the slightest degree influenced either by himself or any member of his Government. Neither was it the result of chance or good fortune; it was solely brought about by the nice calculation of the anti-Corn Law party, who had resolved to prolong the debate on the Coercion Act until the Corn Bill would be passed. And as soon as they heard the aforesaid drowsy Masters in Chancery make the welcome announcement, *they* were satisfied, and the division took place.

During the session, the Peel Government proposed and carried several measures for the employment of the people of Ireland, the principal of which were:—1. An Act for the further amendment of the 1st Victoria, cap. 21; 2. An Act empowering Grand Juries at the Assizes of 1846 to appoint extraordinary presentment sessions for county works; 3. An Act to consolidate the powers hitherto exercised by the Commissioners of Public Works in Ireland; and, 4. An Act to facilitate the employment of the labouring poor for a limited period in the distressed districts. Up to the 15th of August, 1846, there was expended for the relief of Irish distress the sum of £733,372; of which £368,000 was in loans, and

£365,372 in grants. The sum raised in voluntary subscriptions, through the Relief Committees was £98,000. The largest number of persons employed at any one time in this first season of relief was 97,000; which was in August, 1846.[94]

There was very considerable delay in affording relief to the people under the above acts. New Boards—new Commissioners—new Forms—new everything had to be got up, and all were commenced too late; it was, therefore, long, provokingly and unnecessarily long, before anything was done. The Rev. Mr. Moore, Rector of Cong, in one of his letters, complains that he was superciliously treated at the relief office in Dublin Castle, and finally told relief was only to be had in the workhouse. He then wrote to the Lord Lieutenant asking for a consignment of meal to be sold in his neighbourhood, undertaking to be responsible to the Government for the amount. A promise was given to him that this would be done, but I cannot discover that it was ever fulfilled.

Great numbers were in a starving condition in the southern and western counties, and in districts of Ulster also. A correspondent of the London *Morning Chronicle*, writing from Limerick under date of the 16th of April, says: "The whole of yesterday I spent in running from hut to hut on the right bank of the Shannon. The peasantry there were in an awful condition. In many cases they had not even a rotten potato left. They have consumed even the seed potatoes, unable any longer to resist the pangs of hunger." The Rev. Mr. Doyle, of Graig, in the county Kilkenny, writing on the 13th of April, says, he had made a visitation of his parish and found five hundred and eighty-three distressed families, comprising two thousand seven hundred and thirty individuals; of this number fifty-one had constant employment, two hundred and seventy none at all; the rest got occasional work; three-fourths of the whole had not three days' provisions. Sir Lucius O'Brien, (afterwards Lord Inchiquin), as Chairman of the Ennis Board of Guardians, took occasion to remark, "on the heartlessness of some of the Dublin papers, when speaking of the famine." "Everyone acquainted with the country, knew," he said, "that at this moment the people are in many places starving."[95]

The people assembled in considerable numbers in parts of the South calling for food or employment. A man died of starvation on the public works in Limerick. At a meeting in Newry for the purpose of taking measures against the scarcity, and whilst some were denying its existence in that locality, the Right Rev. Dr. Blake, the Catholic bishop, said, that since he had entered the meeting, a letter had been handed to him stating that a person had just died of starvation in High Street. In April and May potatoes had risen to a famine price in the provinces. They were quoted in Galway and Tuam at 6d. a stone, but in reality, as the local journals remarked, the price was double that, as not more than one-half of those bought could be used for food.

The humane and philanthropic, who went about endeavouring to save the lives of the people, often asked, as they travelled through the country, "Are the landlords making any efforts? "The common answer was, with very rare exceptions, "None whatever." The correspondent of a Dublin newspaper,[96] writing from Cashel, quotes a notice he had copied in Cahir, which was posted all about the town.

It ran thus:—

> "The tenantry on the Earl of Glengall's estate, residing in the manor of Cahir, are requested to pay into my office on the 12th of May, all rent and arrears of rent due up to the 25th of March, otherwise the most summary steps will be taken to recover same.
>
> > "JOHN CHAYTOR,
> > "1st April, 1846."

The same correspondent, in a letter from Templemore, informs his readers that a certain noble proprietor was just after paying a visit to his estate in that locality, and he had no sooner taken his departure, than notices were served on his tenantry to pay the November rent. The tenants asked time, saying they had only a few black potatoes left. The bailiff's reply was characteristic, and no doubt truthful:—"What the d— do we care about you or your black potatoes?—it was not *us* that made them black—you will get two days to pay the rent, and if you don't you know the consequence."[97]

When the relief depots, the local committees, and the public works got into gear, much was done during the summer months to alleviate the terrible distress; but as soon as the Government advances and subscriptions to the committees began to be exhausted, the cry for food was again heard from many parts of the country.[98]

At this time there were one hundred and twenty-three workhouses open, and great as the people's aversion was to them the inmates went on steadily increasing. In the month of December, 1845, the total number in those workhouses was 41,118; in March, 1846, 50,717; and on the 13th of June, the highest point attained during the year was arrived at, there being, on that day, 51,302 persons receiving in-door relief. On the 29th of August, owing, of course, to the harvest having come in, the number had fallen to 43,655. In ordinary years, when there was neither blight, nor fear of blight, it was deemed good husbandry to procure foreign seed potatoes, and if this could not be done, farmers at least tried to procure "strange" seed, grown at a distance from their own farms. A larger and in every way a better crop was the usual result of this practice. After the potato blight of 1845, the procuring of sound, and if possible of foreign seed, for planting in Ireland was of the utmost importance, and indeed Sir Robert Peel had included, in his new tariff, the admission of foreign potatoes free, in the hope of securing good seed for the planting of 1846; but as the Corn and Customs' Bill did not become law until the end of June, this provision could be of no avail for that year.

The Peel Government was defeated on the Irish Coercion Act on the 25th of June, and the Duke of Wellington and Sir Robert Peel announced their resignation on the 29th in the Upper and Lower Houses respectively.

The Duke contented himself with the simple announcement; but Sir Robert made a speech, reviewing and defending his conduct whilst minister. Of Ireland he said little, except that he had the full intention of serving her in every way, by dealing with the land and other questions, telling us patronizingly, that she was entitled to a "complete equality of municipal and political rights." But this was only the old stereotyped liberality of a beaten minister—beaten on an Irish Coercion Act— speaking by anticipation from the Opposition benches, and endeavouring to plant thorns in the path of his successful rival. The sentiment, such as it was, was received with much cheers, and *some murmurs*. Strange enough the *murmurs* are not to be found in Hansard, although reported in the newspapers of the day.

The Liberal party being for a long time the free trade party, and Sir Robert Peel and his friends being only neophytes, he knew, even though they did carry free trade, that they could not claim the merit of doing so, only having taken it up, when it had attained such a position before the country as to make it all but irresistible. Neither did he wish the incoming Russell-Whig party to get credit for it; he therefore turned aside, in a rather unusual manner, and gave the merit of it to Mr. Cobden. "I said before, and I said truly," Sir Robert begins his eulogy on that distinguished man, "that in proposing our measures of commercial policy, I had no wish to rob others of the credit justly due to them. I must say with reference to honorable gentlemen opposite, as I say with reference to ourselves, that neither of us is the party which is justly entitled to the credit of them. There has been a combination of parties generally opposed to each other, and that combination and the influence of Government, have led to their success. But the name which ought to be associated with the success of those measures is not the name of the noble lord, the organ of the party of which he is the leader, nor is it mine. The name which ought to be, and will be associated with the success of those measures, is the name of one who, acting, I believe, from pure and disinterested motives, has with untiring energy, made appeals to our reason, and has enforced

143

those appeals with an eloquence the more to be admired, because it was unaffected and unadorned: it is the name of Richard Cobden." Sir Robert's peroration to this speech was an elaborate one, and consisted in praises of himself. Here are his closing words: "I shall leave a name execrated by every monopolist, who from less honorable motives clamours for protection, because it conduces to his own individual benefit; but it may be, that I shall leave a name sometimes remembered with expressions of good will, in the abodes of those whose lot is to labour, and to earn their daily bread by the sweat of their brow, when they shall recruit their exhausted strength with abundant and untaxed food, the sweeter because it is no longer leavened with a sense of injustice."[99]

Although Sir Robert Peel lived four years after this defeat, he never returned to the treasury benches. In opposition, however, he was almost as powerful as when minister; giving to Lord John Russell's Government an independent and most valuable support, without which it could not have continued to exist. On the 28th of June, 1850, he spoke in the House on the celebrated Don Pacifico's claims against the Greek Government, and refused his support to Mr. Roebuck's motion approving of Lord Palmerston's foreign policy. He rode out next day—SS. Peter and Paul's day—his horse shied and became restive, whilst he was saluting a lady on Constitution Hill; he was thrown heavily; on being taken up, partly insensible, he was conveyed to his house, where, having suffered much pain, he died three days afterwards.

Sir Robert Peel's father, a very wealthy cotton spinner, and also a Member of Parliament, had early made up his mind that his son should become a public man. As soon as he was of age he was returned by the borough of Cashel to the House of Commons, where he soon began to display those qualities for which his family was distinguished—prudence, industry, discreet reserve, with a remarkable ability for utilizing the brains of others. His father, who was made a baronet by Mr. Perceval, became a millionaire by cotton spinning, yet in a generation remarkable for invention, neither he nor one belonging to him originated any of the improvements for preparing or spinning cotton; when one was made, however, its utility soon became apparent to the practical good sense of the Peels; they secured it, and thus founded a house and built up a princely fortune to sustain it; while, too often, the man whose original genius discovered the improvement, lived and died in comparative poverty.[100] Sir Robert Peel carried this second-rate, but most valuable quality, into statesmanship. He was not the originator of any great political amelioration; he was invariably found, at first, in opposition to every measure of the kind; but he did not refuse to examine it; on the contrary, he studied it carefully, weighed the reasons put forward in support of it, watched with nervous anxiety the tide of public opinion, and when that could no longer be resisted with safety, he took the question up and sustained it by the arguments he had been combating before—remodelled, to be sure, occasionally, but still the same; threw the weight of his high character into the scale, and thus not only contributed to its success, but secured it. Such is the history of Catholic Emancipation and the repeal of the Corn Laws. Hence a bitter political adversary of his, who has drawn his public character with much candour and ability, and not in an ungenerous spirit either, says of him, that "his life was one of perpetual education." Elsewhere he puts pretty much the same idea in a severer and more sarcastic form, when he asserts that Sir Robert Peel's mind "was one vast appropriating clause."[101]

Some of his eulogists assert that he had made up his mind on the great measures he carried through Parliament long before he had given them his support, but that he was awaiting a favourable opportunity to declare his views, whilst he was in the meantime educating his party. If this be intended as a compliment, as it seems to be, it is a very doubtful one. Assuming it to be true, he must for many years of his life have been a mere hypocrite. The opinion that he himself was gradually educated into these views would seem to be the truer as it is also the kinder one; besides his own declarations coincide with it. There was what is called a Bullion Committee in 1811, and another in 1819, Sir Robert (then Mr.) Peel being chairman of the latter. The former was called Mr. Hooner's

Committee. In 1819, speaking of the inconvertible paper money, he recanted his views of 1811, as his opinions with regard to the question had undergone "a material change." "He had," he said, "voted against Mr. Hooner's resolutions in 1811, he would now vote for them if they were brought forward." In his Memoirs, speaking of the Corn Laws, "he had," he says, "adopted at an early period of his public life, without, he fears, much serious reflection, the opinions generally prevalent of the justice and necessity of protection to domestic agriculture, but *the progress of discussion* had made a material change in the opinions of many persons" [himself of course amongst the number] "with regard to the policy of protection to domestic agriculture." It is true, then, that this eminent statesman was at school all his life, a diligent student, willing and anxious to learn, but always conducting his studies from a Conservative standpoint. It is no discredit to him—far from it. And although the tide of progress carried him to the extent of breaking up his own party, in doing so he was acting, he considered, for the interests of England. Nothing can be more absurd and wicked in a statesman than to allow himself to be impounded within the narrow iron-bound circle of party, and to persevere in sustaining the views and principles of that party against justice, conscience and fact.

Great and varied as were the powers of Sir Robert Peel as a public speaker, he was not an orator in the strictest and highest sense of that word. True oratory is the offspring of genius, and he, gifted though he was, had not the sacred fire of genius in his soul. In the style which he adopted, and which was probably the best suited to his natural powers, he was all but perfect: lucid, argumentation, frank, at least in seeming, bland, persuasive; always singularly respectful not only to the House, but to the humblest member of it; his speeches partook more of the lecture and less of oratorical display than those of most other public men with anything like his reputation; but they were admirably suited to an educated and deliberative assembly like the House of Commons—and hence he influenced—almost ruled it, as no other man did before or since. Knowing this, he never felt so happy or so much at home as in that scene of his labours and his triumphs. His gesture was inferior: he used it but seldom, and when he did it added neither to the grace nor effectiveness of his delivery. He sometimes appeared to be at a loss to know what to do with his arms: at one time he would thrust his thumbs into the armholes of his vest; at another he would let his arms fall into a sort of swinging motion at his sides, where he allowed, rather than used them, to toss back his coatskirts in a confused, undignified manner.

He never spoke on important questions without careful preparation, as was always evident from the facts and arguments of which his speeches chiefly consisted, as well as from their careful arrangement. His voice was fine, and he had the skill, rare enough in public speakers, of modulating it with excellent effect.

The happiest portions of his speeches were those in which he endeavoured, by artful appeals to the good sense and patriotism of his hearers, to win them over to his views; and the frequent success that attended such efforts is their highest praise. He seldom attempted an ambitious flight, and when he did his best friends felt it was not his true line. He dealt but little in figurative language, except when argument failed him; still he has left some specimens of much beauty in this style. In his great speech introducing Catholic Emancipation in 1829, he told Parliament it had but two courses to follow—to advance or to recede; to advance by conceding the Catholic claims, or to recede by reimposing those portions of the penal laws already repealed. Dwelling on the impossibility and insanity of the latter course, he said: "We cannot replace the Roman Catholics in the position in which we found them, when the system of relaxation and indulgence began. We have given them the opportunity of acquiring education, wealth, and power. We have removed with our own hands the seal from the vessel in which a mighty spirit was enclosed; but it will not, like the genius in the fable, return within its narrow confines to gratify our curiosity, and to enable us to cast it back into the obscurity from which we evoked it." Here is another specimen from his speech on the Reform Bill of 1832. He opposed that Bill with all his energy, as is well known. Lord Durham, a very advanced reformer for his time, and son-in-law to Earl Grey, the Prime Minister, was known to have influenced that nobleman in retaining the most liberal clauses of the bill. For his years he was a very juvenile looking man, which gave point to Sir Robert Peel's words when he said so happily: "It would appear as if the reins of the State had been confided to some youthful and inexperienced hands; and who, left without any guiding principle, or any controlling sense of duty, were rushing on with headlong violence which wiser men could neither moderate nor restrain . . . They should have said to any one of these persons, whose ambition made him press for an employment so fraught with danger to himself and injury to others,

'—non est tua tuta voluntas.
Magna petis, Phaëton, et quæ nec viribus istis
Munera conveniant, nec tam puerilibus annis!'

They should have given him the salutary caution that the fiery steeds which he aspired to guide required the hand of restraint and not the voice of incitement—

'Sponte suâ properant; labor est inhibere voluntas;
Parce, puer, stimulis, ac fortius uteri loris.'

If the caution had not been given, or if it had been disregarded, let them hope, at least, that the example of their suffering might be a warning to others, and that another lesson to the folly and rashness of mankind might be read by the light of their conflagration."

The manner in which he dealt with the potato blight, and consequent Irish Famine, is indefensible. His policy from first to last was a policy of delay—delay in a case in which delay was ruin. He went on by slow and almost imperceptible degrees preparing his colleagues for his altered views on the Corn duties; talking and writing all the time pathetically, about the deep apprehensions he entertained of an impending famine in Ireland, while his whole heart was set on quite another object. To aid this masked policy of his, there was Commission after Commission—the Scientific Commission, the Castle Commission, the Police inquiry; and these went on analyzing, printing, and distributing hundreds weight of query sheets, and making reports, long after it was proved, beyond all doubt, that half the food of the Irish people had been irretrievably lost, the money value of which was estimated at from eight to ten millions of pounds sterling. So early as the end of October, 1845, Dr. Playfair, his own scientific investigator, expressed to him his opinion that fully one half of the potatoes in Ireland were perfectly unfit for human food; he said he had made a careful tour of the potato shops of Dublin, and had found that those potatoes picked as sound had nineteen bad for fourteen good! Sir Robert Peel knew this in October, 1845; admitted its truth more than once during the session of Parliament that followed, and yet the bill which he persisted in regarding as the only panacea for such a national calamity, did not become law until the 25th of June, 1846, eight months afterwards; but of course four millions of foodless Irish must battle with starvation until the Premier had matured and carried his measure for securing cheap bread for the artizans of England; and further, those same famishing millions had, day after day, to submit to be insulted by his false and hollow assertion, that all this was done for them. Nor can it be urged in his favour, that the delay in repealing the Corn Laws was the fault of his opponents, not his own; for no one knew better than he, a shrewd experienced party leader, that every available weapon of Parliamentary warfare would be used, as they were used, against his bill for the repeal of the Corn Laws, in order to strike it down by sheer defeat if possible, but if not, at least to maim and lop it of its best provisions.

FOOTNOTES:

88.   Mr. Culhoun.
89.   During the debate in the House of Lords on the Address, in January, 1846, Lord Brougham stated his views about the repeal of the Corn Laws; the

reasons why they should be repealed, and the effects of that repeal. These views must have seemed to many at the time strange enough, if not eccentric, but they have turned out to be singularly correct. He said:—"It was my opinion that an alteration in the commercial policy of this country with respect to corn, as well as to other commodities, was highly expedient; I will not say solely, but principally, and beyond all comparison most chiefly wanted, not for the purpose of lowering the price of corn and food (which I never expected it could do, which I urged it could not do, which I endeavoured to show it had no tendency to do, any more than the Corn Laws had a tendency to keep up the prices of food); but because I thought it would tend to remodel the whole of our commercial system, and cause it to assume such a shape and position with respect to Foreign Powers, as to prevent them from excluding our manufactures, by opening our ports to their corn, and such as would give us a reasonable prospect that their restrictions would be removed, and our manufactures allowed to penetrate into these foreign markets." And further on in the same speech, "I shortly restate," he said, "the ground on which I rested for the repeal or the modification of the Corn Law system. I did not, because I could not, hold to the people of this country—I could not honestly hold out to them, that it would make bread cheap . . . I did not argue that the Corn Law was the cause of famine, that it was the cause of disease, that it was the cause of crime, that it was the cause of mortality, in this country."—*(Hansard)*.

90.   Smith O'Brien occupied far more of the time and attention of the House of Commons, during the Session, by his refusal to serve on a railway Committee than by his speeches. This refusal gave rise to some delicate questions of constitutional law, and consigned the hon. gentleman to prison for twenty-five days. See note B, APPENDIX.

91.   Lord George Bentinck: a political biography, 5th edition, revised, p. 158.

92.   Lord George Bentinck, a Political Biography, by Benjamin D'Israeli.

93.   Sir Robert Peel's Memoirs, part 3, page 310. Any one can see how little poor famine-stricken Ireland was before Sir Robert's mind, when he penned the above lines.

94.   The Irish Crisis, by Sir Charles E. Trevelyan.

95.   This observation was, in all probability, levelled at the *Dublin Evening Mail*, a newspaper which Sir Lucius would be sure to read, being one of the organs

of his party, and which had, sometime before, with a heartless attempt at humour, called the blight "the potato mirage."

96. The *Freeman's Journal.*

97. *Ibid.* This correspondent tells an anecdote of a peasant whose heroic generosity contrasts strongly with the conduct of the above noble proprietors. He (the correspondent) stood by a pit of potatoes whilst the owner, a small farmer, was turning them for the purpose of picking out and rejecting the bad ones. The man informed him it was the *fourth picking* within a fortnight. At the first picking, he said the pit contained about sixty barrels, but they were now reduced to about *ten.* Whilst this conversation was going on, a beggar came up and asked an alms for God's sake. The farmer told his wife to give the poor woman some of the potatoes, adding—"Mary, give her no bad ones, God is good, and I may get work to support us."

"I am warranted in saying," he concludes, "that by the 10th of May there will not be a single potato for twenty miles around Clonmel."

98. There were twenty principal Government Food Depots established in various parts of Ireland in 1846, at which the following quantities were issued:—

	Tons.	cwts.	qrs.	lbs.
Indian Corn	30	00	00	00
Indian Corn Meal	11,593	11	00	19
Oat Meal	528	00	3	24
Biscuit	6	3	00	7
	—	—	—	—
Total	12,157	15	0	22

R.J. ROUTH, Commissary General.

—*Famine Reports. Commissariat Series. Vol. 1, p. 2.*

The number of Relief Committees in this, the first year of famine, was 600. In 1847, they numbered nearly 2,000.

99. "On Monday at five o'clock, the public notification of the resignation of the Ministry was made by Sir Robert Peel to a crowded house, and in a remarkable speech . . . It included an unparliamentary eulogium on Mr. Cobden, whom it mentioned, to the surprise of the House, by name, and it terminated with a

panegyric of himself, elaborate, but rather clumsily expressed."—*Lord George Bentinck, a Political Biography, by Benjamin D'Israeli.*

"On the conclusion of this speech cheers burst forth on all sides . . . The House adjourned to the 3rd of July. Sir Robert Peel went out resting on the arm of his friend, Sir George Clerk, the member for Stamford. A great crowd thronged the approaches, on seeing him all took off their hats, opened their ranks to let him pass, and accompanied him in silence to the door of his house."—*Memoirs of Sir Robert Peel, by M. Guizot*

100.   See Baines' History of the Cotton Manufacture.
101.   Benjamin D'Israeli.

* * * * *

CHAPTER V.

LORD JOHN RUSSELL Prime Minister—He confers important offices on some Irish Catholics—His address to the electors of London—Its vagueness—Addresses of some of the other new Ministers—The Irish difficulty greater than ever—Young and Old Ireland—The *Times* on O'Connell and English rule in Ireland—Overtures of the Whig Government—O'Connell listens to them—The eleven measures—Views of the advanced Repealers—Lord Miltown's letter to O'Connell—Dissensions in the Repeal Association—The "Peace Resolutions"—O'Connell's letters—He censures the *Nation* newspaper—Debate in the Repeal Association—Thomas Francis Meagher's "Sword Speech"—The Young Ireland party leave Conciliation Hall in a body—Description of the scene (*note*)—Reflections—Sir Robert Peel's Speech after his resignation—Lord John Russell's speech at Glasgow—His speech on the Irish Coercion Bill—His speech after becoming Prime Minister—The Potato Blight re-appears—Accounts from the Provinces—Father Mathew's letter—Value of the Potato Crop of 1846—Various remedies, theories and speculations—State of the weather—Mr. Cooper's observations at Markree Castle—Lord Monteagle's motion in the House of Lords for employing of the people—Profitable employment the right thing—The Marquis of Lansdowne replies—It is hard to relieve a poor country like Ireland—Lord Devon's opinion—The Premier's statement about relief—The wonderful cargo of Indian meal—Sir R. Peel's fallacies—Bill for Baronial Sessions—Cessation of Government Works—The Mallow Relief Committee—Beds of stone! high rents on the poor—The Social Condition of the Hottentot as compared with that of Mick Sullivan—Mr. Gibson's views—Mr. Tuke's account of Erris (*note*)—Close of the Session of Parliament.

Sir Robert Peel's defeat on the Irish Coercion Bill made it a matter of course that Lord John Russell, the leader of the Opposition, should be called upon to form a Government. In fulfilling this task his first anxiety seems to have been to conciliate every section of the Liberals. Important offices were given to several Irish Catholics. This fact was accepted by some as a desire on his part to act justly towards Ireland; while others looked upon it with suspicion; regarding it as an attempt to buy up independent liberal representatives, corrupt the national leaders, and thus crush the agitation for a repeal of the Legislative Union. Richard Lalor Sheil was appointed Master of the Mint; Mr. Thomas Wyse was made one of the Secretaries of the Board of Control, and Mr. Redington was sent to Dublin Castle as Under-Secretary. A popular Irish nobleman, the Earl of Bessborough, accepted the post of Lord Lieutenant; the Chief Secretaryship was given to an English gentleman, Mr. Labouchere—a name which at first sounded strangely enough in Irish ears, but which soon became as familiar to them as the tritest O or Mac in the country.

There appeared to be in the public mind not only a pre-disposition to allow the new Government to come in peaceably, but even a desire to sustain and strengthen it was pretty generally manifested. All those members who had to seek re-election on account of having accepted office, were triumphantly returned. Their speeches and addresses to the various constituencies were, of course, looked to with much interest, as likely to indicate, or in some way foreshadow their future measures; but they were much more inclined to be reticent than communicative. Lord John himself, in his address to the citizens of London, dealt in those vague generalities under which politicians are accustomed to veil their intentions, or their want of definite plans. He told them they might feel assured that he would not desert in office the principles to which he had adhered when they were less in favour than at the time he was addressing them. He rejoiced at the removal of commercial restraints, and those that yet remained, he hoped to see removed without anything that could be called a conflict. These words were intended chiefly for the English mind,—his choicest specimen of the political generality he reserved for Ireland. "Our recent discussions," he writes, "have laid bare the misery, the discontent, and outrages of Ireland; they are too clearly authenticated to be denied—too extensive to be treated by any but the most comprehensive measures." No doubt the miseries of poor Ireland were laid bare enough; whatever other charges she had to bring against her English governors, she had not the shadow of a complaint to make on the score of inquiry,—of the laying-bare system. Countless volumes of blue books, ponderous with Irish grievances, lay dusty and moth-eaten on the shelves of Government offices for years; comprehensive measures to be founded on them were on the lips of statesmen in power, and expectant statesmen, who were climbing to it—but that was all.

The new Chief Secretary threw the Irish portion of his speech into a pretty antithesis. "I go to Ireland," he said, to support the law—that it may be respected, and to amend the law—that it may be beloved."

Lord Palmerston, of course, was a man not to be beaten in the vague-generalities line. In fact it was a line in which he quite surpassed his chief. When speaking of Ireland to the electors of Tiverton, the new Foreign Secretary said, with a dignified and generous philosophy,—"Ireland must present itself to the mind of all men as a subject which required an enlarged, an enlightened view; the most anxious and sincere desire to do equal justice to all; which requires energy of purpose, firmness of spirit, and zealous co-operation on the part of those upon whose support the Government must found its existence."

Thomas Babington Macaulay, in his speech at Edinburgh, showed a more real anxiety for the welfare of this country than any of his colleagues. In his peroration he said: "If the present Government did not exert itself to elevate the condition of the people of Ireland socially as well as politically, and above all, if it did not endeavour to ameliorate the relations between landlord and tenant, that Government will deserve to be expelled from office with public contempt." These manly words were uttered in the presence of an audience hostile to Ireland, and hostile to himself, on account of his sympathy for her: an audience, which at a former election, drove him from the representation of their city, because he had supported the endowment of Maynooth in Parliament.

Ireland is generally regarded as one of the chief difficulties of English Cabinets, but at no period was it a greater difficulty than on the day Lord John Russell accepted the seals of office, as First Minister of the Crown. Nine millions of people were passing through the terrible ordeal of a famine year; a far more awful year of famine was before them; the Repeal of the Union was still regarded by them as the only true remedy for their grievances; the hopes awakened by the great public meetings of Clifden, Mullaghmast, and Tara were still clung to and fostered; whilst the fierce indignation resulting from the sudden, and therefore treacherous suppression of the projected meeting at Clontarf; and above all, the prosecution and unjust imprisonment of O'Connell and his compatriots, caused the Irish people to turn a deaf ear to every promised concession short of complete legislative independence. But, like the keen-eyed warrior of classic story, the English minister detected a flaw in the armour of this bold, defiant nation,—it was the old and fatal one of disunion. The men whose influence, lofty patriotism, and burning eloquence, had marshalled the whole people into one mighty phalanx, began to differ among themselves. The Liberator, who had been long proclaiming himself the apostle of a new doctrine, namely, that "no political amelioration was worth one drop of blood," now began to insist upon it more frequently than ever; probably on account of the warlike tone assumed by some of the young fiery spirits who followed, but hardly obeyed him. Thomas Francis Meagher, as their mouthpiece, proclaimed his conviction that there were political ameliorations worth many drops of blood; and adhesion to one or the other of these principles cleft in two the great Irish Repeal party, namely, into Old and Young Ireland. Of the former O'Connell was of course the leader, and William Smith O'Brien allowed himself to be placed at the head of the latter.

No English Government could hope to win or seduce to its side the Young Ireland party—the soul of that party being its opposition to every Government that would not concede a Repeal of the Legislative Union; but to the Old Ireland section of Repealers Lord John Russell's Cabinet looked with hopefulness for support, both in the House of Commons and with the country. It was only through O'Connell this party could be reached; the Government, therefore, and the Government press, were not slow in making advances to him. The *Times*, which can always see what is right, and just, and true, when it is useful to English interests to do so, commenced praising O'Connell; and that journal, which for years had heaped upon him every epithet of insolence and contempt, now condescends to call him "Liberator," and warns the Government to coalesce with him: "Assisted by him," it says, "but not crouching to him—it [the Government] may enlist the sympathies of the majority on its side, and thus be able to do real good."[102] In its next issue it follows up the subject, saying, "O'Connell is to be supported, if possible, by the Government, but at least by the feeling and sympathies of the English people, against agitation of the worst kind—convulsive civil war." "Hitherto," it continues, "no Government had come into immediate contact with the sympathies of the people. *The power of the Executive has been felt in acts of harshness, seldom of beneficial or parental interference.*[103] A Government which should employ itself in improving the material and social condition of the Irish people would awaken sentiments of gratitude, affection and joy, such as no people hitherto had shown to their rulers. But a Government beginning to act thus would need an interpreter between itself and the people. Such an interpreter would O'Connell be, if he would consent to prefer the prosperity and happiness of his country, to hopeless struggle for an ideal advantage." There can be little doubt that the foregoing passages are from what are termed "inspired" articles,—inspired if not actually written by some member of the Government. They contain a bold bid for the support of O'Connell and his adherents.

Whether it was that he thought Repeal would not be granted, or that the concession of some measures of substantial benefit, besides being good in themselves, would strengthen his hands to carry Repeal; or that he feared the people might be driven into a hopeless rebellion, entailing disaster upon the country; or that his high spirit was subdued by his late imprisonment, or his intellect impaired by the incipient inroads of that malady of which he died within a year; or from all those causes combined, O'Connell did not by any means turn a deaf ear to the overtures of the Whigs. The first time he appeared in the Repeal Association after they had entered upon office, he made a speech which showed his inclination to support them, provided they would make certain concessions to Ireland. He, on that occasion, detailed eleven measures which he required them to pass during the current session. They consisted of three Acts for enlarging the franchise, and simplifying the registration of voters; an Act for a full and effective municipal reform; an Act to secure the perfect freedom of education for all persuasions in Ireland; one for tenant right; one for giving compensation for all valuable improvements; one for taking away in certain cases the power to distrain for rent; one for the abolition of the fiscal powers of grand juries, substituting instead a County Board;[104] and finally an Act to tax absentees twenty per cent. The whole of these could not be even introduced during the remnant of the session which remained, it being now July. It is noteworthy that the abolition of the Established Church in Ireland was not called for by O'Connell on this occasion. Lord John Russell was known to be opposed to such a measure. As to Repeal, he said, even if he got those eleven measures, he would not give it up. But the advanced Repealers took a different view, and believed he was either about to relinquish Repeal, or at least to put it in abeyance to avoid embarrassing the new Government. His line of action with regard to the elections was calculated to increase the suspicion; he said he would not sanction any factious opposition to the re-election of the liberal Irish members who had accepted office: if he could find honest Repealers to put forward to contest the seats he would contest them, but he would be no party to opposition for opposition sake. Smith O'Brien, the organ of the other section of Repealers took the opposite view. Writing from Kilkee, under date of July the 9th, he says, Repeal candidates must be put in opposition to the Government candidates, no matter how good they might be.

At this time Lord Miltown, a nobleman who seldom touched politics, addressed a public letter to O'Connell, which, like the *Times'* articles, had the appearance of being inspired from higher quarters. The object of writing the letter is contained in a single sentence of it. It is this: "Without presuming to ask you to forego your exertions in favour of Repeal, might I," his lordship writes, "suggest the policy of your postponing them for a session to give time to form *an Irish Party*, to assist the Ministry, if willing; to urge them on, if lagging; in procuring justice for Ireland." O'Connell replied in a letter, rich with the vigorous trenchant logic of his very best days. He reviews the many attempts made, at various times, to form an Irish party, all of which ended in unmitigated failure. His answer to Lord Miltown, therefore is, that he cannot comply with his request—he cannot consent to postpone, even for an hour, the agitation for Repeal.

For a considerable time the dissensions in the Repeal Association were painfully evident to the whole country. O'Connell saw a rupture must be the result, and he accordingly made preparations for it. On the 13th of July, he, as chairman of a committee appointed for the purpose, brought up a Report reiterating the principles on which the Association had been founded, and in which were embodied the "Peace Resolutions," as they were called. "There are already upon record," says the Report, "the following declarations and resolutions of the Repeal Association:—The basis of the Repeal Association was laid on the 15th of April, 1830. The following were the three first propositions constituting such basis:— '1st. Most dutiful and ever inviolate loyalty to our most gracious and ever-beloved Sovereign, Queen Victoria, and her heirs and successors for ever.'

"'2nd. The total disclaimer of, and THE TOTAL ABSENCE FROM ALL PHYSICAL FORCE, VIOLENCE, OR BREACH OF THE LAW; or, in short, any violation of the laws of man, or the ordinances of the eternal God, whose holy name be ever blessed.'

"'3rd. The only means to be used are those of peaceable, legal, and constitutional combinations of all classes, sects, and persuasions of her Majesty's loyal subjects, and by the power of public opinion, concentrated upon most salutary and always legal means and objects.'"

The Report gave rise to a stormy discussion, but in the end it was adopted all but unanimously, Thomas Francis Meagher alone saying "no" to it.

A fortnight later, after a fierce debate of two days' duration, the complete and final separation between Old and Young Ireland occurred on the 28th of July. Monday, the 27th, was the usual day for the weekly meeting, and on that day the business commenced by Mr. Ray, the Secretary, reading a letter from O'Connell, who had gone to London to attend Parliament, in which he expressed his sorrow at the miserable dissensions which had arisen amongst them, at a period, too, when unanimity was most necessary, and most likely to be useful. He, in substance, repeats the principles contained in the Report adopted a few days before:—"Here we take our stand," he writes, "peaceable exertions and none others—no compromise, no equivocation—peaceable exertions and none others." "Let it, however, be borne in mind that these peaceable doctrines leave untouched the right of defence against illegal attack or unconstitutional violence." "It had become," he adds, "more essential than ever to assent to those peace principles, as the Association was sought to be involved in proceedings of a most seditious nature, stated in the *Nation* newspaper to have been perpetrated in and by the writers for that publication."

Smith O'Brien was the first to speak. Although he might, he said, be in error, he conceived that the present discussion had been raised with a view to call upon the Association to say that there are no circumstances, in this or any other country, to justify the use of physical force for the attainment of political amelioration—a doctrine to which he did not subscribe. He instanced various countries which had attained their liberty by means of physical force. Then referring to the period of 1782 in Ireland—"I say," said Mr. O'Brien, "if the Parliament of England refused to accede to the national demand of the Volunteers to have a free constitution, that the Volunteers would have been fully justified in taking up arms in defence of the country." He, however, for his part, considered the question a merely speculative one, as, so far as he knew, no one contemplated an appeal to physical force, under the present circumstances, which would be madness, folly, and wickedness. He considered it very unwise to be putting those tests when there was no occasion for them. He declared against permitting those Liberals, who had taken place under the Whigs, to have a walk over; they should, he maintained, be opposed by Repeal candidates, as nothing in the Whig programme called for the anticipative gratitude of Ireland. Finally, he expressed the hope that no rash attempt would be made to expel certain members of the Association. "Let nothing," he said, "be done rashly; let nothing be done to destroy this glorious confederacy, the greatest and most powerful that ever existed for the preservation and achievement of the liberties of a people."

Mr. John O'Connell, in a clever speech, replied to Smith O'Brien. He defended the course his father had taken in not giving immediate opposition to the Whigs, as several excellent measures might be expected from them; besides, if they were driven from power they must be succeeded again by the Tories, and although he was far from becoming the defender of the Whigs, still they were better than the Tories; "if the antecedents of the Whigs were bad, the antecedents of the Tories," said he, "were most criminally bad." With regard to the graver question, the chief cause of difference in the Association, the Peace Resolutions, he said, "My honorable friend [Smith O'Brien] has deeply regretted the resolutions that have passed here this day fortnight. He says he would have come up here to modify them, if he were aware that they were about to be brought forward. There may have been, unfortunately, a form wanting; and I regret that any form of the Association should have been wanting in any proceeding that he complains of. There may have been a want of the form of giving notice; but perhaps this may have been an excuse for the want of that notice—namely, that the resolutions of this day fortnight were proposed by the founder of this Association, as simply and entirely the literal and the sole reiteration of the resolutions upon which he founded this Association. He had no doubt upon the subject. It is a maxim that all pledges and tests are to be taken in the sense and in the spirit of the person who gives or proposes the tests, otherwise they should be refused to be accepted. Now, my father moved these resolutions this day fortnight, in order to bring back to men's minds the principles on which this Association is founded—in order to remove from gentlemen any real ground of complaint, if they find in this Hall an opposition to their doctrine of physical force, by shelving them that we don't want to prevent them from expressing such opinions if they go elsewhere, but that we do object to it in an Association expressly founded on the exclusion of physical force." Mr. O'Brien, he continued to say, called the opinion about physical force a speculative opinion; he, Mr. O'Connell, denied it to be such; for the moment the loophole which he seeks to establish is admitted, we place the Association in danger, and it would be the duty of Government to put it down. He then clearly indicated that, unless the Young Ireland party acceded to the Peace Resolutions, they could not continue to be members of the Association. He said: "It is time now to settle this point once and for ever. If, in pressing this question to a point now, any of those talented, warm, enthusiastic and patriotic men, who have hitherto held out to us the prospect of most able and valuable assistance, should oppose the Peace Resolutions, so as to render their retirement from the Association necessary, that would, indeed, be a great calamity. But Ireland must be saved at any price; on the other hand, if those who stood by the Peace Resolutions found themselves in a minority, they would retire—with deep regret, and with fears for the safety of the Association—they would retire, but not into inaction, they would still work for the cause, and redeem the pledge they had given their country, to labour without ceasing, until they succeeded in achieving her independence."

Several other members addressed the meeting. At its close Mr. O'Brien suggested that, if both parties wished, everything which had transpired on that day, regarding the questions in dispute, should be laid aside, binding neither party to any course of action, and reserving any measures to be adopted, so as to apply to what might occur at the meeting of next day. John O'Connell replied that, in his opinion the Association was in the greatest peril, and it would be therefore necessary to have "Yea" or "Nay" to the Peace Resolutions.

At the adjourned meeting next day, the Secretary read a letter from Mr. Charles Gavan Duffy, the proprietor of the *Nation* newspaper. That journal had been charged by several members of the Association with inciting the people to overthrow English rule in Ireland by armed force. Mr. Duffy's letter was written to explain and defend the articles of the *Nation*, which were said to have such a tendency. It must be admitted that, in his earlier days of agitation, O'Connell did not seem to hold the single-drop-of-blood theory; on the contrary, he often threatened England, at least indirectly, with the physical strength of the Irish millions. The Young Ireland party, in defending themselves, referred to this, but Mr. John O'Connell explained in his speech of the previous day, that all those allusions to physical force pointed but to a single case in which it could be used—"the resistance of aggression, and defence of right." The Liberator himself, in the letter quoted above, also fully admits this one case, when he says it is to be borne in mind that those peaceable doctrines leave untouched the right of defence against illegal attack, or unconstitutional violence. Referring to this admission, Mr. Duffy, in a postscript to his letter, writes—"Mr. O'Connell says his threatening language pointed only to defensive measures. I have not said anything else. I am not aware of any great popular struggle for liberty that was not defensive."

Mr. John O'Connell again spoke at great length on the second day; his speech mainly consisting in a bill of indictment against the *Nation*. He quoted many passages from it to show that its conductors wrote up physical force. Mr. John Mitchell, in an able speech, interrupted by cheers, hisses, and confusion, undertook to show that O'Connell was, to all appearance, formerly for physical force. He was accustomed, he said, to remind his hearers that they were taller and stronger than Englishmen, and had hinted, at successive meetings, that he had then and there at his disposal a force larger than the three armies at Waterloo. "I cannot," said Mr. Mitchell, "censure those who may have believed, in the simplicity of their hearts, that he did mean to create in the people a vague idea that they might, after all, have to fight for their liberties. It is not easy to blame a man who confesses that he, for his part, thought when Mr. O'Connell spoke of being ready to die for his country, he meant to suggest the notion of war in some shape; that when he spoke of 'a battle line,' he meant a line of battle and nothing else."[105]

Tom Steele having addressed the meeting for some time, Mr. Thomas Francis Meagher rose and delivered what was subsequently known as "the sword speech," a name given to it on account of the following passage: "I do not disclaim the use of arms as immoral, nor do I believe it is the truth to say that the God of Heaven withholds his sanction from the use of arms. From the day on which, in the valley of Bethulia, He nerved the arm of the Jewish girl to smite the drunken tyrant in his tent, down to the hour in which He blessed the insurgent chivalry of the Belgian priests, His Almighty hand hath ever been stretched forth from His throne of light, to consecrate the flag of freedom, to bless the patriot's sword. Be it for the defence, or be it for the assertion of a nation's liberty, I look upon the sword as a sacred weapon. And if it has sometimes reddened the shroud of the oppressor; like the anointed rod of the High Priest it has, at other times, blossomed into flowers to deck the freeman's brow. Abhor the sword and stigmatize the sword? No; for in the cragged passes of the Tyrol it cut in pieces the banner of the Bavarian, and won an immortality for the peasant of Innspruck. Abhor the sword and stigmatize the sword? No; for at its blow a giant nation sprung up from the waters of the far Atlantic, and by its redeeming magic the fettered colony became a daring free Republic. Abhor the sword and stigmatize the sword? No; for it scourged the Dutch marauders out of the fine old towns of Belgium back into their own phlegmatic swamps, and knocked their flag, and laws, and sceptre, and bayonets into the sluggish waters of the Scheldt. I learned that it was the right of a nation to govern itself, not in this Hall, but upon the ramparts of Antwerp. I learned the first article of a nation's creed upon those ramparts, where freedom was justly estimated, and where the possession of the precious gift was purchased by the effusion of generous blood. I admire the Belgians, I honour the Belgians, for their courage and their daring; and I will not stigmatize the means by which they obtained a citizen king, a Chamber of Deputies." Here Mr. John O'Connell rose to order. He said, the language of Mr. Meagher was so dangerous to the Association, that it must cease to exist, or Mr. Meagher must cease to be a member of it. Mr. Meagher again essayed to speak, but failed to obtain a hearing. Mr. John O'Connell continued: Unless, he said, those who acted with Mr. Meagher stood by the Peace Resolutions, they must adopt other resolutions and another leader; upon which Mr. O'Brien and the Young Ireland party abruptly left the Hall, amid much excitement and confusion. They never returned to it: the rupture was complete.

Thus, at a most critical moment, standing between two years of fearful, withering famine, did the leaders of the Irish people, by their miserable dissensions, lay that people in hopeless prostration at the mercy of the British Cabinet, from which, had they remained united, they might have obtained means of saving the lives of hundreds of thousands of their countrymen.[106]

It matters but little now which party was in the right and which in the wrong. Looking back, however, through the cool medium of a quarter of a century, it would seem that each side had something of right to support its views. In the earlier part of his career, O'Connell did not disclaim the use of physical force, nor denounce the employment of it, in the cause of liberty, as it became his habit to do towards the close of his life; and if ever he did so, it was usually after telling his audience, as Mr. Mitchel said, that Ireland contained seven millions of people, as brave as any upon the face of the earth. Subsequent professions of loyalty, and assurances of his never intending to have recourse to the bravery of those millions, were interpreted by the people as nothing more than a clever touch of legal ability, to keep himself out of the power of the Crown lawyers, who were ever on the watch to catch him in his words. O'Connell himself may have never contemplated any effort beyond legal and constitutional agitation, but the fear that he might intend something more, founded on his bold allusions to the strength and courage of those whom he led, gave undoubted force to the demands he made upon the Government— in a strictly legal and constitutional manner. When the "single-drop-of-blood" principle became the guiding star of his political life, his demands had public opinion, and their own inherent justice only to support them; so that physical force no longer played a part in Irish politics, except from the fact that, inasmuch as it undoubtedly still existed, it might some day act without him, or in spite of him, or act when he should be dead and gone. It is hard to think that a people who had been resisting English oppression for twenty generations, with nothing else but physical force, ever believed him in earnest, when he told them they should win their rights by legal and constitutional means alone. The more educated may have given some credence to his words, but I do not think the great bulk of the people ever did.[107] At any rate, the principle was distasteful to them; and when the *Nation* newspaper began to publish what seemed to them the good old threatening physical force articles, and when a talented band of young gentlemen, in the Repeal Association, began to

166

pronounce eulogiums on the physical force patriots of other countries in fervid eloquence, they soon became the prime favourites of the people; and it was not long until the *Nation* surpassed, in circulation, every other journal in the country. Those enthusiastic young men saw that the oft-repeated maxim, that "no political amelioration is worth one drop of human blood," took the strength and manhood out of the agitation; so they determined to return to the older doctrine of moral force—a doctrine which neither makes it independent of physical force, nor antagonistic with it, but rather its threatening shadow. A principle well expressed by the motto on the cannon of the Volunteers of '82—"Free Trade, or else."—a motto often quoted by the Liberator himself, with a disclaimer, to be sure, in order to avoid the law, as the people believed. Smith O'Brien was right, then, when he said he could not see the utility of continually assuring England that, under no circumstances whatever, would Ireland have recourse to any but peaceable means to right her wrongs, quoting at the same time Davis's happy definition of moral force—

"When Grattan rose, none dared oppose
The claim he made for freedom;
They knew our swords to back his words
Were ready, did he need them."

Had Mr. O'Brien and his friends stopped here, all would have been well; but they did not. The two parties in the Repeal Association, having the same object in view—the good of Ireland—chose different and diverging routes for arriving at it; and every day saw them further and further from each other. The Young Ireland party, to the sorrow of their best friends, and, exposing themselves to the sneers of their enemies, drifted rapidly into an armed outbreak, feeble and ill-planned, if planned at all, and ending in miserable disaster. The Old Ireland agitation went on; but the hand of death was upon the mighty spirit who alone could sustain it, and it may be said to have expired with him.

Moral force, with physical force in the not too dim perspective behind it, was a giant power in the hands of O'Connell, and it won emancipation; physical force by itself, when brought to the test, eventuated in ridiculous failure.

English parties, instead of legislating for Ireland as an integral part of the Empire, have been in the habit of using her for the promotion of their own ambitious views. The party out of place seeks her aid to help to reinstate it in power; whilst those in power, profuse of promises before they had attained to it, forget, or postpone the measures which, in opposition, they had pronounced essential to her welfare.

When Sir Robert Peel was resigning, he took especial care to lay down the doctrine, that Ireland was fully entitled to all the rights and privileges of Great Britain. His successor, Lord John Russell, expressed the same view only a short time before he was summoned to the Councils of his Sovereign. A few days after his unsuccessful attempt to form a government, at the close of 1845, he was invited by the people of Glasgow to accept the freedom of their city. In the speech which he addressed to them, on that occasion, he said, "My opinion is, that Scotchmen should have the same privileges as Englishmen, and that Irishmen ought to have the same privileges as both Englishmen and Scotchmen." The sentiment was received with cheers. He further said: "I consider that the Union was but a parchment and unsubstantial union, if Ireland is not to be treated, in the hour of difficulty and distress, as an integral part of the United Kingdom; and unless we are prepared to show, that we are ready to grant to Irishmen a participation in all our rights and privileges, and to treat them exactly as if they were inhabitants of the same island. I, therefore, could never listen to, or agree with the assertion, that they ought to be considered as aliens. Nor could I consent to any laws which were founded on this unjust presumption." These sentiments were received by his audience with repeated applause. During the absorbing debate on the Irish Coercion Bill, in June, he not only opposed that measure, but, in some sense, became the apologist of those outrages, which the

Government alleged had made it necessary. After quoting, very fully, from the evidence given before the Devon Commission, he goes on to say: "This, sir, differs from the account given by the noble lord, the Secretary for Ireland; and it is evidence which, I think, this House can hardly neglect or deny. However ignorant many of us may be of the state of Ireland, we have the best evidence that can be produced—the evidence of persons best acquainted with that country—of magistrates for many years, of farmers, of those who have been employed by the Crown; and all tell you, that the possession of land is that which makes the difference between existing and starving amongst the peasantry, and that, therefore, ejections out of their holdings are the cause of violence and crime in Ireland. In fact, it is no other than the cause which the great master of human nature describes, when he makes an oppressed nature violate the law:—

> "Famine is in thy cheeks,
> Need and oppression starveth in thine eyes,
> Upon thy back hangs ragged misery;
> The world is not thy friend, nor the world's law;
> The world affords no law to make thee rich;
> Then be not poor, but break it."

This quotation was received by the House with a "hear, hear." "Such," continued the noble Lord, "is the incentive which is given to the poor Irish peasant to break the law, which, he considers, deprives him of the means, not of being rich, but of the means of obtaining a subsistence." Having pointed out the difficulties of giving out-door relief under the Poor Law, he goes on to suggest what seemed to him to be, and what undoubtedly was, a far better remedy for Irish poverty and Irish famine: "There is," said he, "another source of benefit—namely, the cultivation of the waste lands. On that subject I do not see the difficulties which beset the propositions with regard to the Poor Laws. It seems to me some great scheme, with regard to the cultivation, preparation, and tillage of the waste lands, would somewhat abate the severe competition for land, and diminish the cause of crime." Repeated cheers greeted these observations.

Lord John met Parliament as Prime Minister on the 16th of July; on which occasion he gave a brief outline of the Government business for the remainder of the session. He said they would take up, and endeavour to pass some of the measures of the late Administration. As to Irish bills, he postponed the most important one, the Tenants' Compensation Bill, which, he said, was complicated, and was therefore reserved for further consideration. Referring to the waste lands, the reclamation of which he had, a short time before, put so prominently forward, he said he would make preparation for the introduction of a general measure on the subject. Thus were disposed of in a very brief speech, and in a very cool manner, the eleven measures which O'Connell required to be passed before the rising of the Session, and on the passing of which he had grounded any support he intended to give the Whig Government.

Whilst people were absorbed with the change of Ministry, and the wretched conflict in Conciliation Hall, the fatal blight began to show itself in the potato fields of the country. Its earliest recorded appearance was in Cork, on the 3rd of June. Accounts of its rapid increase soon filled the public journals, and the gloomiest forebodings of the total loss of the crop of 1846, immediately took hold of the public mind. Here are a few specimens of the manner in which the dreadful calamity was announced: "Where no disease was apparent a few days ago all are now black." "Details are needless—the calamity is everywhere." "The failure this year is universal; for miles a person may proceed in any direction, without perceiving an exception to the awful destruction." The South and West suffered more in 1845 than the North; but this year the destroyer swept over Ulster the same as the other provinces. "We have had an opportunity," says a writer, "of observing the state of the potato crop from one end of the county Antrim to another, and saw only one uniform gloomy evidence of destruction. The potatoes everywhere exhibit the appearance of a lost crop." The same account was given of Tyrone, Monaghan, Londonderry, and, in fact, of the entire province. On the 18th of August, the fearful announcement was made, that there was not one sound potato to be found in the whole county of Meath! Again: "The failure of the potato crop in Galway is universal; in Roscommon there is not a hundred weight of good potatoes within ten miles round the town." "In Cavan, Westmeath, Galway, and Kerry, the fields emit intolerable effuvia." "The failure this year is universal in Skibbereen."[108]

In a letter published amongst the Parliamentary papers, Father Mathew writes: "On the 27th of last month [July] I passed from Cork to Dublin, and this doomed plant bloomed in all the luxuriance of an abundant harvest. Returning on the 3rd instant [August] I beheld with sorrow one wide waste of putrefying vegetation. In many places the wretched people were seated on the fences of their decaying gardens, wringing their hands and wailing bitterly the destruction that had left them foodless."[109]

Such were the words of terror and despair in which the destruction of the food of a whole people was chronicled; a people who had but just passed through a year of deadly famine; a people still surrounded with starvation—looking forward with earnest and longing expectancy to the new harvest—but, alas! their share of it had melted away in a few short days before their eyes, and, there they were, in their helpless myriads before Europe and the world, before God and man, foodless and famine-stricken, in a land renowned for its fertility, and this, ere the terrible fact could be fully realised by many of their countrymen at home; whilst it was doubted, or only half believed by unsympathizing absentees; who, distant from the scene, are always inclined to think, with a grudging suspicion, that accounts of this kind are either false or vastly exaggerated, to furnish an excuse for withholding rent, or for appealing in some way to their pockets.

The failure of 1845 did not prevent the people from planting potatoes very largely in 1846, in which year, according to one account, the quantity of land under potatoes in Ireland, was one million two hundred and thirty seven thousand four hundred and forty one acres; the produce being valued at £15,947,919 sterling;[110] but according to another account it was very much larger, being, as estimated by the Earl of Rosse, two millions one hundred thousand acres, valued at £33,600,000.[111] The great discrepancy between these two accounts arises from there being no authoritative official returns on the subject. The truth, no doubt, lies somewhere between them.

The crop looked most healthy in the earlier part of Summer. Towards the close of July, the potato fields were in full blossom, and in every way so promising, that the highest hopes of an abundant yield were entertained, and the people had so little fear on the subject of the blight, that there was no appearance of that nervous anxiety which was so strongly manifested at the same period of the previous year.[112] A strong opinion prevailed that imported potatoes, at least, would resist the blight, but there was no considerable importation of them into Ireland in 1846. There is no doubt that new or strange sets, if of a good quality, produce a healthier and a better crop than seed raised on the same or neighbouring land, but from the general prevalence of the potato blight, it is very doubtful if there would have been much advantage in importing seed. An admittedly surer way of producing sound tubers is to raise them from the actual seed as ripened and perfected on the stalk in the apples, as the notch berries are commonly called in Ireland, yet Mr. Niven,[113] an excellent authority— being Curator of the Botanic Gardens belonging to the Royal Dublin Society, says: "The seedlings I have had, both of 1845 and 1846, have been equally affected with the leaf disease, as have been the plants from the tubers; whereas the seedlings I raised on the experimental ground in the Royal Dublin Society's Botanic Gardens, in Glasnevin, in 1834, at the time I instituted my first experiments, were not at all infected with the root disease then prevalent, but were, without an exception, sound and perfect as could be desired."

The blight of 1846 was identical with that of 1845, but more rapid and universal. The leaves of the potato plant were spotted in the same way; the stalk itself soon became discoloured—not completely, but in rings or patches; it got cankered through at those places, and would break short across at them like rotten wood. Moisture, it was observed, either brought on or increased the blight, yet the rainfall of 1846 rose very little above the average of other years; probably not more than from two to three inches; but the rain fell very irregularly, being most copious at those times when it was likely to do most injury to the crops. The Spring was harsh and severe; snow, hail and sleet fell in March; at Belfast, there was frost and snow even in the first week of April. In contrast with this, the greater part of June was exceedingly warm, which must have stimulated vegetation to an unnatural degree, thus exposing the growing crops all the surer to danger, whenever the temperature should fall. It fell suddenly and decidedly, and the month closed with thunderstorms and heavy rains. On the 19th, it was reported that the weather at Limerick underwent a sudden change from tropical heat to copious rain, with thunder, and lightning, followed by intense cold—there were hail showers on the 24th. St. Swithin, true to his traditional love of moisture, ushered in his feast, the 15th of July, with a downpour of rain, and next day a fearful thunderstorm broke over Dublin, followed by a deluge of rain. The same sort of weather prevailed in almost every part of the country throughout July and August.

On the evening of the 3rd of the latter month, Mr. Cooper, of Markree Castle, observed a most singular cloud, which extended itself over the east of the range called the Ox Mountains, in the County Sligo, accurately imitating, in shape, a higher range of mountains somewhat more distant; afterwards an extremely white vapour, resembling a snow-storm, appeared along the southern declivity of the range. Mr. Cooper remarked to a friend at the time, that he thought this vapour might be charged with the fluid causing the disease in the potato. The friend to whom this observation was made, being a resident near those mountains,

Mr. Cooper requested him to make enquiries on the subject. He afterwards informed him that on the same evening, or night, the blight fell upon the whole of that side of the mountain, where they had witnessed the strange appearance. It was noticed in various districts, that some days before the disease appeared on the potatoes, a dense cloud, resembling a thick fog, overspread the entire country, but differing from a common fog in being dry instead of moist, and in having, in almost every instance, a disagreeable odour. It is worthy of remark that from observations made by Mr. Cooper for a series of years, the average number of fogs for each year was a fraction under four,—the night fogs for each year not being quite two. In the year 1846, the night fogs were ten, the day two, being a striking increase of night fogs, in the year of greatest potato blight in Ireland.[114]

On the last day of July, Lord Monteagle brought forward, in the House of Lords, a motion for the employment of the people of Ireland, of which he had given notice whilst the Peel Government were yet in office. He gave credit to that Government for good intentions in passing several Acts for the employment of the people, but these Acts were not, he said, so successful as was expected, or as the wants of Ireland required. Without any desire of being an alarmist, he told the Government that the prospects of the coming year were infinitely worse than those of the year then passing away, and that precautionary measures were much more necessary than ever. The hopes that were at one time entertained by physiologists, that potatoes raised from the seed might be free from the infection, had entirely vanished, and there was every reason to anticipate a failure of the plant itself. Such a failure would, in his opinion, be the worst event of the kind that had ever happened in Ireland. No antecedent calamity of a similar nature could be compared with it. He was, he said, well acquainted with the calamity of 1823, but that was as nothing compared with the one from which the people had just escaped. Alluding to the sums of money given by Government, and by private individuals, he praised the generosity of landlords, naming three or

174

four who had given considerable subscriptions, one of them belonging to a class who had been frequently and unjustly attacked, the class of Absentees.[115] Of the aid given by Government, he said, that although the funds had been administered as wisely as the machinery of the law allowed, he entirely denied that they had been economically or quickly administered for the relief of distress. To a certain extent the Board of Works must be pronounced a failure. How had it acted when the duty was confided to it of finding employment? In the County of Clare, an application was made by Lord Kenmare and himself, to put them in the way of giving productive employment to the people about them, and their lordships would, he said, scarcely credit him when he stated that, up to the present time, they had not been able to obtain the preliminary survey, so as to enable them to take a single step. His lordship moved, that an humble address be presented to her Majesty, on the subject of encouraging industry and employment amongst the people of Ireland.

Some weeks later, Lord Monteagle, addressing himself to the same subject, said he agreed in the propriety of the Government not purchasing the Indian corn which would be required that year; at the same time, he approved of the steps they had taken the year previous, in purchasing Indian corn. He called upon their lordships to recollect that the peasantry of Ireland grow their own food, and they were, by this disease of the potato crop, deprived of the first necessary of life. Under these circumstances, therefore, however they might respect the doctrines of strict political science and non-interference, *yet they would not be doing their duty as legislators, if they stood by and allowed the people to perish without interfering to prevent it.* Of the Bill before them, [a Bill for the employment of the poor of Ireland,] he said, that *its groundwork should have been the profitable employment of the people*; but if they set their baronial sessions to work without reference to profitable employment, they would be making relief the only object, whilst they would be wasting capital, and destroying the funds that would employ labour.

The President of the Council, the Marquis of Lansdowne, in offering some remarks on the speech of Lord Monteagle, said he wished to God he could differ from him, in the expectations which he entertained of the too probable, he would not say certain, but the too probable recurrence of that alarming evil, which was even then staring them in the face. Of course, he said, the Government would endeavour to discharge its duty with efficiency, in every circumstance which arose from the general necessities felt in administering to the wants of a poor country; but he could not be expected, at that moment, to enter more fully into the question. He referred, in terms of approbation, to the measures taken by the late Government, in November, 1845, to meet the famine; of their prudent foresight in *supplying Indian meal, he entirely approved.*

It was a matter of course, according to Lord Lansdowne, that the Government would try to discharge its duty, but he more than hints at the difficulty of relieving a poor country, like Ireland. Yes, he spoke the truth, Ireland was poor—poor with the poverty brought upon her by wicked laws, enacted to make her poor, and keep her so; and that poverty is flung in her face by an English Minister, at a time when the effects of those laws had brought her people to the brink of one common grave— not the grave of a slaughtered army, but the vast monster-grave of a famine-slain nation. "Was there ever heard of such a thing," writes Lord Cloncurry, "as the almost yearly famine of this country, abounding in all the necessaries of life, and endeavouring to beg or borrow some of its own money to escape starvation."[116]

The Earl of Devon, a man eminently qualified to offer an opinion at such a crisis, touched the true point, when he said, there was a matter which he regarded as of still greater importance than public works, and that was *the employment of the people in improving the soil and increasing the productive powers of the country.*

All relief from Government ceased, as we have seen, on the 15th of August. On the 17th, the Prime Minister went into a general statement of what had been done by Sir Robert Peel's Government to meet the

Irish Famine. He detailed the measures adopted by them, in a spirit of approval, like Lord Lansdowne, and dwelt, of course, with especial laudation on the celebrated purchase of Indian meal;—its wisdom, its prudence, its generosity, its secrecy—not disturbing the general course of trade; its cheapness, coming, as it did, next in price to the potato, which the Irish had lost. Beyond doubt, there never was such a wonderful hit as that cargo of Indian meal. Sir Robert Peel flaunted it, with simpering modesty, to be sure, as his wont was, but flaunt it he did, in the face of every member who ventured to ask him what provision he had made against starvation in Ireland; and here again his successor seems to think that even he, who had nothing whatever to do with it, can take shelter under the ample protection it affords to all shortcomings with respect to the Irish Famine. But however good and praiseworthy this purchase of Indian meal was, the precedent it afforded was not to be followed; for, says the First Minister, "if it were to be considered as establishing a principle, for the Government to apply the resources of the Treasury *for the purchase of food in foreign countries*, and that food were afterwards to be sold by retail at a low rate, it was evident that all trade would be disturbed, and *those supplies which would be naturally a portion of the commerce of this country would be applied for the relief of the people of Ireland.*" Loud cheers hailed the announcement. "Likewise, that portion of the local trade in Ireland, which referred to the supply of districts, would be injured, and the Government would find itself charged with that duty most impossible to perform adequately—to supply with food a whole people."

The miserable, transparent, insulting fallacy that runs through this statement, is also found in almost all Sir Robert Peel's speeches on the famine, namely, that there was not food enough in Ireland for its people; and that it must be brought from foreign countries through the channels of commerce. Let any one look at the tables of our exports of food during the famine years, and he will see how the case stood. The food was in the country, on the very ground where it was required—beside the starving peasant, but was taken away before his eyes, while he was left to travel day after day three, four, five, and in many cases six or seven miles for a pound or two of Indian meal, carried three thousand miles to replace the wheat and oats of his own country, of which he was deprived; and there are recorded instances of men falling down dead at their own threshholds, after such journeys, without having tasted the food which they had sacrificed their lives to procure.[117]

It was a question of money also. The Government would not advance enough of money to buy the wheat, oats, or barley of the country; there must be a food found that was nearest in price to the potato. England could find a hundred millions of money to spend in fighting for the Grand Turk; she could find twenty millions for the slave-owners of her colonies; she could find twenty millions more for the luxury of shooting King Theodore, but a sufficient sum could not be afforded to save the lives of five millions of her own subjects.[118]

Lord John having announced the intention of the Government, to bring in a bill empowering the Lord Lieutenant to summon baronial and county sessions, for the purpose of providing public works for the Irish people, proposed that the Commissioners of her Majesty's Treasury should issue Exchequer bills for £175,000 as a grant, and for £255,000 as a loan, to pay for the works that might be undertaken. He concluded in these words: "Sir, as I stated at the commencement, this is an especial case, requiring the intervention of Parliament. I consider that the circumstances I have stated, of that kind of food which constitutes the subsistence of millions of people in Ireland being subjected to the dreadful ravages of this disease, constitutes this a case of exception, and renders it imperative on the Government and the Parliament to take extraordinary measures of relief. I trust that the course I propose to pursue will not be without its counterbalancing advantages: that it will show the poorest among the Irish people that we are not insensible, here, to the claims which they have on us in the Parliament of the United Kingdom; that the whole credit of the Treasury and means of the country are ready to be used, as it is our bounden duty to use them, and will, whenever they can be usefully applied, be so disposed as to avert famine, and to maintain the people of Ireland; and that we are now disposed to take advantage of the unfortunate spread of this disease among the potatoes, to establish public works which may be of permanent utility. I trust, sir, that the present state of things will have that counterbalancing advantage in the midst of many misfortunes and evil consequences."[119]

The 15th of August was fixed for the cessation of the Government works, as well as the Government relief, because it was considered that relief extended beyond that time would be, as the Chancellor of the Exchequer said, in reply to a question from O'Connell, "an evil of great magnitude." When the relief was withdrawn, and the blight had manifested itself in such giant proportions, the friends of the people saw nothing but famine with all its attendant horrors at their doors. At this time I find the Secretary of the Mallow Relief Committee, the Rev. C.B. Gibson, calling the urgent attention of the Commissioners of Relief, in Dublin Castle, to the state of his district, and his facts may be taken as a fair specimen of the state of a great portion of the country at the moment. He had just made a house-to-house visitation of the portion of the country over which the operations of his committee extended, and he says, the people were already starving, their only food being potatoes no larger than marbles, the blight having stopped their growth. He took some of the best of those potatoes to his house, and found that twelve of them weighed just four ounces and a-half—merely the weight of one very ordinary sized full-grown potato. They sickened the people instead of satisfying their hunger. In many places the children were kept in bed for want of clothing, as also to enable them to silence, to some extent, the pangs of hunger; some of them had not had any food for a day and a-half. And such beds as those starving children had! Of many he describes one. It consisted of a heap of stones built up like a blacksmith's fire-place, (these are his words), with a little hay spread over it; bed clothes there were none. One of the children of this family had died of starvation a fortnight before. The people in every house were pallid and sickly, and to all appearance dying slowly for want of sufficient nourishment. Mick Sullivan, a specimen of the labouring class, was the owner of a cabin in which Mr. Gibson found two starved and naked children; this man was obliged to pay a rent of £1 15s. a year for that cabin, and £2 5s. for half an English acre of potato garden, or rather for half an acre of mountain bog. He paid for these by his labour at 6d. a day. It took one hundred and sixty days' clear work to pay for them, and of course his potato garden was no use to him this year. Mr. Gibson valued the furniture in another cabin, John Griffin's, at 15d. A week before Mr. Gibson's visit, the parish priest had found in the same district, a mother dividing among three of her children that nourishment which nature only intended for their infancy. And this was the moment at which the Government relief was withdrawn, because the harvest had come in. It is not matter for wonder that the Rev. Secretary of the Mallow Belief Committee indignantly asks, "Is not the social condition of the Hottentot, who was once thought to be the most wretched of mankind, superior to that of Mick Sullivan, or John Griffin, whose furniture you might purchase for fifteen pence? I will not compare the condition of such an Irish peasant to that of the red man of North America, who, with his hatchet and gun and bearskin, and soft mocassins, and flashy feathers, and spacious wigwam (lined with warm furs, and hung about with dried deer and buffalo), may well contemn the advantages of our poor countryman's civilization. The Irishman has neither the pleasure of savage liberty, nor the profit of English civilization."[120] "I think," adds Mr. Gibson, "the present the proper time for noticing the panegyric passed by Lord Monteagle on the gentry of this country for their liberality.[121] He gives two or three examples; but they may be the exceptions, instead of the examples of the class; and as his Lordship is one of the class he seeks to protect, his testimony cannot be received as impartial. I shall now furnish you with more satisfactory data, from which to draw a conclusion. According to the Poor Law Valuation, the yearly rental of Rahan, the parish a part of which I have already described, is £5,854. From those who hold the possession in fee of this pauper parish, we received thirty-five pounds; from a gentleman farmer we received three pounds; in all, thirty-eight pounds. If this is benevolence, the inhabitants of Rahan would soon starve upon it. If it had not been for the exertions of the Mallow Relief Committee, a number of those people would not be alive this day."

With regard to the Treasury minute, announcing the stoppage of the Government works, he expresses his conviction that if they cease the result around Mallow will be starvation and death. In view of the facts placed before the Commissioners by Mr. Gibson, which could, he says, be verified on oath by every member of the Mallow Relief Committee, he calls upon them not to leave the people to starve, their only resource being their potato gardens, which are utterly destroyed.

Parliament rose on the 28th of August. The Queen's Speech was read by the Lord Chancellor. Her Majesty referred with thanks to the public spirit shown by the members of both Houses, in their attention to the business of the nation, during a laborious and protracted session She, of course, lamented the recurrence of the failure of the potato crop in Ireland, and had given, she said, her cordial assent to the measures framed to meet that calamity. After the fashion of most royal speeches, she expressed her satisfaction at the diminution of crime—not throughout the United Kingdom—but in Ireland.

FOOTNOTES:

102.   *Times* of 31st July, 1846.
103.   The italics are the Author's.
104.   "Grand Juries feared neither God nor man."—*Times*, August 22, 1846.
105.   Mr. Mitchell evidently alludes to the passage so often found in O'Connell's speeches, commencing—
        "O Erin, shall it e'er be mine
        To wreak thy wrongs in battle line," etc.
        It is a curious fact that the Liberator, in the lapse of years, forgot where he had originally found the passage, as the following extract from

the proceedings of the Repeal Association, on the 12th of April, 1844, will show:—

"Mr. O'Connell—As Mr. Steele began by correcting some errors which had crept into a published report of some of his observations, there is quite enough in that fact to justify me in following his example. The errors to which I allude appear in a book recently published by a Frenchman, the Viscount D'Arlingcourt, whom I met accidentally at Tara, and who felt somewhat surprised and mortified, on being informed that I had not heard of him before. In his work he speaks of the meeting, and he makes me state to him that six lines which I wrote in an *album* he presented to me for the purpose, were my own composition. Now, I am a plain prose writer, and I neither wrote, nor said I wrote, the lines in question. You may recollect them; they are as follows:—

O Erin, shall it e'er be mine
To wreak thy wrongs in battle line,
To raise my victorhead and see
Thy hills, thy dales, thy people free,—
That glance of bliss is all I crave,
Betwixt my labours and my grave! (Cheers.)

The rhythm is perfect, the versification excellent, and my disinclination to take the parentage is not because of any defect in them; but it is a matter of fact, there is only one word which I inserted, and which I claim as my own composition—that word is 'Erin.' In the original lines the word was 'Scotland;' they are from a poem of Miss Mitford, called "'Wallace '—a poem not as well known as it ought to be."

"Mr. Maurice O'Connell—The lines are by Miss Holcroft."

"Mr. O'Connell—My son differs with me as to the authorship, but I cannot help that; but there is one thing we cannot dispute about, and that is, the lines are not mine."

Although Mr. Maurice O'Connell undertook to set his father right, he was equally at fault himself, for the lines are Scott's.

In the Lord of the Isles, canto 4, stanza 30, King Robert says:—

"O Scotland! shall it e'er be mine
To wreak thy wrongs in battle line;
To raise my victorhead and see

Thy hills, thy dales, thy people free,—
That glance of bliss is all I crave,
Betwixt my labours and my grave."
Then down the hill he slowly went, etc.

106.   The author was present at the two days' discussion. As Smith O'Brien, on leaving, went towards the door, several persons seizing him by the hands and arms, said to him, in a spirit of earnest, but friendly appeal—"Sure you are not going away, Sir. O'Brien?" He only answered by a determined shake of his head, and moved on. For some time after the departure of Smith O'Brien and his supporters silent depression reigned in the Hall. John Augustus O'Neill, in an eloquent speech, endeavoured to put the meeting in good spirits again, but with very limited success. Every one seemed to feel that a great calamity had occurred. O'Brien and Mitchel spoke with cool, collected determination—more especially the latter. John O'Connell took his stand on the Rules of the Association, as embodied in the Peace Resolutions. I was near him during his speech on each day; and although evidently labouring under the gravity of the occasion, he never ceased to be master of himself. His style was clear, but his voice being neither powerful nor resonant, he failed to make that impression upon his hearers which was warranted by his reasoning. Meagher's delivery of the sword speech had more of ostentation than grace in it. A common gesture of his (if it can be called such) was to place his arms a-kimbo, and turn his head a little to one side, suggesting the idea that this attitudinizing was meant to attract admiration to himself rather than to his argument. His voice was good, but his intonation unmusical, and he invariably ended his sentences on too high a note; but his fiery rhetoric carried the audience almost completely with him, and he was cheered again and again to the echo.

107.   Many a fine, stalwart peasant said to me, during the great era of the Monster Meetings, "I'm afraid, sir, we'll never get the union without fighting for it." I know for a fact, that wives and daughters and sisters endeavoured to dissuade fathers and husbands and brothers from going to the great Tara Meeting—suspecting, as they said, that "bad work would come out of it," *i.e.*, fighting.

108.   *Daily and Weekly Press. Census of Ireland, 1851.*

109.   *Correspondence relating to the measures adopted for the relief of the distress in Ireland (Commissariat Series), p. 3.*

110. This estimate is said to have been compiled from the best available sources for Thom's Almanac and Directory for 1847. The quantity of potatoes in each of the four Provinces, and their probable value were:

Ulster,	352,665 acres, valued at	£4,457,562
Munster,	460,630	6,030,739 10s.
Leinster,	217,854	2,814,150
Connaught,	206,292	2,645,468
	1,237,441	£15,947,919 10s.

111. Letters on the state of Ireland, by the Earl of Rosse: London, 1847. *Halliday Pamphlets, vol. 1993.* These letters were originally sent to the *Times*, but that journal having refused them insertion, the noble author published them in a pamphlet. The Rev. Theobald Mathew said, I do not know on what authority, that two millions of acres of potatoes were irrevocably lost, being worth to those who raised them £20 an acre. This estimate would make the loss £40,000,000.

112. *Mayne on the Potato Failure.* The potato crop, for the most part, continued to look well up to the end of July, but the blight had appeared, in the most decided way, during the first half of that month, although not then very apparent to a casual observer. Mr. Mayne, like many persons at the time, attributed the blight to an insect which some called *Aphis Vastator*, others *Thrips minutissima*. There was a glass case in the Dublin Exhibition of 1853, showing this insect feeding on the leaves and stalks of the potato plant. Mr. Mayne and those who agreed with him, seem, in this instance, to have mistaken cause for effect. Indeed the insect, it would appear, was a natural parasite of the potato, and some observers have gone so far as to assert that the *Aphis Vastator* abounded more on healthy plants than upon those affected with the blight.

113. *Letter to the Duke of Leinster quoted in Irish Census for 1851.* M. Zander, of Boitzenberg, in Prussia, published, about this time, a method by which full sized potatoes could be produced in one year from the seed, and he further stated that the seedlings so produced had resisted the blight. The old idea was, that it took three years to produce full-sized potatoes from the seed. M. Zander's method was tried in various parts of Ireland and England, its chief peculiarity being that the seed was sown on a light hot bed, and the

plants so produced were transferred to the ground in which they were to produce the crop. Full-sized potatoes were the result, each plant producing, on an average, 1½ lbs. of potatoes, or rather more than 29 tons to the Irish acre. This method appeared satisfactory to those who interested themselves about it, but it does not seem to have been followed up.

114.   Proceedings of the Royal Dublin Society.

This opinion as to fogs preceding or accompanying the potato blight was corroborated from various parts of the United Kingdom. A correspondent of the *Gardener's Chronicle*, under date 14th Nov., 1846, writes: "In the early part of August, 1846, there was not a diseased potato in the North Riding of Yorkshire. Late in August, I think the 25th, a very thick dense fog prevailed. The air was not, however, at all *chill*. The heat and closeness was most oppressive. This continued all night, and anything similar to it I never before saw, with so high a temperature. It occurred also on the following night. *On the morning after the fog, the whole of the potato fields had precisely the disorganized appearance they have after a night's frost.* They soon became black, and the disease followed in a very few days."

In the *Gardener's Chronicle* of the 5th of September, it is mentioned that shortly before, and about the time the disease appeared at Aberdeen, "there was a succession of unusually dense fogs, followed by great warmth."

In one of the Orkney Islands it was remarked by a farmer that "a very dense fog rested in patches on certain parts of the island; at times it was so defined, that the observer could point out the exact measure of ground over which it rested. It hung low, and had the appearance of a light powdering of snow. In passing, it fell down on his small farm, and *he smelt it very unpleasant*, exactly like, he says, the bilge water of a ship—a sulphurous sort of stench. After the wind rose and cleared off those clouds or lumps of fog, there *remained on the grass* over which they had hung, as well as on the *potato shaws*, stalks,. *an appearance of grey dew or hoar frost. The next morning he noticed the leaves of his potatoes slightly spotted* . . . Before ten days, not a shaw was in his potato patch more than if it had been a bare fallow . . . *Everywhere through the island, the disease, after the fog, began in spots and corners of fields*, and spread more slowly over all."—*Observations on the probable cause of the Failure of the Potato Crop, by David Milne, Esq., p. 37. Halliday Pamphlets*, vol. 1, 994.

115.   See post, p. 165.

116.   Public Letter of 25th of August.

117. In the debate on the "Fever (Ireland) Bill," on the 18th of March, Mr. Scrope said, "He must observe that he held to the opinion that the first resource for the people of Ireland which should have been looked to, on the failure of the potato crop, should have been the oats which they themselves had grown by the side of their potatoes, and that the burthen should have been thrown upon the Unions of taking care that a sufficient stock of those oats should have been stored to provide against necessity."

   In replying to Mr. Scrope, Sir James Graham called this "a forced purchase of oats which would be most injurious, by increasing the demand for the article." Mr. Wakley addressing himself to that observation, said "he would ask, was not England open to the same or similar effects? Did not the guardians of the poor in this country make purchases upon the spot? Surely, meat, flour, and other provisions for the workhouses were purchased in the immediate neighbourhood of such workhouses—in short, was not everything given in the workhouses obtained in the immediate vicinity of them?"—*Hansard, vol. 150. Columns 1168 and 1191.*

118. "Gentlemen, when I reflect that as much as £30,000,000 of money have been expended in one year in contending with foreign countries for objects of infinitely less importance to us."

   Sir H.W. Barren (interrupting) "£30,000,000 per annum."

   Lord Stuart—I stated so—infinitely of less importance than assisting to relieve an immensity of our fellow-countrymen from starvation. I have not, nor can I feel any distrust in those to whom her Majesty has entrusted the government of the country so as to believe they could hesitate . . . in granting a sixth of that sum for rendering Ireland prosperous and contented."—*Speech of Lord Stuart de Decies* at Dungarvan, recommending the Government to reclaim the waste lands, November 13, 1846.

119. Hansard, vol. 154, p. 776.

120. "I have visited the wasted remnants of the once noble Red Man, on his reservation grounds in North America, and explored the "negro quarter" of the degraded and enslaved African, but never have I seen misery so intense, or *physical* degradation so complete, as among the dwellers in the bog-holes of Erris."—*Visit to Connaught in the Autumn of 1847, by James H. Tuke, of York.*

121. Ante, p. 158.

* * * * *

CHAPTER VI.

The Labour-rate Act passed without opposition: entitled, An Act to Facilitate the Employment of the Labouring Poor—Its provisions—Government *Minute* explaining them—Heads of Minute—Rate of wages—Dissatisfaction with it—Commissary-General Hewetson's letter—Exorbitant prices—Opinion expressed on this head by an American Captain—The Government will not order food as Sir B. Peel did—Partial and unjust taxation—Opposition to the Labour-rate Act—Reproductive employment called for—Lord Devon's opinion—Former works not to be completed under the Act—Minute of 31st of August—Modified by Mr. Labouchere's letter of 5th of September—People taxed who paid a rent of £4 a year—In many cases a hardship—Barren works the great blot of the Labour-rate Act—Arguments against the Act—Resources of the country should have been developed—Panic among landowners—Rev. Mr. Moore's letters—Level roads a good thing—Food better—A cry of excessive population raised—Ireland not overpeopled—Employ the people on tilling the soil—Sir R. Routh takes the same view—Belief Committee of Kells and Fore—Reproductive employment—Plan suggested—Address to the Lord Lieutenant—True remedy—O'Connell on the Famine—Writes from Darrynane on the subject—Money in the hands of Board of Works—Compulsory reclamation of waste lands—Drainage Bill—Mr. Kennedy's opinion—Who is to blame?—The Government, the landlords, or the people?—O'Connell for united action—Outdoor relief will confiscate property—Proposed Central Committee—Several Committees meet in Dublin—Mr. Monsell's letter—

His views—Against unproductive labour—Money wasted—Appeal to the Government—Cork deputation to the Prime Minister—His views—He *now* sees great difficulties in reclaiming waste lands—Platitudes—Change of views—Requisition for meeting in Dublin—Unexpected publication of the "Labouchere Letter" authorizing reproductive works—Verdict of the Government against itself.

The 9th and 10th of Victoria, cap. 107, the Act framed by the Government to provide against the Famine, sure to result in Ireland from the Potato Blight of 1846, was passed through Parliament without opposition. It was entitled, An Act to Facilitate the Employment of the Labouring Poor for a limited period in distressed districts in Ireland; but it became commonly known as the Labour-rate Act. The principal provisions of that measure were:

1. On representation being made to the Lord Lieutenant of the existence of distress in any district, he was empowered to assemble an extraordinary presentment sessions for that district.
2. Such sessions were authorized to present for public works.
3. A schedule of the works presented for, was to be signed by the Chairman of the Sessions, and forwarded to the Lord Lieutenant for his sanction; it should also receive the approval of the Treasury.
4. On its being approved, the Treasury was to make advances for such works to the Board of Public Works in Ireland, and authorize them to be executed.
5. County surveyors were to assist in the execution of those public works.
6. The advances from the Treasury were to be repaid in half-yearly instalments; such instalments not to be less than four, or more than twenty; the tax by which they were to be repaid to be levied under grand jury presentments, according to the Poor Law valuation, and in the manner of the poor rate; the occupier paying the whole, but

deducting from his landlord one-half the poundage rate of the rent to which he was liable—in short, as under the Poor Law, the occupier was to pay one-half, and the landlord the other. Thus, by this law, the whole expense of supplying food to the people during the remainder of the year 1846, and the entire year of 1847, was made a local charge, the Treasury lending the money at five per cent, per annum, which money was to be repaid at furthest in ten years. The repayments required by the previous act, under which operations ceased on the 15th of August, had to be made on the principle of the grand jury cess, which laid the whole burthen upon the occupier. The Labour-rate Act got rid of that evident hardship, and charged the landlord with half the rate for tenements or holdings over £4 a-year, and with the *whole rate* for holdings under that annual rent.

The Lords of the Treasury published, on the 31st of August, a *Minute* explaining how the provisions of this law were to be carried out, which Minute was published to the Irish people in a letter from the Chief Secretary for Ireland.

1. This *Minute* directs the Board of Works to be prepared with plans and estimates of those works in each district where *relief is as likely to be required*, on which the people might be employed with the greatest public advantage; an officer from the Board to be present at the presentment sessions, in order to give such explanations as might be called for. 2. It being apprehended by the Government that the public works would be calculated to withdraw from the husbandry of the country a portion of the labour necessary for the cultivation of the soil, the three following rules were laid down in the Minute, which, "in their lordships' opinion, ought to be strictly observed":—"No person should be employed on any relief works who could obtain employment on other public works, or in farming, or other private operations, in the neighbourhood. The wages given to persons employed on relief works should, in every case, be at least, twopence a day less than the average rate of wages in the district.[122] And

189

the persons employed on the relief works should, to the utmost possible extent, he paid in proportion to the work actually done by them." 3. Under the former Act, the members of Relief Committees had authority to issue tickets, which entitled persons to obtain employment on the Public Works; a system which, it was found, led to abuses, numbers having obtained employment on such tickets who did not require relief. The Treasury *Minute*, therefore, confines the powers of Relief Committees to the *preparation of lists* of persons in need of relief by employment on the works, noting them in the order in which they are considered to be entitled to priority, either on account of their large families, or from any other cause; these lists to be supplied to the officers in charge of the works, who are to revise them from time to time. 4. With regard to donations from Government, in aid of private subscriptions, "their lordships consider that they may be made as heretofore, where necessary, from public funds placed at the disposal of the Lord Lieutenant for that purpose, and in the proportion of from one-third to one-half of the amount of the private subscriptions, according to the extent of the destitution, and the means of the subscribers; but in consequence of such assistance, their lordships are of opinion, that the proceedings of such Relief Committees should be open to the inspection of Government officers, appointed for the purpose." 5. The Relief Committees are to exercise great care in the sale of meal or other food provided by them; such sale not to be made except in small quantities, and to persons who are known to have no other means of procuring food. 6. As to the Government depôts of food, their lordships "desire that it may be fully understood that even at those places at which Government depôts will be established for the sale of food, *the depôts will not be opened while food can be obtained by the people from private dealers, at reasonable prices*; and that even when the depôts are opened, *the meal will, if possible, be sold at such prices as will allow of the private trader selling at the same price, with a reasonable profit*."[123] The rule to allow private dealers to sell at a reasonable profit, excellent in itself, required an amount of supervision which it did not receive, and in consequence, the starving poor were often obliged to pay unjustly exorbitant prices for their food supplies. Commissary-General Hewetson, writing from Limerick on 30th December, 1846, says: "Last quotations from Cork: Indian corn, £17 5s. per ton, ex ship; Limerick: corn not in the market; Indian meal, £18 10s. to £19 per ton. Demand excessive. Looking to the quotations in the United States markets, these are really famine prices, the corn (direct consignment from the States) not standing the consignee more than £9 or £10 per ton. The commander of an American ship, the 'Isabella,' lately with a direct consignment from New York to a house in this city, makes no scruple, in his trips in the public steamers up and down the river, to speak of the enormous profits the English and Irish houses are making by their dealings with the States. One house in Cork alone, it is affirmed, will clear £40,000 by corn speculation; and the leading firm here will, I should say, go near to £80,000, as they are now weekly turning out from 700 to 900 tons of different sorts of meal ... I sometimes am inclined to think houses give large prices for cargoes imported for a market, to keep them up; it is an uncharitable thought, but really there is so much cupidity abroad, and the wretched people suffering so intensely from the high prices of food, augmented by every party through whose hands it passes before it reaches them, it is quite disheartening to look upon."[124]

The Government further determined not to send any orders for supplies of food to foreign countries, as was done by Sir Robert Peel, in the case of the cargo of India meal; and their depôts would be only established in those western and north-western districts, where, owing to the previous almost universal cultivation of the potato (or rather owing perhaps to its universal use), no trade in corn for local consumption existed.

The system of relief thus provided was extensive and expansive enough, as it laid the entire soil of Ireland under contribution. Whether or not the country would, in the long run, be able to pay for it all, the Government acted well in making the landlords understand and feel their responsibilities in such a terrible crisis. But they should not have stopped there. Those who had mortgages on Irish estates, and their name was legion, should have been compelled to contribute their due proportion; the commercial and monied interests of the country should have been taxed, as well as the land; no one able to bear any portion of the burthen should have been exempted from it, at such a moment of national calamity. Instead of taxing one species of property, namely land, to meet the Famine, the *whole* property of the country should have been taxed for that purpose; and this partiality was justly complained of by the landed interests.

But a much more formidable opposition than that of the landed interest, as such, rose up against the Labour-rate Act, and for a very sufficient reason. The employment to be provided under it could not, and was not intended to be reproductive; the public works which it sanctioned being, as Secretary Labouchere said, in his letter, only undertaken with a view of relieving the temporary distress occasioned by the failure of the potato crop. On this account, the dissatisfaction with the measure was very general from every section of politicians; not that it was thought, except perhaps by some few, that the Government were unwilling to provide against the great Famine which all felt was already holding the Irish nation in its deadly grasp, but because it was felt and believed, that the mode chosen for that purpose was the very worst possible. Under the Labour-rate Act, not so much as one rood of ground could be reclaimed or improved. The whole bone and sinew of the nation, its best and truest capital, must be devoted to the cutting down of hills and the filling up of hollows, often on most unfrequented by-ways, where such work could not be possibly required; and in making roads, which, as the Prime Minister himself afterwards acknowledged, "were not wanted," but which Colonel Douglas, a Government Inspector, more accurately described "as works which would answer no other purpose than that of obstructing the public conveyances." This radical defect of the Act was well and happily put by Lord Devon, when he said it authorized "unproductive work to be executed by borrowed money."

The Act was criticised for other reasons too. It made no provision for the completion of the works taken in hand to relieve the people in 1846; and those works must be finished by the 15th of August of that year, or not at all, a full fortnight before the Labour-rate Act had become the law of the land. Of course many of them were unfinished at that date. Clearly, this was wrong; for on the supposition that they were works of at least some utility, and not mere child's-play to afford an excuse to the Government for giving the people the price of food, they should have been completed. They consisted chiefly in the making or altering or improving of roads—and everybody knows that unfinished road-work is worse than useless,—it is a positive injury. Parts of innumerable roads in Ireland were impassable for years after those works had closed; and many a poor man, whose horse and dray got locked in the adhesive mud of a cut-down but unshingled hill, vented his anger against the Board of Works in the most indignant terms.

The sudden closing of the works of 1846, some even regarded as a breach of faith with the public. The *Minute* of the 31st of August, no doubt, left a course open for their completion, when it ruled, "that if the parties interested desired that works so discontinued should afterwards be recommenced and completed, it was open to them to take the usual steps to provide for that object, either by obtaining loans, secured by Grand Jury presentments, or by other means." But this suggestion (for it was no more) did not free the Government from the charge of a breach of faith, for they called upon the country to complete works begun by themselves, and to do so under new and very different conditions. Besides, it was pretty evident that Grand Juries would not present for the completion of works commenced by the Government, on its own responsibility. That the Government felt there was some ground for the charge brought against them, of a breach of faith with regard to those works, is evident from a letter from Mr. Trevelyan to Lieutenant-Colonel

Jones in the beginning of October. In that letter he says, the works under the Labour-rate Act must, as far as the Act is concerned, come to an end on the 15th of August, 1847; and he adds, that "if Parliament should determine that the Irish proprietors shall support their poor after the 15th of August, 1847, by payments out of the current produce of the Poor-rate, instead of by loan from Government, the transfer from one system to the other may take place *without our being liable* to any demands like those which have been lately made upon us *to finish what we had begun,* on pain of being considered guilty of a breach of faith." This, says Mr. Trevelyan, is the full mind of the Chancellor of the Exchequer.[125]

The Minute of the 31st of August was modified somewhat by a letter from Mr. Labouchere, dated September 5th. In that letter the Secretary says it is his Excellency's pleasure that all works stopped on the 15th August should be proceeded with as far as the sums which may have been so sanctioned for them respectively would admit. Should the balance not be sufficient, a presentment under 10 Vict. cap. 107, should be sought for at the Presentment Sessions, provided the work were a desirable one to undertake.

Nor did the new arrangement, under which the landlord paid one moiety of the rate, and the occupier the other, pass without censure. It was, to be sure, considered an improvement on the rule which compelled the occupier to pay the whole; still it was urged that great numbers of the occupiers of small holdings would be as much in need of relief as any portion of the community, and in no position whatever to pay rates. That was true enough, but a line must be drawn somewhere, and when they determined to make the soil responsible, it is hard to see to whom they were to look for rates, had they exempted the small farmers from them. The exemption they made, namely, of those whose rent was under £4 a-year, was probably not liberal enough, but there does not seem to have been any great reason for finding fault with it.

But the great and fatal blot in the Labour-rate Act was, that under its provisions the people could not be employed on works capable of making a profitable return. Lord John Russell's Government followed the precedent set by its predecessors as to the class of works upon which employment was to be given; but there was this important difference in their legislation,—the former made no grants under their Labour-rate Act, while the latter supplied about half the cost of the Public Works from the Treasury, the remainder being a loan. Against this Act several arguments were employed, and, for the most part, very cogent ones. 1. It was said that as the country was taxed for the whole outlay, whatever it might be, the Government had no right to apply the money to unprofitable works, thus taking from our capital (already far too small) a vast sum that could not return to it. 2. Moreover, no matter whence the money came, it was urged that to employ it on barren works was wrong in principle, especially in a country like Ireland, with millions of reclaimable acres, which would, if brought under cultivation, return in almost every case ten per cent, for capital expended. 3. Again, it was put forward with reason, that the employment for the past year was meant to relieve transient distress only; but now the case was very different—a new, a far more extensive and complete failure of the potato had occurred. There was now no question of transient distress; the potato, the principal—almost the only—food of five millions of the people of Ireland, had not only failed a second time, but, to all appearance, had failed permanently and finally: such was the apprehension at the moment. In face of that alarming state of things, why talk of cutting down hills, or of making useless roads,—provide rather some substitute for the doomed esculent, and let the labour-power of the country be, at least in the first instance, employed upon it, to secure food for the next year. 4. Even if it were desirable to continue employing the people upon those public works, where were they to be always found? "In many districts it was impossible last year to find useful public works. Hills were cut down, and new roads made, which, under ordinary circumstances, no one would have thought worth the expense which they entailed on the baronies in which they were situated. In such districts, where are hills and roads to be found upon which the people may, this year, be employed?"[126] Was it not passing strange, that, with such difficulties existing, the Government would neither apply labour to profitable work, nor even allow the old unfinished works to be completed?

At the time of the Famine it was an unquestionable fact, and (to the shame of the Government be it said) it is an unquestionable fact to-day, that no country with any pretence to civilization required its resources to be developed more than Ireland; in no country could a government be more imperatively called upon to foster—nay, to undertake and effect—improvements, than Ireland. In a country so circumstanced, how disappointing, then, and heart-sickening must it not have been to good and thoughtful men, to find the Government passing a bill for the employment of our people on unproductive labour. Not only did the Labour-rate Act exclude productive labour from its own operations, but its direct tendency was to discourage and put a stop to improvement on the part of others. This is manifest enough. The baronies—that is, the lands of the baronies—were to be taxed to pay for all the works undertaken to give employment to the starving people. No one could foresee where or when that taxation was to end. There could be no more effectual bar to useful improvements. What landowner could afford the double outlay of paying unlimited taxation, and at the same time of making improvements on his property? Then, he had to look forward to other probable years of famine, and he naturally trembled with dismay at the prospect, as well he might. So far from making improvements, the commonest prudence warned him to get together and hold fast whatever money he could, in order to maintain himself and his family when his property would be eaten up—confiscated—by taxation expended upon barren works. Private charity, too, was paralysed; private exertion of every kind was paralyzed; everything that could sustain or improve the country was paralysed, by this blind, or wicked, or stupid, or headstrong legislation of Lord John Russell's Government, by which the energies and the capital of the country were squandered upon labour that could not, and was not intended to, make any remunerative return whatever.

Whilst the value of the general principle of employing labour on profitable rather than on unprofitable works was evident enough, and accepted by almost everybody, the practical carrying out of that principle was not without its difficulties. Those who endeavoured to solve them brought forward plans varying from each other in some particulars; but, taking them collectively, there was sufficient good sense in them to enable the Government to frame a system of reproductive employment for the exigencies of the period.

Fears were entertained by many that much of the arable land would remain unfilled in the ensuing spring, by which the Famine would be perpetuated; and it was thought the labour of the country ought to be made available for that purpose. A kind-hearted, charitable clergyman, the Rev. William Prior Moore, who endeavoured most zealously to relieve the sufferings of the people, put forward this view very strongly, in letters addressed by him to the Chief Secretary. In those letters he accuses the Government of being mere theorists, ignorant of the practical way of relieving Ireland. "The Labour Act," he says, "was worse than *absurd*—it was in many respects *pernicious*. The Chief Secretary's letter (I speak with all respect), though well meant, was in many cases impracticable; and the late Treasury Minute, also well-intentioned though it be, is for the most part *incomprehensible*; and when the three are taken together, or brought partially into operation together, as in some places is attempted, the Irish gentry would require a forty-horse power of intellect to understand or avail themselves of them."[127] "I do not say, as many do," Mr. Moore continues, "that the roads will be spoiled by cutting down the hills; on the contrary, it will be of the greatest advantage to have level highways through the land; but I do say, that there could not by possibility have been a more absurd misapplication of the labour and the power of the country. *Level roads are a good thing, but food is better.* And what will level highways do for the poor of Ireland next year, if they have nothing to eat?"[128] When Mr. Moore penned these lines he

197

assumed, we must suppose, that all roads undertaken by Government would be completed, which would, in its way, be an improvement; but such was not the case.

At this time a class of landowners, and an extremely numerous one, raised the cry of "excessive population." They were anxious to clear their lands, not of rocks or briars, but of human beings; and in their opinion the country could be saved only by a vast system of emigration. Mr. Moore denies that such excess existed, and therefore condemns emigration. "*It is not a fact,*" he says, "*that Ireland is over-peopled;* the contrary is the fact. But the strength of Ireland, her bone and sinew, like her unequalled water-power, is either unapplied or misapplied."[129] "Simply two things," in his opinion, were required—"immediate occupation for the people, and that that occupation shall, as far as possible, be made conducive towards providing for the exigencies of coming seasons ... WE WANT EMPLOYMENT WHICH CAN BE MADE IMMEDIATELY AVAILABLE FOR THE PRODUCTION OF FOOD—and *nothing will or can answer this purpose, save only to employ the people in tilling and cultivating the soil; and not a moment is to be lost!*"[130] One is inclined to doubt the feasibility of sending the labouring population of Ireland in upon the tillage farms, to trench, and dig, and plough, and sow; but Mr. Moore had his practical plan for doing it; and although he does not go into details, it does not seem to offer insuperable difficulties. "The plan I would suggest," he writes, "is briefly this: to HIRE THE LABOURERS TO THE SMALL FARMERS ALL THROUGH THE COUNTRY, AT HALF-PRICE, TO TILL THE GROUND. The farmers would be delighted at the arrangement."[131]

The necessity of applying labour to the cultivation of the soil was also most strongly insisted upon by a high Government official, Sir Randolph Routh, the head of the Commissariat Relief Office, Dublin Castle, whose experience was of the most extensive and valuable kind, he having superintended the relief works through Ireland in 1846. He says: "Under the circumstances which you describe, I recommend you to call a meeting of the proprietors, to explain to them the state of the country;

to state the liberal intentions of the Government to give a grant equal to the amount subscribed, when the Workhouse is full; to explain to them that this grant is tantamount to selling them the supply at half-price, as their funds, being doubled, go twice in the purchases they require. Point out to them also the dreadful responsibility the whole country will incur, if they neglect the cultivation of the soil. The transition from potatoes to grain," he says, "requires a tillage in the comparison of three to one between grain and potatoes. All this requires a corresponding increase of labour; and wages so paid are a mere investment of money, bringing a certain and large profit." He adds these remarkable words: "It is useless to talk of emigration, when so much extra labour is becoming indispensable to supply the extra food. Let the labour first he applied, and then, it will be seen whether there is any surplus population, and to what extent. If industrious habits can be established, and the waste lands taken into cultivation, it is very doubtful whether there would be any surplus population, or even whether it would be equal to the demand."[132] These were sound views, except in so far as they threw upon landlords and people the duty of cultivating the soil; the people could do nothing, and many of the landlords had not capital: moreover, *as a class*, they were wholly disinclined to make any adequate effort. From the terms of the memorandum just quoted, it is evident that, in their intercourse with Commissary Hewetson, they were clamouring for emigration. If the Government were sincerely anxious to produce food, and save the country, they ought not to have leaned on such rotten reeds. They should have put their own hand more thoroughly to the work, and framed an Act which would, at least indirectly, have compelled proprietors to second their efforts, and discharge those duties, which, as men and as Christians, they refused to attend to or acknowledge.

Besides the numerous letters called forth by the publication of the Treasury Minute, that important document came prominently under discussion at baronial sessions, and the meetings of Relief Committees. At a meeting of the Relief Committee for the districts of Kells and Fore, in the County of Meath, held in the Court House of Kells on the 5th of September, and presided over by the Marquis of Headfort, the principal question debated was, "the nature of the employment which ought to be provided for the poor during the ensuing season." A report to his Excellency the Lord Lieutenant was agreed to. It was based upon the sound, common-sense principle, "that the labour for which the land is compelled to pay, should be applied in developing the productive powers of the land." From this stand-point they proceed to make practical suggestions, as to the manner in which its principle is to be carried out. Assuming that a rate sufficient to provide for the employment of labour should be levied in each district, and that this labour should be paid for by landlord and occupier, according to the Poor Law valuation, as enacted by the Labour-rate Act, they suggest:

1. That instead of the money being taken from the farmers, and wasted in useless and unproductive works, each person liable to pay this rate should have the option of expending it upon his own land, in additional labour, upon works tending, as far as possible, to promote the increased production of food; and that the most suitable and profitable works in each locality would be best ascertained by inviting proposals from the ratepayers—each for his own land. 2. That in the event of landlord and tenant not agreeing in the works to be undertaken, each should be entitled to expend the portion of rate paid by himself. These suggestions were certainly calculated to avert the most threatening danger of the moment—the danger of not having sufficient attention paid to the cultivation of the land, in order to produce food for the coming year. 3. Those ratepayers next express their opinion, that landlords and others, having sufficient interest in lands, should be encouraged by the offer of loans to undertake extensive and permanent profitable improvements, such as the draining and reclaiming of land—the making of roads to come under the designation of profitable improvements, only so far as they would be the means of facilitating cultivation. All the works undertaken to be under the superintendence of the Board of Works. 4.

The ruling and controlling power in the case to be a local committee of landlords and ratepayers, which committee, on the completion of each work within the time agreed upon, should have notice to that effect; and who should have power to order an inspection of such works, if they thought it necessary. Upon being satisfied that the outlay was fairly and honestly made, according to the terms of agreement, a certificate to be given to that effect, *which should be taken* in payment *of the rate*. The Kells and Fore Committee add, with truth, that this labour, being carried on under the ordinary relations of employer and employed, would be free from the difficulties of superintendence, and the demoralizing effects which "charity works" are apt to produce in the labourer.

After expressing these views and making these suggestions they prepared a formal address to the Lord Lieutenant to impress upon him the urgent necessity that existed for employing the labour of the country in the raising of food. The duties which devolve on those in power this year, they tell him, are very different from those of last year. Last year, when it was found that a great portion of the food of the people had perished, the evident duty of the Government and the country was to provide a sufficient supply, until the harvest would come in. This was done by securing additional wages for the people, with which to buy food; wages paid for the public works then undertaken being the readiest means to meet a transient emergency; but the Committee are convinced, they assure his Excellency, that the calamity of the current year is not transient but permanent. Not one of them, they say, entertains the expectation that the next year's potato crop will put an end to the difficulties of the country, by supplying sufficient food for the population: "the question is not now of the distribution but of the production of food. We have not to relieve a temporary distress, but to make provision for the food of a people." To buy food in foreign markets with money paid for unproductive labour at home, they of course, designate as it deserved. The true and permanent remedy is only to be found in the employment of additional capital and labour on the land. "To anticipate the available resources of the country," they urge, "and to compel or induce the outlay of them on public works not productive of food, or of any commodity which could be exchanged for food, must fearfully aggravate the dangers of our position." Finally, they tell the Lord Lieutenant frankly, that they feel it to be their duty to deprecate the continuance of a system which tends to discourage the exertions of landlord and farmer, and to misapply the labour of the people—closing their admirably reasoned address by repeating the principle with which they had set out: *"That the labour for which the land is compelled to pay should be applied in developing the productive powers of the land."*

O'Connell, as was to be expected, took the greatest interest in the perilous state of his countrymen at this critical period; and he expressed his views in public on several occasions. His great anxiety was for united action. In a letter written from Darrynane, dated 17th of September, and addressed to the Secretary of the National Repeal Association, he says, the system of public works is, in its nature, sufficiently comprehensive, if carried actively and energetically into effect, to afford employment to the great bulk of the adult population; but he feels convinced, that to be satisfactory it requires the most active co-operation of landowners and farmers. The great difficulty, he thinks, is not in want of employment, but in the want of food, and to leave to commercial speculators the supply of food for the people will keep it at a famine price. In his opinion, therefore, the intervention of the Government was absolutely necessary. Such intervention, he admits to be surrounded with great difficulties, and calculated to impose an enormous additional burthen upon them; it must, however, he holds, be done, or the people will starve. In reply to those who called for loans, at a low rate of interest, to be expended on the improvement of the land, he says, it is to be remarked that there are already a million of pounds sterling in the hands of the Board of Works, to be lent for the drainage of Irish estates, and but few had availed themselves of that fund.[133]

But this is no complete answer to the call made for reclaiming Irish lands, because the money held by the Board of Works was only lent when applied for. The advocates for reclaiming waste lands in order to give employment to the starving people wanted a Special Bill empowering the Government to call upon the owners of estates either to reclaim their waste land themselves, or to permit the Government to do so on equitable terms. To some this seemed an interference with the rights of property; but even if it were, the occasion was sufficient to justify it; for when a whole nation is in the throes of famine—threatened with annihilation, as Ireland then was— *salus populi suprema lex* should become the guiding principle of a government. Extraordinary evils call for extraordinary remedies. Nor would such a law be one whit more of an interference with the rights of property than the law which enables a railway company to make their line through a man's estate whether he likes it or not, giving him such compensation as may be awarded by an impartial tribunal. And this is just, for no private individual ought to have the power of preventing what is for the general prosperity. But important as the construction of a railway may be, there is no comparison between its importance and that of saving the lives of a whole people, for whose benefit railways are constructed, and all material improvements projected and carried out.

That some compulsory clauses were necessary in the Drainage Bill is clear from the statement of O'Connell, that but few availed themselves of its provisions. Speaking of this Bill, a gentleman whose opinion must carry much weight with it, says, that all acquainted with the subject admit the whole cost of thorough draining would be returned by the first crop, or the first two, or at least by the first three crops.[134] "Under such circumstances," he asks, "how can the country be exposed to danger or suffering from an infliction such as now threatens? It is impossible, unless we assume all the parties interested—whether the government, the landed proprietors, the farmers, or the labourers—to be inert, and forgetful of their respective interests to an extent of which the world has not yet seen a parallel... Is it possible to imagine that such a cooperation can be withheld: can the alienation and errors infused among classes be so great, that they will perish rather than follow their concurrent interests!!!" "The Drainage Act of 1846 made the expense of drainage works a first charge upon the land, and that Act could be easily expanded and adjusted to the present emergency of the country. *This principle, alike equitable, comprehensive, and applicable to our case, is the law; and it only requires that it should be judiciously and extensively used in order to effect the most rapid and beneficial change that ever occurred in any country.*"[135] That want of co-operation amongst men for their respective interests of which this well-informed writer asserts the world had seen no parallel, occurred in Ireland. Millions of acres were in a wretched half barren condition for want of being drained; the money for the purpose, already granted by Parliament, was in the coffers of the Board of Works, and more would have been supplied; the return for the outlay would have been quick and remunerative; but the money remained unused and sterile; the land was not drained, and the people in myriads died of hunger.

We must not, however, be unjust to the parties named in the quotation given above. The farmers and labourers were powerless for good, unaided by the landlords and the Government. The last-named gave the landlords the power of draining their estates on terms not merely just, but really easy, generous, and remunerative; they refused to avail themselves of that power; on them, therefore, first and above all others, rests the weighty responsibility of neglecting the most solemn duty that could devolve upon them, as accountable beings—that of saving the lives of their fellow-countrymen; a duty not only within their reach, but one that could be discharged with the greatest advantage to their own interests. The next party that failed in its duty was the Government, who should have compelled the owners of land to that, which, of their own motion, they had so culpably neglected. Had the Government done this, the farmers and labourers would have been but too happy to unite with it and the landlords, in an undertaking so evidently for their own advantage, as well as for the general weal.

O'Connell, knowing well that if he could secure united action for practical good amongst the landed interests, everything necessary to save the people would be comparatively easy, laboured to effect this in the letter above referred to. He threatened them, too, with the danger of losing their properties, unless they so acted. "The Government plan of succour," he says, "is calculated to produce throughout Ireland a more extended Poor Law, necessarily calculated to extend outdoor relief to all adult labourers and their families, in a state of destitution, as well as to all other destitute poor. The English statute of Elizabeth is being extended to Ireland, and the poverty of the country is about to be placed for support upon the property—especially upon the landed property." And again: "The English plan of out-door relief, in its worst form, will be almost insensibly communicated to Ireland, and their [the proprietors,] estates not only burthened but actually confiscated." The remedy for this, he says, is combination amongst the owners of land. The baronial sessions proved the possibility of such a combination, but they lasted only a part of a day—there should be a great central permanent committee in Dublin, appointed by the landowners, and communicating between them and the Government. Such a body would be most influential, and could organize the best plans for obtaining Government and local relief.

Several Relief Committees assembled in Dublin, but not one of them was constituted after the plan suggested by O'Connell, although many influential persons expressed their warm approval of it, one landlord, whilst he did so, offensively applying to its originator the vile quotation:— *fas est ab hoste doceri.*

Towards the end of September Mr. Monsell, of Tervoe,[136] addressed a letter to the Irish Chief Secretary, in which he reminds him that the Labour-rate Act was framed and passed into law at a time when the Government did not foresee that the potato rot would be making fearful ravages in every electoral division in Ireland by the first of September;— that in a number of those there would not be a potato fit to eat on the first of October, and that, in all probability there would not remain in the country any considerable quantity of potatoes suitable for human food by November. In view of this terrific state of things, he thinks it is no exaggeration to say, that for ten months to come labour must be found for five hundred thousand men, the cost of which could not be under five millions of pounds; and as destitution in the South and West was greater than in the other parts of the country, a great portion of this sum should be raised in Munster and Connaught. The people were starving, and be the law good or bad they must be employed under it, as it was the only way the poor could, for the time, be relieved. He reviews the provisions of the Labour-rate Act, and like so many other enlightened men of the period—whose opinions he may be fairly taken to represent, he is alarmed at the principle of unproductive labour upon which it was based. The money necessary for the support of the people must, for the most part, be raised from the land, and as this vast sum, so raised, does not "revolve back again upon the land," it would be impossible, he thought, for the nation to recover from such a shock. It was universally acknowledged that the want of sufficient capital was one of the great evils—if not *the* great evil of Ireland. There was abundant scope for the profitable expenditure of capital, "in every corner of Ireland—in every barony—almost in every townland; the money expended upon its improvement would return a large interest of at least ten per cent., [the usual estimate made by practised men was higher, but he, being anxious to avoid exaggeration, leaves it at ten], and the capital of the country would, of course, be largely increased by such expenditure … an increasing capital would give more labour, a decreasing capital less."

1. The first important point, in Mr. Monsell's opinion, was to consider how they were to spend the large sum necessary to sustain the people. Is it, he asks, to be spent on productive or unproductive labour? If on the former, the capital of the country would be vastly increased, and the means of giving future employment increased in proportion; if on the latter, every pound so spent would be taken away from that capital, and the means of employing labour proportionably reduced. It seemed, therefore, to follow very evidently that, as the leading feature of the Labour-rate Act was to employ the people on unproductive labour, its direct tendency was not only to pauperize the country, but to run

it into complete ruin. 2. Another fault in the Act, but one of inferior magnitude, was that it necessitated the congregating together of large masses of the people upon public works, which tends to demoralize the labouring classes; and inflicts, besides, a great hardship upon them, by compelling them to walk great distances to and from those works, making it almost impossible for them to have their mid-day meal carried to them. 3. The experience of the last year proved that fully one-fourth of the money granted to support the labouring poor was expended on the purchase of land, on horse labour, and on blasting rocks. Hence, according to his estimate of the money required for the coming year, there would be a million and a-quarter of it diverted from its intended purpose—the relief of the destitute. "The Government cannot," he says, "by act of Parliament compel drainage or fencing; but they can compel the owner of land to employ the poor, and make those who refuse to employ them on productive labour pay for their employment on public works." Appeals to public spirit, social duties, and so forth, have no effect; nothing will avail but an appeal to self-interest. Make it, then, the interest of landowners who neglect their duties to employ the destitute poor upon profitable labour, by taxing them to pay those poor for public works—unprofitable labour. As the Labour-rate Act did nothing of this kind, it inflicted a positive injustice on the good improving landlord, by taxing him equally with the landlord who never made an improvement; who, in many instances, was an absentee, forgetful and culpably ignorant of the state of his property, his sole aim being to get as much as possible out of it, without expending anything. The tenants of such a man would be sure to be more destitute than those of an improving landlord, who is thus taxed unfairly to support them,—taxed in another way too,— taxed by giving employment, whilst the other gives none. Indiscriminate taxation was, therefore, a positive injustice to the improving landlord, and an actual bar to improvement; for, of course, he would be rated higher on account of his improvements. Such, however, was taxation under the Labour-rate Act.

Mr. Monsell concluded his able letter in the following words:—"I am convinced that these evils cannot be avoided without a change in the law. No matter how the managing of the public works may be extended, you will still find that unless there is an absolute power given to the owners and occupiers of land, to have the money raised from the land expended upon it, you will have such a mass of jobbing and jealousy to contend with, that very few works of private benefit, very few productive works, will be executed. I am sure that if you agree with the views that have now been laid before you, you will announce it speedily in order to prevent the carrying out of the present ruinous system on any scale larger than that required to meet our immediate wants, and that you will not hesitate to recommend that Parliament should be called together at once. This course may be inconvenient, but such an emergency requires inconveniences to be encountered. History presents no parallel to our circumstances. There is no other instance on record of the whole food of a people becoming rotten before it was ripe. Of course the system of public works would go on more smoothly than any other that can be suggested. It would give far less trouble to the Government than the system which it is proposed to substitute for it; but what would the end of it be? Never since the connexion of Ireland with England has so awful a power been placed in the hands of any statesman as in yours. The whole country is, as it were, fused in your hands—on you depends the future shape which it will assume. If you use your opportunities well—if you develope its resources—if you increase its capital—if you improve its agriculture—if you distribute its wealth as it ought to be distributed, its progress in the next two or three years will be greater than the progress ever made by any country in the same time. If you take the easy course—if you throw away the opportunity placed by Providence in your hands—if you allow the vast sums of money which you have to direct the distribution of to be spent unprofitably, we shall retrograde as fast as under the other alternative we should have advanced; and those who have been year after year hoping against hope, and labouring against the tide, will fold their arms in despair."

A deputation from Cork waited on the Prime Minister to urge upon his attention the utility and necessity of employing the people in productive instead of non-productive works. He read to them a reply, in which he said he thought the measures that had passed through Parliament ought to be sufficient to meet the existing emergency; but whilst he expressed this view he, using the time-honored official style of replying to deputations, promised that the subject should receive the deepest consideration during the ensuing session of Parliament. There were, he said, subjects of great difficulty to be encountered in legislating for a country circumstanced as Ireland was. The lands held by Government might be at once improved, but the case was different with respect to those that were the property of individuals. Still, he would not shrink from the necessity or duty of Government interfering even in the latter case; neither did he deny that while property had its owners and its rights, that such ownership and rights should not be allowed to interfere with the operations intended to develop the resources of the soil, and improve the social condition of the people. The Premier here uses the far-famed sentiment, almost the very words, of Secretary Drummond, that property has its duties as well as its rights; but a sentiment, however just, is but an empty form of words, unless it receives a practical application at the proper time. The threadbare and almost insulting platitudes—insulting from the very frequency of their use—about developing resources and improving the social condition of the people, were strangely out of place at a moment when coroner's juries, in various parts of Ireland, were beginning to return verdicts of "Death from starvation." Lord John, now that he was Minister, talked of difficulties in legislating for Ireland, especially with regard to the reclamation of land; when he was only an expectant of office, his expressed sentiments were quite different. In his speech on the Coercion Bill, two or three months before, he said:—"There is another source of benefit, namely, the cultivation of the waste lands. On that subject I do not see the difficulties which beset the propositions in the regard of the Poor-laws." Now it is the very reverse. He sees difficulties in reclaiming the waste lands of Ireland, but finds none in putting into operation the most objectionable part of the Poor-Law system——outdoor relief; for, his Labour-rate Act was, substantially, a gigantic system of outdoor relief.[137]

Meantime the following requisition was put in circulation and numerously signed, both by peers and gentry: "We, the undersigned, request a meeting of the landowners of Ireland to be held in Dublin on the _ *day of* _ next, to press upon her Majesty's Government the importance of at once adopting the necessary measures to alter the provisions of the Act, entitled the 9th and 10th Vic., chap. 107, so as to allow the vast sums of money about to be raised by presentment under it, to be applied to the development of the resources of the land, rather than in public works of an unproductive nature."

The principle of the Labour-rate Act was doomed; no voice was raised in its defence, nor could there have been. The Government having turned a deaf ear to the call for an Autumn Session, the Repealers were anxious there should be a demonstration in Dublin that would, as far as possible, bear the similitude of an Irish Parliament. The above requisition, very probably without intending it, sustained and strengthened this idea; the Prime Minister and his colleagues became alarmed, and the Lord Lieutenant, on the 5th of October, suddenly and unexpectedly issued, through his Chief Secretary, the famous Proclamation known as "Labouchere's Letter," which, if it did not entirely repeal the Labour-rate Act, changed its whole nature. In that document the Irish public are told that the Lord Lieutenant has had under his consideration the various representations which had been made to him of the operation of the poor employment Act, and the difficulty of finding "public works" upon which it would be expedient or beneficial to expend money to the extent requisite for affording employment to the people during the existence of distress; and to obviate the bad effects of a great expenditure of money in the execution of works *comparatively unproductive,* he desires that the Commissioners of Public Works would direct their officers, in the respective counties, to consider and report upon such works of a *reproductive character and permanent utility*, as might be presented at any Sessions held under the above Act; and his Excellency would be prepared to sanction and approve of such of those works as might be recommended by the Board, and so presented, *in the same manner* as if they had been strictly "public works," and presented as such in the manner required by the Act.[138]

Never did any Government pronounce against itself a more complete verdict of ignorance and incapacity. The Government had framed the Act; every clause of it was its own handiwork; it was passed through Parliament without being modified, amended, or in the slightest degree opposed, and yet, before it was brought into practical operation—for a single work had not been commenced under it at the date of the Proclamation—that same Government virtually repeal it, well knowing that for such proceeding it must come before Parliament for an Act of Indemnity.

FOOTNOTES:

122. This rule gave great dissatisfaction, the wages in many places being already far too low, in proportion to the price of provisions. When the Cork deputation waited on Lord John Russell, the Chancellor of the Exchequer said, in reply to Rev. Mr. Gibson, that the Minute of the Lords of the Treasury requiring that wages should be twopence under the standard of the country *was not the law*, and if necessary could be modified.

123. The italics are their lordships'.

124. Letter to Mr. Trevelyan, Commissariat Series, Part I, p. 439, who did not like it all, and sent in reply, on the part of the Treasury, an elaborate defence of high prices and large profits; although the people in many districts could only purchase one meal a day with the wages they received on the public works, as is testified by Commissary-General Doree's letter (p. 444); and by numberless other letters from almost every part of the country; hence men in full employment on the Government works died of starvation, or of dysentery produced by it. And why should they not? They were earning

8-1/4d. a day at task work, whilst meal was 3s. a stone; and the next shop in which it was sold for that sum was often a great distance from them—in some cases twenty, and even five-and-twenty miles!

The following paragraph went the round of the newspapers at the close of December:—"A FACT JOB LORD JOHN RUSSELL.—Mr. Bianconi, ex-Mayor of Clonmel, had shipped to him on the 14th of December, at New York, a small lot of best Indian corn, at *twenty-three shillings* per quarter of 480 lbs.; and the same post which brought the invoice brought a letter stating the price at Liverpool was *seventy-two* shillings. What will Lord John Russell say to this?

125. Board of Works' Series, vol. L., p. 97.
126. Mr. Monsell's Letter to Lord Devon.
127. The case of Ireland, etc., contained in two letters to the Right Hon. Henry Labouchere, Chief Secretary of Ireland, by the Rev. William Prior Moore, A.M., Cavan, p. 6. Halliday Pamphlets, vol. 1991.
128. *Ib.* p. 7.
129. *Ib.*
130. The Case of Ireland, etc., p. 11.
131. *Ib.* p. 11, 12. The capitals and italics in the above quotations are Mr. Moore's.
132. Memorandum to Commissary-General Hewetson. Commissariat Series, p. 452.
133. "A great deal of delay on the part of the Board of Works in the respect of drainage was occasioned by that body involving themselves in legal intricacies which were not necessary under the Act." *O'Connell's Speech at the Baronial Sessions of Caherciveen.*
134. *Correspondence on some of the general effects of the failure of the potato crop and its consequent relief measures. By J.P. Kennedy, formerly an officer of the corps of Royal Engineers, and late Secretary of the Land and Relief Commissions. Dublin: Alex. Thom, 1847. Halliday Pamphlets, vol. 1993.*
135. *Ibid.* The italics are Mr. Kennedy's.
136. Now Lord Emly.
137. "The works under the 9th and 10th Vict., cap. 107, (the Labour-rate Act,) were to be sanctioned for sake of this relief, and not for sake of the works themselves."—*Mr. Trevelyan's Letter to Lieutenant-Colonel Jones, Board of Works' Series of Blue Books, vol. L., p. 97.*

138.   See Proclamation, in Appendix, Note D. "The intended meeting in Dublin will be *now* abandoned, as the promoters of it must be satisfied with Lord Bessborough's Proclamation."—*Mr. Pierce Mahony to the Earl of Clarendon, 6th October, Commissariat Series of Blue Books, vol. I., p. 123.*

Mr. Pierce Mahony was a very well-known Dublin solicitor; a man of position, and evidently in the confidence of Lord Clarendon. He writes from the Stephen's-Green Club, the recognised representative body of the Whigs in Ireland. How anxious the Government must have been that a chief effect of their proclamation would be to prevent the intended demonstration in Dublin is patent from the hurry with which Mr. Mahony transmits the intelligence to the President of the Board of Trade.

* * * * *

CHAPTER VII.

The Measures of Relief for 1846-7—Difficulties—Shortcomings of the Government—Vigorous action of other countries—Commissary General Routh's Letter on the state of the depôts—Replies from the Treasury—Delay—Incredulity of Government—English Press—Attacks both on the Landlords and People of Ireland—Not the time for such attacks—View of the *Morning Chronicle*—Talk about exaggeration—Lieutenant-Colonel Jones—Changes his opinion—His reason for doing so—Mr. Secretary Redington's ideas—Extraordinary Baronial Presentments—Presentments for the County Mayo beyond the whole rental of the county!—The reason why—Unfinished Public Works—Lord Monteagle—Finds fault with the action of the Government, although a supporter of theirs—Expenses divided between landlord and tenant—Discontent at rate of wages on public works being 2*d.* per day under the average wages of the district—Founded on error—Taskwork—Great dissatisfaction at it—Combination—Attempt on the Life of Mr. W.M. Hennessy—True way to manage the people (*Note*)—Stoppage of Works—Captain Wynne—Dreadful destitution—Christmas eve—Opposition to Taskwork continues—Causes—Treasury Minute on the subject—Colonel Jones on Committees—Insulting his officers—Insult to Mr. Cornelius O'Brien, M.P.—Captain Wynne at Ennistymon—A real Irish Committee—Major McNamara—His version of the Ennistymon affair (*Note*)—Charges against the Gentry of Clare by Captain Wynne—Mr. Millet on Ennistymon—Selling Tickets for the Public Works—Feeling of the Officials founded often on ignorance and prejudice—The Increase of Deposits in the Savings Banks a Proof of Irish Prosperity—How explained by Mr. Twistleton, an official—Scarcity of silver—The Bank of Ireland authorized to issue it—The Public Works of 1845-6 brought to a close in August, 1846—The Labour-rate Act—Difficulty of getting good Officials—The Baronies—Issues to them—Loans—Grants—Total—Sudden and enormous Increase of Labourers on the Works under the Labour-rate Act—How distributed over the Provinces—Number of Officials superintending the Public Works—Correspondence—Number of Letters received at Central Office—Progress of the Famine—Number employed—Number seeking employment who could not get it—The Death-roll.

To have met the Potato Famine with anything like complete success, would have been a Herculean task for any government. The total failure of the food of a nation was, as Mr. Monsell said, a fact new in history; such being the case, no machinery existed extensive enough to neutralize its effects, nor was there extant any plan upon which such machinery could be modelled. Great allowance must be therefore made for the shortcomings of the Government, in a crisis so new and so terrible; but after making the most liberal concessions on this head, it must be admitted that Lord John Russell and his colleagues were painfully unequal to the situation. They either could not or would not use all the appliances within their reach, to save the Irish people. Besides the mistakes they made as to the nature of the employment which ought to be given, a chief fault of their's was that they did not take time by the forelock—that they did not act with promptness and decision. Other nations, where famine was far less imminent, were in the markets, and had to a great extent made their purchases before our Government, causing food to be scarcer and dearer for us than it needed to be. Thus writes Commissary-General Routh to the Treasury on the 19th of September:—"I now revert to the most important of our considerations, the state of our depôts. We have no arrivals yet announced, either at Westport or Sligo, and the remains there must be nothing, or next to nothing. The bills of lading from Mr. Erichsen are all for small quantities, which will be distributed, and perhaps eaten, in twelve or twenty-four hours after their arrival. It would require a thousand tons to make an impression, and that only a temporary one. Our salvation of the depôt system is in the importation of a large supply. These small shipments are only drops in the ocean." The Treasury replies in this fashion, on the 22nd, to Sir R. Routh's strong appeal:—"With reference to the remarks in your letter of the 19th instant, as to the insufficiency of the supplies for your depôts, the fact is that we have already bought up and sent to Ireland all the Indian corn which is immediately available; and the London and Liverpool markets are at present so completely bare of this article, that we have been obliged to have recourse to the plan of purchasing supplies of Indian corn which had been already exported from London to neighbouring Continental ports."[139] And again, on the 29th of the same month, Mr. Trevelyan thus explains the difficulties the Treasury laboured under in endeavouring to purchase the supplies for which the Commissary-General had been so emphatically calling:—"It is little known what a formidable competition we are suffering from our Continental neighbours. Very large orders are believed to have been sent out to the United States, not only by the merchants, but by the Governments of France and Belgium, and in the Mediterranean markets they have secured more than their share; all which will appear perfectly credible, when it is remembered that they are buying our new English wheat in our own market."[140]

Here at home, the fatal error of awaiting events, instead of anticipating them, and by forethought endeavouring to control and guide them, was equally pernicious. The most considerable persons in the kingdom— peers, members of Parliament, deputy lieutenants, magistrates without number—pronounced the potato crop of 1846 to be hopelessly gone early in August. But although several members of the Government expressed their belief in this, and spoke about it with great alarm, they seem not to have given it full credence, until it was too late to take anticipatory measures; in short, they regarded it, like everything Irish, as greatly exaggerated. The most influential portion of the English newspaper press supported and encouraged this view, making, at the same time, fierce attacks on Irish landlords for not meeting the calamity as they ought, and as they were bound in duty and conscience to do. Equally bitter and insolent was their tone towards the Irish people, accusing them of many inherent vices—denouncing their ignorance, their laziness, their want of self-reliance. Whatever of truth or falsehood may have been in those charges, it was not the time to put them forward. Famine was at the door of the Irish nation, and its progress was not to be stayed by invectives against our failings, or by moral lectures upon the improvement of our habits. Food, food was the single and essential requisite; let us have it at once, or we die; lecture us afterwards as much as you please. But there was something to be said on the other side about our habits and failings; and a liberal English journalist, taking up the subject, turned their own artillery upon his countrymen, telling them that those vices, of which they accused the Irish people, were not an essential part of Celtic nature. Has not the Irish Celt, he asks, achieved distinguished success in every country of Europe but his own? The state in which he is to be found in Ireland to-day must be, therefore, accounted for on some other theory than the inherent good-for-nothingness of his nature. "The sluggish, well-meaning mind of the English nation," he continues, "so willing to do its duty, so slow to discover that it has any duty to do, is now perforce rousing to ask itself the question, after five centuries of English domination over Ireland, how many millions it is inclined to pay, not in order to save the social system which has grown up under its fostering care, but to help that precious child of its parental nurture to die easy? Any further prolongation of existence for that system no one now seems to predict, and hardly any one longer ventures to insinuate that it deserves."

"This is something gained. The state of Ireland—not the present state merely, but the habitual state—is hitherto the most unqualified instance of signal failure which the practical genius of the English people has exhibited. We have had the Irish all to ourselves for five hundred years. No one has shared with us the privilege of governing them, nor the responsibilities consequent on that privilege. No one has exercised the smallest authority over them save by our permission. They have been as completely delivered into our hands as children into those of their parents and instructors. No one has ever had the power to thwart our wise and benevolent purposes; and now, at the expiration of nearly one-third of the time which has elapsed since the Christian era, the country contains eight millions, on their own showing, of persecuted innocents, whom it is the sole occupation of every English mind to injure and disparage; on ours (if some of our loudest spokesmen are to be taken as our representatives) of lazy, lawless savages, whose want of industry and energy keeps them ever on the verge of starvation; whose want of respect for life and property makes it unsafe for civilized beings to dwell among them. England unanimously repudiates the first theory; but is the other much less disgraceful to us? An independent nation is, in all essentials, what it has made itself by its own efforts; but a nation conquered, and held in subjugation ever since it had a history, is what its conquerors have made it, or have caused it to become. Yet this reflection does not seem to inspire Englishmen generally with any feeling of shame. The evils of Ireland sit as lightly on the English conscience as if England had done all which the most enlightened and disinterested benevolence could suggest for governing the Irish well, and for civilizing and improving them. What has ever yet been done, or seriously attempted, for either purpose, except latterly, by taking off some of the loads which we ourselves have laid on, history will be at a loss to determine."[141]

Some of the officers connected with the relief works expressed their opinion, that the failure of the potato crop and the deficiency of food in the country were both exaggerated. They threw doubts on the veracity of those with whom they conversed, and warned the Government to be cautious about believing, to the full, the statements made by individuals, committees, or newspapers. Sir Randolph Routh, the head of the Commissariat Department, in a letter to Mr. Trevelyan, the Assistant-Secretary to the Treasury, says: "In the midst of much real, there is more fictitious distress; and so much abuse prevails, that if you check it in one channel, it presents itself in another."[142] Again, Assistant Commissary-General Milliken, writing to Sir R. Routh from Galway, informs him that he met a considerable number of carts loaded with meal and other supplies; and there did not, he said, appear that extreme want and destitution that he had expected.[143] More than any other did Lieutenant-Colonel Jones, Chairman of the Board of Works, keep the idea of exaggerated and fictitious distress before the mind of the Treasury, although he began his communications in a far different spirit. Writing on the 1st of September to Mr. Trevelyan, he says: "The prospects for the ensuing season are melancholy to reflect upon; the potato crop may now be fairly considered as past; either from disease, or from the circumstance of the produce being small, it has been consumed; many families are now living upon food scarcely fit for hogs." And again: "I am very much afraid that Government will not find *free trade*, with all the employment we can give, a succedaneum for the loss of the potato." Doubtless Colonel Jones soon discovered such views as these to be distasteful to his superiors; so, like a prudent servant, he puts them aside, and in his after communications adopts the very opposite tone. He writes to Mr. Under-Secretary Redington[144] on the 13th of October, from Athlone, this piece of information, intended, he says, for his Excellency: "On the 11th instant I posted from Dublin to Banagher. Along the entire line of road I observed the farmyards well stocked with corn, the crop of the past harvest, unthreshed"—thus assuming that the four millions of people who lived almost exclusively on potatoes had such things as farmyards and corn to put in them. In the same month he writes again to Mr. Trevelyan, that he hears from more quarters than one that the early potatoes, which were left in the ground, now prove to be sound. Although small in size, he says, still from one-third to one-half may be considered available for food. "On my way here from Athlone," he again writes, "I went into a field where a man was digging potatoes. The crop looked good, and he told me that it was an early crop, and that he considered that about half were sound; and I therefore hope that there is much more food of that description than the general outcry about famine would lead strangers to suppose." At the end of December he reports to the Treasury a conversation he had had with an assistant-engineer from Roscommon, who told him his belief was, that there were much more provisions in the country than was generally supposed. He had every day, he said, good potatoes at eight shillings a cwt. When the disease appeared, the people who held conacres threw them up, and the potatoes remained undug. Those that were sound continued so up to the late frost; and the people had, by degrees, been taking them up. This engineer expected a considerable quantity, serviceable for food, would be found during the ploughing of the land in spring.

But the wail of starving millions reached the Lord Lieutenant from every side, and, in compliance with it, he authorized the "Extraordinary Baronial Presentment Sessions" to be held. At those sessions the tone of the speakers was, on the whole, kind and liberal; acknowledging the universality of the failure of the potato crop, and the necessity of making immediate provision against its consequences. Sometimes the presentments for the public works were very large—far beyond the entire rental of the barony; yet they may not have been too great to meet the starvation which the assembled ratepayers saw everywhere around them. At Berehaven, in the County Cork, a place certainly fearfully tried by the Famine, the presentments at the sessions—at the very first sessions held in the barony—were said to be quadruple the rental of the entire barony! This, however, was only one district of the largest Irish county; but the presentments for the whole County of Mayo, the most famine-stricken, to be sure, of all the counties, are worth remembering; and so is their explanation. They were forwarded to the Board of Works by the County Surveyor. The number of square miles in the county are given at 2,132, the rent value being £385,100. The County Surveyor recommended to the Sessions presentments amounting in the aggregate to £228,000, nearly two-thirds of the entire rental. The Baronial Sessions, however, were far from resting contented with this. The ratepayers and magistrates assembled in their various baronies, presented for works to the amount of £388,000, nearly £3,000 in excess of the entire rental of the county; but which was finally cut down by the Board of Works to £128,456 8s. 4d. Prudent people and political economists will at once be inclined to exclaim, "Very right; it was most fortunate to have an authority to check such recklessness." But, softly; let there be no hasty conclusions. Hear the end. The County Surveyor gives the population of Mayo at 56,209 families, *of whom 46,316 families*, he says, *were to be employed on the relief works!* Taking those families at the common average of five and a-half individuals to each, the total number would be 254,738 persons. The presentments allowed would thus give about ten shillings' worth, of employment for each individual, with nine or ten foodless months before them. The conclusion is inevitable; the presentments allowed were utterly inadequate to meet the Famine in Mayo, the fearful consequences of which we shall learn as we proceed.[145]

Many of the speakers at the Presentment Sessions charged the Government with a breach of faith, in not finishing the works which were prematurely closed on the 15th of August, 1846. Those works were commenced under the law passed by Sir Robert Peel's Government, whereby the baronies, or, in other words, the ratepayers, paid *one-half the expense*, and the Government the other; so that even if Lord John Russell's Government took them up anew, under the Labour-rate Act, *the whole expense* should, according to the terms of that Act, fall upon the baronies. This was looked upon as a grievance, and at the Glenquin Sessions, in the county Limerick, Lord Monteagle, a friend and supporter of the Administration, put the grievance in the shape of a resolution, which was unanimously adopted. In moving the resolution, his lordship said: "We claim that we have a right to ask from the Government one-half of the expenses incurred by the completion of these works, on the terms and conditions upon which we entered into the engagement. The Government are bound to do this in point of justice." The resolution was: "That whilst we express our full approval of these works, yet the magistrates and ratepayers feel that it is also their duty to express their strong and unanimous opinion, that the just construction of the arrangement between this barony and the Government for the completion of such works as have been commenced under the Act 9 Vic. c. 1, requires an adherence to the terms of that contract."

Some, whilst finding fault with the illiberality of the Government, still expressed their satisfaction at the expenses under the new Act being equally divided between landlord and tenant; a proper responsibility being thus placed upon landlords, which was not the case under the former Act. Very general discontent was manifested at the rule by which the rate of wages on the public works was to be twopence a day under the average wages of the district in which the works were being carried on. Wages ruled so excessively low at the time, it was felt that, with rapidly advancing markets, the labourer on the works could not get food sufficient for his family. The object of this rule, however, was obvious and well meant enough; it was framed to induce agricultural labourers to remain at their usual employments, in order that the crops might be sown. Had the Government been well informed of the relations subsisting between farmer and labourer in Ireland, they would have known that this arrangement could not have the desired effect, *money-wages regularly paid* being almost a thing unknown to our agricultural population at the time; whilst the Famine made money-wages, regularly paid, the first essential of existence.[146]

When the Government began to insist on task, or piecework, instead of day labour, the greatest amount of dissatisfaction that occurred during the entire Famine manifested itself. The engineers of the Board of Works reported over and over again, that an industrious man, willing to labour, could earn from fifteen to eighteen pence a-day under this arrangement, yet the people rose in combination—almost in rebellion—against it, whilst daily wages ranged from eight to tenpence only. They assaulted overseers; refused to work for them; threatened their lives, and in one instance at least, attempted the life of a Government functionary. At the village of Clare, in the county of that name, some short distance south of Ennis, the capital, this insubordination seems to have become rather formidable, as a murderous outrage was committed there on the head steward of the works, Mr. W. Hennessy, half-way between Clare and Ennis. He was fired upon by one of four men whom he observed inside the road ditch, as he passed along. The weapon used was a blunderbuss. It was charged with some of the blasting powder belonging to the works, and duck shot; so that although Mr. Hennessy received the contents in his right side, he was not mortally wounded, and recovered in a little time. Captain Wynne, the local inspector, giving an account of this outrage to his Board, says, the cause of the outrage was because Mr. Hennessy was trying to get the men into proper training. Quite likely. But it must be taken into account, that a duty of that kind might be done in such a way as neither to offend the men, nor lose their respect or esteem; and it might be done in an offensive insolent manner, calculated to exasperate them, especially as they were in a state of excitement at the period.[147] Captain Wynne further says, that the perpetrator of the outrage was known, but could not be brought to justice. The Board of Works, to mark its indignation at this murderous attack upon one of its servants, stopped the works in the locality, and the inhabitants, miserably off before, sank into a state of the most heartrending destitution, as is testified by Captain Wynne, writing from the same place a fortnight or three weeks after, to Colonel Jones.[148] "I must again," he says, "call your attention to the appalling state in which Clare Abbey is at present. I ventured through that parish this day, to ascertain the condition of the inhabitants, and although a man not easily moved, I confess myself unmanned by the extent and intensity of suffering I witnessed, more especially among the women and little children, crowds of whom were to be seen scattered over the turnip fields, like a flock of famishing crows, devouring the raw turnips, and mostly half naked, shivering in the snow and sleet, uttering exclamations of despair, whilst their children were screaming with hunger. I am a match for anything else I may meet with here, but this I cannot stand. When may we expect to resume the works?" This letter does much credit to the feeling and manly heart of Captain Wynne. He says the wretched beings were devouring the raw turnips they found in the fields, but surely very little such was to be found among the snowdrifts in the last days of December, for, sad to say, his letter was written on Christmas Eve! Such a Christmas for the people of Clare Abbey, and of a thousand places besides!

Beyond doubt, the Government, and those under them, had enormous difficulties to contend against. Every new scheme, or modification of a scheme, proposed by them had its inconveniences. Inspectors, engineers, and overseers appeared to regard the opposition to task work as the dislike of the lazy Celt to labour for his daily bread, and to his wish to get the "Queen's pay," as the wages on the works were termed, without doing anything for it. Hence they were of opinion almost from the outset, that the sooner the system of task work was enforced the better, as the people, they said, seemed to be generally under the impression that no work was really required from them. This was a very wrong and demoralizing notion, if it were entertained to any considerable extent. Very probably it had a percentage of truth in it, but no more. Worthless idlers, in no very urgent distress, must from the nature of things, have got employed upon works so extensive, but the officials were too fond of founding general conclusions on isolated, or at least on an insufficient number of cases. The opposition to task work arose from more than one cause. Lazy unprincipled people were opposed to it, because they were lazy and unprincipled; a far larger class were opposed to it, because it was no secret that the works were carried on not for sake of their utility, but to keep the people from being idle. Had this class been employed upon really useful works, such as reclaiming land, tilling the soil, draining, subsoiling, or railroad-making, they would, no doubt, have had more heart for their daily labour. There is a natural repugnance in the mind of a man to apply himself in earnest to what he has been told is useless,—to what he sees and feels to be useless. If a labourer were hired, and even given good wages, for casting chaff against the wind, I make bold to say, he would soon resign his employment, from sheer inability to work at anything so much opposed to his common sense. A third and a very large class of the labouring population were opposed to task work, because they were able to earn so very little at it. "Those who choose to labour may earn good wages," writes Colonel Jones to Mr. Trevelyan; but he forgot, or was ignorant of the fact, that great numbers of the working class had been already so weakened and debilitated by starvation, that they were unable to do what the overseers regarded as a day's work; and it is on record that task work frequently brought industrious willing workmen less money than they would have received under the day's-work system.[149]

At the end of October a Treasury Minute was published to the effect that such prices were to be allowed for Relief Works, executed by task, as would enable good labourers to earn from one shilling to one shilling and sixpence a day; the day's work system, at the wages fixed by the Treasury Minute of the 31st of August, was to be in future confined to those who were unable or unwilling to work by task. There was some concession in this. Under it the labourer could choose piece work or day's work as seemed more advantageous to himself. The spirit, at least, of the August Treasury Minute was, that all should work by task. "The persons employed on the Relief Works," says that Minute, "should, to the utmost possible extent, be paid in proportion to the work actually done by them." In a few instances task work was reported to have given satisfaction, but in the great majority of cases it was resisted by the labourers, and it sometimes resulted in serious disturbances, as we have seen. The local Committees, who had much to do with preparing the lists of those whose circumstances made them proper objects for the public works, were repeatedly complained of by the Government officials. Lieutenant-

Colonel Jones, who appears to have been more severe and distrustful than his subordinates, accuses Committees of insulting his officers, producing improper lists, and even of balloting amongst themselves for the persons who were to be put upon the works.

With regard to the first accusation there was generally a counter-charge from the Committees, accusing the Board's officers of being insulting and overbearing to them. One of the most noteworthy cases of this kind occurred at Ennistymon. Captain Wynne, the Board of Works' inspector, writes a long complaint about the treatment he had received from the members of the Committee there; it being, amongst other things, he says, proposed that he should be kicked out of the Court-house, where the Committee was assembled. The well-disposed few, he writes, advised him to stay at Ennistymon for the night, or to take an escort of police with him, should he persevere in his intention of returning to Ennis; "but," he continues, "with my double gun, a rifle, and three cases of pistols, Mr. Gamble, myself, and Mr. Russell returned home. Mr. Russell was very anxious to see a Clare Relief Committee. He was indeed astonished. He said he would not have supposed matters were so bad."[150] There is a fine dash of the sensational in this. Mr. Russell's anxiety was very laudable, being evidently akin to that thirst for information which excites travellers like Captain Cook or Dr. Livingstone to seek an assembly or encampment of "natives" in some previously unexplored region; but there happened to be members of the Ennistymon Relief Committee in every respect the equals, and in some the superiors of Captain Wynne and Mr. Russell. Major M'Namara, one of the members for the county, thus gives his version of the affair to the Chief Secretary, Mr. Labouchere: "I feel it to be my duty towards myself and the constituency of this county, to state to you, as the organ of the Government, that I was present on Thursday at Ennistymon, when Mr. Wynne, an inspecting officer of the Board of Works, gave my colleague, Mr. O'Brien, in the presence of several magistrates and gentlemen assembled at the Ennistymon Relief Committee, the most unprovoked insult, by stating that he treated what Mr.

O'Brien said with utter contempt, although Mr. O'Brien merely observed that certain letters containing what we all believed to be unfounded charges against the Liscannor Committee, afforded evidence of a vile conspiracy." Captain Wynne being called on by the authorities for an explanation, charged the gentry of Clare with putting their servants and dependants on the lists for public works without being proper objects for them, and that they were indignant with him because he took such persons off in great numbers. He did not, however, deny the insult Major M'Namara had charged him with giving his brother representative for the county, Mr. Cornelius O'Brien.[151]

As to the complaint made by Colonel Jones about the preparation of the lists, there does not seem to be much in it. Men of influence would naturally try to get their own people on the works in preference to others, but the efforts of such parties would be calculated to neutralize each other. The balloting for the lists is explainable on very legitimate grounds. Great as the extent of the Relief Works undoubtedly was, these works were lamentably short of the wants of the time. Let us suppose that five hundred men in a district were, every one, urgent cases for the Relief Works, and let us suppose employment could not be given to them all, a very common occurrence indeed, what more natural—what more just than to select by ballot those who were to be recommended? It is hard to see what else could be done, unless the system of influence and favoritism against which Colonel Jones complained, were adopted. The ballot, in short, would seem in many instances the only means of defeating that system. It might be said that five hundred equally pressing cases could not be found in the same district. Very true. But what was unfortunately found in many districts was, twice—thrice as many cases as there was employment for, the least urgent of which might be well pronounced very urgent. Such, for instance, was the fact in the whole county of Mayo.

After Skibbereen, Bantry, and Skull, there was scarcely any place in the South so famine-stricken as Ennistymon. The gentry of the place knew the real wants of the population, and pressed them on the Government officials; while they, on the other hand, in obedience to orders, felt bound to keep the labour lists as low as possible. To have reduced those lists always served an inspector at head-quarters. In such cases it is no wonder that unpleasant differences sometimes arose between Committees and inspectors. That Ennistymon was sorely tried appears from many communications to the Board of Works. A very short time after Captain Wynne's unpleasant quarrel with the Committee there, I find Mr. Millet, the officer, I suppose, who succeeded him, writing to the Board from that town, that he was besieged in his house by men trying to compel him to put them on the works, on which account he could not get out until half-past four o'clock in the evening. "Some of the men make a list," he writes, "and get it sent by the Committee whether men are wanting or not. The people think this is sufficient authority."[152] From this it seems clear that the works at Ennistymon were quite insufficient for the number of the destitute. The starving people wanted to get employment, *whether men were wanting or not*. What a complaint! Good Mr. Millet, the question with the people was not whether you required workmen or not, but it was, that they and their families were in the throes of death from want of food, and they saw no other way of getting it but by being employed on those works. Besides, your masters began by stating that the Public Works were not undertaken on account of their necessity or utility, but for the purpose of rescuing the people from famine, by giving them employment.[153]

The inspectors and the local Committees had such frequent differences, that the Board had it under serious consideration to dispense with those Committees altogether. This idea was abandoned, but the important privilege of issuing tickets for the Works was taken away from the Committees, by an order of the Board, bearing date the 9th of December. Besides the various other complaints forwarded to Dublin of the way in which tickets were issued by the Committees, one officer writes that he finds they had become a "saleable commodity" in the hands of the labourers. A man, he says, obtains a ticket, disposes of it for what he can get, and goes back for another, feeling sure that amongst the numberless applicants he would not be recognized as having been given one before. This practice, which was not and could not be carried on to any great extent, was but another proof that the works were insufficient to meet the demand for employment. Instead of the issue of tickets by Committees it was ruled by the Board, that the inspecting officer should furnish to the check clerk, for the engineer, a list of the men to be employed on any particular work.[154]

As before remarked, an undercurrent of feeling pervaded the minds of officials that there was not at all so much real distress in Ireland as the people pretended, and that there was a great deal more food in the country than there was said to be. This was sometimes openly asserted, but more frequently hinted at and insinuated in communications to the Board of Works and the Treasury. It was founded partly on prejudice, and partly on ignorance of the real state of affairs, which was far worse than the most anxious friends of the people asserted, as the event, unfortunately, too truly proved. That there was some deception and much idleness, in connection with the public works, cannot be doubted for a moment; such works being on a gigantic and ever increasing scale, effective supervision was impossible. The mistake of many of the officials, although not of all, was, that they regarded such exceptional things as an index to the general state of the country, built theories upon them, and sent those theories up to their superiors, which helped to make them close-handed and suspicious. Those officials did not, and, in many cases, could not sound the depths of misery into which the country had sunk; the people were dying of sheer starvation around them, whilst they were writing reports accusing them of exaggeration and idleness. What the Rev. Jeremiah Sheahan of Clenlure, in the County Cork, said of his parishioners was equally true in hundreds of other cases: "The most peaceable have died of want in their cabins. More than twelve have done so in the last six days."[155]

One of the proofs brought forward that the Irish people were not so badly off as they pretended—in fact that in many instances they were concealing their wealth, was, *the increase of deposits in the Savings Banks*. At a superficial glance there would appear to be much truth in this conclusion; but we must remember that the millions whom the potato blight left foodless, never, in the best of times, had anything to put in Savings' Banks. They planted their acre or half acre of potatoes, paid for it by their labour; they had thus raised a bare sufficiency of food; and so their year's operations began and ended. An official of the Irish Poor Law Board, Mr. Twistleton, gave a more elaborate and detailed answer to the Savings' Banks argument. Writing to the Home Secretary, Sir George Grey, under date of the 26th of December, he calls his attention to leaders in the *Times* and *Morning Chronicle* on the subject. One of those articles is remarkable, he says, since it "seemed to treat the increase in the deposits as a proof of *successful swindling on the part of the Irish people*, during the present year." So far from this being true, an increase, in Mr. Twistleton's opinion, might show "severe distress," inasmuch as when times begin to grow hard, deposits would increase for the following reasons:

1. People in employment, who were thoughtless before and did not deposit, would begin to be depositors in bad times.
2. People in employment, who were depositors before, would increase their deposits.
3. Thrifty people, who would at other times have gone into little speculations, would now be afraid to do so, and they would become depositors instead.
4. Persons of a higher class, say employers, in such times cease to be employers and become depositors.

An increase of deposits, Mr. Twistleton admits, may arise from prosperity; he only wishes to show that such increase is not always a certain sign of it. We know too well now, that the increase of deposits in some of our Savings' Banks during the Famine, was no sign whatever of prosperity; yet the *journals* named above, at once built upon the fact a theory most damaging to the existing destitution of our people, and most injurious to their moral character; basing this theory on one of those general principles of political economy, which often admits of grave exceptions, and sometimes breaks down utterly, when put to the test of practical experience.

Amongst the minor difficulties with which the Board of Works had to contend, were scarcity of silver, and the impossibility of having suitable tools manufactured in sufficient quantity. Gold and bank notes were of little or no use on pay day,—and where works were opened in wild out-of-the-way places, there was no opportunity of exchanging them for silver coin. Representations on this head having been made by the Inspectors, the "Comet," a government vessel, was sent to deliver as much silver as was required, to the various banks in the towns round the coast of Ireland; but this system was not long persevered in. Towards the end of October, Mr. Secretary Trevelyan announced that the Treasury would return to the ordinary mode of supply. The Bank of England, he informed the Board, is the appointed distributor of silver coin, which is supplied to it for that purpose by the Treasury; but as there might be some inconvenience in sending to England, the Board of Works are to apply to the Bank of Ireland, which is authorized to give silver coin when they have it, and when it is not in their own vaults, they will procure it for the Board from the Bank of England.[156] In this manner the want was met, but there is very little in the official correspondence about the channels through which it reached the various parts of the country where it was required; secrecy on the subject being, no doubt, thought necessary to avoid danger.

The public works projected and carried on by the Government to meet the distress of 1845-6 were brought to a close on the 15th of August of the latter year. The Treasury Minute, empowering the Board to begin anew public works in Ireland under the provisions of the Labour-rate Act, was published on the 31st of the same month; so that the officials whom the Board had added to their ordinary staff, when entrusted with the management of the previous public works, were, we may assume, still in their hands, when they received their new commission from the Treasury. Although numerous, they were miserably insufficient for the vast and terrible campaign now before them. Indeed, throughout those trying and marvellous times, a full supply of efficient officers the Board was never able to secure; the pressure was so great, the undertakings so numerous and extensive, that this is by no means matter for surprise. A few figures selected from their accounts and reports, will serve to show the sudden and extraordinary expansion of their operations.

The baronies to which loans had been issued up to the 31st of December, 1846, under the Labour-rate Act, numbered *three hundred and twenty-two*, and the total sum issued up to the same time was £999,661 4s. 2d.—a million of money, in round numbers. Besides this, many of those baronies (but not all) had obtained loans under previous Acts; whilst baronies, which had as yet made no application for loans under the Labour-rate Act, were also indebted to Government for money borrowed under previous Acts. The number of baronies which had taken out loans under the Acts of 1 Vic., cap. 21, and 9 and 10 Vic., cap. 124, was four hundred and twenty-four. The account between the baronies and the Government stood thus on the 31st of December, 1846:

Loans to baronies under Acts passed previous to the Labour-rate Act	£186,060 1 5
Grants	229,464 8 0
Loans to baronies under the Labour-rate Act	999,661 4 2

Making in all	£1,415,185 13 7

£229,464 8s. 0d. being the amount of grants, and £1,185, 721 5s. 7d. being the amount of loans; besides which there was expended by the

Board of Works under various drainage Acts, for the year ending 31st December, 1846, a sum of £110,022 14s. 4d.

In the week ending the 3rd of October, there were 20,000 persons employed on the public works in Ireland; in the week ending the 31st of the same month, there were over 114,000. In the very next week, the first week of November, there were 162,000 on the works; and in the week ending the 28th of November, the returns give the number as something over 285,000! A fortnight later, in a detailed account of the operations of the Board, supplied to the Treasury, this remarkable sentence occurs: "The works at present are in every county in Ireland, affording employment to *more than* three hundred thousand persons."[157] The increase went on rapidly through December. In the week ending the 5th of that month, there were 321,000 employed; and in the week which closed on the 26th, the extraordinary figure was 398,000![158]

The number of persons employed was greatest in Munster, and least in Ulster. At the beginning of December, they were thus distributed in the four Provinces: Ulster, 30,748; Leinster, 50,135; Connaught, 106,680; and Munster, 134,103. At the close of the month the same proportion was pretty fairly maintained, the numbers being: for Ulster, 45,487; for Leinster, 69,585; for Connaught, 119,946; and for Munster, 163,213. According to the Census of 1841, there were in Ulster 439,805 families; in Leinster, 362,134; in Connaught, 255,694; and in Munster, 415,154. From these data, the proportion between the number of persons employed on the relief works in each Province, and the population of that Province, stood thus at the close of the year 1846: in Ulster there was one labourer out of every nine and two-thirds families so employed; in Leinster there was one out of about every five and a quarter families; in Munster, one out of every two and a-half families; and in Connaught, one out of every two and about one-seventh families.

At the end of November, the number of employees superintending the public works were: 62 inspecting officers; 60 engineers and county surveyors; 4,021 overseers; 1,899 check clerks; 5 draftsmen; 54 clerks for correspondence; 50 clerks for accounts; 32 pay inspectors, and 425 pay clerks—making in all 6,913 officials, distributed over nine distinct departments.

The gross amount of wages rose, of course, in proportion to the numbers employed. At the end of October, the sum paid weekly was £61,000; at the end of November, £101,000; and for the week ending the 26th of December, £154,472.

The number of Relief Committees in operation throughout the country at the close of 1846, was about one thousand. Indeed, everything connected with the Public Works and the Famine tends to impress one with their gigantic proportions;—even the correspondence, the state of which is thus given by the Board in the middle of December: "The letters received averaged 800 a-day, exclusive of letters addressed to individual members of the Board, on public business; the number received on the last day of November was 2,000; to-day, (17th December,) two thousand five hundred."

All this notwithstanding, the Famine was but very partially stayed: on it went, deepening, widening, desolating, slaying, with the rapidity and certainty which marked the progress of its predecessor, the Blight. The numbers applying for work without being able to obtain it, were fearfully enormous. From a memorandum supplied by the Board of Works to Sir Randolph Routh, the head of the Commissariat Department, dated the 17th of December, we learn that the labourers then employed were about 350,000, whilst the number on Relief Lists (for employment) was about 500,000,—that is, there were 150,000 persons on the lists seeking work, who could not, or at least who did not, get it. Those 150,000 may be taken to represent at least half a million of starving people;—how many more were there at the moment, whose names never appeared on any list, except the death-roll!

FOOTNOTES:

139.   Commissariat Series of Blue Books, Correspondence, vol. I., pp. 80 and 83.
140.   *Ib.* p. 98.

141.   *Morning Chronicle* quoted in *Freeman's Journal* of October 7th, 1846. The *Standard*, commenting on a letter which appeared in the *Times* shortly before on the same subject, and written in the same spirit of hostility to the Irish people, says it would be "indecent" at any time; at present it is "intolerably offensive" and "greatly mischievous." "That the Irish are not naturally an idle race," continues the *Standard*, "every man may satisfy himself in London streets, and in the streets of all our great towns, where nearly all the most toilsome work is performed by Irish labourers."

142.   Letter in Commissariat Series of Blue Books, vol. I., p. 360.

143.   *Ib.* p. 349.

144.   Afterwards Sir Thomas Redington, Knt.

145.   Mr. Brett, County Surveyor of Mayo to the Board of Works. Board of Works Series of Blue Books, vol. L, p. 125.

146.   "*Employment*, with wages in *cash* is the general outcry."—*Com. Gen. Hewitson to Mr. Trevelyan; Commissariat Series, p. 12.*

147.   "Those at taskwork had fivepence, and in some cases as low as threepence per diem. In other cases, again, an opposite extreme existed, and as much as two shillings and twopence per diem was found in two instances to have been paid . . . I fear there was not, in all cases, sufficient sympathy for the present sufferings of the poor—a feeling quite compatible with a firm and honest discharge of duty. This inflames the minds of the people against the system generally, and they become victims alike to their own intemperance, and the mismanagement of those placed over them. Throughout the country, in the majority of cases, disturbances are attributable wholly, or in a great degree, to such errors, overseers acting more as slave-drivers than as the messengers of benevolence to an afflicted but warm-hearted people."—*A Twelvemonth's Residence in Ireland during the Famine and the Public Works, with suggestions to meet the coming crisis. By William Henry Smith, C.E., late conducting Engineer of Public Works. London, 1848; p. 94.*

Again: "I much regretted leaving, and but for the circumstance of some imperative engagements recalling me to London, my intended sojourn of two or three months, which I originally named to the Commissioners, would probably have been prolonged even beyond what it eventually was, amongst a people whom I saw no reason to fear, even when using necessary severity, but on the contrary every reason to admire, from their strongly affectionate dispositions and resignation in deep suffering: they treated it as the will of God, and murmured, 'Thy will be done.'"—*Ibid. p. 18.*

148.   "In cases where disturbances arose in any one district, the works of the whole barony were suspended, inflicting injury upon all, the guilty and innocent indiscriminately."—*Ibid. p. 93.*

149.   See Note p. 203, from Mr. Smith's valuable book, *A Twelvemonth's Residence in Ireland.*

150.   Board of Works Series, vol. L, p. 53.

151.   On the 8th of February, 1847, during the debate on the "Poor Relief (Ireland) Bill," in the House of Commons, Lord Duncan said, "He found it stated in the Blue Book he had referred to, that the two members for Clare had put tenants upon the relief-rate who were paying them considerable rents. He trusted that they would be prepared to deny this serious imputation."

    Major M'Namara rose and said:—"Sir—As one of the members for Clare, I beg to say, that every sentence in Captain Wynne's letter is a malicious falsehood. (Some sensation, amid which the hon. member resumed his sat)."

152.   He thus complains in italics: "*None of the gentry will take our part except one.*" Board of Works Blue Books, vol. L, p. 352, Appendix.

153.   "The works under 9 and 10 Vic., c. 107, are sanctioned for sake of the relief and not for sake of the works themselves." Mr. Trevelyan to Lieut.-Colonel Jones, 5th October, 1846.

154.   The duty of check clerks was to visit the works frequently, to count the labourers, and prepare the pay lists.

155.   Memorial to Lord John Russell, Dec. 14, 1846.

156.   Letter to Lieutenant-Colonel Jones, 28th October, 1846.

157.   Board of Works' Series of Blue Books, vol. L (50), p. 352.

158.   Another account makes it only 376,133. It is easy to see that perfect accuracy with regard to the number of persons employed on the works at any given time was, for obvious reasons, not to be attained. The figures given above from the official returns are, therefore, only an approximation to the truth, but they may be accepted as substantially correct.

* * * * *

CHAPTER VIII.

Operations of the Commissariat Relief Department—Not to interfere with Mealmongers or Corn Merchants—Effects of this Rule—Deputation from Achill *(Note)*—Organization of the Commissariat Relief Department—Reports on the Potato Crop—The Blight in Clare—Commissary-General Hewetson's Opinion—Commisary-General Dobree's Report—Depôts—Universality of the Blight—Rules with regard to Food Depôts—Fault of the Treasury—Scarcity of Food—Depôts besieged for it in the midst of harvest—Depôts to be only on the West Coast—What was meant by the West Coast—Coroner's Inquests at Mallow—Rev. Mr. Daly—Lord Mountcashel—Famine Demonstration at Westport—Sessions at Kilmacthomas—Riot at Dungarvan—Capt. Sibthorpe's Order—Mr. Howley's Advice—Attempt to rescue Prisoners—Captain Sibthorpe asks leave to fire—Refused by Mr. Howley—Riot Act read—Leave to fire given—People retire from the town—Two men wounded—The carter's reason for fighting—Lame Pat Power—Death of Michael Fleming, the carter—Formidable bands traverse the country—Advice of the Clergy—Carrigtuohill—Macroom—Killarney—Skibbereen—March on that town by the workmen of Caheragh—Dr. Donovan's account of the movement—The military, seventy-five in number, posted behind a schoolhouse—Firmness and prudence of Mr. Galwey, J.P.—Biscuits ordered from the Government Store—Peace preserved—Demonstration at Mallow—Lord Stuart de Decies—Deputation from Clonakilty to the Lord Lieutenant—Ships prevented from sailing at Youghal—Sir David Roche—Demonstrations simultaneous—Proclamation against food riots—Want of mill-power—No mill-power in parts of the West where most required—Sir Randolph Routh's opinion—Overruled by the Treasury—Mr. Lister's Account of the mill-power in parts of Connaught—Meal ground at Deptford, Portsmouth, Plymouth, and Rotherhithe; also in Essex and the Channel Islands—Mill-power at Malta—Quantity of wheat there—Five hundred quarters purchased—The French—The Irish handmill, or quern, revived—Samples of it got—Steel-mills—Mill-power useless from failure of water-supply—Attempt to introduce whole corn boiled as food.

Two Governmental departments were told off to do battle with the Irish Famine; namely, the Board of Works and the Commissariat Relief Office. The duty of the former was to find employment for those who were able to work, at such wages as would enable them to support themselves and their families; the latter was to see that food should be for sale within a reasonable distance of all who were necessitated to buy it, and at fair market prices; but more than this the Commissariat Office was not empowered to do. Corn merchants, food dealers, and mealmongers were not to be interfered with; on the contrary, they were to be encouraged in carrying on their trade. It was only where such persons did not exist, or did not exist in sufficient numbers, that the Commissariat depôts were to sell corn or meal to the people. No food was to be given away by Government; none was to be sold under price, it being assumed that the people could earn enough to support themselves. Government feared that, if they began to undersell the merchants and dealers, those classes would give up business, which, in the Government's opinion, would be a very great evil. Mealmongers and food dealers are generally very shrewd men; and it was believed, with much reason, that they succeeded in raising prices when it suited them, and in many cases in realizing even large fortunes, by working on the apprehensions of the Government in respect to this very matter.[159]

The Commissariat Relief Department was organized at the close of 1845, for the purpose of managing the distribution of Indian meal, imported at that time by Sir Robert Peel, to provide against the anticipated scarcity of the spring and summer of 1846. Its head-quarters were in Dublin Castle, and its chief was a Scotch gentleman, Sir Randolph Routh—a name which, like some others, must occur pretty frequently in these pages. The Commissariat people, as is usual in such cases, began by instituting extensive inquiries. They ordered their subordinates to furnish reports of the state of the potato crop throughout the country.

The Assistant Commissaries-General and others employed in this service, in due time, made their reports, which in the main agreed with the statements in the public journals, and with the opinion prevalent everywhere among the people; thus differing with those officers of the Board of Works who held that there were more sound potatoes in Ireland than was generally admitted. So early as the 11th of August, Mr. White, writing from Galway to Assistant Commissary-General Wood, makes a most unfavourable report of the state of the crop in Clare; the Blight, he says, was general and most rapid in its effects, a large quantity of the potatoes being already diseased, and a portion perfectly rotten. "I am, therefore, clearly of opinion," he continues, "that the scarcity of the potato last year will be nothing compared with this, and that, too, several months earlier."[160] Commissary-General Hewetson sent specimens of diseased potatoes to the Secretary of the Treasury in the middle of August, with this information: "The crop seems to have been struck almost everywhere by one sweeping blast, in one and the same night. I mentioned a hope that the tubers might yet rally, many of the stalks having thrown out fresh vegetation; I fear it is but a futile hope."[161] Just about the same time, Assistant Commissary-General Dobree reports to the same quarter: "It is superfluous to make any further report on the potato crop, for I believe the failure is general and complete throughout the country, though the disease has made more rapid progress in some places than in others. In a circuit of two hundred miles, I have not seen one single field free from it; and although it is very speculative to attempt a calculation on what is not yet absolutely realized, my belief is that scarcely any of the late potatoes will be fit for human food."[162]

Considerable stores of oatmeal and Indian corn remained in the Government depôts throughout the country, when they were closed in August. By a Treasury Minute, these were ordered to be concentrated at six points; two in the interior, namely, Longford and Banagher, and four on the coast, Limerick, Galway, Westport, and Sligo.

Like the heads of the Board of Works, the Commissariat officials thought they would have had some time to arrange their various duties, appoint their subordinates, fit up their offices, such as had any, in a snug and convenient manner, and print and circulate query sheets without number; and all this in spite of their own observations and reports—in spite of this overwhelming fact, which, if they adverted to it at all, does not seem to have impressed them—namely, that they were in the middle of a great famine, and not at the beginning of it; that they were entering on the second year of it with exhausted resources, while the blight which caused it was far more general and destructive than it had been the year before; in short, that it was universal, sweeping, immediate, terrible.

The Government depôts already in existence, as well as those to be established, were only to be in aid of the regular corn and meal trade; and no supplies were to be sold from them, until it was proved to the satisfaction of the Assistant Commissary-General of the district that the necessity for so doing was urgent, and that no other means of obtaining food existed. This rule was, in some instances, kept so stringently, that people died of starvation within easy distance of those depôts, with money in their hands to buy the food that would not be sold to them. The Treasury, rather than Commissary-General Routh or his subordinates, was to blame for this; their strong determination, many times expressed, being, that food accumulated by Government should be husbanded for the spring and summer months of 1847, when they expected the greatest pressure would exist. This was prudence, but prudence founded

240

on ignorance of the real state of things in the closing months of 1846. The dearth of food which they were looking forward to in the coming spring and summer arose fully FIVE MONTHS before the time fixed by the Government; but they were so slow, or so reluctant to realize its truth, that great numbers of people were starved to death before Christmas, because the Government locked up the meal in their depôts, in order to keep the same people alive with it in May and June! "It is most important," says a Treasury Minute—these were the days of Treasury Minutes—"it is most important that it should be remembered, that the supplies provided for the Government depôts are not intended to form the primary or principal means of subsistence to the people of the districts in which the depôts are established, but merely to furnish a last resource, when all other means of subsistence, whether derived from the harvest just got in, or from importations, are exhausted, and the depôts are, therefore, in no case to be drawn upon while food can be obtained by purchase from private parties."[163] This Minute is addressed to Sir Randolph Routh, who had written to the Treasury ten days before, pressing upon them the necessity of large and immediate purchases of corn. "We have no arrivals yet announced," he says, "either at Westport or Sligo, and the remains there must be nothing, or next to nothing. The bills of lading from Mr. Erichsen are all for small quantities, which will be distributed, and perhaps eaten, in twelve or twenty-four hours after their arrival. It would require a thousand tons to make an impression, and that only a temporary one. Our salvation of the depôt system is in the importation of a large supply. These small shipments are only drops in the ocean." And further on in the same letter: "We began our operations on the 1st of September or thereabouts; and here, in the midst of harvest, before any Commissariat arrangement for supplies from abroad could be matured, we find the country besieging our depôt for food, and scarcely a proprietor stirring in their behalf."[164]

Government depôts were only to be established where it was probable that private enterprise would not offer a sufficient quantity of food for sale. On this principle, the north, east, and south were left to be supplied through the usual channels of commerce; the depôt system being confined to the west coast. What was meant precisely by the west coast does not seem to have been settled at the outset, but in answer to an enquiry from Sir R. Routh on the subject, the Treasury, on the 31st of October, defined it to be the country to the west of the Shannon, with the County Donegal to the north, and Kerry to the south, with a small corner of Cork, as far as Skibbereen, because that town was on the western coast.[165]

We have seen the rapid increase of labourers on the Relief Works from October to December, yet famine was always far ahead of the Government. Their arrangements for the first famine year were made with reference to the closing of all operations at harvest time, in 1846, but there was no harvest that year *for the poor*, their crop had vanished before the destroyer, and they were actually worse off at the end of August, 1846, than they had been since the beginning of the Potato Blight. In that year, the potatoes never came to maturity at all, and any that were thought worth the labour of digging, were hurried to market, and sold for any price they fetched, before they would melt away in the owners' hands. One of the Commissariat officers asked a farmer's wife, who was selling potatoes of this kind, what was the price of them; "two pence a stone, sir," she replied, "is my price," but lowering her voice, she *naively* added, "to tell you the truth, sir, they are not worth a penny." Even in September—it was on the 18th of that month—a resolution was passed by the Mallow Relief Committee, that from information laid before them, and from the verdicts of several coroner's inquests, held during the previous few days, disease of the most fatal character was spreading in the districts around them, in consequence of the badness of the food purchasable by the working classes. A little later, the Rev. Mr. Daly announced to the ratepayers at the Fermoy sessions, that at the moment he was addressing them, numbers of persons were living on cabbage leaves, whose countenances were so altered, and whose whole appearance was so changed by starvation and wretchedness, that he could hardly recognise them. Lord Mountcashel, the Chairman of the sessions, on the same occasion used these remarkable words: "The people are starving; they have no employment; they require to be attended to immediately, for, starvation will not accommodate itself to any man's convenience." Nothing truer. Many landlords throughout the country made similar observations; but to all such, the representatives of the Government replied, and not without a good show of reason, that whilst landlords talked in this manner, they themselves, with rare exceptions, did nothing to employ the people, nor did they, in any way, relieve the fearful pressure upon the Public Works.

The earliest famine demonstration seems to have taken place in Westport on the 22nd of August. On that day a large body of men marched four deep, and in a very orderly manner, to Lord Sligo's residence, beside the town. They made their intention known beforehand to the inspector of police, and asked him to be present to show they had no illegal designs. They were chiefly from Islandeady and Aughagown. Lord Sligo, accompanied by some gentlemen, who were staying with him, received them at his hall door. They said they wanted food and work. His lordship assured them that he had already represented, in the strongest terms, the necessity of measures being taken to secure a supply of both, and that he would repeat his application. They seemed satisfied with this, and quietly retired.

Towards the end of September, however, the state of the country became very unsatisfactory and even alarming. The low rate of wages fixed by the Government; the high price of provisions; the closing of the Government depôts; the large quantities of corn which they saw sent daily to England, whilst they who raised it starved, were amongst the chief causes which excited the people to acts of intimidation. In several instances they went in formidable bodies to the presentment sessions, apparently under the impression that the ratepayers, there assembled, had something to do with fixing the amount of wages, which of course was a popular error. On Monday, the 28th of September, a special sessions was appointed to be held at Kilmacthomas, some fourteen miles from Dungarvan, and notices were extensively circulated the day before, by unknown hands, calling on the people to assemble at Dungarvan on that day, as the military would be away at the sessions. The avowed object of this assemblage was to seize provisions by force, or at least to lay down a scale of prices beyond which they should not be raised. The authorities had, of course, timely notice of this movement, and left a sufficient force in the town to protect it. The precaution was not an idle one, for soon after the dragoons took their departure for Kilmacthomas, about five thousand men entered Dungarvan, led by a person named Power, well known in the locality as "lame Pat." The town was guarded by sixty soldiers and fifty-four police, but in the face of such numbers, their officers considered it the best policy to stand upon the defensive, and do nothing until a breach of the peace had been committed. They, however, cautioned the people, and advised them to return to their houses; they did not take their advice, but went round to the various places in which corn was stored, and threatened the owners, if they attempted to export any of the produce they had purchased. They next proceeded to the shops where Indian meal was on sale, and uttered similar threats against the vendors if they charged more than one shilling a stone for it. Meantime Captain Sibthorpe, the officer in command of the detachment of the 1st Royal Dragoons that had gone to Kilmacthomas in the morning, finding the number of people there assembled less than he had anticipated—only five hundred or so—and being aware that a much larger body was expected at Dungarvan, asked permission from the magistrates to return to that town. At first, they were very loath to grant his request, but having at length yielded, he left forty-eight policemen for their protection, and marched his men back to Dungarvan. It was a journey of three or four hours. On their arrival they found the people under Power had concluded their preliminary business of visiting the stores and shops, and not being provided with a commissariat to supply them with rations, they were levying contributions from the bakers of the town. Seeing this, Captain Sibthorpe ordered his dragoons to ride them down, and drive them off, which they did. Some prisoners were taken, lame Pat Power, their leader, being of the number. The prisoners having been secured, Mr. Howley, the resident magistrate, addressed the people; he explained to them the illegality and folly of their proceedings, and assured them he would forward to the Government any document detailing what they considered as their grievances, provided that it was couched in respectful language; and further, that he would do all he could to have any reasonable request of theirs complied with. Upon this they retired and drew up a statement which they handed to him, and which he promised to send to the Lord Lieutenant. So far so good. The day's proceedings might be fairly supposed to have ended here—but no—what about the prisoners? The people refused to go away without them. The magistrates would not release them, but assured their comrades that their punishment should be light. This did not satisfy them, and they commenced to use violent language and to throw stones. Orders were given to clear the square, which service was performed by the dragoons, who drove them into the neighbouring streets; but as the stone-throwing was continued, the police were sent to drive them away; failing to do this, the dragoons were ordered to advance, whereupon, it is said, a shout was raised in Irish by the people to "kill them," which was followed by a shower of stones. Things began to look so critical, that Captain Sibthorpe asked permission from Mr. Howley to order his men to fire, but that gentleman refused the permission. Captain Sibthorpe then asked Mr. Howley to allow him to take that responsibility upon himself, but he still refused, saying that as an important trust had been reposed in him, he would retain that trust, and allow no firing until their lives were imperilled. The stone-throwing continued; Mr. Howley at length said to the other magistrates that there was no use in talking any more to the people, and that he must read the riot act, which he accordingly did. He then warned them of the dangerous course they were pursuing—a shower of stones was the response. Captain Sibthorpe now told Mr. Howley that he would withdraw his men from the town, unless they were permitted to fire. The order was given; the dragoons were drawn up in sections of four—each section firing in its turn. In this manner twenty-six shots were fired, each round being answered by a volley of stones. When the firing had continued for some time, the people retired from the town; they were followed by the dragoons, but entrenching themselves behind the walls and ditches, they prepared to renew the conflict, under more favorable circumstances, but the opportunity was not afforded them. It grew late—the town, at any rate, was cleared, and the success of the troops being by no means so certain upon this new battle ground they were withdrawn by the magistrates. On their return to town, they found two men had been wounded, and as usually happens in such cases, one of them had no connection whatever with the business, being a carter employed in carrying baggage for the troops. When asked how he came to be among the belligerents, having no interest in the matter, he replied, that he was under the impression the troops had orders not to fire on the people, or if they did, it should be with blank cartridge; he was confirmed in this belief by the fact, that the first four or five shots took no effect; but, "at any rate," he added, "when I saw the fun going on, I could not resist the temptation of joining in it."

The persons arrested on the occasion, fifty-one in number, were brought up for trial before the sitting barrister in about a month afterwards. All pleaded guilty, and received merely nominal punishment, with the exception of "lame Pat," their leader. He, poor fellow, was sentenced to one year's imprisonment, although he declared he had been four days and four nights living on cabbage leaves and salt, previous to his misconduct. But the saddest part of this Dungarvan tale is, that the poor carrier, whose name was Michael Fleming, died of his wounds on the 26th of October, in the Workhouse, to which he had been removed for medical treatment.

Formidable bands went about, in some portions of the country, visiting the houses of farmers, and even of the gentry, warning them not to raise the price of provisions, and also asking for employment. Notices continued to be distributed, and posted up in public places, calling assemblies of the people in various towns of the South, in order to discuss their existing state and future prospects. A notice posted on the chapel of Carrigtwohill, calling one of those meetings, warned such as absented themselves that they would be marked men, as there was famine in the parish, and they should have food or blood. The priests of the place advised and warned their flocks against those illegal proceedings, and the evils to themselves which must necessarily spring from them. This had the desired effect, and the objects contemplated by the promulgators of the notice were entirely foiled. At Macroom, crowds of working men paraded the streets, calling for work or food. Food they urgently required, no doubt, for two of those in the gathering fell in the street from hunger. One, a muscular-looking young man, was unable to move from the spot where he sank exhausted, until some nourishment was brought to him, which revived him.[166] At Killarney, a crowd, preceded by a bellman and a flag of distress, paraded the streets, but the leaders were arrested and lodged in Bridewell. In the neighbourhood of Skibbereen, the people employed in breaking stones for macadamizing the roads struck work, and marched into the town in a body, asserting that the wages they were receiving was insufficient to support them. The overseer alleged that enough of work had not been done by the men, and that task work should be introduced. Their answer was, that the stones given them to break, being large field stones, *were as hard as anvils*, and they could not break more of them in a given time than they had done; and that death by starvation was preferable to the sufferings they had already endured.

Those men worked some miles from Skibbereen, at a place called Caheragh, and before their arrival, the wildest rumours were afloat as to their coming and intentions. It was Wednesday, the 30th of September. At twelve o'clock on that day, the principal inhabitants met to consult with Mr. Galwey, the magistrate, as to what course they should adopt in the emergency. Whilst thus engaged, Dr. Donovan, who had been on professional duty, rode in from the country, and announced that a body of men, consisting, as far as he could judge, of from eight hundred to a thousand, appeared on the outskirts of the town. They were marching in regular order, ten deep. Twenty-two years after the event, Dr. Donovan thus narrates the cause of this extraordinary movement, and the impression made upon his mind by the terrible phalanx, on its appearance before the trembling town of Skibbereen: "Some difficulty," he says, "occasionally arose in making out the pay lists," and as the people were entirely dependent for their day's support on their day's wages, great suffering and inconvenience resulted from the slightest delay. In addition to these causes of inconvenience, supplies of food had sometimes to be procured, and on this particular occasion serious consequences had nearly resulted from the obstinacy of an official, (a Mr. H—,) a commissariat officer, who boasted of his experience in matters of the kind, during the Peninsular campaigns of the Duke of Wellington, and who refused to allow any food to be sold to the people, although ready money was offered on the spot. An additional difficulty arose when it was made known that extensive works in the neighbourhood, upon which over one thousand persons had been employed, were stopped. Great excitement was the result, and it was determined by the whole body of workmen employed upon the Caheragh relief works, to march into Skibbereen, levy contributions, and enforce compliance with their demands. About twelve o'clock in the day, a number of persons, amounting to about a thousand, marched in the direction of the town, and had nearly reached their destination before the fact was made known. I believe I was, myself, one of the first who saw the approach of those once stalwart men, but now emaciated spectres; and cannot describe adequately the interesting appearance of the body, as they marched along, bearing upon their shoulders their implements of labour, such as spades, shovels, etc., which, in the glitter of a blazing sun, produced a most surpassing effect. Immediately a most exciting scene took place. Under the apprehension that shops would be rifled, shutters were put up and doors were closed. The servants in charge of children hastened to their respective habitations, and everything denoted that a serious onslaught was unavoidable. The military force in the town amounted to seventy-five men, and by the sound of trumpet they were at once summoned to their post, and positive directions were given that under no circumstances should the invading party be allowed to enter the town. The interposition of a long schoolhouse prevented the military from being seen until the party were within twenty yards of the school. The orders were then given to prime and load, and I cannot describe what my feelings were as the clink of the ramrods clearly denoted what was likely to follow. Fortunately, the force upon this occasion was under the command of Mr. Michael Galwey, J.P., a gentleman remarkable for his firmness and courage, his kindness and humanity, and extraordinary influence among the people. When a sanguinary affray was almost inevitable, he took advantage of a temporary lull, and cried out in a stentorian voice: "Three cheers for the Queen, and plenty of employment to-morrow," a call which was immediately responded to in the best manner that the weakened vocal powers of the multitude would admit of. The threatening aspect of affairs was completely changed. Mr. G., in his own familiar phraseology, said, "H—, we must get the biscuits, and we will all then go home in good humour." No sooner said than done. The stores were opened, the biscuits were distributed, the price was paid, the effusion of blood was avoided, and this neighbourhood was saved from what in the commencement threatened to be a most fearful calamity.[167]

It may be further mentioned that the people were four hours at the entrance to the town before they finally retired, although repeatedly called upon to do so by Mr. Galwey, who had resorted to the extreme measure of reading the riot act. The people's constant reply was, that they might as well be shot as not, as they had not tasted food for twenty-four hours. Several of the neighbouring gentlemen took an active part in the day's proceedings, as well as Mr. Galwey, more especially Mr. M'Carthy Downing, the present worthy member for the county.

A body of men, numbering about five hundred, marched through Mallow, on their way to the Workhouse, where they began to scale the walls, at the same time exclaiming that they were starving and wanted food. Temporary relief was distributed to them outside the Workhouse, upon which they retired. It was reported that an attack had been made upon Lord Stuart de Decies, on occasion of his attending the special sessions at Clashmore, during which it was said that several persons cried out, "Knock him down;" but his Lordship, in a letter to the newspapers, gave a complete contradiction to this report. A deputation from the magistrates of Clonakilty, consisting of the Rev. Mr. Townsend, the rector, and John O'Hea, Esq., waited on the Lord Lieutenant on the 5th of October. They stated they were deputed by the clergy of all denominations, the magistrates, the gentry, and the people of the district, to lay before Government the utter desolation caused by the destruction of the potato crop; the poor having been for some time past living on cabbage leaves and food of that description. They pressed upon his Excellency the urgent necessity which existed for sending an immediate supply of provisions into the locality. The magistrates, they stated, had directed them to say that they would not be responsible for the peace of the district, if such a supply as would check the exorbitant price of meal were not sent forthwith. At Youghal two ships laden with corn for exportation were stopped by the people, and for some time prevented from sailing. Large numbers assembled at Macroom, with the apparent intention of making an attack upon property; but, through the advice and judicious conduct of Sir David Roche, they dispersed. Horses engaged in carrying corn to the coast for exportation were sometimes shot. In a few places, especially in Connaught, convoys of meal and flour were seized and carried off.

The troops and police had a hard time of it. Detachments of either, or both, had to be despatched to those places in which disturbances had occurred, or were apprehended. Numerous arrests were made in every instance.

A very alarming symptom in those assemblages was that they occurred almost simultaneously, many of them even on the same day, although there is no trace of this being the result of previous organization. At the moment, the whole framework of society in Ireland was shaken and disjointed, and, in fact, on the point of falling into utter confusion; yet there were no manifestations of reckless wickedness—the demands of the people did not go beyond the cry for food and employment, at fair wages.

The Lord Lieutenant issued a proclamation against those food and labour riots, calling on magistrates and others to assist in protecting "the lawful trade in the articles of food." He also announced that the Government works would be stopped, wherever those employed on them manifested a disposition, "by violence, to obtain a higher rate of wages," or to resist the arrangements made by the officers of the Board of Works. His Excellency added, that he desired in an especial manner to thank the ministers of religion, of all persuasions, for their useful and exemplary conduct on the trying occasion of those riots.

The want of conveniently situated mill-power, to grind the Indian and other corn purchased by the Government, caused them for some time great anxiety. It was of the utmost importance to have the means of grinding corn as near as possible to their depôts. Economy, convenience, regularity, despatch, would be secured by it. In reply to inquiries on the subject, it was found that the quantity of corn required for current demands could not be ground within reach of those depôts at all. At Broadhaven and Blacksod Bay, on the western coast, both in the midst of a famished population, there was no available mill-power whatever. Even where mills existed, a new difficulty arose. The policy of the Government was to encourage, as much as possible, private enterprise in supplying food for the people; and this private enterprise had the mills, in many places, pre-engaged. For instance, such was the case at the important stations of Westport and Limerick. Sir Randolph Routh, pressed by this difficulty, wrote to the Treasury, to say he could not altogether forego the Government claim to have, at least, some corn ground at Westport. As to the mill-power at Limerick, it was so uncertain, so dependant on the weather, and so very much required there by the merchants, that he would make no demand upon it. Mr. Lister, however, the official at Westport, dissuaded him from grinding any corn even there. Quoting from a recent Treasury Minute, the passage about not opening the depôts, while food could be obtained by the people from private dealers, at reasonable prices, he continues: "To delay resorting to this alternative, and in order to stimulate exertion, it is, I beg to repeat, absolutely essential that the trade should have the full and exclusive benefit of all the mill-power in its own locality."[168] In a Treasury Minute of September the 8th, the head of the Commissariat is informed that, considering the limited mill-power in the neighbourhood of Westport, and how important it was that private merchants, who had ordered consignments of Indian corn to that port, should have ready means of grinding it, "My Lords" express their opinion, that the supplies intended for the Government depôt at Westport should, if possible, consist only of meal; and they promise to give directions that not only that depôt, but all the Government depôts in Ireland, should, as far as practicable, be replenished with that article.

Mr. Lister, in the letter just cited, encloses to Sir R. Routh, in a tabular form, an account of the mill-power in Westport, Newport, and along the coast of Mayo and Connemara. He informs his Chief that there were, in the extent of country named, ten ordinary mills and twenty "gig" mills in all, capable of grinding one hundred and seventy tons of oatmeal per day. Five of those mills were fit to grind Indian corn, and wheat could be ground at all, except the gig mills. The mill-power of Galway and its vicinity, taking in Loughrea, Gort, Cong, and Tuam, was not so considerable. In that extent there were thirteen mills, capable of grinding about five hundred and twenty tons a-week; but some of these were not available for Government business. All could grind Indian corn. They were entirely dependant on the water-supply: when it failed, which generally happened about the end of September, they had to cease working.[169] Foreseeing the great difficulty of being able to command sufficient mill-power near those places in which their depôts were, the Treasury ordered a return of the mill-power at the chief government victualling establishments on the English coast, as there would be no difficulty in sending meal to Ireland from those places. It was found that the combined available mill-power of Deptford, Portsmouth, and Plymouth could turn out no more than two hundred and fifty quarters a-day.[170] However, it was put in requisition as soon as possible. In addition, Indian corn was ground at the King's mills, Rotherhithe, and by some private mills engaged for the purpose. There were one thousand tons of barley ground in Essex, and some even in the Channel Islands. The mill-power at Deptford was, meantime, increased by an additional engine. If anyone be curious enough to enquire, how the numberless sacks necessary to carry all this meal and corn to Ireland were supplied, the answer is— the Ordnance Department undertook that service, and supplied as many sacks as were required, at 1s. 7-3/4d. each.

The Treasury also put themselves in communication with the authorities in Malta, relative to its mill-power, and the facilities that might exist there for purchasing grain in quantity. The Comptroller of the Victualling Department informed them, that he had twenty pair of stones worked by mules, and twelve pair by steam, and that many private mills could be engaged for hire. All the mills, however, which were worked by mules were required for the fleet, and could not be employed for any other purpose. Referring to the enquiry as to the purchase of grain, he reports that large quantities of wheat were generally kept on sale at Malta. As to quality, he says, Odessa wheat is hard and good, but can only be ground by "lava stones;" Egyptian inferior, the biscuit made from it not being liked; oats were to be had in abundance; barley scarcer, but both of good quality. Mr. Trevelyan, on the part of the Treasury, writes back in these terms to Deputy Commissary-General Ibbotson: "It is my wish that a considerable quantity of grain should be purchased at once, consisting altogether of Indian corn, if it is to be procured, or, if not, partly of Indian corn, and partly of barley, oats, and *wheat of an inferior, but wholesome quality.*"[171]

In compliance with this order, a purchase of five hundred salms, or quarters, of Indian corn was at once made, and the mills were set to work; but there were not such stocks of grain in Malta as reported at first, and once again the Secretary of the Treasury expresses his suspicions that the French had been making food purchases in the Mediterranean.[172]

To enable the people to be, to some extent, independent of mill-power, it occurred to the authorities to revive the use of the old Irish hand-mill, or quern. This very ancient and rude contrivance had been employed in many countries as well as our own; nor had it as yet fallen into complete desuetude in parts of Scotland and the Shetland Islands. Mr. Trevelyan had seen it with the army in India, and he hoped by getting samples of various kinds of quern, to have one constructed that would be of considerable importance in the present crisis, especially in very out-of-the-way districts. In September, Lord Monteagle, who showed much practical good sense and kindheartedness throughout the famine, called the attention of the Treasury to this matter, and requested that some steel mills and querns should be placed at the disposal of the Commissariat officer on duty in his district; for, said he, the markets are rising, and the people, by buying corn and grinding it for themselves, will have food cheaper than if they bought meal; and moreover they can thus occupy old people for whom no other employment can be found. The quern, adds his lordship (alluding to Matt. c. 24, v. 41) is literally the Scripture mill—"two women shall be grinding at the mill," etc. As to the steel mills, such as those used for grinding coffee, they were considered too expensive to be brought into use; mills of this description, specially tempered to grind Indian corn, not being purchasable even in quantity at a less cost than from four to five pounds each. Curiously enough, the Treasury could not obtain specimens of the Scotch or Irish quern, so they procured an Indian one, from the museum of the India House. They also got a French hand-mill, which was considered superior at least to the Indian one. The attempt to revive the use of the quern had no success except in a single instance. Captain Mann, the officer in charge at Kilkee, induced a coast-guard there to take to quern making. This man turned out querns at from ten to twelve shillings each, and got a ready sale for them; Mr. Trevelyan recommended them to all, but it would seem their sale was confined to the locality.

The Irish mill-power given above was considerable for the extent of the district, but as the machinery was worked exclusively by water, the mills, of course, were idle when the water supply failed. Towards the end of September the mills in and about Westport could not, on this account, execute the orders of the corn merchants, to say nothing of the Government business. Captain Perceval, who had charge of the district, under the Relief Commissariat Department, called attention to this fact, and suggested that *whole* corn should be issued from the depôt, which could be cooked without being ground into meal. He says he had made a trial of this plan, by steeping the grain at night, and boiling it next morning; in this manner it made what he terms "a very nice podge," like pease-pudding, and, to his taste, preferable to stirabout. The Treasury called Sir R. Routh's attention to this suggestion, deeming it important to be able to turn Indian corn into a palatable food, without being either ground or bruised. Commissary-General Hewitson prepared a memorandum on the subject, and put it in circulation, especially amongst the Relief Committees. How far the recommendation was acted on does not appear.[173]

FOOTNOTES:

159.   A deputation from the island of Achill had an interview with Sir R. Routh, at his office, on Saturday night, October the 10th. The deputation stated the peculiar circumstances of Achill—the total destruction of the potato

crop there, and the absence of grain crops in any quantity, owing to the exposed position of the island. The principal object of the deputation was to procure a supply of food from the Government Stores, for which the inhabitants were ready to pay. Sir R. Routh replied, that no supply of food of any consequence could be expected before the latter end of November, and that even then it was not his intention to recommend to the Government to sell the food at a price lower than that demanded by the merchants, as it was essential to the success of commerce that the mercantile interests should not be interfered with. Rev. Mr. Monahan, one of the deputation, remarked that the Government acted differently last year, and sold cheap for the purpose of bringing down the markets. Sir R. Routh admitted the fact, but regretted it, as it gave bad habits to the people, and led them to expect the adoption of a similar course now, whereas the Government was determined not to interfere with the merchants, but to act more in accordance with the enlightened principles of political economy. Rev. Mr. Monahan said he could not understand why the Government was to be fettered by notions of political economy at such a crisis as this. Sir R. Routh remarked that nothing was more essential to the welfare of a country than strict adherence to free trade, and begged to assure the rev. gentleman that, if he had read carefully and studied Burke, his illustrious countryman, he would agree with him, Sir R. Routh.

This interview called forth much sarcastic commentary from the press. "And so," writes the *Nation*, "there is a military gentleman in Dublin, having the control of all public relief operations throughout the country, whose answer to all deputations—whose sole fixed idea—whose Bible and Articles-of-War—appears to be the 'strict rules' and 'the enlightened principles of political economy.' People come to him from the extreme west, and tell him there is in their parish neither potatoes nor corn—that they have neither stores at home, nor trade from other places; and ask him, as 'Commissary-General,' and public relief officer, what he is to do with them? The epauletted philosopher strait replies that trade must take its course (such was the word of command), that 'nothing was more essential to the welfare of a country' (so it was written in the orderly book) 'than strict adherence to the principles of free trade;' and that if the deputation doubted it, they might read Burke." A leading morning journal remarked, that Sir R. Routh's reply to the Achill deputation had not even the merit of originality; for there was an Eastern story, in which it was related how a deputation of Sheiks came, once upon a time, to the Calif, and announced the sad intelligence that all their date trees had withered, and his subjects were perishing throughout the region whence they had come. They demanded assistance: but before the Calif could make any reply, an old Moollah, who stood by, told them to return home *and read the Koran,—Freeman's Journal.*

160.   Commissariat Series, p. 6.
161.   *Ib.* p. 15.
162.   *Ib.* p. 16.
163.   Treasury Minute, Sept. 29. Commissariat Series, p. 63.
164.   Letter to Mr. Trevelyan, dated 19th Sept. Commissariat Series p. 80.
165.   Commissariat Series, p. 208.
166.   *Cork Examiner.*
167.   MS. Memoir of his experience during the Famine, kindly written for the author by Daniel Donovan, Esq., M.D., Skibbereen.
168.   Commissariat Series, part I, p. 46.
169.   Commissariat Series, part I, p. 55.
170.   *Ib.* p. 50.
171.   Commissariat Series, p. 122.
172.   Mr. Trevelyan gives the following caution to the Commissary-General at Malta: "I am told that the Egyptian wheat is mixed with the mud of the Nile; and if such be the case, it will, of course, be washed before it is ground."— Commissariat Series, p. 156.

   Salm was the word used at Malta for "quarter," being, probably, a corruption of the Spanish *salma*, a ton.
173.   In some parts of Ireland there existed a custom of boiling new wheat in this manner, but without steeping. It was merely intended as a mess for children, in order to give them the first of the wheat at reaping time, but was not continued as a mode of cooking it. This mess was called in, Irish *gran bruitead*, (pron. *grawn breehe*), *boiled* or *cooked grain.*

* * * * *

CHAPTER IX.

The Landlords and the Government—Public Meetings—Reproductive Employment demanded for the People—The "Labouchere" Letter—Presentments under it—Loans asked to construct Railways—All who received incomes from land should be taxed—Deputation from the Royal Agricultural Society to the Lord Lieutenant—They ask reproductive employment—Lord Bessborough answers cautiously—The Prime Minister writes to the Duke of Leinster on the subject—Views expressed—Defence of his Irish Famine policy—Severe on the Landlords—Unsound principles laid down by him—Corn in the haggards—Mary Driscoll's little stack of barley—Second Deputation from the Royal Agricultural Society to the Lord Lieutenant—Its object—Request not granted—The Society lectured on the duties of its Members—Real meaning of the answer—Progress of the Famine—Deaths from starvation—O'Brien's Bridge—Rev. Dr. Vaughan—Slowness of the Board of Works—State of Tuam—Inquest on Denis M'Kennedy—Testimony of his Wife—A Fortnight's Wages due to him—Received only half-a-crown in three weeks—Evidence of the Steward of the Works; of Rev. Mr. Webb; of Dr. Donovan—Remarks of Rev. Mr. Townsend—Verdict—The *Times* on the duties of landlords—Landlords denounce the Government and the Board of Works—Mr. Fitzgerald on the Board and on the farmers—Meeting at Bandon—Lord Bernard—Inquest on Jeremiah Hegarty—The Landlord's "cross" on the barley—Mary Driscoll's evidence; her husband's—*Post mortem* examination by Dr. Donovan—The Parish Priest of Swinford—Evictions—The *Morning Chronicle* on them—Spread and Increase of Famine—The question of providing coffins—Deaths at Skibbereen—Extent of the Famine in 1846—Deaths in Mayo—Cases—Edward M'Hale—Skibbereen—The diary of a day—Swelling of the extremities—Burning beds for fuel—Mr. Cummins's account of Skibbereen—Killarney Relief Committee—Father O'Connor's Statement—Christmas Eve!—A Visit to Skibbereen twenty years after the great Famine.

As events progressed, the landlords of Ireland appeared to grow more and more alarmed, not so much for the people as for themselves; and they held meetings and passed resolutions, censuring the Government for the mode which it had chosen of counteracting the Famine. The Government and its organs returned the compliment by pointing out the inaction and obstructive policy of the landlords.

At those meetings it was invariably one of the resolutions, that labour should be employed upon productive works. The common-sense principle contained in this expression of opinion could not be denied: it was, indeed, the general opinion of the country; still every one felt that it would require time to develop such works—the starving millions must be fed, or at least the attempt must be made to feed them; they could not wait for tedious preliminaries, and more tedious surveys, and no other means existed to supply their daily food, but those afforded by the Labour-rate Act.[174] But very early in the business, as soon as a famine seemed imminent, it was urged by men of weight and character, that reproductive works should and could be found for the people. Yes; and it was a fatal error—it was worse than an error, it was a crime, not to have adopted, at the earliest moment, the principle of reproductive employment. At length the Government felt the force of this logic, and did, although late, make an attempt to lessen the effects of their own great blunder. On the 5th of October, the "Labouchere letter" came out, authorizing reproductive works, the very thing the landlords were agitating for; now that their agitation was successful, what did they do? Nothing, or next to nothing, except that they opened a new cause of disagreement with the Government about boundaries. In the Chief Secretary's letter the Government followed the subdivisions of electoral districts, as they had been doing before; the landlords insisted on townland boundaries, and would not be content with—would not act under—any other. Their opponents said this was merely to cause delay; some even asserted it was an attempt to turn the whole system of public works to their own private advantage; a contrivance of the landlords, they said, to enjoy just so many jobs unmolested. The request about the change of boundaries was not granted; and so the Labouchere letter was not acted upon to the extent which it ought to have been. The entire amount presented under the letter was £380,607, of which presentments were acted on to the gross amount of £239,476. The sum actually expended was about £180,000; and the largest number of persons at any time employed was 26,961, which was in the month of May, 1847.[175]

Another demand which the landlords put in the shape of a resolution was, that the Government should advance loans for the construction of railways in Ireland. This the Government also refused, or rather, they insisted on conditions that amounted to a refusal. They said proper security could not be had for the advancement of the money; they therefore resolved not to make any advances to Irish Railways, except in the ordinary way, namely, by application to the Exchequer Loan Commissioners, when fifty per cent of the subscribed capital would be paid up. Could they not have made railways themselves, as they were afterwards almost compelled to do by Lord George Bentinck, in which case they would have had something for their money?

The landlords also made a demand which must be regarded as a fair one: it was that all who received incomes from the land should be taxed for the relief of the people. This was pointed at absentees, but still more at mortgagees.

The Royal Agricultural Society of Ireland, a society mainly representing landlord and aristocratic views, of which the Duke of Leinster was president, took up, as became it, the great labour question of the moment. A deputation from that body waited on the Lord Lieutenant, on the 25th of September, and laid its views before his Excellency. The members of the deputation open the interview at the Viceregal Lodge by enunciating the good and sound principle, "that it is the clear and imperative duty of the possessors of property in Ireland, to avert from their poor fellow-countrymen the miseries of famine; and that they, therefore, willingly acquiesce in the imposition upon them of any amount of taxation necessary for that purpose." They go on to say, that as a very large sum must be raised on the security of Irish property, and expended upon labour, during the continuance of the distress occasioned by the failure of the potato crop, the expenditure of this sum upon unproductive works will increase the disproportion already existing between labour and capital in the country; which disproportion they look on as the main cause of the want of employment for the people, and of the miserable wages they are sustained by. Reproductive work, they continue, is the only work on which the labour of the population ought to be employed, and plenty of such work was to be found in every part of the country. It would improve the soil, and return the ratepayers a large interest for the capital expended. The Board of Works, they suggest, might be empowered to postpone the public works ordered by the presentment sessions, whenever they saw fit, and also to suspend the portion of money voted for that purpose on any townland, and have it applied to the carrying out of reproductive works, according to the requisition of the owners and ratepayers of such townland; such works, in every case, to be approved of by at least three-fourths of the ratepayers.

Lord Bessborough gave a short, and, of course, a cautious answer to the deputation, saying that he would give his best consideration to the proposal; consult the Government, and in a few days let them know the result. The "Labouchere Letter," authorizing reproductive works, was the response to this memorial of the Royal Agricultural Society. But it received another answer, and that from the Prime Minister himself. The question of productive and non-productive labour was so important, that, some time after the publication of the Labouchere Letter, Lord John Russell discussed it, in a communication addressed by him to the Duke of Leinster, as president of the Royal Agricultural Society.

After a passing allusion to the deputation that waited on the Lord Lieutenant, he at once takes the landlords to task. "It had been our hope and expectation," he says, "that landed proprietors would have commenced works of drainage and other improvements, on their own account: thus employing the people on their own estates, and rendering the land more productive for the future. The Act, [the Labour-rate Act,] however, was put in operation in the baronies in a spirit the reverse of that which I have described . . . When the case was brought before the Government by the Lord Lieutenant, we lamented the wrong direction in which the Act had been turned; but admitting the necessity of the case, and anxious to obtain the willing co-operation of the landlords, we authorized the Lord Lieutenant to deviate from the letter of the law, and gave our sanction for advances for useful and profitable works of a private nature. But after having incurred the responsibility, I am sorry to see that, in several parts of Ireland, calls are made upon the Government, to undertake and perform tasks which are beyond their power, and apart from the duties of Government." The political-economy Premier then enunciates this principle: "Any attempt to feed one class of the people of the United Kingdom by the Government, would, if successful, starve another part—would feed the producers of potatoes, which had failed, by starving the producers of wheat, barley, and oats, which had not failed." He proceeds: "That which is not possible by a Government is possible by individual and social exertions. Everyone who travels through Ireland observes the large stacks of corn, which are the produce of the late harvest. There is nothing to prevent the purchase of grain by proprietors or committees, and the disposal of these supplies in shops furnished on purpose with flour at a fair price, with a moderate profit. This has been done, I am assured, in parts of the Highlands of Scotland, where the failure of the potatoes has been as great and as severe a calamity as it has been in Ireland.[176] There is, no doubt, some inconvenience attending even these modes of interference with the market price of food; but the good over-balances the evil. Local committees or agents of landowners can ascertain the pressure of distress, measure the wants of a district, and prevent waste and misapplication. Besides, the general effect is to bring men together, and induce them to exert their energy in a social effort directed to one spot; whereas the interference of the State deadens private energy, prevents forethought—and after superseding all other exertion, finds itself, at last, unequal to the gigantic task it has undertaken." Towards the end of his letter, the First Minister gives his views on another point or two. "One thing," he writes, "is certain—in order to enable Ireland to maintain her population, her agriculture must be greatly improved. Cattle, corn, poultry, pigs, eggs, butter, and salt provisions have been, and will probably continue to be, her chief articles of export. But beyond the food exchanged for clothing and colonial products, she will require, in future, a large supply of food of her own growth and produce, which the labourer should be able to buy with his wages."

There can be little doubt but the Premier intended this letter as a defence of his Irish-famine policy. As such it is not very conclusive. It is quite true to say, that the landlords should have exerted themselves far more than they did, to employ the people in improving their estates, by draining, subsoiling, and reclamation; which works were sure to be remunerative, and at no distant time. But had they done all this, Lord John Russell could take no credit to himself for it, having done nothing to induce or compel them to do so. When he says he expected it, he shows great ignorance or forgetfulness. The Irish landlords, as a class, were not improvers of their properties before the Famine;—how could he expect them to become so at such a crisis, when many of them feared, with reason, that both themselves and the people would be swallowed up in one common ruin? Besides, most of the wealthy proprietors were Englishmen or absentees, who, with few exceptions, never saw their tenants; took no friendly interest in them, but left them in the hands of agents, who were prized by their employers in proportion to their punctuality in sending the half-yearly remittances, no questions being asked as to the means by which they were obtained.[177] How could the Prime Minister pretend to think that such men would rush into the midst of a famine-stricken people, to relieve, employ, and improve them? He knew, or ought to have known, they would do no such thing, except on compulsion, and there was no compulsion in the case; he being, he said, for "willing co-operation" only. His government has certainly a right to be credited with the praiseworthy attempt it made to turn the labour of the Irish people to profitable work, but it came too late for immediate practical purposes. Planning, surveying, and laying out improvements take much time. The principle contained in the "Labouchere Letter" should have been embodied in an Act of Parliament, and reclamation of waste lands made compulsory, as had been advocated by many. The publication of that letter was, no doubt, the confession of a previous error, but it was also a concession to a present demand, and with active hearty co-operation it could be still turned to great advantage. Lord John is right in blaming the landlords for not making use of the powers conferred by it. They, above all others, called the loudest for reproductive employment, but when it was sanctioned, they raised new difficulties about boundaries and other matters, which looked very like a determination not to carry into practical effect the permission granted, it may be fairly said, at their own request.

When Lord John says, that "any attempt to feed one class of people of the United Kingdom by the Government, would, if successful, starve another part," he is rather puzzling. One is tempted to think that he originally wrote—"Any attempt to feed one class of people of the United Kingdom *at the expense of another class*, would, if successful, starve the latter," and that by some mistake of the writer or printer, the words in italics were omitted. As the sentence stands in his letter, it is strangely inexact. 1. In case one portion of the people had raised more food than was required for their own wants—a most common case, they would not surely starve by the fact of the Government buying their surplus for another portion who were starving—no, but they would thank the Government very much for buying it. There would be no danger of their finding fault with the quality of their customer, provided they got their price. 2. What are Governments for, if not for the good of the people?—and the Government that sees millions of its people dying of starvation, with none others to help them, neglect the very first duty of a Government—the *salus populi*—unless they make all the efforts in their power to relieve and save them. 3. Besides, to feed one part of the people—the starving Irish people—is just the thing Lord John's Government did attempt to do, although badly. There is, moreover, a fallacy in calling the Irish people, in every instance, a class of people of the United Kingdom, for they have often been, and still are, treated as a distinct and separate nation, or class of people. In such a case it is assumed that our interests and those of England and Scotland are identical, whereas they are no such thing. We used to be legislated for separately, and in many instances we are so legislated for to-day, which need not be the case if Lord Russell's assumption were true. Again: England is a great manufacturing country, whilst Ireland has no manufactures; from the nature of things the interests of two such peoples could not be identical, and yet Lord John Russell and many others talk and write about Ireland as a portion of the people of the United Kingdom, in the sense that we are partakers of the great material prosperity that manufactures have brought to England, which is supposing that a fair proportion of the manufactures of the United Kingdom are established and flourishing in Ireland: but so far from this being the case,—so far from Lord John's political ancestors having supposed the interests of England and Ireland to be identical, they never ceased, until by a code of unjust and tyrannical commercial laws, they destroyed all the manufactures we had, in order, as they avowed, to encourage the same manufactures in England. What position did we then occupy as a class of people of the United Kingdom?

Where were Lord John's wonderful free trade principles then? The time had not come for them. No; but when his countrymen had monopolized our manufactures by shameful prohibitions; when England had become supreme as a manufacturing nation, and when she wanted cheap bread for her artizans and markets for her wares, then arose the anti-Cornlaw League; then, but not till then, did Free Trade become the only saving gospel with enlightened English politicians.

Lord John speaks of the corn in the haggards of Ireland. There was, I believe, much corn in some of them, at the time he addressed his letter to the Duke of Leinster. Why did not the Government buy it, instead of sending to America and Malta for Indian corn and bad wheat? Had his lordship ascertained, before he wrote, how many of the stacks in Irish haggards *had the landlord's cross upon them for the rent*, like poor Mary Driscoll's little stack of barley at Skibbereen? *It stood in her haggard* while her father, who resided with her, died of starvation in a neighbouring ditch![178]

About the middle of November, the Royal Agricultural Society again approached the Queen's representative in Ireland by memorial. It was not this time for leave to commence reproductive works,—that had been already granted; they came now to prove that reproductive works could *not* be undertaken under the provisions of Mr. Secretary Labouchere's letter. They assure his Excellency that the letter gave them much satisfaction; that, on its appearance, they directed their immediate attention to the introduction of reproductive works in their respective districts; but on account of one or more of the reasons they were about to lay before him, their opinion was, that, in the majority of cases, it was "impossible" to carry out his Excellency's views in the manner required by the Letter: 1. Because it was scarcely possible to find works in any electoral division of such universal benefit as would render them profitable or reproductive to all owners and occupiers in such divisions.[179] 2. Because by the terms of the letter, *drainage in connection with subsoiling* appeared to be the only work of a private character allowed as a substitute for public works, whereas, in many districts, this class of work was not required, whilst others, such as clearing, fencing, and making farm roads, were. 3. Because, in case of works, the cost of which was to be made an exclusive charge on the lands to be improved, as specified in the letter, it was necessary for the just operation of the system, that each proprietor should undertake his own portion of the sum to which the electoral division would be assessed, and unanimity, so essential on this point, was seldom attainable. For instance, townlands were chiefly in the hands of separate proprietors, of whom many were absentees, whose consent it would be almost impossible to obtain; others were lunatics, infants, tenants for life, in which cases impediments existed to the obtaining of the required guarantee; others again were embarrassed; some, too, might prefer the work on the public roads to private works, and their opposition could counteract the wishes of the majority. 4. In practice it could not be expected, that a proprietor would submit both to the direct charge incurred for drainage or other improvement of his property, and likewise to that proportion of the general rate, which would be cast upon him by the refusal of other proprietors to undertake their own portion. Such a state of things would not only involve the enterprising proprietor in a double expense, but would, in precisely the same proportion, relieve his negligent neighbours from their allotted share of the burthen.

The memorialists, therefore, prayed that each proprietor, or combination of two or more proprietors, who might be willing to charge their proportion of the rate for employing the poor upon any particular land to be improved thereby, should be relieved to that extent, from the payment of rate, and that the works so to be undertaken should not be confined to drainage or subsoiling, but might include all works of a productive nature, suited to the wants of the locality for which they were proposed, provided only, that such works should meet the approbation of the Board of Works.

This carefully prepared memorial was met by a refusal, the reasons given for which do not seem very cogent; the real reason, in all probability, not having been directly given at all; the impossibility of supervising townland improvements, with such care as to avoid the malversation and misapplication of funds, having, it is reasonable to suppose, great influence on the decision of the Government. The reasons given by Lord Bessborough for the refusal were: 1. That he saw great practical difficulties would be attendant on any attempt to carry the townland-boundary plan into execution; and—2. That he also believed it would be inconsistent with the primary object of the Poor Employment Act, which, he said, was meant to meet, as far as possible, the present exigency of the season, by providing sustenance for the destitute, through the means of labour, in the most available manner of which the circumstances of the case would admit. In giving the option of reproductive work, his Excellency said he had taken upon himself "a responsibility;" but that the option was conceded with as little departure as possible from the spirit of the measures sanctioned by Parliament; whereas the adoption of the townland, instead of the electoral division, would, in many cases, lead to the greatest expenditure, where the amount of destitution was least. Perhaps his Excellency gave his real reason, when he concluded with something stronger than a hint to the Royal Agricultural Society, which comprised, as he said, the leading gentry of the country. He calls upon them to discharge their duties in their various localities, and to avoid or prevent the misapplication of the funds given for the relief of the really destitute. He cannot, he says, forego the opportunity of expressing an earnest hope that they will, in their various relief committees, lend their aid to the Government in resisting a practice which, he has reason to fear, has very extensively prevailed—namely, "that of allowing persons, who are by no means in a destitute condition, to be employed upon the public works, thus depriving the really distressed of the benefit which was intended for them, as well as withdrawing from the ordinary cultivation of the soil the labour which was essential to the future subsistence of the people."[180]

The latter part of the answer means just this: that the landlords were already turning the public works to their private gain, by getting numbers of their well-to-do tenants, often with their carts and horses, upon those works, in order to obtain their own rents more securely; a practice of which they were repeatedly accused by the Board of Works' people; and that, therefore, if townland boundaries were conceded, the landlords would have increased power, and a still greater amount of the same kind of jobbing would be the inevitable result.

It is not surprising that at this period society in Ireland was shaken to its foundations. Terror and dismay pervaded every class; the starving poor suffered so intensely, and in such a variety of ways, that it becomes a hard task either to narrate or listen to the piteous story; it sickens and wrings the heart, whilst it fills the eyes with the testimony of irrepressible sorrow. To say the people were dying by the thousand of sheer starvation conveys no idea of their sufferings; the expression is too general to move our feelings. To think that even one human creature should, in a rich and a Christian land, die for want of a little bread, is a dreadful reflection; and yet, writes an English traveller in Ireland, the thing is happening before my eyes every day, within a few hours of London, the Capital of the Empire, and the richest city in the world.

O'Brien's Bridge is a small town on the borders of Limerick, but in the County Clare. The accounts received from this place during the first half of October were, that nothing could restrain the people from rising *en masse* but an immediate supply of food. On one of the admission days, one hundred and thirty persons were taken into the Scariff Workhouse, out of six thousand applicants! Scariff is the union in which O'Brien's Bridge and Killaloe are situate. Of Killaloe, the Rev. Dr. Vaughan, afterwards Bishop of the Diocese, wrote, about the same time, that there was some promise of fifty or sixty being employed out of six hundred. The Relief Committee, of which he was a member, had to borrow money on the stones broken by the poor labourers for macadamizing the roads, in order to pay them their wages. Being paid, they were dismissed, as the Committee could not, in any way, get funds to employ them further. "We are a pretty Relief Committee," exclaims the reverend gentleman, "not having a quart of meal, or the price of it, at our disposal." He adds, with somewhat of sorrow and vexation of spirit: "When those starving creatures ask us for bread, we could give them stones, if they were not already mortgaged."

Employment was not, and, with the appliances in the hands of the Board of Works, perhaps, could not be given rapidly and extensively enough for the vast and instant wants of the people. Hunger is impatient, and the cry of all men—loudest from the South and West—was one of despair, mingled with denunciations of the Government and the Board of Works for their slowness in providing work, and, if possible, still more, for their refusal to open the food depôts. "I am sorry to tell you," writes the correspondent of a local print, "that this town [Tuam] is, I may say, in open rebellion. They are taking away cattle in the open day, in spite of people and police . . . They cannot help it; even if they had money, they could not get bread to buy." Works were often marked out for a considerable time before they were commenced. At a place called Lackeen, in the South, they were in that state for three weeks or more, without any employment having been given. If this goes on, writes a resident of the locality, there must be an increase of coroners, and a decrease of civil engineers. "It is coffins," says another, "must now be sent into the country. I lately gave three coffins to bury some of the poor in my neighbourhood." This was bad enough; but a time was at hand when the poor had to bury their dead without coffins.

Three weeks had scarcely elapsed from the day on which the labourers engaged on the Caharagh road had shouldered their spades and picks, and marched to Skibbereen, when an inquest upon one of them laid open a state of things that no general description could convey. A man named Denis M'Kennedy was employed on those works. He was found dead on the side of the road one day, and a coroner's inquest was held upon his remains in the historic graveyard of Abbeystrowry. The evidence will tell the rest. Johanna M'Kennedy, the wife of the deceased, was the first witness examined. She said her husband died on Saturday, the 24th of October, and had been at work on the Caharagh road *the day he died*. He had been so engaged for about three weeks before his death. He did not complain of being sick. She explained to the coroner and the jury what they had had to support them during the week, on the Saturday of which her husband died. Her family was five in number. She had nothing, she said, to give them on Monday; and then the poor woman varied her mode of expression by saying they had nothing at all to eat on Tuesday. On Wednesday *night* she boiled for her husband and the family one head of cabbage, given to her by a neighbour, and about a pint of flour, which she got for a basket of turf she had sold in Skibbereen. On Thursday morning her husband had nothing to eat. She does not account for Friday; but on Saturday morning she sent him for his breakfast less than a pint of flour baked. Poor creature! she had but a pint for the whole family; but in her loving anxiety to sustain her husband, who was trying to earn for them, she only kept "a little" for the children. "The rest was sent to him," said Mrs. M'Kennedy, through her choking grief, "but it was too late; before it arrived he was dead." Thus, through the whole of that, to her dreadful week, she had for her family of five persons about half a weight of potatoes,[181] small and bad, which were given to her by a kind neighbour, Mick Sweeney (God bless him, she said, for he often relieved us), two pints of flour, and one head of cabbage. It is no great marvel that the man who was trying to work on his share of such provision was dead on Saturday. In M'Kennedy we have a specimen of the people to whom the Board of Works insisted on giving task work. "For the three weeks he was at work," said his wife at the inquest, "he got two shillings and sixpence, being one week's pay." There was a fortnight's wages due to him the day he died. "Even if his hire was regularly paid," she added, "it would not support the family; but it would enable us to drag on life, and he would be alive to-day."

Jeremiah Donovan, the steward of the works at Caharagh, deposed that M'Kennedy was at work the morning of the day on which he died. On that morning he saw the deceased leave his work and go to the ditch-side; seeing him stop so long, he told him to return to his work. He did not return, but said to deponent, "How can a man work without food?— a man that did not eat anything since yesterday morning." Deponent then handed him a bit of bread. He took it in his hand and was putting it to his mouth when it fell from him. He died in two or three hours after. His pay was eight pence a day.

The Rev. Mr. Webb, incumbent of Caharagh, then volunteered a statement—hear it, ye rich, who have not that mercy and compassion for His poor, which the God of all so strictly requires at your hands,—"I have been told by some on the road," said the Rev. gentleman, "that this poor man has frequently divided amongst the labourers his own scanty food."

There were two physicians at the inquest, of whom Dr. Donovan was one; having made a *post-mortem* examination, no disease was discovered that could account for death. There was no food in the stomach or small intestines, but a portion of raw, undigested cabbage. The physicians said they had seen hundreds of dead bodies, but declared they had never seen one so attenuated as that of M'Kennedy. The representative of the Board of Works, when asked to explain why it was that a fortnight's wages was due to M'Kennedy, said, that the money was sent to the wrong pay-clerk. It had really come, but through some mistake, had been sent to Mr. Notter, and was by him expended in payment of his own district, when it should have been paid on the Caharagh line. "But these stories," he added, "received in gossip, are turned against the Board of Works." It is not very clear what this official meant by stories, but there is one thing plain enough in the matter: Mr. Notter's men must have been in arrear of their pay as well as those on the Caharagh works, or there could be no opportunity of expending the Caharagh money upon them. If Mr. Notter had got his own money together with the Caharagh money, he certainly would not require both remittances. There is another thing pretty obvious too: if the money had been directed to the overseer of the Caharagh works, Mr. Notter would not be justified in paying it away to his workmen. In reference to the flippant pertness of the Board's officials, the Rev. Mr. Townsend, the incumbent of Abbeystowry, said: "We have here M'Kennedy's death and the cause of it sworn to. That evidence proves that our people are dying by the ditch-side for want of payment of their hire. We take no such statements, sir, on gossip, nor shall we be told we do." The jury returned the following verdict: "We find that the said Denis M'Kennedy, on the 24th day of October, in the year aforesaid, at Caharagh, in the county aforesaid, died of starvation, owing to the gross negligence, of the Board of Works."

The *Times*, commenting on Lord John Russell's letter to the Duke of Leinster, said: "We in England consider it the first duty of the landlord to provide extraordinary employment to meet extraordinary distress; we do not wait until an Act of Parliament converts a duty into a necessity. In Ireland, even with special facilities, it has been very sparingly and tardily done."[182] This remark about Irish landlords has much truth in it. They took every means of shifting responsibility upon the Government; they lost no opportunity of publicly declaring and of endeavouring to prove that the duty of employing the people rested with the Government and not with them: then, when the vast system of Relief Works which sprang up under the hands of the Government in two or three short months did not prove perfectly satisfactory, it became quite the fashion with the landlord class to denounce the Board of Works, and through it the Government. To be sure there was much reason for this, but the landlords, of all others, had no right to cast the stone; for, in the interests of truth and justice it must be said, that the Government made some efforts to save the people, whilst the landlords as a body, made none whatever. Their views were put in a striking manner at a meeting of landowners and farmers held at Aghada, in the County Cork. Mr. Fitzgerald, a landowner, attacked the Board for doing unprofitable work.

They had, he said, a staff of incompetent officers, who were, moreover, absurdly numerous, there being, he asserted, an officer for every workman in the works at Whitegate. The reply to this attack is obvious enough. If the Board of Works were doing unprofitable work, they could not help it, they were compelled by Act of Parliament to do it; and when the Government enabled the country to undertake profitable works, where were the landlords? They were in conclaves here and there, elaborating objections to the Government plan, instead of affording aid to carry it into execution; they seemed to make it a point to throw obstacles in its way, and certainly showed anything but a disposition to make it a success. Very likely, the Board of Works had too many officers; doubtless they could not all be competent, or even trustworthy persons, there being ten or eleven thousand of these raked together from all quarters in three months. Mr. Fitzgerald next attacked the farmers for not employing the workmen. In fact, according to him, every class of the community had responsibilities—was called on to make exertions and sacrifices to save the people from famine, except the landlords—the owners of the soil of the entire kingdom. He expressed his opinion, that the proper way to begin the business of the meeting was, to pass a vote of censure on the Board of Works and send it to the Lord Lieutenant. The Chairman, Richard G. Adams, thought Mr. Fitzgerald's suggestion a good one. So it was, from the landlord's point of view; it being their policy to turn attention away from themselves and their shortcomings, and make the Board of Works the scapegoat of all their sins. Mr. Fitzgerald proceeded: the farmers, he said, were banking their money. He had cut out of the *Times* the article on the increase of deposits in the Irish Savings' Banks, which he intended to have read for the meeting, but he had unfortunately mislaid it. No matter, there could be no doubt of the fact. No one present opened his mouth in defence of the unfortunate Board of Works, but a Mr. Kelly took up the cudgels for the farmers. He said, few farmers in that district had money to put in Savings' Banks, but if the farmers had hundreds, as was asserted, surely the gentlemen ought to have millions. When the gentlemen complained of want of means, no wonder the farmers did the same. There was not, Mr. Kelly maintained, enough of corn in the haggards of the country to last until the 1st of June,—

Mr. Fitzgerald: The haggards are in the Savings' Banks.

Mr. Kelly: You will find them in the pockets of a great many landlords. I don't say in yours.[183]

In Bandon there was a somewhat similar meeting. Lord Bernard, who presided, told his hearers in solemn accents that the Government was awfully responsible for not either assembling Parliament, as they were called upon to do, or at least providing effectively for the relief of the people. His lordship recommended the suspension of the Poor Laws as a measure that would be advantageous at the present emergency! Undeveloped though the poor law system was in Ireland at the time of the famine, it still afforded much relief in many places. It is hard to see what Lord Bernard hoped to gain from the suspension of the Poor Laws during the famine, unless exemption from his own share of the rates.

Turning over the public journals during this period is the saddest of sad duties. It is like picking one's way over a battle-field strewn with the dead and dying. "Starvation and death in Dingle;" "Deaths at Castlehaven;" "Death of a labourer on his way to the Workhouse;" "Coroner's inquests in Mayo;" "Four more deaths on the roads at Skibbereen." Such are specimens of the ghastly headings that lie before us. One of those deaths at Skibbereen calls for more than a passing word; it is that of Jeremiah Hegarty. As in M'Kennedy's case we have here what is seldom attainable, an account of the evidence given at the inquest upon his remains. He was a widower and lived with his married daughter, Mary Driscoll, at Licknafon. Driscoll, his son-in-law, was a small farmer. He had a little barley in his haggard, some of which he was from time to time taking privately out of the stack to keep himself and his family from dying of starvation, although Curley Buckley, his landlord's driver,[184] *had put a cross and keepers on it.*

Mary Driscoll, daughter of the deceased, being examined, deposed that her father eat a little barley stirabout on Saturday morning, but had not enough; "none of us," she said, "had enough. We all lived together—nine in family, not including the infant at my breast. My father went to work; my husband worked with him; three pints of barley meal was the only thing we had from Thursday before. *I had no drink for the infant,*" she said; by which, I suppose, the wretched being meant the nourishment which nature supplies to infants whose mothers are not in a state of starvation; "it ate nothing. On Thursday we had nothing but a quarter weight of *Croshanes*.[185] We had but a little barley—about a barrel, and, God help us, we could not eat any more of that same, as the landlord put a cross on it, I mean it was marked for the rent." She here gave the name of the landlord, on being asked to do so. He wanted, she said, to keep the barley for the last rent, £2 17s. She simply and frankly acknowledged they had been taking some of it, but their condition was such that it melted the heart of the landlord's driver, Curley Buckley, who told them "to be taking a little of it until the landlord would come." The poor Driscolls were not bad tenants, they owed their landlord *the last rent only,* but they were responsible for another debt. "We owed," Mary Driscoll said, "ten shillings for the seed of the barley; we would sooner die, all of us, than not to pay. Since a fortnight," continued this wretched woman, in her rude but expressive English; "since a fortnight past, there was not one of us eat enough any day."

Driscoll, the husband of the last witness, was examined. He said: "If he" (meaning the deceased) "was paid the wages due to him for working on the road, it would have relieved him, and he might be now alive; but," he added, "even if we had received the money, it would be hardly sufficient to keep us alive." Referring to his own case, he said he was but one day working on the road, and that he was six weeks looking for that same.

Dr. Donovan had made a *post mortem* examination. He found the stomach and upper part of the intestines totally devoid of food. There was water in the stomach, but nothing else. Want, the doctor said, was the remote—exposure to the cold the immediate—cause of death. The jury found that the deceased, Jeremiah Hegarty, met his death in consequence of the want of sufficient sustenance for many days previous to his decease; and that this want of sustenance was occasioned by his not having been paid his wages on the Public Works, where he was employed for eight days previous to the time of his death.

Instead of providing employment for the tenants on their estates, which the Premier, and his commentator, the *Times*, looked upon as a mere ordinary duty, many Irish landlords began to evict for non-payment of rent. The parish priest of Swinford concludes a letter, detailing the sufferings of his people, thus: "One word as to the landlords. There are several owners of land in this parish (Kilconduff), but not one of them resident. We made an effort to create by subscription a fund for the purpose of keeping a supply of provisions in Swinford, to be sold to the poor in small quantities. The non-resident landlords were applied to, but not *one* of them responded to the call. They are not, however, idle. Their bailiffs are on the alert, distraining for rent, and the pounds are full."[186] In the County Sligo, thirty families were evicted together by one landlord; they must have been one hundred and fifty individuals in all. They were somewhat in arrear. But in other cases the corn was distrained in the beginning of October for rent falling due the previous May. This, in the second year of the Famine, meant eviction, purely for the sake of clearing the soil of its human incumbrances.

A portion of the English press, but a very small one, sympathised with those miserable beings who were cast out of their dwellings to perish by the roadside. The *Morning Chronicle*, in one of its leaders, thus dealt with the subject: "We shall here state at once our opinion, in plain terms, respecting this clearing system, by which a population, which has for generations lived and multiplied on the land, is, on the plea of legal rights, suddenly turned adrift, without a provision, to find a living where there is no living to be found. It is a thing which no pretence of private right or public utility ought to induce society to tolerate for a moment. No legitimate construction of any right of ownership in land, which it is for the interest of society to permit, will warrant it. We hold, at the same time, that to prevent the growth of a redundant population on an estate is not only not blameable, but it is one of the chief duties of a landowner, having the power over his tenants which the Irish system gives. As it is his duty, so it is, on any extended computation, his pecuniary interest. He is to be commended for preventing over population, but to be detested for tolerating first, and then exterminating it."

As the year 1846 wore on to its close, the Famine deepened in intensity, and every day extended itself more and more. The cold, which was very severe in December, became its powerful auxiliary. Wherever the blame is to rest—at head-quarters in Dublin, or with the clerks at the works— the irregularity with which wages were paid by the representatives of the Government, caused terrible suffering and innumerable deaths. Many of those recorded at this period occurred from the taking of food by persons who had been without it for a long time. "Carthy swallowed a little warm milk and died," is the simple announcement of one man's death from starvation; but, with slight variations, it might be given as the record of thousands of deaths as well as Carthy's.

The means of providing coffins for the victims of famine was becoming a serious question, as the survivors in many a poor family could not now attempt to purchase them, as the outlay of a small sum for a coffin might be the cause of further deaths from starvation in the same family. At a meeting in Skibbereen, in the beginning of December, Dr. Donovan said that, since his return from Glandore that morning, he had been followed by a crowd of applicants, seeking coffins for their deceased friends; and he had, he said, just visited a house in the Windmill,[187] where he saw two dead bodies lying, awaiting some means of burial. His opinion was, that they were on the eve of a pestilence that would reach every class. "And," said a gentleman, interrupting, "when I asked a presentment for coffins at the sessions, I was laughed at." Dr. Donovan continued: The case of a man named Sullivan was a most melancholy one. His children began to drop off without any apparent disease, after they had entered the Workhouse. From scarcity of beds, the father and son—the latter being sick and weakly—had to sleep together; and one morning the son was found dead alongside of his father, while another child died in the mother's arms next day. He (Dr. Donovan) had asked Sullivan why he did not tell him his children were sick. His answer was, "They had no complaint." Mr. D. M'Carthy said it would be for the meeting to consider whether they should not pronounce their strong condemnation upon the conduct of an official in the town, who, with starvation staring them in the face, would not give out a pound of food except at famine price, though he had stores crammed with it. "He'd give you," said Mr. Downing, "for £17 a-ton what cost our paternal Government £7 10s."

Dr. Donovan, writing to one of the provincial journals at this time, says: "Want and misery are in every face; and the labourers returning from the relief works look like men walking in a funeral procession, so slow is their step and so dejected their appearance."

The South and West were the portions of the country in which the Famine committed its earliest ravages; but before the close of 1846 considerable parts of Leinster and Ulster were invaded by it, and deaths from starvation began to be recorded in those comparatively wealthy provinces. In Maryborough, a man named William Fitzpatrick died of starvation in the beginning of December. He and his family were for a considerable time in a state of destitution. He tried to earn or obtain food for them, but without success. At the inquest, his wife said that, when she pressed him to eat such scanty food as they could occasionally procure, he often said to her, "Eat it yourself and the children." A kind neighbour, having heard how badly off this poor family was, gave an order for some bread; but, as occurred in so many cases, this act of Christian charity came too late. Fitzpatrick was unable to eat, and so he died. At Enniskillen, a poor girl, who had been sent for Indian meal, fell down near her dwelling and expired. She had not gone out more than eight or nine minutes, when she was discovered lifeless, and clutching a small parcel of Indian meal tied up in a piece of cloth. In parts of Ulster, the applications for employment on the Government works were very numerous; in one parish alone (Ballynascreen) there were sixteen hundred such applications. In West Innishowen, within twelve miles of Londonderry, twelve persons died of starvation in one week.

Thus had the great Famine seized upon the four Provinces before the end of 1846; Munster and Connaught, however, enduring sufferings which, in their amount and terrible effects, were unknown to Leinster or Ulster. In the West, Mayo, up to this time, had suffered most, which, from its previously known state of destitution, was to be expected; in the South, Cork seems to have been the county most extensively and most fatally smitten. This, however, may not have been actually the case. Clare and Kerry suffered greatly from the very beginning, but their sufferings were not brought so prominently before the public as those of Cork. This county had many and faithful chroniclers of her wants and afflictions—a fact especially true of Skibbereen. That devoted town and its neighbourhood were amongst the earliest, if not the very earliest, of the famine-scourged districts; and their story was well and feelingly told by special correspondents, and, above all, by Dr. Donovan, the principal local physician, whose duties placed him in the midst of the sufferers. There can be no doubt that even at this comparatively early period of the famine, parts of Connaught, especially Mayo, suffered as much as Skibbereen, but the results were commonly told in briefer terms than in parts of the South. "More deaths from starvation in Mayo;" "Dreadful destitution in Mayo;" "Coroners' inquests in Mayo." Such are the headings of brief but suggestive paragraphs, during the latter part of November, and all through December. Many of the Mayo inquests may have been the occasion of more dreadful revelations than even those of Skibbereen, but they did not receive the same extensive and detailed publicity. Here are two or three starvation cases from that county. Patrick M'Loughlin, in the parish of Islandeady, was ordered by the Relief

Committee a labour-ticket, in consequence of earnest representations as to his starving condition. He did not get the ticket for five days, he, his wife and five children not having a morsel of food in the interval. Having at length obtained the ticket, he produced it, and went to labour on the Public Works. He got no pay for the first three days, and in the meantime his wife died from actual starvation. Being unable to purchase the timber for a coffin in which to bury her, poor M'Loughlin held over the remains for upwards of forty-eight hours; but yet anxious to earn what would give her decent sepulture, and at the same time procure food for his children, he went each of the two days her remains were in his cabin to labour, and spent the night in sorrowing over his departed wife. At length the story came to the ears of the parochial clergy, one of whom immediately furnished the means of interment, and she was consigned to the grave *at night*, in order that the survivors might not lose the benefit of M'Loughlin's toil on the following day.[188] Bridget Joyce, a widow with four children, was found dead in a little temporary building, which had been erected in a field to shelter sheep. One of the children was grown enough to give some attention to her dying mother, but had nothing to moisten her parched lips but a drop of water or a piece of snow. The woman died, and so poor were the people of the locality, that for want of a few boards to make a coffin, she remained uninterred for eight days. There is a melancholy peculiarity in the case of a young lad named Edmond M'Hale. When he had been a considerable time without food, he became, or seemed to become, delirious. As his death approached, he said from time to time to his mother—"Mother, give me three grains of corn." The afflicted woman regarded this partly as the mental wandering of her raving child, and partly as a sign of the starvation of which he was dying. She tried to soothe him with such loving words as mothers only know how to use. "*Astore*," she would say, "I have no corn yet awhile— wait till by-and-by;" "Sure if I had all the corn in the world I'd give it to you, *avour-neen*;" "You'll soon have plenty with the help of God." A neighbouring woman who was present at the touching scene searched the poor boy's pockets after he had died, and found in one of them three grains of corn, no doubt the very three grains for which, in his delirium, he was calling. Many of the deaths which happened are too revolting and too horrible to relate; no one could travel any considerable distance in Mayo at this period without meeting the famine-stricken dead by the roadside.

Still it would be hard to surpass Skibbereen in the intensity and variety of its famine horrors. Dr. Donovan, writing on the 2nd of December, says: Take one day's experience of a dispensary doctor. It is that of a day no further off than last Saturday—four days ago. He then proceeds with the diary of that day: his first case was that of Mrs. Hegarty, who applied to him for a subscription towards burying her husband and child; the doctor had not prescribed for them, and he asked why he had not been applied to; the answer was as in other cases—they had no disease, and he could be of no use to them. His second case was that of a boy named Sullivan, who came to him for some ointment for his father. This application was somewhat out of the usual course, ointment being a peculiarly useless thing as a remedy against famine. There was, however, need of it. The boy's grandmother had died of fever some days before, and his father and mother, with whom she had resided, took it from her. The neighbours were afraid to go into the fever-house, but some of them, kindly and charitably, left food outside the door, and candles to wake the corpse. The mother struggled out of bed to get the candles in order to light them. She succeeded in doing so, but from weakness she was unable to stand steadily, so she reeled and staggered towards where the corpse was laid out, and with the lighted candles set the winding sheet on fire: the thatch caught the flame; the cabin was burned down, and the parents of this miserable boy were rescued with the utmost difficulty. They got more or less burned, of course, and the ointment was therefore required for them. Having escaped death from fire, they almost suffered death from cold, as they were left four hours without the shelter of a roof on a bitter December day, all being afraid to admit them lest they should catch the contagion. The doctor's third case happened at midnight, being called on duty to the workhouse at that hour. It was about a mile from the town—something less perhaps. Halfway on his journey he found a man trying to raise a poor woman out of the dyke. He went to his assistance, and found the woman paralyzed with cold, and speechless. Locked in her arms, which were as rigid as bars of iron, was a dead child, whilst another with its tiny icy fingers was holding a death-grip of its mother's tattered garment. Her story was short and simple, which she was able to tell next day: she had made an effort to reach the workhouse, but sank exhausted where she was discovered.

After a while the effects of famine began to manifest themselves in the sufferers by a swelling of the extremities. Perhaps the severe cold caused this or increased it. However that may be, experience soon taught the people that this puffy unnatural swelling was a sure sign of approaching dissolution.

When the cold weather had fairly set in, it frequently happened that the straw which composed the bed, or the excuse for a bed, occupied by members of a family dying of fever or hunger, or both combined, was, piecemeal, drawn from under them and burned on the hearth to keep up a scanty fire. It was felt, we may presume, that the dying could not require it long, and those who had still some hopes of life were famishing as much from cold as from hunger. An eye-witness, describing such a family in Windmill-lane, Skibbereen, one of whom had already died, thus writes: "The only article that covered the nakedness of the family, that screened them from the cold, was a piece of coarse packing stuff, which lay extended alike over the bodies of the living and the corpse of the dead; which seemed as the only defence of the dying, and the winding sheet of the dead!" The same writer says: "In this town have I witnessed to-day, men—fathers, carrying perhaps their only child to its last home, its remains enclosed in a few deal boards patched together; I have seen them, on this day, in three or four instances, carrying those coffins under their arms or upon their shoulders, without a single individual in attendance upon them; without mourner or ceremony—without wailing or lamentation. The people in the street, the labourers congregated in town, regarded the spectacle without surprise; they looked on with indifference, because it was of hourly occurrence.[189]

The statements in the public journals about the effects of the famine in and about Skibbereen were so new and appalling that many people thought them greatly exaggerated. Finding this feeling to exist, and perhaps to some extent sharing in it, Mr. Cummins, a magistrate of Cork, proceeded to Skibbereen, to examine for himself the state of things there. He was not only convinced but horrified. He published the result of his visit in a letter to the Duke of Wellington, in which he begged that exalted personage to call the Queen's attention to the fearful sufferings of her people. Convinced that he was destined at least, to witness scenes of real hunger and starvation, Mr. Cummins informs us that he took with him as much bread as five men could carry. He began his inquiries at a place called South Reen, in the parish of Myross, near Skibbereen.[190] Being arrived at the spot, he was surprised to find the wretched hamlet apparently deserted. There was no external appearance of life—silence reigned around. On entering some of the cabins he soon discovered the cause. He was at once confronted with specimens of misery, which, he says, no tongue or pen could give the slightest idea of. In the first cabin he entered he found six famished, ghastly skeletons, to all appearance dead, huddled in a corner on a little filthy straw, their sole covering being what seemed a piece of ragged horsecloth; their miserable shriveled limbs were hanging about as if they did not belong to their bodies. He approached them in breathless horror, and found by a slow whining moan that they were alive—four children, a woman, and what had once been a man—all in fever. Mr. Cummins met other cases as fearful, more especially one similar to that described by the writer quoted above, where a corpse was lying amongst the surviving members of the family, sharing their straw bed and their scanty covering.

At a meeting of the Killarney Relief Committee, the Earl of Kenmare being in the chair, the parish priest, the Rev. B. O'Connor, made a statement, which, except as an illustration of the unprecedented misery to which the people had sunk, I would hesitate to reproduce. He said: "A man employed on the public works became sick. His wife had an infant at her breast. His son, who was fifteen years of age, was put in his place upon the works. The infant at the mother's breast," said the rev. gentleman, amid the sensation of the meeting, "*had to be removed*, in order that this boy might receive sustenance from his mother, to enable him to remain at work." Another poor woman, the mother of eight children, when dying of want, was attended by the Rev. Mr. O'Connor. She made her last request to him in these words: "O Father O'Connor, won't you interfere to have my husband get work, before the children die."

"In December, 1846, matters seemed to have come to a climax, and on the evening of the 24th [Christmas Eve] I witnessed a scene which scarcely admits of description. On that day a board was held at the Workhouse, for the admittance of paupers. The claims of the applicants were, in many cases, inquired into, but after some time the applicants became so numerous, that any attempt to investigate the different cases was quite useless, and an order was then given by the members of the Board present, to admit all paupers, and at least to give them shelter, as but little food was to be had. I shall never forget the scene which I that night witnessed: mothers striving, by the heat of their own persons, to preserve the lives of their little ones; women stretching out their fleshless arms, imploring for food and shelter; old men tottering to the destination where they were to receive shelter. The odour from the clothes and persons of those poor people was dreadfully offensive, and the absence of active complaints clearly showed that in many the hope of restoration was not to be expected. On my visiting this scene next morning, eleven human beings were dead."[191]

Some twenty years after the famine-scourge had passed away, and over two millions of the Irish people with it, I visited Skibbereen. Approaching the town from the Cork side, it looks rather an important place. It is the seat of the Catholic bishop of Ross, and attention is immediately arrested by a group of fine ecclesiastical buildings, on an elevated plateau to the left, just beside the road, or street, I should rather say, for those buildings are the beginning of the town; they consist of a cathedral and a convent, with very commodious schools, and a pretty gothic chapel. On the other side of the way is the schoolhouse, in shade of which the military were concealed on the day the Caharagh labourers invaded Skibbereen. A short distance beyond the town, the wooded hill of Knockomagh, rising to a considerable height, overhangs Lough Hyne, one of the most beautiful spots in Ireland. Some miles to the westward lies the pretty island of Sherkin, which with Tullough to the east, makes the charming little bay of Baltimore completely landlocked. Out in front of all, like a giant sentinel, stands the island of Cape Clear, breasting with its defiant strength that vast ocean whose waves foam around it, lashing its shores, and rushing up its crannied bluffs, still and for ever to be flung back in shattered spray by those bold and rocky headlands. The town of Skibbereen consists chiefly of one long main street, divided into several, by different names. This street is like a horse-shoe, or rather a boomerang, in shape. Coming to the curve and turning up the second half of the boomerang, we are almost immediately in Bridge-street, a name well known in the famine time; not for anything very peculiar to itself, but because it leads directly to the suburb known as Bridgetown, in which the poorest inhabitants resided, and where the famine revelled— hideous, appalling, and triumphant. Bridgetown is changed now. In 1846 it contained a large population, being not much less than half a mile in length, with a row of thatched houses on each side; when the Famine slaughtered the population, those houses were left tenantless in great numbers, and there being none to reoccupy them, they fell into ruins and were never rebuilt. Hence instead of a continuous line of dwellings at either side, as of old, Bridgetown now presents only detached blocks of three or four or half-a-dozen cabins here and there. Coming towards the end of it, by a gradual ascent, I accosted a man who was standing at the door of his humble dwelling: "I suppose you are old enough," I said to him, "to remember the great Famine?" "Oh! indeed I am, sir," he replied, with an expressive shake of his head. "Were there more people in Bridgetown and Skibbereen at that time than now?" "Ay, indeed," he replied, "I suppose more than twice as many." "And where did they all live—I see no houses where they could have lived?" "God bless you, sure Bridgetown was twice as big that time as it is now; the half of it was knocked or fell down, when there were no people to live in the houses. Besides, great numbers lived out in the country, all round about here. Come here," he said, earnestly; and we ascended the road a little space. "Do you see all that country, sir?" and he pointed towards the north and west of the town. "I do." "Well, it was all belonging to farmers, and it was full of farmers' houses before the famine; now you see there are only a couple of gentlemen's places on the whole of it. The poor all died, and of course their houses were thrown down." "And where were they all buried," I enquired. "Well, sir," he replied, "some of them were buried in the old chapel yard, near the windmill; a power of them were buried in Abbeystrowry, just out there a bit, where you are going to, but—" he suddenly added, as if correcting himself—"sure they were buried everywhere—at the Workhouse over—in the cabins where they died—everywhere; there was no way, you see, to bring them all to Abbeystrowry, but still there were a power of them, sure enough, brought to it."

My informant was quite right about my going to Abbeystrowry. I had already enquired the way to it, and had learned that it was half-a-mile or so beyond Bridgetown. I wished my interesting informant good evening, and pursued my walk. Coming to the highest point of the road beyond Bridgetown, a very charming landscape opened before me, made up of the Valley of the Ilen and the agreeably undulating country beyond it. The river at this place is wide and shallow; but, judging from the noble bridge by which it is spanned, it must be sometimes greatly swollen. The evening was bright and pleasant; the sun had gone far westward, and the effect of his light, as it played on the scarcely rippled water, and shone through the high empty arches of the bridge, standing like open gateways in the shallow stream, made me pause for a moment, to take in the whole scene. It was during this time that I discovered, immediately beyond the river, the object of greatest interest to me—the object, in fact, of my journey—the churchyard of Abbeystrowry. There was the spot in which a generation of the people of Skibbereen was buried in a year and a half! Those places in which poor humanity is laid to rest when life's work is done have been always regarded as holy ground; cities of the dead, solemn and suggestive. But this was more; in its lonely seclusion, in its dark and terrible history, it was exciting in its impressiveness. In the still sunlit evening, wooed to rest, one could imagine, by the gentle murmurs of the Ilen, its little clump of gnarled trees grouped around its scanty ruin was a picture of such complete repose as to make the most thoughtless reflective. I entered. Immediately inside the gate, a little to the right, are those monster graves called by the people "the pits," into which the dead were thrown coffinless in hundreds, without mourning or ceremony—hurried away by stealth, frequently at the dead of night, to elude observation, and to enable the survivors to attend the public works next day, and thus prolong for awhile their unequal contest with all-conquering Famine. A difficulty arose in my mind with regard to the manner of interment in those pits. Great numbers, I knew, were interred in each of them; for which reason they must have been kept open a considerable time. Yet, surely, I reflected, something resembling interment must have taken place on the arrival of each corpse, especially as it was coffinless. The contrivance, as I afterwards learned, was simple enough. A little sawdust was sprinkled over each corpse, on being laid in the pit, which was thus kept open until it had received its full complement of tenants.

To trace one's steps, slowly and respectfully, among the graves of those who have reached the goal of life in the ordinary course, fills one with holy warnings; to stand beside the monument raised on the battle-field to the brave men who fell there, calls up heroic echoes in the heart, but here there is no room for sentiment; here, in humiliation and sorrow, not unmixed with indignation, one is driven to exclaim:—

O God! that bread should be so dear,
And human flesh so cheap.

Although thus cast down by earthly feelings, divine Faith raises one up again. Divine Faith! the noblest and brightest, and holiest gift of God to man; always teaching us to look heavenward—*Excelsior* in its theme for ever. And who can doubt but the God of all consolation and mercy received the souls of his famine-slain poor into that kingdom of glory where He dwells, and which He had purchased for them at so great a price. Even in their imperfections and sins, they were like to Him in many ways; they were poor, they were despised, they had not whereon to lay their head; they were long-suffering, too; in the deepest pangs which they had suffered from hunger and burning thirst (the last and most terrible effect of hunger), they cursed not, they reviled not; they only yearned for the consolations of their holy religion, and looked hopefully to Him for a better world. It is one of the sweetest consolations taught us by holy Faith that the bones now withered and nameless in those famine pits, where they were laid in their shroudless misery, shall one day, touched by His Almighty power, be reunited to those happy souls, in a union that can know no end, and can feel no sorrow.

FOOTNOTES:

174.   "It cannot be too strongly lamented, the opportunity which has been lost for the present, of adopting reproductive employment; but it is not now a question of productive or non-productive employment, it is a question of life or death to those famishing and destitute, anxiously waiting for the means of procuring food . . . A general and well-digested Drainage Bill, applicable to Ireland, cannot be hastily prepared; if so it may be again a nugatory one, and it is *some great* measure, and *great* expenditure for some years to come, under a Drainage and reclaiming of waste lands Bill, that is to be of permanent and effectual relief to this impoverished country."—*Mr. Lambert of Brookhill's letter to the Lord Lieutenant, October 4th.*

175.   Irish Crisis, p. 68.

176.   If the word of a Scotch farmer may be accepted, this seems a great exaggeration. Mr. Hope, of Fentonbarn, at the monthly meeting of the Haddington Farmers' Club, said, lately: "It was only *after* the great disaster of 1845 that potatoes began to be grown to any extent in Scotland."—*Irish Farmers' Gazette for 16th Nov., 1872, p. 399*. But Lord John was only too glad to praise the Scotch at our expense.

177.   Some time ago, an English gentleman, who is an Irish landlord, and one in no bad repute either, was told that, for reasons detailed to him, he ought not to continue a certain agent in his employment: he answered—"I do not care for all that—he gets me my rent."

178.   See Inquest on Jeremiah Hegarty, p. 263.

179.   This view differs considerably from that put forward in the Memorial of the 25th of the previous month, in which the Society tells his Excellency, "that, from their experience as the Royal Agricultural Improvement Society of Ireland, they are confident that every part of this country affords the opportunity of at once employing the rural population in the improvement of the soil, and of returning to the ratepayers a large interest for the capital expended, and thus providing an increased quantity of food and certain employment for the working classes in future years."

180.   Letter to Edward Bullen, Esq., Secretary to the Royal Agricultural Society.

181.   A *weight* of potatoes in the South of Ireland varied from 21 to 23lbs.

182.   *Times* of 13th November.

183.   See pp. 214 and 215.

184.   A driver or bailiff is a man employed by Irish landlords to warn tenants of the rent day, serve notices upon them, watch their movements, see how they manage their farms, play the detective in a general way, and supply useful information to the landlord and his agent. They are regarded with pretty much the same feelings as tithe-proctors were, until that historic class became extinct. They are called drivers by the people, because one of their duties is to drive tenants' cattle off their lands, that they may be sold for the rent. When a peasant wishes to speak politely of this functionary he calls him "a kind of under agent." "There are many parts of Ireland in which a *driver* and a *process-server*—the former a man whose profession it is to seize the cattle of a tenant whose rent is in arrear, the latter an agent for the purpose of ejecting him—form regular parts of the landlord's establishment. There

are some in which the driver, whether employed or not, receives an annual payment from every tenant." *Journals, Conversations and Essays relating to Ireland. By Nassau William Senior, Second Edition, vol. 1, p. 33.*

185.   An Irish word, so given in the report, but more correctly *Creacan* or *Criocan*. It is used to express anything diminutive, when applied to potatoes, it means they are small and bad.

186.   Letter of Rev. B. Durcan, P.P., Swinford, Nov. 16, 1846.

187.   The Windmill is a bare rock, or collection of rocks, which is used as a Fair-field. It overlooks the town. It derives its name from the fact that a windmill had been formerly in use there. Hence, several lanes leading to it are called Windmill Lane.—*Letter from Rev. C. Davis, Administrator of Skibbereen.*

188.   Letter of Rev. K. Henry, P.P., Islandeady.

189.   Special Correspondent of *Cork Examiner*, writing from Skibbereen, 14th December, 1846.

190.   The first case of death, clearly established, as arising from starvation, occurred at South Reen, five miles from the town of Skibbereen. The case having been reported to me, as a member of the Relief Committee, I procured the attendance of Dr. Dore, and proceeded to the house where the body lay. The scene which presented itself will never be forgotten by me. The body was resting on a basket which had been turned up; the head reclined on an old chair; the legs were on the ground. All was wretchedness around. The wife, miserable and emaciated, was unable to move, and four children, more like spectres than living beings, were lying near the fire place, in which, apparently, there had not been a fire for some time. The doctor, of course, at once communicated with the Committee."—*Letter of Mr. M'Carthy Downing, M.P., to the Author.*

191.   MS. Memoir of his famine experiences, by Dr. Donovan. "Up to this morning, I, like a large portion, I fear, of the community hooked on the diaries of Dr. Donovan, as published in *The Cork Southern Reporter*, to be highly coloured pictures, doubtless intended for a good and humane purpose; but I can now, with perfect confidence, say that neither pen nor pencil ever could pourtray the misery and horror, at this moment, to be witnessed in Skibbereen." *Mr. Mahony, the artist of the Illustrated London News, in his letter from Skibbereen to that journal, Feb. 13, 1847, p. 100.*

* * * * *

CHAPTER X.

The Landlords' Committee—A new Irish party—Circular—The "Great Meeting of Irish Peers, Members of Parliament and Landlords" in the Rotunda—The Resolutions—Spirit of those Resolutions—Emigration-Great anxiety for it—Opening of Parliament—Queen's Speech—England on her Trial—Debate on the Address—Lord Brougham on Irish Landlords—Lord Stanley on the Famine—Smith O'Brien's Speech—Defends the Landlords—Mr Labouchere, the Irish Secretary, defends the Government—The Irish Agricultural population were always on the brink of starvation, and when the Blight came it was impossible to meet the disaster—The views of the *Morning Chronicle* on the Government of Ireland—Mr. Labouchere quotes the Poor-Law Enquiry of 1835 and the Devon Commission—Change of the Government's views on the Famine—Griffith's estimate of the loss by the Blight—Extent of Irish pauperism—Lord George Bentinck points out the mistakes of the Government—The people should have been supplied with food in remote districts—He did not agree with the political economy of non-interference—Mr. D'Israeli's manipulation of Lord George's speech—Letter of Rev. Mr. Townsend of Skibbereen—Fourteen funerals waiting whilst a fifteenth corpse was being interred—Quantity of corn in London, Liverpool and Glasgow—Lord John Russell's speech—He regarded the Famine as a "national calamity"—Absurd reason for not having summoned Parliament in Autumn—Sir Robert Peel's view—The Prime Minister on the state of Ireland—His views—His plans—Defends the action of the Government—Defends unproductive work—Reason for

issuing the "Labouchere letter"—Quotes Smith O'Brien approvingly—
Mr. O'Brien's letters to the landlords of Ireland (*note*)—Confounding the
questions of temporary relief and permanent improvement—Fallacy—
Demoralization of labour—The Premier's "group of measures"—Soup
kitchens—Taskwork—Breakdown of the Public Works—Food for
nothing—Mode of payment of loans—£50,000 for seed—Impossibility
of meeting the Famine completely—The permanent measures for
Ireland—Drainage Act—Reclamation of waste lands—Sir Robert
Kane's "Industrial Resources" of Ireland—Emigration again—Ireland
not overpeopled—Description of England and Scotland in former times
by Lord John Russell—His fine exposition of "the Irish question"—
Mr. P. Scrope's Resolution—A count out—Bernal Osborne—Smith
O'Brien—The good absentee landlords—The bad resident landlords—
Sir C. Napier's view-Mr. Labouchere's kind words—Confounds two
important questions—Mr. Gregory's quarter-acre clause—Met with some
opposition—Irish liberals vote for it—The opponents of the quarter-
acre clause—Lord George Bentinck's attack on the Government (*note*).

About the middle of December, there was formed in Dublin a
committee of landlords, which assumed the name of the Reproductive
Works Committee. Its objects were excellent. It was to be the beginning
of a real Irish party, whose members were to lay aside their differences,
political and religious, that, by a united effort, they might carry the
country through the death-struggle in which it then was, and lay the
foundation of its future progress to prosperity. Many of the best men in
the whole nation were active promoters of this movement; but, viewed
as a whole, it was little more than the embodied expression of the fears
of the landlords, that they would be swamped by the rates levied to feed
the people, and of their hopes that, by uniting, for the occasion, with
the popular leaders, they would be able to compel the Government so
to shape its course, that, at any rate, *they* would come forth safe from the
ordeal. Neither the Committee, nor the landlords who met in Dublin at

their call, intended to form a permanent Irish party; in fact, it could not be done in the sense indicated by them. In a circular which was issued the first week of January, they say:

"That, at this awful period of national calamity, it becomes the first duty of every Irishman to devote his individual efforts to the interests of Ireland, and that neither politics, parties, nor prejudices should influence his mind in the discharge of such a duty."

"That, as we feel deeply convinced that our own divisions have been the leading causes of our own misfortunes, and, by weakening our influence in the councils of the empire, have deprived us of our share in the general prosperity, so we are no less firmly persuaded that it is by union alone that we can repair the evils that dissension has created."

"That, if the necessity of joint and united action be urgent and important to Ireland, under ordinary circumstances, it at this moment becomes imperative and vital, as not only the future fortunes, but the present lives of millions, may depend on our exertions, and that dissensions at such an hour is not only a reproach but a crime."

"That, to make such an union binding and effective, it will be necessary not only to feel, but to act together, to take steps to ensure an united support or united opposition to such measures as may be produced with regard to Ireland during this anxious session of Parliament."

"That, for this purpose, we venture to suggest to the Irish members of the Legislature, to meet together at such a time as may be considered most proper and convenient, for the purpose of forming an Irish party for the protection of Irish interests; and we earnestly entreat, that every member of that body should resolve, as far as is possible, to consider and modify his own opinion, so as to meet the united feelings of the general body, and should banish from his mind all considerations of party or prejudice, at a time when the lives and interests of his countrymen are so deeply perilled."

"That we feel confident a union thus formed and carried on, for the protection of all classes, will receive the support and co-operation of all—the aid of the rich, and the confidence of the poor. We pray Divine Providence to bless our efforts in the cause of our afflicted country—to promote amongst us that feeling of united exertion and self-reliance which can alone raise us to our proper place in the great empire to which we belong."

A few days later, the Committee instructed their secretaries to call a meeting of the peers, members of Parliament, and landed proprietors of Ireland, in the Rotunda, on the 14th of January, for the consideration of the social condition of the country, all political and extraneous topics to be strictly excluded. They published at the same time the resolutions they proposed submitting to the meeting, one series of which referred to temporary measures, which, in the opinion of the Committee, were necessary for the immediate wants of the country; another suggested those required for her future prosperity.

The great meeting of Irish peers, members of Parliament, and landlords, as it was called, was held in the Rotunda on the above day. The attendance on the occasion was large, and the meeting was what might be termed a great success. Tickets of admission were issued to fourteen peers, twenty-six members of Parliament, and about six hundred other landed proprietors, from all the four provinces. Admission was only by tickets, and their issue commenced on Tuesday morning, and was continued to an advanced hour on Wednesday evening, the meeting being convened for Thursday. So great, however, was the influx of country gentlemen who were anxious to take a part in the proceedings, that it became necessary to issue a further supply of tickets in the forenoon of that day, notwithstanding which a considerable number were sold at the entrance door. Every phase of Irish politics was represented at the meeting. Amongst the peers were the Marquis of Ormond, the Earl of Erne, Lord Cloncurry, and Lord Farnham; the M.P.'s reckoned, amongst others, O'Connell, Frederick Shaw, William Smith O'Brien, Anthony Lefroy, John O'Connell, and Edward Grogan. The Marquis of Ormond was chairman. The resolutions prepared by the Reproductive Works

Committee were proposed and unanimously adopted. They had, the chairman said, been considered by a committee composed of gentlemen of all shades of parties. Great differences occurred upon almost every word of every resolution. However, personal opinions had been sacrificed with a view of having perfect unanimity at the present meeting—a meeting, as he truly said, of peculiar construction—perhaps the only one of the kind ever assembled in the Rotunda before. The resolutions adopted by this very remarkable assembly were:

1. That we deem it our duty most earnestly to impress upon our representatives, our solemn conviction of the necessity of their now co-operating cordially together in Parliament, for the advancement of the interests of Ireland, and of their uniting to advocate such measures as may appear calculated to raise the social, material, and moral condition of the people; to save society from the ruin by which all classes in the land are now threatened; and to preserve the country from confiscation.
2. That, before and beyond all other considerations, is the salvation of the lives of the people; and we therefore deem it our solemn duty—the present system having signally failed—to call upon the Government, in the most imperative terms, to take such measures as will secure local supplies of food sufficient to keep the people alive, and to sacrifice any quantity of money that may be necessary to attain the object, declaring, as we do, that any neglect or delay in that matter will render the Government responsible for the safety of the people of Ireland, who must perish in multitudes unless supplied with food.
3. That, as the people of this country are suffering from a most extraordinary and incalculably extensive deficiency in the stock of food, we further call upon the Government to remove all artificial impediments to the supply of that deficiency, by the temporary suspension of the navigation laws, and the duties on the importation

of corn, and also to give increased facilities to that importation, by permitting such vessels of her Majesty's navy as can be spared to be employed in the transport of provisions.

4. That we consider it would be most desirable, that the unrestricted use of sugar and molasses in our breweries and distilleries should be permitted, under existing circumstances; in order to save for more useful purposes a portion of the grain now used in those establishments.

5. That we recommend that Relief Committees should be allowed to sell food under first cost to the destitute, in their respective neighbourhoods, and that their doing so should not disentitle them to Government contributions in aid of their funds.

6. That while we affirm, that it is the clear and paramount duty of the state to take care that provision be made for the destitute, we regret that the means hitherto adopted for that purpose have, on the one hand, proved incommensurate with the evil, and on the other hand, have induced the expenditure of vast sums of money upon useless or pernicious works.

7. That this most wasteful expenditure, tending, as it does, to diminish our resources and to increase the probabilities of future famine, has not been the result of neglect on the part of the resident proprietors of Ireland, but of an impolitic and pernicious law, which they have been compelled to carry into effect, notwithstanding repeated protests to the contrary.

8. That, though entirely acquiescing in the justice of imposing upon the land the repayment of all money advanced for reproductive purposes, we solemnly protest, in the name of the owners and occupiers of land in Ireland, against the principle of charging exclusively on their property, the money which they have been forced to waste on unproductive works.

9. That the destruction of the staple food of millions of our fellow-subjects cannot be considered in any other light than that of an

Imperial calamity, and we claim it as our right that the burthen arising from it, so far as it has been expended on unproductive works, shall fall on the empire at large, and not be thrown upon Ireland alone, much less upon those classes in Ireland which have suffered most severely from it.

10. That though considering the present Labour-rate Act as a most mischievous measure, to be laid aside whenever a better system can be introduced, yet, in order to prevent the continuance of the present waste of money, we call upon the Legislature to amend that Act, by enabling each proprietor to take upon himself his proportion of the baronial assessment, to be expended in reproductive works upon his own property, and thereby to discharge himself from any further taxation in respect to that particular assessment; and that the objects to which the taxation shall be applied, should be extended to all permanent improvement of the land.

11. That we have heard with alarm and regret that in many districts of Ireland, the usual extent of land has not been prepared, and cannot be prepared, for cultivation, owing to the poverty of the occupants, and consequently will be waste during the ensuing year; and while we confidently rely on the exertions of the landed proprietors to protect this country from the great evils which must follow from such a neglect, we cannot avoid calling the special attention of Government to the alarming reports which have reached us on this important subject.

That it is an ascertained fact, that the supply of seed in this country will be deficient, and to meet this evil we earnestly recommend that depôts for the sale of seed be established by Government.

12. That powers should be given to the Treasury to advance money, by way of loan, to railway companies that have obtained their acts—such money to be paid out in making the earthworks of the railway. That, as there must be a large amount of population dependent for subsistence, during the year, upon public or private charity,

provision should be made for assisting those to emigrate (with their families) who cannot be supported in this country, by the exercise of independent labour.

[With this resolution ended the suggestions for temporary relief; the remainder regard measures of permanent improvement.]

13. That the direct employment of the great mass of the able-bodied people by the state, has an unavoidable tendency to paralyse industry, and to substitute artificial for natural labour.

That any system of relief to the able-bodied that does not lead to the increase of food, or articles that may be exchanged for food, will diminish the capital of the country, and that just in proportion as capital decreases, poverty will increase.

That, therefore, any measures of relief for the able-bodied ought to have for their object the encouragement of the employment of labour by private individuals in productive works; and that the efficacy of their action, as a stimulus to encourage and force such employment, will be the measure of their utility.

That, in order to place the owners and occupiers of land in a position in which they can be acted upon by such a stimulus, the whole energies of the State should be applied to the absorption of surplus labour, to the affording facilities for private employment, and to the removal of the impediments that now obstruct it.

14. That, to absorb surplus labour, and at the same time to increase the food produce of the country, piers and harbours for fishery purposes, and model curing-houses, with salt depôts attached, should be established along the coast.

That, with the like object of absorbing labour, and increasing our food supplies, a systematic plan should be adopted for the reclamation of waste lands throughout the country.

That, in any such system, an option should be given to the proprietors of waste lands to undertake the reclamation themselves; and, in order to enable them to do so, means should be placed at their disposal for obtaining public loans for that purpose—the security of such loans to be confined to the land improved—and (subject to due protection of reversionary interest), every possible facility should be afforded them in alienating their waste lands for the purpose of reclamation. That, with the further view of absorbing labour, our representatives be entrusted to lay claim to such expenditure upon works and objects of a national character—such as naval dockyards, safety harbours, and packet stations—as ought of right to be allotted to this country.

That, in addition to these measures, a scheme of systematic colonization would, in our opinion, provide the means of subsistence to a large portion of our destitute population—would relieve many districts in this country, which are unable to support their inhabitants—would benefit the Colonies by supplying them with labour—would increase the supply of food throughout the world, by bringing fresh land into cultivation—and would largely extend the market for home manufacture.

That the class which it is desirable to see emigrating cannot do so by their own resources; and that no one of the other classes benefited by the operation would, separately taken, find it so profitable as to ensure their carrying it out upon a large scale.

That it is, therefore, peculiarly the province of the State, which represents and protects the interests of all collectively, to promote emigration by direct intervention, as well as by assisting, with information and pecuniary aid, the efforts of individuals and public bodies in promoting this most desirable result.

15. That, for affording facilities for private employment, we recommend that the Drainage Acts should be simplified and consolidated; that tenants for life, and other proprietors having a limited estate, should be enabled to obtain public loans (to be a charge exclusively on the land improved), for other permanent improvements of land, besides drainage, without any application to the Court of Chancery, provided such permanent improvements shall increase the value of the land

seven per cent, per annum; that all such public advances shall be repaid on the principle of the million act, in twenty-two annual instalments, and that a certain percentage shall be fixed, beyond which preliminary expense and expenses of inspection shall not extend.

That, with a like object, we also recommend that tenants, with the consent of their landlords, should have power to apply for public loans in the same manner as the proprietor himself, and to charge the lands improved with the repayment of the money advanced—the tenant rendering himself responsible for the annual instalments that shall accrue due during the period of his occupation; and that in order to encourage the investment of the tenant's own capital upon his land, his right to compensation for permanent improvements, in case of his removal, should be recognised by law.

16. That, to remove the obstacles that now obstruct employment, the laws which regulate the management of estates under the Courts of Equity should be revised and amended, and facilities should be given to landed proprietors to sell portions of their estates for the payment of charges.

That, with a like object, and to diminish the enormous expense and delays that now exist in these matters, cheap and simple modes should be devised for the transfer, partition, and exchange of landed property.

17. That, in addition to these measures for the absorption of surplus labour, for the affording facilities for private employment, and for the removing of the obstacles that now obstruct it, we are of opinion that other measures of an economical and social nature are imperatively called for.

That, among the most prominent of these is an amendment of the present Grand Jury system; and as great inconveniences have arisen from the want of permanent bodies for the administration of county affairs, we would recommend that all the fiscal powers of Grand Juries should be transferred to county and baronial Boards.

That, in such, a change, we would recommend that the present system of road-repair contracts should be modified; and that all roads should be kept in repair under the superintendence of the baronial Boards.

18. That, in addition to an amendment of the Grand Jury Laws, we deem it highly expedient to raise the social state of our agricultural labourer; and that, as we believe, one of the most efficacious means of effecting this will be the improvement of his habitation, we are of opinion that measures should be adopted to enable proprietors to improve the dwellings upon their properties of the labouring poor, and by proper sanitary regulations to render it the interest of all landholders that every dweller on their estates should have a good and healthy habitation.

That we likewise deem it expedient to increase and disseminate agricultural knowledge,—and, with this view, we are of opinion that baronial Boards should have the power of establishing model farms in each barony, presided over by proper agriculturists.

19. That, among the most prominent evils of the present land system, is the want of a cheap and simple mode of checking waste, and therefore we are of opinion that measures should be taken to remedy this.

That, with the view of relieving the owners and occupiers of the soil from any burthens that unfairly press upon them, we would recommend that the expense of jails, lunatic asylums, and criminal prosecutions shall no longer remain a charge upon landed property, and that, in future, all classes who derive an income out of land shall bear their equitable proportion of the taxation which affects it.

20. That, having suggested above what appears to us to be the best means of absorbing surplus labour, and removing the obstacles which fetter private enterprise, we at the same time desire to express our firm and deeply fixed conviction that any system of relief for the support of the destitute, which is not based on the principle of distinguishing

between the proprietor who performs his duty, and him who neglects it, by exempting the former from any taxation that may be rendered necessary by the default of the latter, will be most injurious to the interests of every class in the community.

21. That the Reproductive Employment Committee be requested to continue their labours, and be empowered to call meetings, similar to the present, at any time during the session of Parliament, if such shall appear to be necessary; or to take such other steps as may appear expedient for the carrying out the objects of the meeting.

22. That the secretaries be requested to communicate with those landed proprietors who have been unable to attend the meeting to-day, with a view of obtaining their support to the above resolutions.

23. That an address be presented to her most gracious Majesty, the Queen, setting forth in the most respectful, but, at the same time, the most urgent manner, that the present state of provisions in Ireland is inadequate to support the people of that country; that the resources of the landed proprietors, gentry, and merchants, are altogether unequal to meet the present emergency; and that we, therefore, pray that her Majesty may be graciously pleased to direct her Parliament, immediately on their assembling, to take into consideration the speediest and most effectual means of importing provisions into Ireland, so as to provide, as far as possible, the necessary food for the people.

These resolutions go very fully into the state of the country, its evils and their remedies. They contain much that is wise and well intended, and some of the measures suggested in them will be found in the programme of the Government, or, as their plan was called by their friends,—the "group of measures," by which the present and future of Ireland were to be settled to the satisfaction and advantage of all parties. The Rotunda meeting having been held only a few days before the assembling of Parliament was just in time to exercise an influence on the measures the Government had in preparation, to meet the existing Irish difficulty; and very possibly it had that effect. One thing the landlords who met in the Round-room had evidently set their hearts on—there was to be an extensive emigration—the land was to be cleared. If half the improvements suggested in the resolutions were undertaken, instead of a surplus population, labour enough could not be had for the purpose of carrying them out: if piers and harbours were taken in hand, and if the earthworks of the projected railways were commenced, and if the reclamation of the waste lands were seriously taken up, the labour wasted on the barren road-making would be found insufficient for such gigantic undertakings: but the piers were not built; the harbours were not deepened or improved; the waste lands were not reclaimed; the railway earthworks were left to private enterprise—but EMIGRATION—Oh! that darling object was always in favour with the ruling class, and most effectively promoted by wholesale eviction. The people were sent to benefit the colonies, as the 14th resolution suggested, by their labour; sent "to increase the supply of food throughout the world [except in Ireland], to bring fresh land under cultivation," and above all to "largely extend the market for home manufacture." Yes, that last was a happy hit to secure the willing ear of the "mother country;" as for the poor "sister island," from which all those people were to emigrate, she had no manufactures to open a market for. But the Rotunda people would send away another class too. The last clause of the 12th resolution reads thus: "that as there must be a large amount of population dependent for subsistence, during the year, upon public or private charity, provision should be made for assisting those to emigrate, with their families, who cannot be supported in this country by the exercise of independent labour." (!) This is no slip of the pen. Almost every word of every resolution, the noble chairman said, was carefully discussed. The suggestion, then, is, that those who are *unable to work*, from age, weak health, or, who, having got chronic coughs, asthma, or rheumatism, by working for 6d. or 8d. a day, "wet and dry," on the land that gave them birth, and are now unfit to work any longer;

or, in rosewater phrase, "who cannot be supported in this country by the exercise of independent labour," are to be "shot," like so much rubbish, upon the shores of the western hemisphere—provided the crazy barques into which they are to be huddled do not go down with them bodily, in the middle of the Atlantic. Surely, of all other people, such were unfit for emigration, being unfit to earn their bread; but they were a burthen, a real burthen on the soil here, and so that the clearance took place, the manner of it and its results to the exiled were held to be of small account indeed.

Parliament was opened by the Queen in person, on Tuesday, the 19th of January. She read the speech from the throne, about two-thirds of which related to Ireland exclusively. No wonder. The state of that country had become the theme of public writers, politicians and philanthropists in both hemispheres. England was on her trial before the civilized world. Could not she, the richest nation of the earth, whose capitalists searched the globe for undertakings in which to invest their vast and ever accumulating wealth—could not she—or *would* not she—save the lives of those starving Irish, who were her subjects, and who, if not loved by her like others of her subjects, were at least useful in giving size and importance to the empire, and in fighting those battles which helped her to keep her place among first-class nations; useful in opening up, with the bayonet's point, those foreign markets so essential to her iron and cotton lords—nay, to all her lords? England was on her trial; England's Government was on its trial; and the Queen's speech was to shadow forth their line of defence for past legislation, and to indicate those future measures which were to stay the famine, and prevent its recurrence. Here is the portion of the speech relating to Ireland:

"My LORDS AND GENTLEMEN,—
    "It is with the deepest concern that, upon your again assembling, I have to call your attention to the dearth of provisions which prevails in Ireland, and in parts of Scotland.

"In Ireland, especially, the loss of the usual food of the people has been the cause of severe sufferings, of disease, and of greatly increased mortality among the poorer classes. Outrages have become more frequent, chiefly directed against property, and the transit of provisions has been rendered unsafe in some parts of the country.

"With a view to mitigate these evils, very large numbers of men have been employed, and have received wages, in pursuance of an Act passed in the last session of Parliament. Some deviations from that Act, which have been authorized by the Lord Lieutenant of Ireland, in order to promote more useful employment, will, I trust, receive your sanction. Means have been taken to lessen the pressure of want, in districts which are most remote from the ordinary sources of supply. Outrages have been repressed, as far as it was possible, by the military and police.

"It is satisfactory to me to observe, that in many of the most distressed districts, the patience and resignation of the people have been most exemplary.

"The deficiency of the harvest in France and Germany, and other parts of Europe, has added to the difficulty of obtaining adequate supplies of provisions.

"It will be your duty to consider, what further measures are required to alleviate the existing distress. I recommend to you to take into your serious consideration, whether, by increasing, for a limited period, the facilities for importing from foreign countries, and by the admission of sugar more freely into breweries and distilleries, the supply of food may be beneficially augmented.

"I have also to direct your earnest attention to the permanent consideration of Ireland. You will perceive, by the absence of political excitement, an opportunity for taking a dispassionate survey of the social evils which afflict that part of the United Kingdom. Various measures will be laid before you, which, if adopted by Parliament, may tend to raise the great mass of the people in comfort, to promote agriculture, and to lessen the pressure of that competition for the occupation of land, which has been the fruitful source of crime and misery."

In the House of Lords, the debate on the address in reply to the Queen's speech was not very remarkable. All the speakers admitted that which it was impossible to deny, the terrible reality of the famine, unequalled, as Lord Hatherton said he believed it to be, in past history, and certainly not to be paralleled in the history of modern times. Lord Brougham made a joke and raised a laugh at the expense of the Irish landlords. He inclined, he said, to the opinion that Parliament ought to have been called together sooner, but it was objected that such a course would have the effect of bringing the Irish proprietors to England at a time when their presence at home was much needed. "God forbid," exclaimed his lordship, "that I should be instrumental in bringing the Irish proprietors over to this country."[192] He further said, in one of those involved sentences of his, "that he held it to be impossible that, when the cry of hunger prevailed over the land—when there was a melancholy substance as well as the cry—when the country was distracted from day to day by accounts of the most heartrending spectacles he had ever seen, heard, or read of—that at a time when there was deep misery and distress prevailing, and proved in Ireland—rendered only the more heartrending, because the more touching, by the patience—the admirable and almost inimitable patience—with which it seemed to be borne—that at a time when that great calamity existed—when there were scenes enacted all over those districts, which they could find nothing existing in the page of disease and death and pestilence, ever following in the train of famine—to which nothing existing was to be found in the page of Josephus, or on the canvas of Poussin, or in the dismal chant of Dante . . . that they should be in circumstances like these, and yet be able calmly and temperately to take up questions of permanent policy, he held to be absolutely and necessarily impossible."

More to the point were some of the remarks made by Lord Stanley, then in opposition. With regard to the awful visitation which afflicted the sister island from one end to the other, he said he believed that no exaggeration could, in many instances, exceed the dreadful reality. He was quite content, that for the prevention and palliation of the evil, *for the purpose of rescuing the country from the guilt of permitting a large portion of its people knowingly to* STARVE, there is no sacrifice, no efforts which her Majesty's Government can call upon the people of this country to make, which will not be cheerfully responded to by the members of your Lordships' house, and by the representatives of the people, who will, in this case, represent the deliberate and cordial sense of the whole country. The Labour-rate Act he pronounced "a great blunder." With regard to the non-establishment of food depôts, he said that if he could accuse the Government of an error on that head, they were led into it by too rigid an adherence to the principles of political economy—to the *abstract* principles of political economy, that were meant for the permanent improvement of the people; but the question might arise as to the propriety of acting against such principles, in order to meet an extraordinary emergency.

In the House of Commons, one of the earliest speakers on the address was Smith O'Brien. He said, he thought he would be wanting in his duty to his country if he did not, on that occasion, make an appeal to the House on behalf of those whose sufferings could not be exaggerated— could not be described. He was asked, by assenting to the address, if he was prepared to say that the Government had been altogether guiltless of having produced that frightful state of things; and if he were called upon to affirm, that everything had been done by the Government, which might have been done by them, he would answer, that *he believed it was in their power, to prevent one single individual from dying of starvation in Ireland.* He did not impute to them the wilful intention of bringing about a state of things so disastrous, but it was his opinion, and the opinion of others in Ireland, that they had not introduced those measures which were suitable to the condition in which Ireland was placed, and had thus brought about the state of things which was now witnessed. "To the declaration of the Prime Minister, last session, that there was to be no legislative interference with the price of food, he believed they owed many of the disasters which had taken place in Ireland." This sentiment was received with cheers. Mr. O'Brien then made a point in favour of the Irish landlords. Was this, he asked, to be considered as a local calamity, or was it to be considered as a national calamity? If the Irish members were legislating in an Irish parliament, it would be considered by them as a national calamity, and all classes—the fund holder, the office holder, the mortgagee, the annuitant, would be called on to contribute to the general exertion to alleviate distress. He wished to learn whether the House considered this as an Imperial calamity or not; and whilst he, for his own part, refrained from any supplication to the Imperial treasury, he could assure the House, that there were millions in Ireland, who did not consider the Union a union in which all the advantages ought to be on the part of England. England had the advantage of the Irish absentee rents, and the advantage of applying all the resources of Ireland; and the Irish people did not consider that it ought to be looked upon as a union for the advantage of England alone, and no union when it was for the interests of Ireland. Nothing, he thought, could be more outrageous than that one class, who suffered most from the disasters which had taken place—namely, the landlords of Ireland—should be called upon to bear the whole burthen of this calamity.

Smith O'Brien was quite right in saying it was most unreasonable that the Irish landlords should be called upon to bear the whole expense of the Famine, but it is equally true, that, as a body, they made no effort worth the name to stay or mitigate the Famine, until it had knocked at their own hall doors in the shape of rates, present and prospective, that threatened them with the confiscation of their properties.

Mr. Labouchere, the Irish Chief Secretary, as was to be expected, was put up to defend the Government, and to foreshadow the future measures of relief. His line of defence was a strange one for an English minister to adopt. It was, that the agricultural population of Ireland, vast in its numbers, were always on the brink of starvation; so that when the potato blight swept the country from sea to sea, it was impossible for the Government to meet the disaster fully. An English journal of high repute,[193] whose words have been already quoted in these pages, truly said, that for five hundred years Ireland had been completely in the hands of England, to mould and fashion her as she pleased; and now at the end of those five centuries, a British statesman does not blush to urge, as an argument in favour of the Government of which he is a member, that the normal state of Ireland was—to be on the brink of starvation. This defence, weak and inconclusive from every point of view, served his colleagues and himself, of course, but little, while it was calculated to cover his nation with shame and confusion. He goes on to prove the fact, alas! too easily proved; he goes to Lord Devon's Commission, and tells us from it, that it is no exaggeration to say, that the people of Ireland are the worst housed, the worst clothed, and the worst fed of any people in Europe. It is a country, proceeds the Secretary, of which I find an account given from a most unexceptionable source, the Commission of Poor Law Enquiry in 1835. From this Report it appeared, that Ireland then contained 1,131,000 agricultural labourers, whose average earnings did not exceed from two shillings to two shillings and six pence a week; and that of these one-half were destitute during thirty weeks of every year. "This," said he, "is the ordinary condition of Ireland, and it is upon such a country as this that the calamity has fallen—a calamity which I believe to be without a parallel in modern times."

Such was the defence of the Irish Chief Secretary. And here it is worth while remarking, that in the earlier stages of the Famine it was the practice of the government organs to throw doubt on the extent of its ravages which were published, and the Government, apparently acting on these views, most culpably delayed the measures by which the visitation could be successfully combated. *Now*, their part was to admit to the fullest extent the vastness of the Famine, and make it the excuse for their want of energy and success in overcoming it. On the same principle, Mr. Labouchere, relying on figures supplied by Mr. Griffith, goes into what appears to be a fair statement of the actual money value of the loss Ireland suffered from the potato blight. The money value of the potatoes destroyed by the Blight of 1846, he estimates at £11,250,000: the loss of the oat crop of that year he calculates to be £4,666,000, making the whole loss in oats and potatoes £15,916,000. Still this sum, he says, is under the actual loss; the money value of the loss not at all representing the real loss to the people; and the House, he added, would form a very inadequate notion of the nature and extent of the loss which had befallen Ireland, if they merely considered the money value of the crop which had failed, or the stock of human food which had been supplied.

The chronic poverty and misery of Ireland, as set forth in the Report which the Poor Law Commissioners published in 1835, seems to have been the favourite armoury whence Mr. Labouchere loved to draw his logical weapons, for the defence of the Government on this occasion. In that Report he finds it stated that "Mayo alone would furnish beggars to all England."[194] Be it remembered, that the Poor Law Commissioners had published their Report eleven years before Mr. Labouchere made this speech, but he does not inform us what measures the British Government had in the meantime adopted, or if they had adopted any, to raise the people out of such a state of misery and degradation; but he clearly thinks he has brought forward a clever argument in his own and his colleagues' defence, when he states that one of the thirty-two counties of Ireland, had such abundant and redundant pauperism. Yet this was in the "sister country"—the sister of that great and wealthy and enlightened England of which, no doubt, the Irish Secretary felt proud to be a native.

After offering some defence for the free-trade policy of his chief, and having indicated the measures the Government had prepared for Ireland, he resumed his seat, and was followed by Lord George Bentinck.

Lord George had, within a short time, attained to great importance in the House of Commons. After the protectionist party was deserted ("betrayed" was their own word), by Sir Robert Peel, that large-hearted and high-minded nobleman was installed in his place, as their leader. On the present occasion, without being severe or unkind towards the Government, he pointed out their shortcomings and mistakes with regard to the Irish crisis. Speaking for himself and the party with whom he acted, he said: "We shall be prepared to give our calmest and best attention to any measures her Majesty's ministers may be prepared to bring forward as remedies for that destitution which unhappily exists. But, sir, at the same time, we must be expected to deal frankly with the conduct of ministers, and whilst we are not disposed to say that ministers acted wrongly in declining to call Parliament together, not disposed to censure them for having overridden the law, and suspended the duties of the legislature itself, we are disposed to say, that the measures to which they have had recourse are not those to which we can altogether agree. It is impossible to view the operation of their poor-employment Act, and say that it has answered any good purpose." He held strongly the opinion, that the Government should have supplied food to the people, at least in remote districts, where it could not be otherwise procured. On this point he thus expressed his sentiments: "With respect to the supply of food to the people he, for one, cannot agree altogether in those principles of political economy which had been advanced by the Right Hon. gentleman, the Irish Secretary. This political economy of non-interference with the import and retail trade may be good in ordinary times, but in times such as the present, when a calamity unexampled in the history of the world has suddenly fallen upon Ireland—when there are no merchants or retailers in the whole of the West—when a country of which the population has been accustomed to live upon potatoes of their own growth, produced within a few yards of their own doors, is suddenly deprived of this, the only food of the people, it was not reasonable to suppose that, suddenly merchants and retailers would spring up to supply the extraordinary demands of the people for food. Therefore, I should say that this was a time when her Majesty's Ministers should have broken through these, the severe rules of political economy, and should, themselves, have found the means of providing the people of Ireland with food. The Right Hon. gentleman has said, that ministers have done wisely in adhering to this decision, but I think differently from them. When, every day, we hear of persons being starved to death, and when the Right Hon. gentleman himself admits that in many parts of the country the population has been decimated, I cannot say, that I think ministers have done all they might have done to avert the fatal consequences of this famine."[195] Lord George then read a letter from the Rev. Mr. Townsend, of Skibbereen, in which it was stated that in one month from the 1st of December to the 1st of January, there were one hundred and forty deaths in the workhouse of that town; the people having entered the workhouse, as they said, "that they might be able to die decently under a roof and be sure of a coffin." The Rev. Mr. Townsend also mentioned that in the churchyard of his parish there were, at one time, fourteen funerals waiting, whilst the burial of a fifteenth corpse was being completed. In the next parish to his, there were nine funerals at once in the churchyard, and in two other adjoining ones, there were six together in each. To prove his assertion that the Government should have done more in supplying food to the people, his lordship said: "At this moment, we know that there are between 300,000 and 400,000 quarters of corn in stock on hand in the different ports of London, Liverpool and Glasgow. I want to know, then, what was to have prevented ministers from sending any part, or all of this food to the West of Ireland, to feed the starving people there? . . . It would have kept the retailers and forestallers in order, and prevented them from availing themselves of the Famine to obtain undue prices. What do we see with regard to Indian meal? Why Indian corn is, at this moment, selling in New York at three shillings, and at Liverpool and in Ireland at nine shillings per bushel."[196]

The Prime Minister spoke towards the close of the debate, and, with the apparent intention of answering a question put by Smith O'Brien, said he was quite willing to consider what had occurred in Ireland as "a national calamity," and that the national resources were fitly employed in endeavouring to meet it. The reason he gave for not having summoned Parliament in the Autumn, as O'Connell and many others had suggested, or rather demanded, was a striking proof of the evils of absenteeism. "We had to consider," he said, "that if we did meet Parliament, we should be acting against the opinion of the Irish Government, and against the opinion of almost every one I saw who was connected with Ireland, who thought that to take away at that time—at the commencement of the severe pressure—every person connected by property with Ireland, would inflict a very great injury upon that country, and that, consequently, Parliament should not be called together at that time."[197] If it could be looked upon as a great injury to Ireland to have the comparatively few proprietors who are resident there absent for even one short month, doing important business for Ireland, how terrible the evil must be of having the owners of £4,000,000 of her rental continually absent, and to have her representatives in both Houses of Parliament absent, not merely for a month, but for about seven months out of every twelve!

Sir Robert Peel supported the Premier's view, and in a sentence remarkable for the same sort of logic, said—"He believed nothing effectual ever would or ever could be done in Ireland, without the active, earnest, and unremitting cooperation of the landlords of that country." No doubt, it is the very truth; but how can landlords co-operate for the good of Ireland unless they reside in it, and try to understand something about it? Let them, therefore, reside, or reimburse the country for the evil and loss of their non-residence.

The address was, of course, voted without a division.

The First Minister made no unnecessary delay in bringing the state of Ireland formally before Parliament. On the 25th of January, six days after the opening of the session, he rose in a full house; expressed his sense of the great responsibility under which he laboured, and claimed its indulgence whilst he endeavoured to explain what had been already done to counteract the disastrous results of the potato blight in Ireland; to call their attention to those measures which the Government considered necessary to meet the existing emergency, and finally to submit to its consideration other measures, which, in the opinion of her Majesty's advisers, were calculated to improve the general condition of that country, and lay the foundation of its permanent improvement.

He proceeded to develope this somewhat pretentious programme.

Like other members of the Government, he commenced by quoting the reports of Poor Law Commissioners, to prove that even in what were regarded in Ireland as prosperous times, that country was on the verge of starvation. A pretty confession for an English Prime Minister, to be sure; yet such was his argument and his excuse. It may be imagined, he said, how those who, in the most prosperous years, were scarcely able to maintain themselves, and may be said to have been on the brink of famine, were utterly unable to resist the flood of calamity which poured in upon them with a crop so lamentably deficient; a calamity almost without a parallel, because acting upon a very large population, a population of eight millions of people,—in fact he should say it was like a famine of the 13th century acting upon a population of the 19th century. He then went into some figures to show how vast the operations of the Board of Works were. At present, he said, they had 11,587 officials, and half a million of people at work, at a weekly cost of between seven and eight hundred thousand pounds. He took up the objections against the Labour-rate Act, and the reproductive works authorized by the "Labouchere Letter." Very soon after the Labour-rate Act had come into operation there came, he said, on the part of the proprietors and country gentlemen of Ireland, a complaint that the works were useless, that they were not wanted, and that they were not reproductive. The First Minister, strange to say, did not attach any great value to these objections. "I think," he said, "the object being relief, and to combine relief with a certain amount of work, to show that habits of industry have not been entirely abandoned, that the productive nature of the work was a question of secondary importance. We spend in Ireland upwards of £1,000,000 a-year in poor-rates, and I do not believe that if enquiry were made it would be found that any productive works were the result." So much the worse; and it was one of the great objections to the Irish Poor-law system, that under it no provision was made for the profitable employment of able-bodied paupers. To call the productiveness or non-productiveness of the labour of half a million of men a matter of secondary importance was, certainly, most cool assurance on the part of a professed political economist, who must hold as a central dogma of that science that labour is the principal producer of capital. Everybody admitted that the crying want of Ireland was the want of capital; yet here is a Minister, holding in his hands her destinies during a life-and-death struggle for existence, and an ardent disciple of Adam Smith besides, expressing his belief that to expend in useless and even pernicious works the labour of half a million of men was a matter of secondary importance; and because it was, he did not attach any great weight to the objection! It was not, therefore, he said, such an objection that caused the Government to sanction a modification of the law as was announced in the letter of the Irish Chief Secretary, but because it was desirable to obtain the co-operation of the landed gentry of Ireland, and, if possible, to have the labour made reproductive, that the plan of reproductive works was sanctioned. But this plan did not win the Irish landowners, and they began a new agitation for townland divisions. On this point he quoted the following passage from a letter of Smith O'Brien, in which the Prime Minister said he fully concurred: "This plan had the merit of being intelligible, simple, and effective. It is undoubtedly better that the population should be so employed than in destroying good land, by making new lines of road which are wholly unnecessary, or in otherwise doing absolute mischief. It will, however, have the effect of still further pauperizing the labour of the country. To elucidate this result in the simplest manner, let us suppose that there are one hundred labourers in a district which belongs to two landlords, whose incomes are equal, and one of whom now employs fifty independent workmen, whilst the other does not employ a single labourer. It is at present necessary to provide for the maintenance of fifty unemployed labourers. These are now set to work upon the roads, and the expense of their maintenance falls upon the two proprietors in equal proportions. If the proposed plan be adopted, the improving landholder will naturally desire to exempt himself from taxation, without employing more hands than he at present requires. This he could do by dismissing all his present workmen. There would then be one hundred surplus labourers in the district. As these must be maintained at the expense of the two properties, each proprietor would eventually be compelled, in self-defence, to employ fifty. The landholder who originally employed this number will thus escape taxation, without engaging more labourers than he requires; but his labourers will cease to be independent workmen, chosen and paid by himself, and subject to his own control. They will be sent to him by the Relief Committee of the district; they will be placed under the superintendence of an expensive staff of stipendiaries appointed by the Board of Works, and will be paid out of the funds raised for the relief of the poor. A system not very dissimilar to this was acted upon in several parts of England, previous to the Poor Law Amendment Act of 1834, and was found to produce effects most demoralizing to the labouring population—paralyzing all the energies of independent labour and of individual enterprise, and in many respects operating most unjustly upon particular classes of property."[198] Referring to the value of independent labour, the Premier said: "I admit the evils of the present system, but I think that still greater danger would have ensued if we had done that which I conceive to be one of the most pernicious acts which a Government can do, the depriving labourers of their independence, and thus permanently injuring the great and important class to which those labourers belonged."

Through all the Famine time, there is nothing more remarkable than the manner in which the expounders of the views of Government, as well as many others, managed, when it suited them, to confound two things which should have been kept most jealously distinct,—(1.) What was best for the Famine crisis itself; (2.) What was best for the permanent improvement of the country. The confounding of these two questions led to conclusions of the most unwarrantable and deceptive kind. In the present instance, the Prime Minister himself seems to fall into the same mistake; or he goes into it with his eyes open, that he may be able to draw conclusions to suit his purpose. The proposition laid down by him is by no means unreasonable in itself; in fact it may be accepted as true: the fallacy is, that he keeps out of sight the peculiar circumstances of the case, and puts his proposition stripped of those circumstances, which should greatly modify it, when applied to Ireland, as she then was. Here is the Premier's argument: Smith O'Brien, in the extract quoted, said it was found to be a great evil in England, before the Poor-laws were revised, that employers, instead of choosing their own workmen, had them sent to them by the parish authorities. This produced two bad results: (1.) The men did not give a good day's work, and so the employer was injured; (2.) In practice it was found most demoralizing to the labourers themselves, destroying their independence, and paralyzing individual enterprise. Lord John assents most approvingly to all this, and then applying it to the existing state of Ireland, says, that by such a system still greater dangers would have ensued, and that one of the most pernicious acts which a Government could do would be to adopt it, for it would deprive labourers of their independence, and thus permanently injure the great and important class to which they belonged. The fault in this reasoning is plain enough. If the system recommended for ensuring reproductive employment were to be a permanent arrangement, the evils which resulted from it in England would, in all likelihood, result from it here—for the time being; but the demoralization of labour would not, in the case, be greater than that already in existence on the Public Works, from which there was no reproduction; nor could it be near so great as what he was about to propose that the people should be fed without any labour, or labour test whatever. But nothing done to counteract the Famine should be regarded as a permanent arrangement, suitable to the ordinary wants of the country; on the contrary, the extraordinary means adopted to meet an extraordinary crisis should, from the nature of things, pass away with the crisis. The Famine once over in Ireland, labour would soon return to its ordinary channels. The simple question: "Was it better to employ the labour of the country on productive rather than on non-productive works during the Famine?" became involved and obscured by the enunciation of principles which applied only to an ordinary state of society. It is an amusing commentary on the line of argument adopted above by the First Minister, that he concludes this very speech with two distinct sets of measures for Ireland, one temporary, to meet the Famine, and another permanent.

The first great means he proposed for arresting the progress of the Famine was to establish soup-kitchens, and to give the people food without any labour test whatever. Was the townsland boundary system, which he had just condemned, half so demoralizing to the labourer as this? Certainly not; but this had the excuse, that there was now no time for anything but the immediate supply of food: exactly so; but when there was time, it was wasted in needless delay, and misused in barren discussions about questions of political economy, and the probable extent of the Famine, when its real extent was already well known.

The question of task work has been dealt with already. It was insisted on at a time when a very large number of the working poor were so exhausted with starvation that their physical capacity for work of any kind was almost completely gone. This fact is more than sufficiently proved by the evidence given at various coroners' inquests; still the Government persevered in insisting upon it, and Colonel Jones was amongst the most determined in doing so. In addressing the House on the present occasion, Lord John Russell said it was reported to the Government that the people on the Public Works were seen loitering about the roads; that the Government then introduced task work; that it met great opposition, but that the Lord Lieutenant remained firm, and had it carried out; an announcement which was received with "loud cheers." And no one would be inclined to find fault with task work, if the people had strength enough left to earn fair wages at it, but they had not—a fact which was, long before, evident to everybody but the Government; but even they saw it, or at least were compelled to acknowledge it at last, and then the Prime Minister is furnished with a convenient letter from the same Colonel Jones, so late, he tells the House, as the 19th of January, in which that gentleman informs the Premier that it would be better to give the people food for nothing than to give them any more money; and as for task work, the Colonel says of them, that "their strength was gone, and they had not power to exert themselves." This looks wonderfully like a letter written to order. The people, for many months, had been quite unequal to task work, but the Colonel could never see it until the line of policy resolved upon by his chief required him to clear his vision. "Sir," continued Lord John, "the opinion of the Government previously to the receipt of this letter was, that the system had become so vast in itself, while at the same time destitution and want of food had so greatly increased, that it was desirable, if possible, to attempt some temporary scheme by which, if possible, some of the evils which now met us might be mitigated, and with so vast an expenditure of money, some more effectual relief might be afforded." He then laid his new scheme before the House. 1. His first proposal was to form the country into districts, with a relief committee in each, empowered to receive subscriptions, levy rates, and receive donations from the Government. By these means the committees were to purchase food, and establish soup-kitchens in the different districts, where food was to be distributed without any labour test; the labourer, however, was to be allowed to work on his own plot of ground, for the next harvest. The Lord Lieutenant, he said, and the Board of Works were consulted about this, and approved of it. The system was to be carried out in the first instance by a preparatory measure, and then by a Bill to be proposed to Parliament. 2. As soon as circumstances would permit, by an easy transition, and without disturbing existing arrangements, no further presentments would be made, and no new public works undertaken. The Lord Lieutenant was of opinion that if the roads which had been already begun should be left in an unfinished state, much evil would result, and he therefore suggested that those roads should be completed. With respect to the money which had been already expended, and was being expended, on public works in Ireland, a claim had been made that it should not wholly be a burthen upon that country. Sir, said the Premier, passing by the remote causes of these evils, and looking at the present resources of Ireland, I think it would not be right that the whole burthen should remain on Irish property. We shall, therefore, propose, on a future day, that an arrangement shall be made by Parliament, by which, in each succeeding year, when an instalment becomes due, the payment of one-half of that instalment shall suffice, and that the other half shall be remitted. We purpose, however, that the whole debt shall be kept up until the half of it be paid; thus providing that one-half of the whole charge shall fall upon the public. "I should state," he continued, "that with regard to the financial part of the question, the sums paid have been issued out of the Consolidated Fund, and that there is not contemplated any new issue of Exchequer bills. At the same time it must be considered, when I make this proposition to Parliament, that it is placing a very considerable burthen on the finances of the country; and that by placing that burthen upon its finances, I do feel myself disabled from making some proposition, which otherwise I should be called on to make, and which would involve further advances, but which I think it is now hardly fair to the people of this country to propose. When it is said—'Let the burthen be borne by the Consolidated Fund, or by the Imperial Treasury, and the Imperial Exchequer,' I must always recollect that these sums are not granted by

Government or by Parliament without the most serious consideration, and that they are sums derived from the people of this country, by their payment of the taxes upon soap, sugar, tea, and coffee; from the surplus of which we are enabled to come to the assistance of Ireland. And, sir, while I feel that there is a disposition in this country to do everything that is liberal towards Ireland, in this respect, we must also consider the difficulties and privations to which the people of England will be subjected." These words of the First Minister were evidently spoken in a spirit of kindness and compassion; still it is hard for an Irishman to avoid feeling that they are degrading and offensive. Ireland is not regarded as part and parcel of the United Kingdom in any part of the quotation. He speaks of placing a serious burthen on the finances "of this country," meaning England only. Again: the sums advanced are, he feels, derived from the people "of this country," by their payment of taxes on the necessaries of life, from the surplus of which "we are" enabled to come to the assistance of Ireland—of Ireland as an alien—a beggar,—who clings to us and looks to us in her misery, but who has no claim upon us, except her starvation and our great bounty;—to all which an advanced Irish nationalist might well reply—"Why not cut her adrift then, and let her shift for herself, as she has so often craved and demanded?" It would seem to be assumed by the Prime Minister, that Ireland never paid any taxes, never helped to fight any battles for England, never manned any ships, never did anything to entitle her people to be kept from dying of starvation, when the Famine-plague fell upon her. Lord John Russell keenly felt the placing of a considerable burthen upon the finances of England—"this country" was his word. All the unjust, and unnecessary, and extravagant wars ever waged by England, were burthens upon the finances of the country, just as much as the grants to relieve the Irish famine; and it is a question if a Minister ever felt it necessary to make so many apologies in asking the sinews of war from Parliament, as Lord John did, when asking the means of saving millions of the Queen's subjects from death by a famine, for the existence of which they could in nowise be held responsible.

Lord John next proposed a loan of £50,000 for one year, to enable landed proprietors to furnish seed for land. He had, he said, some misgivings about proposing this loan to Parliament, but still the Government thought it right to do so. The loan was not to be made to the small tenants themselves, which he considered would be disadvantageous, but to the proprietors, which course, he thought would be safe and beneficial. His lordship then read an extract from an address signed by the Marquis of Sligo and Mr. George H. Moore, in which the people were earnestly entreated to petition Parliament to take such steps as might ensure an immediate and sufficient supply of food. "I own, sir," he continued, "that I am astonished at this—I am astonished that, at a time like this, men of education—men who seek to relieve their countrymen from the difficulties which encompass them, should tell them to demand from Parliament, such steps as may be necessary for an immediate, a constant and a cheap supply of food. Why, sir, that is a task which it is impossible for us to accomplish—that is a task which they should tell their countrymen, that it is impossible for us to perform—that the visitation under which they are suffering has made it impossible for man; that is a task which is beyond all human power; all that we can possibly do being, in some mode, to alleviate the existing distress—to lighten somewhat the dreadful calamity which has befallen them. They should not imagine that it is in our power to turn scarcity, and even famine into plenty. But, sir, what surprises me all the more in reference to this announcement, is, that it so happens that at Castlebar, where the people of the surrounding country are requested to meet, there is a Union workhouse, which Union workhouse should contain 600 inmates, but which, at present, contains not more than 130—the doors being closed against other persons seeking, and in need of admittance, and the guardians saying, that it is impossible for them to levy the rates, in order to enable other persons in want of food to come to that workhouse for relief. Amongst those who have not paid the rates, who have not furnished the money by which famine might have been, to a certain degree, averted, are some who, we cannot but suppose, are fully able to pay what is due from them; and I cannot but see in this proposal a most unhappy tendency—an unhappy tendency, which I have more than once remarked—to recommend to others to do some vague and impossible thing—to call upon Government, or Parliament to do something, the practicability of which is not considered; to confer some benefit that may be visionary or impossible, whilst the plain practical duty of paying the rates, for the sustenance of starving men, women and children in the neighbourhood, is left neglected and unperformed" (hear, hear, from all sides).

The Premier next proceeded to lay before the House other measures which the Government considered would be of permanent as well as immediate benefit to Ireland.

These measures were three in number: 1. An improved drainage act; 2. An Act for the reclamation of waste lands, and, 3. A system of out-door relief, at the discretion of the guardians of the poor. Of the Drainage Act, which he was about to propose, he said, it would be founded on various previous Drainage Acts, but more especially upon the Act of the previous session, and the Treasury Minute of the 1st of December. According to those Acts and that Minute, he proposed that, "When the improvement of an estate, by draining and other operations, by reclamation of waste lands—when a certain improvement in the value of the lands reclaimed will be produced, so that the legal heirs will not be prejudiced, can be made, a certain advance shall be made from the public funds." The usual rate of interest for such advances from the Treasury used to be five per cent.; by the act of 1846 the rate payable on such advances was reduced to three and a half per cent., with repayment in twenty-two years; making six and a half per cent, in each year, until the expiration of twenty-two years, when the advance, principal and interest, would be repaid. The Government now proposed to take the terms of the Drainage Act, and to extend them to various improvements, not confining the operation of the measure to drainage alone; and to do away with those technical difficulties which arose under the former Act, and which rendered it difficult for tenants for life to borrow money. This Act only applied to private estates, but the Government now intended to consolidate former Drainage Acts of a more general nature, so that the drainage of districts could be carried out by the majority of the proprietors of any district agreeing upon the drainage of such district, the minority being bound by their acts. 2. A further announcement, and a very striking one, was made by the Premier; namely, that the Government intended to propose that the State should undertake the reclamation of a portion of the waste lands in Ireland; he alluded to various reports of Commissions upon the reclamation of waste lands, and to the works of eminent writers, who were of opinion that, in many cases, the reclamation of such waste lands would provide profitable employment for large masses of the people; and would render land, now valueless, of great value, as it would be made capable of cultivation. He quoted Sir Robert Kane (then Dr. Kane), who said, "in his most interesting work on the Industrial Resources of Ireland," that the estimate, that 4,600,000 acres of waste land might be reclaimed, and be reduced to the condition of cultivated land, was by no means an exaggerated estimate. "We propose, then, sir," continued Lord John, "to devote a million to this purpose, and that the land reclaimed should, if the proprietor is willing to part with it, be purchased from him, but that if he does not improve it in the method just before stated, by loan, or by his own resources, and *if he refuses to sell it, there should be a compulsory power in the Commissioners of Woods and Forests to take and improve all such waste lands, so situated, as are below a certain annual value, namely two and sixpence per acre.*" This announcement was received by the House with an approving "hear, hear." He went on to say, that lands of this nature were only to be improved and reclaimed so far as general operations were concerned, such as the making of roads through them, general drainage, and necessary buildings; that the lands so reclaimed should be divided into lots, which should not be below nor above a certain amount.

Without binding himself to any precise amount, he would say, by way of illustration, not less than twenty-five, and not more than fifty acres; that when so reclaimed and subdivided, the lands might be either sold or let to poor tenants for a certain number of years, with the determination, that the portion thus let should likewise be sold at the end of the term. "I own, sir," said his lordship, "that I expect a very great advantage gradually to arise from the adoption of this plan. I expect that great numbers of persons, who have hitherto been driven to despair, and many of them to crime, by the great demand for land in Ireland, will earn a competent livelihood from the produce of these lands. I think, likewise, with regard to those who will purchase the lands, so reclaimed and improved, *that there will arise a class of small proprietors, who will form a very valuable class in the social fabric of Ireland.*" He further expressed his opinion, that he did not think that small holdings were the great evil of Ireland, he rather thought that the particular way in which land was held has often been the source of insecurity and want of cultivation. From the state of the County Armagh he came to the conclusion, he said, that small holdings were not the great evil of Ireland. In that county the greatest subdivisions had taken place, and yet it was one of the most flourishing, and best cultivated counties in Ireland. Compare it, or in fact compare the whole province of Ulster with the province of Munster, and many more small holdings will be found in the former than in the latter.

The whole of the Premier's plan for the reclamation of waste lands in Ireland, was received with marked approbation by the House.[199]

Having at some length explained the principle on which out-door relief was to be given, he adverted to the subject of emigration, about which, he said, the most extravagant expectations had been excited and entertained in Ireland, but which never could be realized. Emigration did not, he said, consist in landing a certain number of people on the shores of America; they should be looked to when they would arrive there; and his opinion was, that the best mode of promoting emigration was by affording aid on the arrival of the emigrants at the place of their destination. This had been extensively done, the previous year, at Montreal, and he should be sorry to give any other stimulus to emigration. He then went on to prove that Ireland was not overpeopled; and as it was not, emigration, in his opinion, had not become a necessity for that country. He again quoted Sir Robert Kane, who had stated that there were resources in Ireland, which, if properly developed, would enable that country to maintain seventeen millions of inhabitants. He, Lord John, did not go so far as that, but he did not think the population of the country was excessive, and there was nothing in the country to prevent the highest improvement. Other countries, he said, had been quite as badly off as Ireland was now asserted to be, which were, at present, in the highest state of prosperity.

To illustrate this he would read a description of a country, in which the following evils were said to exist. The writer, an old English author, says:—"The husbandman be thrust out of their own, or else either by covin or fraud, or violent oppression, they be put beside it; or by wrongs and injuries they be so wearied, that they be compelled to sell all. By one means, therefore, or by the other, either by hook or by crook, they must needs depart away, poor wretched souls—men, women, husbands, wives, fatherless children, widows, woeful mothers with their young babes, and the whole household, small in substance, and much in number, as husbandry requires many hands. Away they trudge, I say, out of their known and accustomed houses, finding no place to rest in. All their household stuff, which is very little worth, though it might well abide the sale—yet, being suddenly thrust out, they be constrained to sell it for a thing of nought; and, when they have wandered about till that be spent, what can they then do but steal, and then justly pardy be hanged, or else go about a-begging? Sir," said the Prime Minister, "is this vivid description unlike the story of an ejectment in Ireland?—of an ejectment, where the wretched families turned out are obliged to sell their little all, and forced in a few days either to steal or go about begging? And yet the description which I have read is a description of England, by Sir Thomas More—a description of the England of his day.[200] And lest it should be considered highly coloured or fanciful, let it be recollected that there are accounts written by magistrates, in which it is stated that in every county there were 200 or 300 persons who lived by thieving—who went about, say the contemporary chroniclers, by sixty at a time—who carried away sheep and cattle, so that no husbandman was secure, and against whom no defence was sufficient: that in one reign alone no less than 70,000 of these marauders were hanged. Sir, this is an account of what England once was—the England in which we now see so much security. And in the absence of the outrages described as formerly existing, I think we have a proof that their existence was owing to the state of society at the time, and not the nature of the country. I will now read you a description of another country, at a different period, at the end of the seventeenth century:—"There are at this day (besides a great number of families very meanly provided for by the Church boxes, with others, who, with living upon bad food, fall into various diseases) 200,000 people begging from door to door. These are not only no ways advantageous, but a very grievous burthen to so poor a country; and though the number of them be, perhaps, double what was formerly, by reason of the very great distress, yet in all times there have been about 100,000 of these vagabonds, who have lived without any regard or submission, either to the laws of the land, or even those of God and nature—fathers incestuously accompanying their own daughters, the son with the mother, and the brother with the sister. No magistrate could ever discover, or be informed, which way any of these wretches died, or that ever they were baptized. Many murders have been discovered among them; and they are not only a most unspeakable oppression to poor tenants (who, if they give not bread, or some sort of provision, to, perhaps, forty such villains in one day, are sure to be insulted by them), but they rob many poor people, who live in houses distant from any neighbourhood. In years of plenty, many thousands of them meet together in the mountains, where they feast and riot for many days; and at country weddings, markets, burials, and other the like public occasions, they are to be seen, both men and women, perpetually drunk, cursing, blaspheming, and fighting together." Such, sir, is a description of industrious, sober, civilized, religious Scotland. Such is a description of what that country was at the end of the seventeenth century. Dare we, sir, say that the particular laws—that the particular state of a country—has no influence; that a country which has been in a perfectly disordered condition—where robberies have been frequent—where industry has been interrupted—may not yet become orderly, civilized, and industrious? We should be unworthy of being members of this British Parliament were we to give way to despair." To prove that the miseries of Ireland could be neither attributed to the soil or the people, the Premier said, at the close of his singularly able and lucid speech: "There is no doubt of the fertility of the land; that fertility has been the theme of admiration with writers and travellers of all nations. There is no doubt either, I must say, of the strength and industry of its inhabitants. The man who is loitering idly by the mountain-side, in Tipperary or in Derry, whose potato plot has furnished him merely with occupation for a few days in the year, whose wages and whose pig have enabled him to pay his rent, and eke out afterwards a miserable subsistence—that man, I say, may have a brother in Liverpool, or Glasgow, or London, who, by the sweat of his brow, from morning to night, is competing with the strongest and steadiest labourer of England and Scotland, and is earning wages equal to any of them. I do not, sir, therefore, think that either the fertility of the soil of Ireland, or the strength and industry of its inhabitants, is at fault."[201]

During the delivery of the speech here summarized, Lord John Russell was frequently interrupted with an amount of applause very unusual in the House of Commons, and at its close he is reported to have sat down amidst vociferous and continued cheering.

And no wonder, for never did an English Minister touch the grievances of Ireland with a bolder or truer hand than he did on this occasion; but amongst his proposals, that which was of the greatest value, the reclamation of the waste lands, was abandoned,—in fact, was never brought forward. May we not well ask, Why were not the permanent measures, now proposed, thought of long before, and passed into laws? Statesmen appear to have understood them well enough: why then did it require a famine to have them brought officially before Parliament? Because it seemed to be the rule with successive Governments to do nothing for Ireland until they were forced to it by agitation, rebellion, famine, or some abnormal state of things, which could not be passed over or resisted. Here we have a plan sketched for the reclamation of the waste lands of Ireland, which, if in operation for twenty years before, would have gone far to make the famine transient and partial, instead of general and overwhelming, as it was. Still the plan was very welcome when it came, as it offered the prospect of great future prosperity for this country; everybody felt this, and hence it was hailed with the most unusual marks of approbation by the House of Commons. But, the turning point of the famine crisis over, one of the most valuable measures ever proposed for the benefit of Ireland was shamefully abandoned. One is inclined to suspect that the Government never really intended to carry the measure,—it was too good—too much to the advantage of the people—too great a boon to this country. Mr. Labouchere, as Irish Secretary, had charge of it; he never seemed in any hurry to bring it forward, and after a notice or two, followed by postponements, it ceased to be heard of. Some excuse for the Government may, perhaps, be found in the fact that the Tories would, in all probability, have opposed it, and Lord John was only Minister on sufferance; he could be displaced at any moment Sir Robert Peel pleased, who expressed himself against the reclamation scheme in his speech during the debate on the Premier's "group of measures" for Ireland, but with this exception, Sir Robert gave his full support to those proposals. He said it was better for Ireland to have self-reliance than be looking to Dublin Castle; and he advised Irish proprietors to act independently of the Castle. "With respect to the proposition for the reclamation of waste lands in Ireland," said Sir Robert, "I shall only so far allude to that proposition as to express a hope that the noble lord will pause before he expends so much of the public money on those lands." The noble lord did pause, and every Minister since his time has continued to pause; so that the four and a-half millions of waste acres are still unreclaimed, and the public money which, as was proved, might be profitably expended on them, has been saved for other purposes, such as foreign wars, which, since the Irish Famine, have cost as much as would reclaim them twenty times over, although no one, I should think, would call those wars "reproductive employment;"—nay, the money spent on the Crimean war alone, undertaken to keep the Grand Turk on his throne, would reclaim them twenty times over.

The Government having evidently abandoned their promise of bringing forward a measure for the reclamation of Irish waste lands, Mr. Poulett Scrope, (an English member!) on the 22nd of June, moved the following resolution in the House of Commons: "That the waste lands of Ireland offer an available resource for the immediate employment and future maintenance of a part of her population, now apparently redundant; and that it is expedient to apply them to this great national object, making equitable compensation to their present proprietors." The hon. member proceeded to speak in support of his resolution, but, says *Hansard*, he had not proceeded far when the House was counted out. (!) With respect to this "count out," the following appeared in the pages of a Dublin morning journal, from its London correspondent: "In my private note of last night I enclosed you a copy of a resolution, which Mr. Poulett Scrope had given notice of his intention to move, with respect to the waste lands of Ireland. When I closed my letter, the hon. gentleman's motion stood next on the paper to that which the Commons were engaged in discussing, but although the House was tolerably full, about a hundred members being present, I expressed my conviction that a 'count out' would abruptly terminate that which ought to be a debate of the greatest possible consequence, The despatch which conveyed my anticipations of another deliberate insult being offered to the Irish nation, was not forwarded from the House of Commons more than an hour before the 'count' took place. There can be little doubt that the Government were privy to this disreputable manoeuvre, as a debate upon the subject of reclaiming Irish waste lands, particularly after their broken promises, would, just at the present moment, and on the eve of a general election, be exceedingly inconvenient and distasteful . . . When the 'count out' took place, there were only thirty members present, including *thirteen* Irish members! Where were the virtuous and conscientious men in whom the constituencies of Ireland had reposed confidence? Why did they not attend in numbers sufficient to prevent Mr. Poulett Scrope's laudable effort on behalf of Ireland from being burked?"[202]

During the debate which followed Lord John Russell's speech on the state of Ireland, Mr. Bernal Osborne accused Parliament of shutting its eyes, for a series of years, to the fact that there were two millions and a-half of destitute poor in Ireland, until honorable members had been suddenly awakened to the circumstance by the potato famine. They were now endeavouring, by convulsive efforts of legislation, to correct evils which had been in a great measure incurred through the neglect and carelessness of that House. "Hear, hear," responded the neglectful and careless House. He thought the Minister would have exercised a much wiser discretion if, in addition to the soup-shops, he had turned his serious attention to the tilling of the land for the next harvest. He combated Lord John Russell's argument drawn from the prosperity of the small farmers of Armagh, inasmuch as that county had manufactures as well as agriculture, and expressed his opinion that small farms were at the root of the evils of Ireland.[203]

Mr. Smith O'Brien (then enthusiastic about a Repeal of the Legislative Union) said that the picture of Irish misery drawn by Lord John Russell was the result of forty-seven years of union with England. Halcyon days were promised to Ireland at the time of the Union, but he called on the House to contrast the progress of Ireland from 1782 to the Union, with the state of Ireland since. He expressed his opinion that the loss in potatoes, considering the value of offal for pigs and the rise in prices, was from twenty to thirty millions of money. He believed the Government could have made such exertion as would have prevented the death of ONE INDIVIDUAL in Ireland from starvation. He thought the legitimate course was to have called Parliament together at the earliest possible moment, (cheers,) and nothing surprised him more than the statement of the Chief Secretary, that the Irish people had not a general desire for Parliament to meet in November.

Sir Robert Inglis, referring to the assertion that absentees did not discharge the duties of proprietors, said he found it stated in a speech of the late Bishop Jebb, in 1822, when there was a similar calamity, that a large subscription was raised in a western county by the resident proprietors, but the absentees, who received out of it a rental of £83,000 a-year, only subscribed £83.

The Chancellor of the Exchequer (the Right Hon. Charles Wood), defended the absentees, but was severe upon local proprietors. He held that the occupiers of land, and not the absentee landlords, were mainly chargeable with the neglect of their duties to the people in this trying crisis. Many of the absentees, he said, were most exemplary in their conduct in alleviating the present distress, amongst whom he named Colonel Wyndham, who was furnishing daily rations to ten thousand people.

I wonder how many more such absentees could the Chancellor of the Exchequer name.

The speakers who were supporters of the Government, and indeed almost all the English members, were excessively severe on the Irish landlords. Mr. Roebuck, in the course of a very bitter speech, during the debate on the address, said: "Now let me say a word about Irish landlords" (sensation). "I had no doubt," he continued, "but that that sentence would be met by some sort of feeling on the part of those, the Irish landlords, for whom the British Parliament has been legislating for the last three hundred years. Yes, it has been legislating for them, as a body, against the people of Ireland—it has been maintaining them against the people of Ireland—it has been permitting them to work for their own personal purposes, the mischief of the people of Ireland."

Sir Charles Napier, in reply to Mr. Roebuck and others who attacked the Irish landlords, said, that whether the landlords of Ireland had or had not done their duty, he did not pretend to say; and more than that, he thought that many gentlemen, who were so violent against the landlords of Ireland, knew just as much about them as he did. Of this he was quite satisfied, that if they had not done their duty the Government were to blame for not having forced them to it, long before the existing calamity appeared. Had the English proprietors, he would ask, who had large estates in Ireland, done their duty? It was not enough to tell him that their agents were doing all in their power, and he maintained that the presence of such men as the Duke of Devonshire, the Marquis of Lansdowne, and other large landed proprietors, upon their estates in Ireland, would do much to relieve the people.

Mr. Labouchere defended the Labour-rate Act, and complained that the Government had not received from the gentry of Ireland, or from the Relief Committees, that cordial support which they had a right to expect. He said, the more the real condition of Ireland was examined, the more tremendous would their difficulties be found. He believed the great majority of the House was disposed to treat Ireland with a becoming and proper spirit, and that no one contended that Ireland was to be considered a mendicant applying for alms to the Imperial Legislature. He thought the relief should be granted as a matter of justice, and that the relation between the two countries should be considered as the relation between the members of a family, whose one member had been afflicted by some great and sudden and tremendous distress; and that just as the other members of the family would be bound, in a spirit of humanity and justice, to come to the relief of the starving member, so it was incumbent on the Imperial Legislature to come forward and relieve the starving members of the United Kingdom, at the present moment. These sentiments were received with marked approbation. He defended the non-interference of the Government in the supply of provisions for Ireland: and in dealing with this, not easy question, he reasoned thus: "We have been blamed," he said, "amongst other things, by honorable members, who have said to us, 'When you had the corn in the country, why did you not sell it under the cost price—why did you not allow the Relief Committees to dispose of it at less than its own cost—it would have been so much better.' His answer was, because the Government thought it of infinite consequence to foster, in every manner, the retail trade of Ireland." There is a confounding of two important questions here by Mr. Labouchere, which should be kept quite distinct, and it even looks like an intentional confounding of them. What certain members of Parliament may have privately said to Mr. Labouchere, we have no means of ascertaining except from the information he here gives; but he was Irish Secretary, and he ought to have known—was bound to know—that the country asked two questions about the supply of food, instead of one: 1. The first was, "Why did the Government allow the corn crop of Ireland to be taken out of the country to feed others, and await their chance of getting Indian meal from a distance of three thousand miles, to save from starving (which they failed to do) the people who raised that crop?" The Secretary's answer to his own-made question, is no answer to that. 2. The second question asked by the country was—why did not the Government sell corn and meal to the starving people at some price or another, in districts where there was no retail trade, and where the creation of it would be the work of years? There is no answer given to that by Mr. Labouchere. It is on record, that the people died of starvation with the money in their hands ready to purchase food, but it would not be sold to them, although thousands of tons of meal were in the Government stores, at the doors of which they knocked in vain. Where were the retailers then, who were to have sprung into existence under the political economy wand of Lord John Russell and Mr. Labouchere? Mr. Trevelyan, their mouth-piece, said that the corn in the Government stores should be held over to meet the pressure expected in May and

335

June. Why did they not keep the Irish corn crop for May and June, or use it for immediate need and import Indian meal for May and June?

After further considerable discussion and many modifications, "The Poor Relief (Ireland) Bill," granting outdoor relief and establishing soup kitchens, became law on the 16th of April. The name of William Henry Gregory, then member for the City of Dublin, and afterwards for the County of Galway, must remain for ever associated with this measure, on account of two clauses which he succeeded in having incorporated with it. The first was to this effect: that any tenant, rated at a net value not exceeding £5, and who would give up to his landlord, the possession of his land, should be assisted to emigrate by the Guardians of his Union, the landlord to forego any claim for rent, and to provide two-thirds of such fair and reasonable sum as might be necessary for the emigration of such occupier and his family; the Guardians being empowered to pay to the emigrating family, any sum not exceeding half what the landlord should give, the same to be levied off the rates. This clause, although not devoid of redeeming features, was proposed and carried in the interest of the landlord-clearing-system, yet it was agreed to without what could be called even a show of opposition. It is, however, on the second clause— the renowned quarter-acre-clause—that Mr. Gregory's enduring fame, as an Irish legislator, may be said to rest. It is well entitled to be transcribed here in full: "And be it further enacted, that no person who shall be in the occupation, whether under lease or agreement, or as tenant at will, or from year to year, or in any other manner whatever, of any land of greater extent than the quarter of a statute acre, shall be deemed and taken to be a destitute poor person under the provisions of this Act, or of any former Act of Parliament. Nor shall it be lawful for any Board of Guardians to grant any relief whatever, in or out of the Workhouse, to any such occupier, his wife or children. And if any person, having been such occupier as aforesaid, shall apply to any Board of Guardians for relief as a destitute poor person, it shall not be lawful for such Guardians to grant such relief, until they shall be satisfied that such person has, *bona fide*, and without collusion, absolutely parted with and surrendered any right or title which he may have had to the occupation of any land over and above such extent as aforesaid, of one quarter of a statute acre." So that by this carefully prepared clause, the head of a family who happened to hold a single foot of ground over one rood, was put outside the pale of relief, with his whole family. A more complete engine for the slaughter and expatriation of a people was never designed. The previous clause offered facilities for emigrating to those who would give up their land— the quarter-acre-clause compelled them to give it up, or die of hunger. In the fulness of his generosity Mr. Gregory had, he said, originally intended to insert "half an acre" in the clause, but, like many well-intentioned men, he was over-ruled: he had, he said, been lately in Ireland, and people there who had more knowledge of the subject than he could lay claim to, told him half an acre was *too extensive*, so he made it a quarter of an acre. It is not hard to conjecture who his advisers were on this occasion.

This clause met with more opposition than the former one, but only from a small band of kind, good-hearted men, Smith O'Brien called it a cruel enactment; but as he had heard the Government were for it, he knew, he said, to remonstrate against it was useless. Mr. Curteis, the member for Rye, said the clause was meant for the benefit of Irish landlords—a class that deserved little sympathy from the House or the country. Sir George Grey, one of the Secretaries of State, supported the clause, because he had always understood that small holdings were the bane of Ireland; from which observation it is clear he accepted it as an exterminating clause. Now, suppose it is admitted that small holdings were the bane of Ireland, who, we may be permitted to ask, created them? The very landlords who now sought to abolish them, at the expense of millions of lives. Again, if small holdings were the bane of Ireland, was the midst of an unparalleled famine the proper time to remove the bane? Ought not such a bane be the subject of legislation, when society was in its normal state? Sir George thought not, and hence he virtually says to the landlords, "Now is your time to get rid of the people; they have served your purpose; they are useful to you no longer; why should they cumber the ground?" Mr. Poulett Scrope objected to carrying the clause so suddenly into execution, as it would be a complete clearance of the small farmers of Ireland, and would amount to a social revolution in the state of things in that country. Mr. Sharman Crawford said he would divide the House against the clause, which he did. Strange as it may seem, some Liberal Irish members present supported the clause. Mr. Morgan John O'Connell said he looked on it as a valuable alteration in the bill. Alderman Humphrey said the phrase "quarter-acre" ought to be changed to five acres; whereupon he was told, almost in terms by Sir George Grey, that he did not understand what he was talking about. Sir George said "he was afraid his honourable friend, Alderman Humphrey, did not really see the effect of his own amendment. All holders of land, up to 4¾ acres, would, according to such an amendment, be enabled to obtain relief without selling their land." "Giving up to the landlord," not "*selling*," is the phrase in the clause. In spite of Sir George Grey's opinion to the contrary, it would seem to ordinary readers that the worthy Alderman knew quite well the force of his amendment; it was meant to feed the starving people, even though they happened to have a little land. Mr Gregory, replying in defence of his clause, used these words: "Many honourable members insisted that the operation of a clause of this kind would destroy all the small farmers. If it could have such an effect, he did not see of what use such small farmers could possibly be;" because, I suppose, they could not survive a famine that threatened the lords of the soil with bankruptcy or extinction, as they were constantly proclaiming. Mr. Gregory's words—the words of a liberal, and a pretended friend of the people—and Mr. Gregory's clause are things that should be for ever remembered by the descendants of the slaughtered and expatriated small farmers of Ireland. On a division, there were 119 for the clause and 9 against it. Here are the nine who opposed the never-to-be-forgotten quarter-acre-Gregory clause: William Sharman Crawford, B. Escott,

Sir De Lacy Evans, Alderman Humphrey, A. M'Carthy, G.P. Scrope, W. Williams. Tellers: William Smith O'Brien and J. Curteis.[204]

FOOTNOTES:

192.   So given, in the daily *journals*, but in *Hansard* the passage is much modified, and the hit at the Irish landlords disappears.

"Allow me an opportunity of correcting the error which is widely diffused among the public, and even in Parliament itself, that in *Hansard's Debates* we have the means of obtaining an authentic report of parliamentary proceedings. This is an entire delusion. *Hansard* is a private publication, dependent on the ordinary newspaper reports, supplemented by such corrections as members make themselves."—*Letter of Mr. Mitchell Henry, M.P., to the Times of July 14th, 1873.*

193.   *The Morning Chronicle.*

194.   In some reports of the speech the words are "beggars enough for all Europe."

195.   Mr. D'Israeli, in his *Political Biography* of Lord George Bentinck, quotes this passage, and, as it seems to me, manipulates it unfairly, by ending it at the word "decimated," as if there were a full stop there, whereas the sense in the original only requires a comma, and so it is in *Hansard*. To make the sense terminate at "decimated," he moulds a sentence and a half into one, thus: "The Chief Secretary says, that the ministers did wisely in this decision, but I differ from him when I hear, every day, of persons being starved to death, and when he, himself, admits that in many parts of the country the population had been decimated;" the censure on the Government contained in the words immediately succeeding, is omitted. The reason why Mr. D'Israeli did this is obvious from what follows, which shows he did not agree with Lord George, in censuring the Government for not opening depôts, and he undertakes to prove that they should not have done so. He uses, amongst others, the old trite argument, when he says: there is reason to believe that the establishment of Government depôts at the end of '46, however cautiously introduced, tended in the localities to arrest the development of that retail trade, which was then rapidly extending throughout Ireland."—*Lord George Bentinck, a political Biography, 5th Ed., pp. 360, 363.*

There is reason to believe, says Mr. D'Israeli; yes, there is the best reason to believe, that tens of thousands died of starvation in Munster and Connaught, because food depots were not introduced, or, at least, because they were not opened for the sale of food to the public. The word "development" which he uses, sufficiently refutes his whole theory. There was no time for development; millions were starving who must die or get food within a few days. What a time to begin to develop a trade in articles of food among a people without capital, who never had such a trade before! The effect of Government not interfering in the sale of food is shown by the prices Lord George quotes a little further on.

196.   Mr. D'Israeli took good care not to quote this passage in his Biography of Lord George Bentinck.

197.   It was more than hinted that he did not follow the advice of the Irish Government in other important matters concerning the Famine.

198.   In the middle of November, Mr. Smith O'Brien commenced a series of letters to the landed proprietors of Ireland. Whilst he was preparing the first of these, which was introductory, and intended to awaken the class he was addressing to a sense of their danger and their duty, the Agricultural Society of Ireland published their objections to the system of carrying out reproductive works laid down in the Chief Secretary's letter; and it was in commenting on their views that he wrote the passage quoted above by the Prime Minister. His second letter dealt with the knotty question of land tenure. In it he urges strongly and well a principle which has become a part of the Land Act of 1870, namely, the tenant's right to compensation. He says: "I begin with the subject of tenure: uniform experience of human nature teaches that men will not toil for the benefit of others as they toil for themselves. You are very sensitive about the maintenance of the due rights of property . . . The same feelings influence your tenant; he will not expend his capital upon your land unless the return of such capital be guaranteed to him." His third letter is devoted to the question of drainage, and the reclamation of waste lands. He undertook to show how advantageous a peasant proprietary would be, changing, as it would, numbers of persons from the catalogue of those who have little to gain by maintaining the rights of property, to that of those who have everything to lose by their violation. He, however, tells the landlords plainly that they will not obtain from the Imperial treasury the money necessary for the undertaking he recommends,

unless they mortgage their estates, and pledge the county rates first. "An Irish member," he writes, "who would propose to apply ten millions of money to the reclamation of land in Ireland, would be laughed to scorn in the British legislature. Yet Parliament would consent almost without a question—perhaps amidst the cheers of all parties—to the expenditure of this amount in piratical incursions, such as those made upon the inhabitants of Affghanistan, Scinde, Syria, and other nations, who have never injured us." The fourth letter is a continuation of the same subjects. The fifth discusses the railway question, then in its infancy. The sixth deals with public works and public instruction. The public works which he specially discusses and recommends are—internal navigation, and fishery piers and harbours; he does not enter into systems of education, he only calls for more liberal grants. The seventh and concluding letter of the series is devoted to what the writer calls fiscal arrangements. These letters showed much practical ability, and knowledge of the true wants of the country. They were written in a calm moderate spirit, but, emanating from a man of his political views, they do not seem to have received the attention they deserved.

No doubt, the difficulty stated by Smith O'Brien, and approvingly quoted by the Prime Minister, did exist in the townland boundary scheme; it was, perhaps, as great a one as the boundary scheme in the Chief Secretary's letter; but sacrifices should have been cheerfully submitted to on such a terrible occasion; and the greatest and realest difficulty of all was, that the landlords, as a body, had little or no sympathy with the people, and were not prepared to make sacrifices to save their lives.

199.   The following is Mr. D'Israeli's account of the waste land reclamation proposal: it does not, by any means, seem to be in accord with the spirit with which that proposal was received by Parliament:—"In the course of the next ten days the Government measures of relief distinctly transpired. One of these was a public undertaking to reclaim a portion of the waste lands of Ireland: but it was finally proposed by the first Minister, sneered at a few days after by his own Chancellor of the Exchequer, and finally fell prostrate before a bland admonition from Sir Robert Peel, who was skilful always in detecting when the Cabinet was not confident in a measure, and by an adroit interposition often obtained the credit with the country of directing the Ministry, when really he had only discovered their foregone conclusion."— *Lord George Bentinck: a political biography, p. 367, 5th Edition.*

200.   In the *Utopia*.

201.   "The people are not indolent. Of that there has been abundant proof. Give them a definite object, a fair chance of profit, and they will work as well as the people of this or any other country. Of this I have had ample opportunity of judging, on works where thousands have been employed, both here England. and in Ireland."—*A twelve months' residence in Ireland, during the Famine and the Public Works in 1846-7, by Wm. Henry Smith, C.E., late conducting Civil Engineer of Public Works.*—London, 1848; p. 120.

        "A foreign railway company, a few months ago, advertised in the English papers for Irish labourers to work on their lines, where they would receive one-third more wages than the French people themselves were receiving. He the Irishman. would do the same amount of work at home, if properly fed; but the principle is much the same as keeping a horse without his oats, and expecting him to get through his work the same as if well fed. The Irishman at the English harvest, or as a railway labourer, and the London heavy goods or coal porter, is not excelled in his willingness or industry."—*Ib.* 196.

        "It is a mistake to suppose the Irish people will not work. They are both willing and desirous to work, and, when in regular employment, are always peaceable and orderly."—*His Excellency Lord Clarendon's Letter to the Lord Mayor of London, on the "Plantation Scheme," dated Viceregal Lodge, June 26, 1849.*

202.   *Freeman's Journal*, 23rd June, 1847.

203.   Armagh could be scarcely said to have had any manufactures at this time, as machinery, erected in the large factories of Belfast and other places, had abolished the hand-looms at which the people worked in their cottages, and the linen trade had been greatly depressed for years before; but no doubt there was a time when it was a material help to the inhabitants of that and other Northern counties.

204.   Immediately after the above clause was added to the "Poor Relief (Ireland) Bill," Lord George Bentinck made the following attack upon the Irish-famine policy of the Government: "The noble Lord," says the report, "proceeded to contend that, if the Government had had recourse to the system he had recommended, it would have raised the condition of the people, and the House would not have heard of the tens of thousands and the hundreds of thousands of deaths; but they could not learn from the Government how many, for there was one point upon which the Irish Government were totally ignorant, or which they concealed, which was, the mortality which had

occurred during their administration of Irish affairs (hear, hear). They shrink (continued the noble lord, energetically) from telling us; they are ashamed to tell us. They know the people have been dying by thousands, and I dare them to inquire what has been the number of those who have died through their mismanagement, their principles of free trade (oh, oh). Yes, free trade; free trade in the lives of the Irish people (laughter, cries of 'oh, oh, oh,' and great confusion); leaving the people to take care of themselves, when Providence has swept away their food from the face of the earth. There were no stores, nor mills, nor granaries. Then why (the noble Lord continued, with much vehemence) don't he give us the information, if he don't shrink from it? Never before was there an instance of a Christian government allowing so many people to perish—(oh, oh)—without interfering (great confusion and cries of 'oh, oh'). Yes, you will groan; but you will hear this. The time will come when we shall know what the amount of mortality has been; and though you may groan, and try to keep the truth down, it shall be known, and the time will come when the public and the world will be able to estimate, at its proper value, your management of the affairs of Ireland (murmurs and confusion)."

* * * * *

CHAPTER XI.

Lord George Bentinck's Railway Scheme; he thought the finishing of the railways would be useful; he was a practical man, and wished to use the labour of the people on useful and profitable work—The State of England in 1841-2—The remedy that relieved England ought to have the same effect in Ireland—Under certain arrangements, there could have been no Irish Famine—Tons of Blue Books—No new Acts necessary for Railways—1,500 miles of Railway were passed—Only 123 miles made—Lord George Bentinck's Speech—Waste of power-traffic—Great Southern and Western Railway—Principles of the Railway Bill—Shareholders—What employment would the Railway Bill give?—Mode of raising the money—£20,000,000 paid to slave-owners—Why not do the same thing for Ireland?—Foreign Securities in which English money has been expended—Assurances of support to Lord George—The Irish Members in a dilemma—The Irish Party continue to meet—Meeting at the Premier's in Chesham Place—Smith O'Brien waits on Lord George—The Government stake their existence on postponing the second reading of Lord Bentinck's Bill—Why?—No good reason—Desertion of the Irish Members—Sir John Gray on the question—The Prime Minister's Speech—The Chancellor of the Exchequer's Speech a mockery—Loans to Ireland (falsely) asserted not to have been repaid—Mr. Hudson's Speech—The Chancellor going on no authority—Mr. Hudson's Railway Statistics—The Chancellor of the Exchequer hard on Irish Landlords—His way of giving relief—Sir Robert Peel on the Railway Bill—The Railway Bill a doomed measure—Peel's eulogium on industry in general, and on Mr. Bianconi in particular—Lord G. Bentinck's reply—His arguments skipped by his opponents—Appoint a Commission, like Mr. Pitt in 1793—Money spent on making Railways—The Irish Vote on the Bill—Names.

No effort of statesmanship to overcome the Famine is remembered with such gratitude in Ireland as Lord George Bentinck's generous proposal to spend sixteen millions of money in the construction of railways, for the employment of its people.

In the autumn of 1846, when the Potato Blight had become an accepted fact by all except those who had some motive for discrediting it, he began to think that to finish the railways, already projected in Ireland, would be the best and promptest way of employing its people upon reproductive works. He was a great enemy to unprofitable labour. To the Labour-rate Act, which became law at the close of the session of 1846, Lord George was conscientiously opposed; because, whilst millions of money were to be spent under it, the labour of the people was to be thrown away upon profitless or pernicious undertakings. His was an eminently practical mind, and, being so, he did not rest satisfied with reflections and speculations upon the plan he had conceived. He took counsel with men who were the most eminent, both for scientific and practical knowledge, with regard to the construction of railways. Among them, of course, was Robert Stephenson. The result of his conference with those gentlemen was, that two engineers of acknowledged ability were despatched by him to Ireland, to examine and report upon the whole question of Irish railways.

Lord George, reflecting upon the perilous state of England in 1841-2, came to the conclusion that it was the vast employment afforded by railway enterprize which relieved the pauperism of those years; a pauperism so great, that it was enough to create alarm, and almost dismay, in the breasts of English statesmen. There were at that time a million and a-half of people upon the rates: between eighty and ninety thousand able-bodied men within the walls of the Workhouses, and four hundred thousand able-bodied men receiving outdoor relief. It seemed to him that this pauperism was not only relieved, but was actually changed into affluence and prosperity by the vast employment which the railway works, then rapidly springing into existence, afforded. "Suddenly, and for several years," says Mr. D'Israeli, quoting Lord George, "an additional sum of thirteen millions of pounds sterling a-year was spent in the wages of our native industry; two hundred thousand able-bodied labourers received each upon an average, twenty-two shillings a-week, stimulating the revenue, both in excise and customs, by their enormous consumption of malt and spirits, tobacco and tea."[205]

Lord George saw no reason why the same remedy, if applied to Ireland, should not be attended with the like success. He was sustained, too, by the reports of Parliamentary Commissioners, as well as by the natural and common-sense view of the subject. Many years before, in 1836, a commission had been issued to enquire into the expediency of promoting the construction of railways in Ireland. The Commissioners, in their report, recommended that a system of railway communication should be established there by Government advances. Ten years had passed; but, of course, nothing was done. Yes, another commission! The noted Devon one was, I should have said, issued some years after the former by another Government, which "confirmed all the recommendations of the Railway Commissioners of '36, and pointed to those new methods of communication, by the assistance of loans from the Government, as the best means of providing employment for the people."[206] Had the recommendations of those Commissioners been carried out, or even begun within a reasonable time, there could have been no Irish famine in the sense in which we are now obliged to chronicle it. There must have been extensive employment at wages that would have afforded great numbers other and better food than the potato. As it was, all that resulted from those commissions, and countless others of the like kind, were the ponderous Blue Books, which contained their reports, and the evidence upon which they were founded. And, indeed, so many tons of those had been, from time to time, produced and stowed away in

Government vaults and rubbish stores, that, had they contained some of the nutritive qualities which, go to sustain human life, they would have been an appreciable contribution towards feeding the starving Irish people during the Famine.

No new Acts were necessary to be passed through Parliament, to authorize the construction of railways in Ireland, in order to justify the Government in advancing the necessary funds. When Lord George Bentinck brought his plan before the House of Commons, there were Acts in existence authorizing the construction of more than 1,500 miles of railway in this country, some of those Acts having been passed so far back as eleven years before; yet, at the close of 1846, only 123 miles had been completed. Here, then, was the field in which Lord George had made up his mind that the superabounding but wasted labour of the famishing people should find profitable employment. After taking the advice of his political friends, and securing their approval and support, he, on Thursday, the 4th of February, introduced his Bill to the House of Commons, in, says Mr. D'Israeli, the best speech he ever made. It was evidently prepared with great care, and was both lucid and argumentative.

His exordium was solemn and earnest, and he seemed much impressed with the importance and magnitude of the subject with which he was about to deal. For the principle of the Bill, and for the faults that principle might contain, he alone, he said, was responsible; but as to the details, they had been wrought out by the ablest minds in England; amongst whom he named Hudson, Stephenson, and Laing. "It is not my intention," he said, "to make a very long preface, or to enter into any general discussion as regards the state or condition of Ireland: suffice it for me, that this great fact stares us in the face, that at this moment there are 500,000 able-bodied persons in Ireland living upon the funds of the State. That there are 500,000 able-bodied persons, commanded by a staff of 11,587 persons, employed upon works which have been variously described as 'works worse than idleness;' by the yeomanry of Ulster as 'public follies;' and by the Inspector of the Government himself, Colonel

Douglas, as 'works which will answer no other purpose than that of obstructing the public conveyances.'" The calamity was great, but he did not, he said, despond. "We, who at one period of the war were expending, upon an average, for three years, £103,000,000 sterling a-year, will not be downhearted at having to provide for a deficiency and for a disaster that may be estimated at £10,000,000." He quoted the two Commissions above referred to, and said that railway Acts had been passed for 1,523 miles of railway, whilst at the moment he was speaking only 123 miles were completed, 164 miles being in course of construction. There must, he thought, be some weakness in Ireland up to this, as 2,600 miles of railway had been constructed in England and Scotland, and Acts passed for 5,400 miles more—8,000 miles in all. The denseness of population, said his lordship, is in favour of Ireland as against England and Scotland. "But, Sir," he continued, "perhaps you will tell me this may be a very good argument as far as population is concerned, but what is the use of population if they have no means of paying for their conveyance by railways? Sir, my friend, who sits beside me (Mr. Hudson) will tell you that in all railway speculation population is held to be the first element of success—property second,"

He then went on to show that the traffic upon the Irish railways already opened, was greater than upon the English and Scotch lines. This argument met the assertions of some persons, who said that if money were advanced to make Irish railways they would never pay; and it would be asked, if they are paying, why not have them done by private enterprise? Lord George confessed that he could not answer this question satisfactorily, but English capitalists would not come forward, partly, he thought, through distrust, and partly through ignorance, whilst the calamity of the Famine had, of course, a great effect in preventing the small amount of Irish capital which did exist from coming forward. The prejudice which English capitalists had against investing in Irish undertakings, is strikingly illustrated by a fact stated by Lord George in the course of his speech. It was this: the Great Southern and Western Railway of Ireland was one of the many the completion of

348

which was arrested by want of funds, yet a portion of it was open for traffic. He compared it with a well known English railway. The Irish one, he said, had cost in its construction £15,000 per mile; the English, upwards of £26,000 per mile; the weekly traffic on the two railways, allowing for some difference in their extent, was about the same on both, varying in amount from £1,000 to £1,300 per week; yet the unfinished British railway was at £40 premium in the market,—the unfinished Irish one at £2 discount.

1. Lord George's railway bill was simple and comprehensive. In order to encourage the making of railways in Ireland, he proposed for every £100 properly expended on such railways, £200 should be lent by the Government, at the very lowest interest at which, on the credit of the Government, that amount could be raised. He undertook to prove "that the State shall not lose one single farthing by the proposition." The current interest was £3 6s. 8d. per cent., but he would assume it to be 3½ per cent., and that the Government was to lend it at that rate, and take the whole security of the railway for the loan; consequently, a line paying £7 upon £300 expended would afford ample security for the £200 lent by the State, at £3 10s. per cent., because, of such £300, one hundred would be laid out by the company, and £200 by the Government, who, taking the whole railway for their security, would have a legal claim upon the produce of the money expended by the shareholders as well as by themselves. He took the returns of traffic on the very lowest line—that from Arbroath to Forfar, to show that even at the lowest traffic yet known on any railway, the Government would be secured against loss.

2. He next dealt with the position of shareholders under his Bill. He said they need not be alarmed at Government taking the whole railway as security, because, as matters stood, the shares of all lines stopped for want of means were valueless, or all but so, in the market; the effect of the Government loan would be to bring those dead shares to life again; for where there was a certainty of any line being finished, there was a

fair prospect of a dividend from that line. The advantage, therefore, of the loan to shareholders was self-evident. He read a letter from Mr. Carr, then chairman of the Great Southern and Western Railway of Ireland, in which the Peel Government were asked, in May, 1846, by that Company, for a loan of £500,000 to go on with their works, they undertaking to employ 50,000 men over those works, provided their request was complied with. The money was not given. No one, said Lord George, can come to any other opinion but that this offer of the Great Southern and Western Railway ought to have been accepted. If the money now asked for be lent, he said, there need be no crowding of labourers on any point, for they can be distributed over the whole country; as, according to the railway bills passed for Ireland, lines will run through every county but four. "Now, Sir," he continued, "in introducing this measure to the House, it has not been my wish to bring forward any proposition either of hostility or rivalry to the Government of my noble friend. I have assured the House publicly and privately, I have pledged my honour to my noble friend the First Minister, that I seek no advantage from the carrying of this measure, and that it is my anxious hope that we may come to the consideration of it as if it were a great private Bill, and we were all selected members of the committee to inquire into its worth."

3. In view of the amount of the loan sought for, and the mileage of the railways to be constructed, how many men, said Lord George, can we employ? Quoting Mr. Stephenson's authority, he answers that on the London and Birmingham line there were employed one hundred men a mile for four consecutive years; but Mr. Stephenson's opinion was that the Irish lines would require no more than sixty men a mile for four consecutive years. Fifteen hundred miles of railway would thus give constant employment for four consecutive years to 90,000 men on the earth works and line alone; but quarrymen, artificers, etc., would give six men more a mile—9,000 men; making fences for securing fields, etc., 9,000 more—in all, 108,000; a number representing 550,000 persons.

350

4. The labourers were specially cared for in the bill. They were to be paid weekly in cash, and decent, suitable dwellings were to be constructed for them along each line.

5. As to the manner in which the money was to be raised, Lord George did not call for a single penny out of the Imperial Exchequer; all he asked was, that the Government of England would pledge its credit to borrow for Ireland the required sum, for which Ireland had full and abundant security to give. The £16,000,000 was not to be raised at once; the loan was to be spread over four years, at the rate of £1,000,000 a quarter. The objection was put forward that the raising of this sum would oppress the money market, but Lord George pointed to the experience they had, with regard to the loan of the £20,000,000, for the slave-owners, which proved that such would not be the case. The illustration was a suggestive one. It said—You have not refused to raise £20,000,000 to free the coloured slaves in your colonies—can you venture to refuse a less sum, not merely to promote the prosperity of Ireland, but to save the Irish nation from dying of starvation? The Irish nation—the sister kingdom, your fellow-subjects, living at your very threshold—as near to you as York or Devon? And yet, I ask for them no such free grant as you gave the slave-owners; I only ask you to lend, for a time, your credit to your starving Irish brethren.

He then bursts into a passage full of heart and manliness: "Send money," he said, "out of the country as you did in 1825—invest £7,000,000 and upwards, as you did on that occasion, in Peruvian and Mexican silver mines; sink your capital, as you did then, in Bolanos (silver), in Bolivar (copper and scrip), in Cata Branca, in Conceicas, in Candonga (gold), in Cobre (copper), in Colombian, in Copaiba, and in no less than twenty-three different foreign mining companies, which the speculators of this country took in hand, because they had no railways to make; and then when your gold goes, never to come back to you, of course the funds will go down, and trade and commerce be correspondingly paralysed. Send

351

£13,000,000 to Portugal, £22,000,000 to Spain, to be sealed up in Spanish Actives, and Spanish Passives, and Spanish Deferred—and the funds will fall of course. Send as you did, in 1836, millions to Ohio for the construction of canals, and millions to Pensylvania, Illinois, and Virginia for the same purpose, to be invested in bonds of those and the other States, the borrowers of which sums set out with the determination to turn public swindlers; and the funds will certainly fall. Spend £100,000,000 in this manner, and it will lead to commercial distress, but it will be otherwise when you come to spend your £100,000,000 on the employment of your own distressed people in productive labour."

6.   Thirty years were to be allowed for the repayment of the loan.

"Sir," said Lord George, "I have heard it said, at different times, that there is danger of an outbreak in Ireland. We have heard this story a thousand times repeated, and as often refuted, 'that the starving peasantry of Ireland are purchasing arms with which to commence an outbreak in that country.' Sir, I do not believe one word of any such representation. I can only express my great surprise that, with the people starving by thousands—with such accounts as we have read during the last two days, of ten dead bodies out of eleven found lying unburied in one cabin; of seven putrid corpses in another; of dogs and swine quarreling over, and fighting for the dead carcasses of Christians; of the poor consigned coffinless to their graves, and denied the decencies of Christian burial, that the price of the coffin saved might prolong for a few days the sufferings of the dying, I, Sir, for one, *look with amazement at the patience of the Irish people.*"

He solemnly promised the House, that if they allowed this Bill to pass, and that the Irish people could have good food and good clothing, he would answer for their loyalty. "I, the Saxon," concluded the noble lord, "with my head, will answer for the loyalty and the honour of the Irish people. Yes, Sir, I, the Saxon, will lead them, through their wants fulfilled—their wishes gratified—their warm sympathies and grateful hearts—not to sever but to cement the union with England." Loud and prolonged cheering greeted this peroration.

When Lord George had concluded his masterly statement, the Prime Minister rose and complimented him on his zealous desire to benefit the people of Ireland, but at the same time declared that the Government did not think employment on the construction of railways the best suited to meet the general distress in that country; he did not deny that there would be a permanent benefit, but with such extreme destitution existing, he did not think it wise to devote £16,000,000 to the promotion of railways, as such an expenditure would check the outlay that was, at the moment, necessary for the support of the people. He would not oppose the first reading of the bill, but announced his determination to resist its further progress. After an animated discussion, in which Mr. Bernal Osborne, Mr. Roebuck, Alderman Thompson, Mr. Hume, Smith O'Brien, Mr. John O'Connell and Henry Grattan took a part, the bill was read a first time, and the 11th of February fixed for the second reading.

The Government had made up their mind to oppose Lord George Bentinck's bill. But seeing that he had a large following, and that the Irish members, and many independent English members too, would support him, they had recourse to the stale trick of weak governments—the threat of resignation. The affairs of the country were at the moment in a most critical position, and every hour's delay in sending relief to Ireland would add hundreds to the deaths from starvation. The confusion which would be caused by resignation, would inflict serious injury on the country that Lord George Bentinck was so anxious to serve: Lord John knew this well, and, therefore, he knew his threat of resignation had a certain coercive power in it. Moreover, the Tory party was split in two; Lord George was at the head of the Protectionists, who had deserted Peel, or rather, who had been deserted by him; Sir Robert had still many adherents, but a fusion of the two sections of the party was, at the moment, next to impossible, so that there could be no Tory Government framed to succeed Lord

John Russell's. What Bernal Osborne prophesied at the time, would in all likelihood have happened, that if the noble lord went out by one door, he would come in by another. Many thought the risk of breaking up the Government too great, considering the state of Ireland; and many Irish liberal members were but too glad of an excuse to keep it in office. If we assume that no action of the Irish representatives would affect any votes but the votes of those returned by Irish constituencies, the division shows that it was beyond their power to secure a majority for the second reading; but it is not unreasonable to suppose that, had the Irish members maintained a united and determined opinion in favour of the bill, English members would see the wisdom and necessity of yielding to them.

Between the 4th and the 11th great activity was shown at both sides. The friends of Lord George Bentinck, who happened to be absent from London, sent him assurances that nothing would prevent them from being present at the division; whilst the Government and their supporters laid their heads together to devise the best means of defeating the measure. One thing they deemed essential—the Irish members must be taken in hand, and their hopes and fears so wrought upon as to prevent them from giving a united and determined support to Lord George. On the day fixed for the second reading of the Bill, the Premier called a meeting of his party at his private residence. Nearly two hundred obeyed the summons. He spoke, on the occasion, against the Irish railway scheme; but his arguments were devoid of force and solidity. He said the money could not be raised, which nobody believed. He said it was generally admitted, that only twenty-five per cent. of the money spent in the construction of railways went for labour; an assertion for which neither he nor the Chancellor of the Exchequer gave any authority, and which Mr. Hudson triumphantly refuted, in his speech on the Bill next day. But Lord John further said, that he was resolved to meet the second reading with a direct negative, and that he would resign if the Government were out-voted; an announcement which, although it lacked argument, had force and meaning in it.

Several of those present at the meeting expressed their views for and against the Bill. The Irish members, especially the Liberal members, felt they were in a dilemma. They knew Lord George's proposal was popular in Ireland—regarded, in fact, as a great boon. They did not at all desire the resignation of the Government, from which they had received many favours, and expected many more. What was to be done? They hit upon a plan, which they considered would lift them out of their dilemma; they resolved to ask Lord George to postpone the second reading of his Bill, for a time, by which arrangement the Premier would not be bound to carry out his threat of resignation; and Ireland eventually might have the benefit of the railway scheme proposed by the Protectionist leader.

The party which was formed some time before, at the Rotunda meeting, and named the Irish party, as representing Ireland and its interests, without reference to politics or religion, continued to meet from time to time, in rooms they had hired in London. Those who joined it, probably, meant well in the beginning; and many of them, no doubt, meant well all through; but they undertook an impossible task, when they pledged themselves to work for their country, irrespective of their individual views, religious and political. In an hour or two after the meeting of the 11th of February, at Lord John's, had broken up, they assembled in their rooms. Some of the Irish members who were present at Chesham-place attended, and gave an account of what had transpired there. The situation was grave. Time was pressing. The second reading of Lord George's Bill would be on in a few hours. The meeting, which consisted of thirty-four Irish peers and members of Parliament, agreed to forward a request to Lord George, to postpone the second reading. The request was contained in the following resolution, with which Smith O'Brien was deputed to wait on him: "Resolved—That Lord George Bentinck be requested to postpone, to such a day as he shall appoint, the second reading of the Railway Bill, in order that the discussion on the Bill may not interfere with the progress of measures now before the House, which are of urgent and immediate importance to the famishing people of Ireland; and also in order that time may be allowed for the expression of public opinion in Ireland upon the merits of the proposal of Lord George Bentinck."

He received Mr. O'Brien in the kindest manner, but frankly told him he could not postpone the second reading of his Bill without consulting his friends. At the same time, he expressed an opinion, that if the Irish members pressed their request, it would be acceded to, provided those who were the cause of the postponement would take the responsibility of it. There was no postponement: the second reading was proceeded with that evening, as originally intended. When it came on, Smith O'Brien, who was probably appointed by the Irish party for the purpose, immediately rose, and appealed to the noble lord to postpone the second reading, saying (as the resolution had said) that the constituents of the Irish members had not had time to express their opinions on the Bill—a most delusive plea, as if, forsooth, the Irish people would at such a moment, or at any time, object to the outlay of £16,000,000 on the improvement of their country. Besides, they were known to be favourable to the Bill. Mr. O'Brien gave the true reason, when he asked Lord George to postpone the second reading, because the Government had staked their existence upon it. A change of ministry, he truly said, would throw into confusion legislation, which was of pressing necessity for Ireland. He tendered his support to the noble lord, but he was anxious to consider the question apart from a change of ministry; and he knew that many members, like himself, wished for a postponement, at least for a few days.

The debate was adjourned to the next day. The proposal of the Irish party to postpone the second reading of Lord George Bentinck's Railway Bill, does not seem to have had much to recommend it. Lord John Russell's Government would have opposed it at any time it might be brought forward, and even with a better show of reason after than before a postponement; inasmuch as the expenditure made in the meantime by the Government, to stay the famine, would be a new argument against such an outlay as Lord George's Bill contemplated. Moreover, the Irish members had no claim upon his Lordship's courtesy When his Bill was ready, he, in a most gracious manner, sent it to them for their opinion, before it was submitted to the House of Commons. After it was some time in their hands, they called a meeting, to hear Lord George explain its provisions, which he did at much length, and with great force and clearness. *He was then given to understand that the proposed Bill met the unanimous approval, and would receive the united support, of the* IRISH PARTY, *in the Upper and Lower Houses of Parliament.*[207] When they submitted to be cowed by Lord John Russell's threat of resignation—when they halted and vacillated, and at length changed, it was too much to expect the noble lord would derange his plans to accommodate such trimmers.

The following passage of a speech, delivered at a public meeting some years afterwards, lets in the light upon the motives which actuated many of the Irish members in their conduct with regard to this famous measure: "I went into a certain room in London," said the speaker, "where some thirty Irish members sat in conclave, after the intimation from Lord John Russell that he would resign if the Bill passed the second reading. The question raised at that private conference was, what was the state of each man's constituency? and it was agreed that, wherever there was a constituency that would not brook a sale, its representative must vote against the Government; but wherever there was an inactive clergy, and local leaders who sought places, and instructed their representatives in making a traffic of the votes of the people, for the purpose of getting cousins, nephews, and other connections appointed to places of emolument and gain, in these cases the representatives were required to vote against the people, and to sacrifice them; because there was a consciousness, on their part, that there were none amongst those they ought to fear, who would call them to account, before God and man, for their treachery and baseness (tremendous cheers). We are dealing here to-night, not so much with theories as facts; and I, therefore, tell you of those things which I have seen, my statements in reference to which I can vouch."[208]

The positions taken up by the proposer of the Bill were not seriously damaged during the discussions which followed. The Chancellor of the

Exchequer was the chief speaker on the Government side against the second reading; but his arguments were characterized by an honorable member as "a mockery." The only effective objection he made to the Bill he put in the foreground, when, he repeated what the Premier had said more than once before, namely, that the Government would not undertake to carry out the noble lord's plan, as they could not do so consistently with their views of public duty. He also asserted that loans to Ireland, as a rule, had not been repaid, and he instanced the loans for the making of canals in that country: a loan given to the Dublin and Kingstown railway had, he admitted, been repaid, which confession elicited cheers from Lord George Bentinck and his friends. The charge made against Ireland of not paying back what she had borrowed was met by Mr. Bernal Osborne. The Chancellor of the Exchequer had said, that he did not wish to see the State become a great money lender; in reply to which Mr. Osborne expressed the opinion, that it would be much better for the State to become a great money lender than to continue a profligate spendthrift—dissipating the funds of the country on the highways of Ireland. "Had not," he asked, "the policy of the State always been to become a great money lender? Since the Union £18,000,000 of money had been lent to England and Scotland, of which £6,000,000 had been repaid, whilst £9,002,000 had been lent to Ireland, of which £7,000,000 had been repaid." The Chancellor of the Exchequer also said in his speech, that he had been informed by a person of great experience on the subject, that only 25 per cent. of the money would go for labour; and that from twenty to thirty men per mile were all that could be employed; taking the highest figure, the noble lord's scheme, he said, would only afford employment to 45,000 workmen. Mr. Hudson, the "railway king," then the great authority on such matters, thus replied to the Chancellor's assertions: "As far as he (Mr. Hudson) could ascertain, there were but two points on which the right hon. gentleman had doubted the statements of the noble member for Lynn—namely, the number of men that would be employed on the lines, and the amount of money that would be expended on labour. As far as he could remember, those two were the only points questioned by the right hon. gentleman, the Chancellor of the Exchequer; and since then, they had been taunted by the right hon. member for Portsmouth, for not having replied to the objections made in those respects to the plan of the noble member for Lynn. He did not know on what authority the Chancellor of the Exchequer had made his statement as to the amount of money that would be expended in labour; but he wondered it had not occurred to the right hon. member for Portsmouth, that even upon the Chancellor of the Exchequer's own showing, the right hon. gentleman must have made a gross mistake. The right hon. gentleman seemed to have forgotten that, under the Bill of the noble lord, the member for Lynn, for every £4,000,000 which the Government would have to provide, the railway companies would provide £2,000,000 more. Now, the right hon. gentleman, Mr. Baring, allowed 25 per cent. for earthworks; but he only allowed that 25 per cent. on the £4,000,000, which would make £1,000,000 to be devoted to earthworks; whereas he ought to have allowed it on the £6,000,000, which would have made the amount £1,500,000. So that, by his own showing, the right hon. gentleman was at least wrong in regard to that point. He (Mr. Hudson) would give figures which would clearly show, that the noble lord's calculation was below the average amount in regard to labour, and that instead of £1,500,000, it would be nearly £4,000,000 that would be expended under that head, under his plan. Take, for instance, the expenses in constructing the North Midland Railway. That line cost, on the average, £40,000 per mile. The land cost £5,500 per mile; the permanent way cost between £5,000 and £6,000 per mile, and the parliamentary expenses about £2,000. There was an expenditure of, say, £13,000 per mile; and to what did the right hon. gentleman suppose the remaining £27,000 were devoted? That was a line of great expense and large works; but there was the York and North Midland, a line of comparatively small expense and small works, and that line cost an average of £23,000 per mile; the land having cost not more than £1,800 per mile, and the permanent way £5,500. Now, he wanted to know in what the remainder was spent? Why, undoubtedly, in labour. In the Leeds and Bradford, again—a more recently constructed line—of which the expenses had been £33,000 per mile, there had been £17,000 per mile to be calculated on the side of labour. The permanent way included sleepers and other things connected with the works. They might, perhaps, say there was a great consumption of bricks; but they could not make bricks without the employment of much labour—and with such facts as these before them, how was it possible they could doubt the accuracy of the statements of the noble lord who had brought forward this measure, and that the right hon. gentleman, the Chancellor of the Exchequer, was grossly mistaken. The right hon. gentleman, too, had said, that the number of men per mile was about twenty-five or thirty; but on the Orleans line there were as many as 130 per mile. He really thought the right hon. gentleman ought to be better informed before he came down to the House and impugned the statements of other gentlemen."[209]

The Chancellor of the Exchequer, in the course of his speech, made a statement which reflected severely on the landlords in some parts of Ireland, but which was no argument whatever against the Bill before the House. He said: A few days since, we received a report of the proceedings of a Relief Committee of a barony in the Queen's County; the subscriptions were raised by persons themselves but little removed from poverty, and with little or no assistance from the resident proprietor. The most beneficial results were produced; the whole sum raised was £176; of this £136 were subscribed by the farmers, the policemen, and the priest, and only £40 were contributed by the proprietors of the soil. I have never, said the Chancellor of the Exchequer, perused a document with greater pleasure and satisfaction, for it gives strong hopes of what may be done if all classes unite their efforts, giving money if they have it, and their personal exertions if they have no money, on behalf of their distressed countrymen. By this means alone can relief be extended to the starving population. And I confess it was with pain I can scarcely describe, that I received, by the same post that brought me the above report, an account of very different proceedings in the county of Mayo. There I find, so far from subscriptions having been entered into to maintain their people, that the landlords, or their agents, are pursuing a system of ejectment, under processes for rent, to an extent beyond what had ever been known in the country. The number of processes entered at the quarter sessions exceed, very considerably, anything they have been before. At the quarter sessions of the barony of Ballina, 6,400 processes have been entered, of which 4,000 are at the suit of the landlords for rent. The same letter further states, that—"these proceedings have almost depopulated the country, the people having fled with all they possessed to prevent their property being seized, or themselves thrown into prison, under decrees. There are districts in this barony where the townlands hitherto occupied by 400 or 500 persons are now uninhabited." This, he said, may account, perhaps, for some of the thousands landed on the quays of Liverpool from the Irish steamers; and if the same course were to be generally pursued, I should despair of the country ever being relieved.

Towards the close of the debate, Sir Robert Peel spoke against the Bill, and made one of those weak, hollow, plausible speeches for which he was justly famous. His two chief objections against it were—(1), that they had not the money to spend which Lord George Bentinck asked for, and (2) if they had, he doubted if they could not find a way of spending it more profitably for Ireland. He doubted:—yes, his habit was to kill every measure he did not approve of by doubts and fears. When Lord John Russell, at the beginning of the Session, proclaimed the determination of his Government to take in hand the reclamation of the waste lands of Ireland, and said he would begin by allocating for that purpose the, not extravagant, sum of £1,000,000, Sir Robert, in his blandest accents, expressed a hope that the noble lord would *pause* before spending so much money on such an object. Now, it is railways, Lord George Bentinck asks the Government to lend, not the public money, but the national credit, to raise a loan for extending railway accommodation, and save the lives of the people; but Sir Robert tells him England has not the money for such a purpose, and if she had, his idea was that some other way of spending it could be devised, which would be more beneficial to Ireland; but he did not favour the House with what, according to his views, that better way was.

Some weeks later, the Chancellor of the Exchequer introduced a Bill, empowering the Government to lend the paltry sum of £620,000 to Irish railways, which Sir Robert also opposed, saying that "the measure of Lord George Bentinck was free from some of the objections which forcibly applied to the present measure." He offered no objection to the giving of money to Ireland, as a pauper, but he would give none for her permanent improvement. Like certain philanthropists, who deliver homilies on alms-giving but spare their pockets, he was most liberal of his advice. He counselled us to have self-reliance, to depend upon ourselves, and not be looking to Dublin Castle or to England; whilst, on the other hand, the First Minister defended his Government against the charge of allowing the people to die of starvation, by asserting that the Irish Famine was a visitation with which no human power could cope.

Before the second reading of his Bill came on, Lord George Bentinck knew it was a doomed measure. The meeting at Lord John Russell's, the threat of resignation, the treachery of many Irish members, the opposition of Sir Robert Peel and his followers, left no doubt that the majority against the second reading would be a large one. Lord George rose after Sir Robert Peel had spoken. His feelings must have been those of a man who had made a great and noble effort for a good and holy purpose, but had failed, mainly for want of support from those who had solemnly promised it, and whose interest and duty impelled them to stand firmly by that promise. He did not spare his opponents in his reply. A good part of Sir Robert Peel's speech consisted of a eulogium upon industry, perseverance, and individual exertion; and to illustrate those valuable qualities he adduced the example of Mr. Bianconi,—a foreigner, an Italian, from Milan, Sir Robert said, who had commenced in the South of Ireland, some years before, with one stage-car: his cars now travel three thousand miles a-day: he received no Government aid. "Let me entreat you," urged the amiable ex-Premier, "to imitate that example."

"Mr. Bianconi and his cars," began Lord George, "appear to be the standing stock-in-trade of the right hon. gentleman. I am sure, that it must be in the recollection of every man who was in the House in 1839, when the Government of Lord Melbourne proposed its scheme for assisting railways in Ireland, that, word for word, what we have heard for the last half hour in the right honourable gentleman's speech, was uttered by him on that occasion. Leave private enterprise, said the right honourable gentleman, to take its own course in Ireland, and you will have railways constructed the same as you have got Mr. Bianconi's cars. But, Sir, seven years have elapsed, and what has been the result? Why, Sir, this: in England you have 2,300 miles of railroad; in Belgium there are 375 miles completed; in Austria and Germany 3,000 miles; in the United States of America, 3,300; whilst Ireland, where private enterprise is left unaided by Government, has only 123 miles of railroad. Would the House listen to this effete policy of the right honourable gentleman, or would they agree with him (Lord George Bentinck) in the opinion, that, as Government aid had succeeded in Belgium, in Austria, in Germany, in the United States of America, the aid of the Government of this country ought to be afforded to Ireland—not to supersede private enterprise, for that he had never proposed to do, but to stimulate private enterprise." Sir Robert Peel had also gone into the state of the finances of the country, to show the passing of Lord George's Bill would imperil them. Addressing himself to that argument, his lordship said, Sir Robert Peel had totally passed by, as all the three Chancellors of the Exchequer who preceded him did, the financial statement which he (Lord George Bentinck) had made a fortnight before to the House, and to which he challenged denial, that the effect of giving to Ireland £4,000,000 a-year for railways would be not only to improve her condition, but to increase the consumption of exciseable articles in Ireland; not to take away from the general taxes of the country, but to add, from the proceeds of Irish taxes, between £600,000 and £700,000 a-year to British revenue. That exposition, he said, had now run the gauntlet of three Chancellors of the Exchequer and a Prime Minister, and he thought they might take it for granted that no man in the House could gainsay it. Turning to the threat of resignation made by the Russell Cabinet, Lord George said, it was only consistent with the independence of that House and the country, that when the Government rejected a measure which the proposer of it believed to be for the good of the country, the author of such a measure ought not to shrink from any responsibility implied by the nature of his proposition; and when those who held the reins of government declared that, in the event of such a measure being carried, they must retire from responsible office, then he did not hesitate to say, that he should be wanting in spirit and independence, if he did not come forward and address the House in the language which they had already heard from him, but nothing that fell from him was conceived in a spirit of hostility to the minister of the crown. He told the Government that if they did not like to carry out the measure, they ought to do what Mr. Pitt did in 1793, appoint a commission—an unpaid commission—to carry it out. "Let them put me," said Lord George, "at the head of that commission, and I will be responsible for carrying out the plan, without the loss of a shilling to the country; if I fail, I am willing to accept the risk of impeachment. I offer no quarter; it is most just that I should receive no quarter. I offer myself to carry out the measure at the risk of impeachment, without its costing the country a single shilling. I am quite willing to be answerable for its success. It is a measure offered on no old party grounds; it is a measure that rests on no religious prejudices; it confiscates no property; it introduces no agrarian law; it will feed the hungry and clothe the naked, by borrowing from the superfluities of the rich. It is my honest and earnest prayer that it may be successful; and, should it fail, I care not if it be the last time I address this or any other mortal assembly."

Although the more usual course would have been for the House to divide after Lord George's address, during which the call for a division was heard more than once, the Prime Minister, as a mark of respect to the House, he said, rose and made a speech, thus giving the Government the last word. He did not intend to reply to the proposer of the Bill, but he wished to give his view of the existing state of things. He did so. It was charged with gloomy apprehensions. He agreed with Sir Robert Peel, that the finances would not bear the strain a loan of £16,000,000 would put upon them.[210] Six hundred thousand persons were receiving wages on the public works in Ireland, representing, he would say, 3,000,000 of the population. There were 100,000 in the Workhouses; and, taking with these the thousands subsisting by private charity, there were, he considered, three and a-half millions of the Irish people living by alms. He repeated, once again (on the authority of some important but nameless person, whom Lord George Bentinck called "the great Unknown"), that only one-fourth of the money expended in making railways went for unskilled labour. It was well into the small hours of the morning before the division bell rung, after a three nights' debate. In a house of 450, the Bill was supported by only 118 votes. A majority of 214 for the Government left them secure in their places.[211]

Of the one hundred and five members returned from Ireland, sixty-six voted—thirty-nine with Lord George Bentinck, and twenty-seven against him. There were Liberals and Tories at both sides. The noble proposer of the Irish Railway Scheme proclaimed—and, no doubt, intended—that it should not be regarded as a party question. After his very effective speech on introducing it, the common opinion was that it would be carried. It was popular in the House and out of it. Everybody in England and in Ireland was sick of spending money on unprofitable work. Lord John Russell saw but one way of defeating the measure, and that was to make it a party question; and so he made it one. We find some of the most decided Irish Tories voting for the Bill, whilst many Whigs and professing patriots voted against it.[212] For some days before the division it was known the Bill would be defeated, but few, if any, thought the majority against it would have been so large. After his seven or eight months of hard work, in preparing and maturing his Railway

Scheme, its rejection touched Lord George keenly; but his lofty spirit would not stoop to manifest his feelings.

He had, however, the gratification to see himself vindicated, not to say avenged, a few weeks afterwards. The Chancellor of the Exchequer, the great opponent and decrier of Lord George's Bill, actually brought in a Railway Bill himself of a similar character. Politicians, in their statements, are ever watchful to leave themselves loopholes for retreat. The Prime Minister, in the discussion on Lord George's Bill, "would not say that money should not be given, under any circumstances, to make railways in Ireland, but," in his opinion, "it should be in a different state of the country." What difference there was between the state of Ireland on the 16th of February, 1847, when the Government opposed and defeated an Irish Railway Bill, and on the 26th of April, of the same year, when the Government brought in a Railway Bill of their own, no one but the Government could see. It is not even a fair statement of the case to name the 26th of April, the day on which the Chancellor of the Exchequer brought in the Government Bill, because that Bill must have been some time in preparation—probably in preparation when they were opposing the generous and manly scheme of Lord George Bentinck. Yet, with his little proposal for a loan of £620,000 to Irish railways, he had the face to go down and tell the House that, "in the present state of Ireland, it was impossible to deny that, by this course, a great impetus must be given to employment, where the advances could be safely made." He even contradicted his own assertion, made with such confidence on the information of "the great Unknown," that only 25 per cent. would go for labour, and admitted, that more would be expended upon it than Lord George Bentinck ever assumed there would. After several members had condemned the proposal in strong terms, that noble lord rose, and assured the Chancellor of the Exchequer that he would not object to the vote going forward. "There was," he said, "more joy over one sinner that repenteth, than over ninety-nine just persons." He greatly rejoiced to find that ministers had at length discovered that it was cheaper for

England to lend her money (receiving interest for it) upon reproductive works, than upon those useless relief works, which were to return no interest and produce no fruits. He greatly rejoiced, also, to hear from the Chancellor of the Exchequer, that, in the course of the last two months, he had become better instructed upon the subject of the number of men to whom the construction of railways would give employment. He (Lord George Bentinck) had proposed to employ one hundred and ten thousand men with £6,000,000, but the Chancellor of the Exchequer then told the House that £6,000,000 laid out in railways would only furnish employment for forty-five thousand labourers. Now, the Chancellor of the Exchequer told the House that £600,000 would employ fifteen thousand labourers; so that, upon his calculations, £6,000,000 would afford employment not merely for one hundred and ten thousand, as he (Lord George Bentinck) had formerly stated, but for one hundred and fifty thousand able-bodied labourers. It must, said Lord George, be a great disappointment to the people of Ireland, to find upon what false grounds they were deprived of their darling measure for the construction of railways. He was glad the right hon. gentleman had at last come to his senses, and proposed to grant a portion, at least, of the £16,000,000. He (Lord George) now found, that his calculation, that £16,000,000 would give employment to one hundred and ten thousand men in Ireland, for a certain number of years, was understated. When it suited the purpose of the Chancellor of the Exchequer, a million of money would give employment to half as many more able-bodied labourers, as it could when it suited his purpose to resist a motion proposed by his opponents. "Let it be remembered, the Chancellor of the Exchequer argues in favour of this measure, that the money he asks for will certainly be paid back, while only one-half, he tells you, of the money advanced or relief works is sought to be reclaimed. Why, Sir, that was just my argument three months ago."

The Chancellor of the Exchequer's Bill was carried by a large majority.

It is a pity that noble-hearted Englishman, Lord George Bentinck, did not live long enough to see how enduring the gratitude of the Irish people has been for the friendly and bounteous hand he endeavoured to stretch out to them, in their hour of sorest need. Seven-and-twenty years have passed away since then; yet that gratitude still survives, nor is it likely soon to die out amongst a people noted for warm hearts and long memories.

FOOTNOTES:

205. Lord George Bentinck, a political Biography, 5th edit., p. 339.
206. *Ib.* p. 340.
207. Special London Correspondent of *Freeman's Journal.*
208. Speech of Dr. (now Sir John) Gray, at the Tuam Banquet, 24th January, 1854.
209. "The speech of the night was that of King Hudson. In a most masterly manner he swept away the rubbish, of the Whig Chancellor."—*Special Correspondent of Dublin Freeman.*
210. "How is it that a war expenditure never alarms our practical public, while half the amount employed among ourselves produces something like a panic? We spent millions on the Affghanistan war, and had a whole army destroyed, with no one result whatever; there was scarcely a remark made about it, and the generals who commanded the expedition that led to defeat and disgrace got peerages and pensions . . . We will put it to any one whether, if Lord George Bentinck had, as a general (and had he continued in the army he might have been one), caused the positive loss for ever of sixteen millions to this country, in a campaign at the other end of the world, he would have been visited with such a torrent of ridicule as that poured upon him on account of his plan for laying out that sum at home, with an absolute certainty of its return? No; his destruction of that amount of capital would have been rewarded with a peerage and a pension for three lives."—*Illustrated London News, May 8th, 1847.*
211. The majority was at first announced to be 204, but it was afterwards found to be 214.
212. The following were the votes of the Irish members on the occasion:

FOR THE BILL.	AGAINST THE BILL.
Colonel Acton,	Viscount Acheson,
Sir H.W. Barron,	R.M. Bellow,
T. Bateson,	R.D. Browne,
Viscount Bernard,	Hon. R.S. Carew,
M.J. Blake,	Viscount Castlereagh,
Sir A.B. Brooke,	Hon. C.C. Cavendish,
Colonel Bruen,	B. Chapman,
W.M. Bunbury,	M.E. Corbally,
P.J. Butler,	Hon. H.T. Corry,
Lord J.L. Chichester,	Hon. T. Dawson,
Hon. H.A. Cole,	Sir T. Esmonde.
Colonel Conolly,	F. French,
E.A. Fitzgerald,	Sir B. Howard,
H. Grattan,	J. O'Brien,
W.H. Gregory,	M.J. O'Connell,
E. Grogan,	O'Connor Don,
J.H. Hamilton,	J. Power,
G.A. Hamilton,	Colonel Rawdon,
Lord E. Hill,	D.R. Ross,
J. Kelly,	Right Hon. F. Shaw,
D.S. Kerr,	Right Hon. E.L. Sheil,
P. Kirk,	J.P. Somers,
Hon. C. Lawless,	Sir W.M. Somerville,
A. Lefroy,	W.V. Stuart,
C.P. Leslie,	W.H. Watson,
Major M'Namara,	H. White,
A. M'Carthy,	T. Wyse.
T.B. Martin,	
Viscount Newry,	
Sir D. Norreys,	
Viscount Northland,	
C. O'Brien,	
W.S. O'Brien,	
D. O'Connell, jun.	
John O'Connell,	
E. Smithwick,	
E. Taylor,	
H.M. Tuite,	
Sir W. Verner.	

CHAPTER XII.

State of the Country during the Winter of 1847—State of Clare—Capt. Wynne's Letter—Patience of the suffering people—Ennis without food. The North—Belfast: great distress in it—Letter to the *Northern Whig*. Cork: rush of country people to it—Soup—Society of Friends—The sliding coffin—Deaths in the streets—One hundred bodies buried together!—More than one death every hour in the Workhouse. Limerick: Experience of a Priest of St. John's. Dublin: Dysentery more fatal than cholera—Meetings—"General Central Relief Committee for all Ireland"—Committee of the Society of Friends—The British Association for the Relief of Extreme Distress in Ireland and Scotland. The Government—Famine not a money question—so the Government pretended—Activity of other countries in procuring food—Attack on Divine Providence—Wm. Bennett's opinion. Money wages not to be had from farmers. Was it a money or food question?—The navigation laws—Freights doubled—The Prime Minister's exposition—Free Trade in theory—protection in practice—The Treasury says it cannot find meal. President Folk's message to Congress—America burthened with surplus corn—could supply the world—Was it a money question or a food question? Living on field roots—Churchyards enlarged—Three coffins on a donkey cart. Roscommon—no coffins—600 people in typhus fever in one Workhouse!—Heroic virtue—The Rosary. Sligo—Forty bodies waiting for inquests!—Owen Mulrooney—eating asses' flesh. Mayo—Meeting of the County—Mr. Garvey's statement. Mr. Tuke's experiences—Inquests given up—W.G.'s letters on Mayo—Effect of

Famine on the relations of landlord and tenant—Extermination of the smaller tenantry—Evictions—Opinion of an eyewitness—A mother takes leave of her children—Ass and horse flesh—something more dreadful! (*Note*). The weather—its effects. Count Strezelecki. Mr. Egan's account of Westport—Anointing the people in the streets! The Society of Friends— Accounts given by their agents. Patience of tho people—Newspaper accounts not exaggerated. Donegal—Dunfanaghy—Glenties—Resident proprietors good and charitable. Skull—From Cape Clear to Skull—The Capers—Graveyard of Skull—Ballydehob—The hinged coffin—Famine hardens the heart. Rev. Traill Hall—Captain Caffin's narrative—Soup-kitchens—Officials concealing the state of the people—Provision for burying the dead—The boat's crew at a funeral. State of Dingle. Father Mathew's evidence. Bantry—Inquests—Catherine Sheehan—Richard Finn—Labours of the Priests—Giving a dinner away—Fearful number of deaths—Verdict of "Wilful murder" against Lord John Russell—The Workhouse at Bantry—Estimated deaths—The hinged coffin—Shafto Adair's idea of the Famine.

The year 1846 closed in gloom. It left the Irish people sinking in thousands into their graves, under the influence of a famine as general as it was intense, and which trampled down every barrier set up to stay its desolating progress. But the worst had not yet come. It was in 1847 that the highest point of misery and death had been reached. Skibbereen, to be sure, ceased to attract so much attention as it had been previously doing, but the people of that devoted town had received much relief; besides, there were now fewer mouths to fill there, so many were closed in death, at the Windmill-hill, in the Workhouse grounds, and in the churchyard of Abbeystrowry. Instead of one, Ireland had now many Skibbereens. In short, the greater part of it might be regarded as one vast Skibbereen. In the Autumn of 1846, the famine, which all saw advancing, seized upon certain districts of the South and West; but as ulcers, which first appear in isolated spots upon the body, enlarge until, touching each other, they become confluent, so had the famine, limited in its earlier stages to certain localities, now spread itself over the entire country. Hence, it is not in any new forms of suffering amongst the famine-stricken people that its increasing horrors are to be looked for: it is in its universality, and in the deadly effects of a new scourge—fever—which was not only manifesting itself throughout the land at this time, but had already risen to an alarming height—a thing not to be wondered at, because it is the certain offspring, as well as the powerful auxiliary, of famine.

In the fall of 1846, several parts of Clare were in a very wretched condition; but, at the opening of the new year, the most prosperous localities in that county had been sucked into the great famine vortex. Writing at this period from Ennis, the chief town, Captain Wynne says: "The number of those who, from age or exhaustion and infirmity, are unable to labour, is becoming most alarming; to those the public works are of no use; they are, no doubt, fit subjects for private charity and the exertions of relief committees, but it is vain to look to these sources for relief at all commensurate with the magnitude of the demand. Deaths are occurring from Famine, and there can be no doubt that the Famine advances upon us with giant strides." Several of the officials who had written to Sir Randolph Routh and others, from different parts of the country, blamed the people for their listlessness, their idleness, and the little interest they seemed to take in cropping their land, in order to secure a future supply of food. Addressing himself to this point, Captain Wynne says: "It is in vain to direct their [the people's] attention to the prosecution of those agricultural operations which can alone place any limit to their present deplorable condition. Agricultural labour holds out a distant prospect of reward—their present necessities require immediate relief. Such is their state of alarm and despair at the prospect before them, that they cannot be induced to look beyond to-morrow; *thousands never expect to see the harvest.* I must say the majority exhibit a great deal of patience, meekness, and submission." Again, in the same letter: "The effects of the Famine are discernible everywhere: not a domestic animal to be seen—pigs and poultry have quite disappeared. The dogs have also vanished, except here and there the ghost of one, buried in the skeleton of one of those victims of cruelty and barbarity, which have been so numerous here within the last two months—I allude to the horses and donkeys that were shot. It is an alarming fact that, this day, in the town of Ennis, there was not a stone of breadstuff of any description to be had on any terms, nor a loaf of bread."[213]

In the chief cities, the pressure of the Famine, day by day, became greater. In Belfast, the flourishing seat of the linen trade, one of the gentlemen appointed to visit the different districts, with the view of ascertaining the real amount of distress amongst the poor, writes in the following terms to the *Northern Whig*: "There is not any necessity that I should point out individual cases of abject want, though in my visitations I have seen many of whose extreme destitution I could not possibly have formed a true estimate had I not seen them. Let it suffice, however, to state, that in many of our back lanes and courts there are families in the veriest wretchedness, with scarcely enough of rags to cover their shivering emaciated bodies; they may be found huddled together around a handful of dying cinders, or endeavouring to fan into flame a small heap of damp smoking sawdust Perhaps when they have not been happy enough to procure even that scanty fuel, they will be found, to the number of five or six—some well, some ill, and all bearing the aspect of pinching hunger—endeavouring to procure warmth by crouching together upon a scanty heap of filthy straw, or mouldering wood shavings, their only covering an old worn-out rag of a blanket or a coverlet, that has been so patched and re-patched that its original texture or colour it would be impossible to discern. On looking around this miserable dwelling, nothing meets the eye save the damp floor and the bare walls, down which the rain, or condensed vapour, is plentifully streaming. Not a stool, chair, or seat of any description, in many instances, is to be seen, nor commonest utensil; and as for food, not so much as would satisfy the cravings of even a hungry infant. Let not this picture be deemed overdrawn. If any one suppose it exaggerated, had that individual been with me, on Sunday last, I could have shown him some instances of suffering, that would have removed all doubt regarding the reality of distress in Belfast. I will merely mention one of them:—"I entered a house to which my attention had been directed; in the kitchen there was not a single article of furniture— not even a live cinder on the cold deserted-looking hearth. In the inner room I found a woman, lately confined, lying upon a heap of chopped-up rotten straw, with scarcely a rag to cover her; beside her nestled two children, pictures of want, and in her bosom lay her undressed babe, that, four days before, had first seen the light. She had no food in the house, nor had she, nor her children, had anything since her confinement, save a little soup procured from the public kitchen. Such was her statement; and the evidence of her wretched dwelling bore but too ample testimony to her melancholy tale."

Large numbers were in a state of utter destitution in the city of Cork. As happened in other cities and important towns, the country people flocked in to swell the misery; and roaming in groups through the streets, exhibiting their wretchedness, and imploring relief, they gave them a most sad and deplorable appearance. Even the houses of once respectable tradesmen, denuded of every article of furniture, and without fuel or bedding, presented a most affecting spectacle of want and misery. And so impressed were the committee of the Society of Friends in Cork with the sufferings of this class, that a separate subscription was raised for supplying them with straw beds and some fuel. The apparatus which this committee had erected for the making of soup was, they thought at first, on too extensive a scale, but it was soon found to be insufficient to meet the calls which were daily made upon it. Their Report of the 1st of February says: "Our distribution of soup is rapidly increasing; during the past week it averaged one thousand and sixteen quarts a-day, and on seventh day it reached the extent of twelve hundred and sixty-eight quarts." It went on increasing until it had, a fortnight later, reached fourteen hundred quarts a-day. Besides the distribution of soup by the Society of Friends, there

374

were four district soup houses, supplying over six-thousand quarts of soup daily; so that, at this time, forty-eight thousand quarts of soup were made and distributed weekly in the city of Cork. There was a nominal charge of a penny or so a quart for some of this soup, but much of it was given away gratuitously. Speaking of the accounts from different parts of the county Cork, the Report says:—"Where the potato crop was most completely annihilated—in the far west—the Famine first appeared, but other quarters were also invaded, as the remnant of the crop became blighted or consumed. Hence, in localities, which until recently but slightly participated in this afflictive visitation, distress and destitution are now spreading, and the accounts from some of these are presenting the same features of appalling misery as those which originally burst upon an affrighted nation from the neighbourhood of Skibbereen." In the postscript of a letter to the *Cork Examiner*, Rev. James O'Driscoll, P.P., writing from Kilmichael, says: "Since writing the above a young man named Manley, in fever at Cooldorahey, had to be visited. He was found in a dying state, without one to tend him. *His sister and brother lay dead quite close to him in the same room. The sister was dead for five days, and the brother for three days.* He also died, being the last of a large family. The three were interred by means of a sliding coffin."

The Cork Workhouse was crowded to excess, and the number of deaths in it, at this time, was simply frightful: they were one hundred and seventy-four in a single week—more than one death in every hour.[214] In one day, in the beginning of February, there were forty-four corpses in the house; and on the 10th of that month one hundred bodies were conveyed for interment to a small suburban burial place near Cork. Several persons were found dead in the streets; numbers of bodies were left unburied for want of coffins. Under a shed at the Shandon guard-house lay some thirty-eight human beings; old and young, men, women, and infants of tenderest age, huddled together like so many pigs or dogs, on the ground, without any covering but the rags on their persons.[215]

The *Limerick Examiner*, in giving an account of the state of the poor in that city, publishes a day's experience of one of the Catholic priests in the Parish of St. John. In one day he was called to officiate at the death-beds of seven persons who were dying of starvation, the families of which they were members comprising, in all, twenty-three souls. The wretched abodes in which he found them were much of the same character—no beds, scarcely any clothing, no food, the children quite naked. In one of those miserable dwellings he could not procure a light, to be used whilst administering the Sacraments to a dying woman; and such was the general poverty around, that *the loan of a candle could not be obtained in the neighbourhood*. His last visit was to a girl in fever, who had had three relapses. He found her father and mother tottering on their limbs from want. The father said he had a dimness in his eyes, and he thought he would become mad from hunger before night.

Dublin, notwithstanding its many advantages, did not escape the all-pervading scourge. In the month of December, 1846, there were seven hundred persons under treatment for dysentery in the South Union Workhouse, besides convalescents. The disease proved more fatal than cholera. Parochial meetings were held, and committees appointed to collect funds for the relief of the starving people; besides which a meeting of the citizens was convened at the Music Hall, on the 23rd of December, to form a general committee for the whole city. In the unavoidable absence of the Lord Mayor, it was presided over by Alderman Staunton, Lord Mayor elect. The meeting was very numerously attended by leading citizens and clergymen of various denominations. Amongst the latter were the Most Rev. Dr. Murray, Archbishop of Dublin, and the Provost of Trinity College. A committee was formed, whose duties were to raise funds, and, "by a due disbursement thereof," for the relief of the necessitous, to endeavour to mitigate "the alarming and unparalleled distress of the poor of the city," and so arrest the progress of "a train of evils that must otherwise follow in the track of famine."

Four days later "The General Central Relief Committee for all Ireland" sprang into existence, under the chairmanship of the Marquis of Kildare, the present Duke of Leinster. This became a very important and useful body, having disbursed, during the year of its existence, over seventy thousand pounds. Greater still were the results achieved by a committee formed on the 13th of November, 1846, by the Society of Friends. That admirably managed body sent members of the Society to the most distressed parts of the country, in order to investigate on the spot the real state of things, and report upon them. This committee received from various parts of the world, the very large sum of £198,326 15s. 5d., two thousand seven hundred of which remained unappropriated when they closed their glorious labours in the cause of benevolence. But of all the charitable organizations produced by the Famine, the most remarkable was "The British Association for the Relief of *Extreme Distress* in Ireland and Scotland."[216] This association received in subscriptions, at home and abroad, over £600,000. The balance in hands, when they drew up their report, was the very trifling one of fourteen hundred pounds; whilst so many of those more immediately connected with this gigantic work laboured gratuitously, that the whole expense of management was only £12,000, barely two per cent. Further on, I shall have an opportunity of speaking more in detail of charitable committees.

There is one curious fact regarding the Government in connection with those committees. It is this: The Government seemed anxious to have it understood, that it was not the money outlay which concerned or alarmed them, but the difficulty of procuring food, and the probability of not being able to procure it in sufficient quantity, by any amount of exertion within their power. "Last year," writes Mr. Trevelyan, "it was a money question, and we were able to buy food enough to supply the local deficiency; but this year it is a food question. The stock of food for the whole United Kingdom is much less than is required; and if we were to purchase for Irish use faster than we are now doing, we should commit a crying injustice to the rest of the country." And again, in the same letter: "I repeat that it is not a money question. If twice the value of all the meal which has been, or will be, bought, would save the people, it would be paid for at once."[217] In face of this assertion, our Government, as we have already seen, allowed the French, Belgians, and Dutch, who were in far less need than we, to be in the food markets before them, and to buy as much as they required—even in Liverpool, which they cleared of Indian corn in a single day. If food were the difficulty, and not money, it is not easy to see what great advantage there was in those charitable associations, formed to receive *money* subscriptions for the purchase of food. Of what use was money, if food were not procurable with it? The aid of such bodies, in investigating cases of destitution and distributing food, would, no doubt, be very valuable; but this service they could render the Government as well without subscriptions as with them. Writing to Sir R. Routh, in December, 1846, Mr. Trevelyan says: "I have continued to forward the plan of a private subscription, as far as it lay in my power, both in Ireland and in England; and Sir George Grey (Home Secretary) has rendered his more powerful assistance. I think it will be brought to bear."[218] It was brought to bear; and in a later communication, he speaks of the British Association with evident satisfaction. "The subscription is going on very well," he says; "six names down for a thousand pounds each, and a good working committee organized."[219]

The Government, it may be fairly said, should not refuse any aid proffered to them. Certainly not; but they did more. They showed a decided anxiety to receive aid in money, not only from landlords, who were bound to give it, but from any and every quarter—even from the Great Turk himself, who subscribed a thousand pounds out of his bankrupt treasury, to feed the starving subjects of the richest nation in the world. And the noblemen and gentlemen who signed the Address of Thanks to the Sultan Abdul Medjid Khan, for his subscription, amongst other things, say to his majesty, that "It had pleased Providence, in its wisdom, to deprive this country suddenly of its staple article of food, and to visit the poor inhabitants with privations, such as have seldom fallen to the lot of any civilized nation to endure. In this emergency, the people of Ireland *had no other alternative but to appeal to the kindness and munificence of other countries* less afflicted than themselves, to save them and their families from famine and death."[220] Besides making the Famine a money question, this address contains the blasphemous attack upon Divine Providence, so current at the time among politicians. William Bennett, one of those praiseworthy gentlemen whom the Society of Friends sent to distribute relief in the Far West, was, however, of opinion that the responsibility of the Irish Famine should not be laid at the door of Divine Providence, at least without some little investigation. In his letters to his committee, he endeavoured, he says, to give a bird's-eye view, as it were, of the distressed portions of Ireland, drawn upon the spot, with the vivid delineation of truth, but without exaggeration or colouring. And what is the picture, he asks? "Take the line of the main course of the Shannon continued north to Lough Swilly, and south to Cork. It divides the island into two great portions, east and west. In the eastern there are distress and poverty enough, as part of the same body suffering from the same cause; but there is much to redeem. In the west it exhibits a people, not in the centre of Africa, the steppes of Asia, the backwoods of America—not some newly-discovered tribes of South Australia, or among the Polynesian Islands—not Hottentots, Bushmen, or Esquimaux—neither Mahommedans nor Pagans—but some millions of our own Christian nation at home, living in a state and condition low and degraded to a degree unheard of before in any civilized community; driven periodically to the borders of starvation; and now reduced by a national calamity to an exigency which all the efforts of benevolence can only mitigate, not control; and under which thousands are not merely pining away in misery and wretchedness, but are dying like cattle off the face of the earth, from want and its kindred horrors! *Is this to be regarded in the light of a Divine dispensation and punishment? Before we can safely arrive at such a conclusion, we must be satisfied that human agency and legislation, individual oppressions, and social relationships have had no hand in it.*"[221] Was it not a money question, when a labourer at task work could only earn 8d. or 8-1/4d. a-day?—not enough to buy one meal of food for a moderate sized family. No, no, answered the Government people; this low rate of wages is fixed, in order not to attract labour from the cultivation of the soil. Now, in the famine time, the labourer, as a rule, could not obtain money wages for the cultivation of the soil—a fact well known to the Government; so that *money wages* of almost any amount must withdraw him from agriculture, from the absolute necessity he was under of warding off immediate starvation. If, therefore, Government wished the labour of the country to be employed in cultivating and improving the soil, why did they not, instead of spoiling the roads, so employ that labour at fair money wages, and subject to just and proper conditions? They were often urged to do it, but in vain. They yielded at last, but at an absurdly late period for such a concession.

Further: if it were solely a food question, the Government should have used all the means in their power to bring food into the country, which they did not do; because they refused to suspend the navigation laws—this free-trade government did, and thus deliberately excluded supplies from our ports. By the navigation laws, merchandize could be brought to these countries only in British ships, or in ships belonging to the nation which produced the merchandize. The importation of corn fell under this *protective* regulation. If those laws were suspended in time, food could be carried to British ports in the ships of *any* nation; and in fact, whilst a great outcry was raised by our Government about the scarcity of food, and the want of ships to carry it, Odessa and other food centres were crowded with vessels, *looking for freights to England, but could not obtain them*, in consequence of the operation of the navigation laws. The immediate effect was, a great difficulty in sending food to those parts of Ireland where the people were dying of sheer starvation. But a second effect was, the enrichment, to an enormous extent, of the owners of the mercantile marine of England; freights having nearly doubled in almost every instance, and in a most important one, that of America, nearly trebled. The freights from London to Irish ports had fully trebled.

The Prime Minister came down to Parliament at the end of January, 1847, and proposed the suspension of the Navigation Laws until the first of September following; in order, he said, that freights might be lowered and food come in more abundantly; but, as one of the members said in the debate that followed, the proposal, good in itself, came too late, being made at a time when the surplus of the harvest of 1846 was to a great extent, disposed of. In his speech proposing the suspension of the Navigation Laws, Lord John Russell used, of course, in its favour the arguments which everybody was tired pressing upon himself for months before; but he especially dwelt upon the great increase of freights. The ordinary freight from the Danube, said his lordship, used to be 10s. the quarter; it is now 16s. 6d. to 17s.; from Odessa, 8s.; it is 13s. to 13s. 6d. at present: from the United States, 5s.; it is now 12s. 6d. to 13s.; and what concerns Ireland still more, he said, the usual freight from London to Cork was 1s. to 1s. 3d. the quarter, and often considerably less; it is now 3s. to 3s. 6d. the quarter, with much difficulty in finding vessels even at those freights.

Lord John and his representatives in Ireland were exceedingly fond of propounding free trade principles to those who complained that the Irish harvest—the natural food of the Irish people—was being taken out of the country. O'Connell, early in the Famine, said: close your ports against the exportation of your corn—open them to the corn markets of the world. This and the like advice was ridiculed as "Protection," and "Ignorance," by those ostentatious apostles of free trade, who kept the Navigation Laws in full force, in order to protect the monopoly of English shipowners; and who, rather than share with other nations the profits arising from carrying the food which would have saved the Irish people, *protected that monopoly*, and left their fellow subjects to die of famine, rather than withdraw the protection. Talk of Lord John and his free trade government after that.

In the letter already quoted from the *Commissariat Series* (p. 409), and bearing date the 24th of December, Mr. Trevelyan, on the part of the Government, says to Sir R. Routh: "You write as if it were in our power to purchase grain and meal at our discretion, but I can assure you that this is far from being the case. The London and Liverpool markets are in a more exhausted state than you appear to be aware of, and the supplies which are to be expected till April, are so totally inadequate to filling the immense void which has been created by the failure of the potato crop, the deficiency of the Spring crops, and the foreign demand, that they give us no confidence . . . You must therefore bear in mind, and impress upon all those with whom you are acting, that even the stock of food at your disposal has a certain fixed limit, and that it must be economized, and made to last the requisite time, like any private stock. The Chancellor of the Exchequer will, on no account, permit you to undertake to provide food for any portion of the Eastern district of Ireland. What we have is insufficient even for the Western district, for which we have undertaken . . . No exigency, however pressing, is to induce you to undertake to furnish supplies of food for any districts, except those for which we have already undertaken."

This letter, written, as all Mr. Trevelyan's were, by the authority of the Treasury, assumes that the Government had a full knowledge of the state of the food markets. And, no doubt, it was their bounden duty to collect such knowledge, by trusty agents, despatched at the earliest moment, to investigate and report upon the harvest-yield in Europe and America. Yet, at the very time it was written, President Polk's message to Congress, delivered in Washington on the 8th of December, arrived in England, containing the following passage: "The home market alone is inadequate to enable them [the farmers] to dispose of the immense supplies of food which they are capable of producing, even at the most reduced prices, for the manifest reason that they cannot be consumed in the country. The United States can, from their immense surplus, supply not only the home demand, but the deficiency of food required by the whole world."

Was it a money question or a food question?

There was, naturally enough, a mournful sameness in the news from every part of the country: starvation, famine, fever, death; such are the commonest headings in the newspapers of the time. Seven deaths from starvation near Cootehill was the announcement from a locality supposed not to be at all severely visited. In Clifden, County Galway, the distress was fearful; 5000 persons there were said to be trying to live on field roots and seaweed. A Catholic priest who was a curate in the County Galway during the Famine, but who now occupies, as he well deserves to do, a high position in the Irish Church, has kindly supplied the author with some of his famine experiences. There are five churchyards in the parish where he then ministered. Four of these had to be enlarged by one half during the famine, and the fifth, an entirely new one, became also necessary, that there might be ground enough wherein to inter the famine-slain people. This enlargement of burial accommodation took place, as a rule throughout the South, West, and North-west. One day as this priest was going to attend his sick calls—and there was no end of sick calls in those times—he met a man with a donkey and cart. On the cart there were three coffins, containing the mortal remains of his wife and his two children. He was alone—no funeral, no human creature near him. When he arrived at the place of interment, he was so weakened by starvation himself, that he was unable to put a little covering of clay upon the coffins to protect them. When passing the same road next day, the priest found ravenous, starved dogs making a horrid meal on the carcasses of this uninterred family. He hired a man, who dug a grave, in which what may be literally called their remains were placed. On one occasion, returning through the gray morning from a night call, he observed a dark mass on the side of the road. Approaching, he found it to be the dead body of a man. Near his head lay a raw turnip, with one mouthful bitten from it. In several of the reports from the Board of Works' inspectors, and other communications, it was said that as the Famine progressed, the people lost all their natural vivacity. They looked upon themselves as doomed; and this feeling was expressed by their whole bearing. The extent to which it prevailed amongst all classes is well illustrated by a circumstance related by the same clergyman. When the Famine had somewhat abated in intensity, he was one day in a field which was separated from the public road by a wall. He heard a voice on the road; it was that of a peasant girl humming a song. The tears rushed to his eyes. He walked quickly towards her, searching meantime for some coin to give her. He placed a shilling in her hand, with a feeling somewhat akin to enthusiasm. "It was," said he to the author, "the first joyous sound I had heard for six months."

From Roscommon the brief, but terrible, tidings came that whole families, who had retired to rest at night, were corpses in the morning; and were frequently left unburied for many days, for want of coffins in which to inter them. And the report adds: The state of our poorhouse is awful; the average daily deaths in it, from fever alone, is eighteen; there are upwards of eleven hundred inmates in it, and of these six hundred are in typhus fever.[222] In a circumference of eight miles from where I write, says a correspondent of the *Roscommon Journal*, not less than sixty bodies have been interred without a coffin. In answer to queries sent to a part of Roscommon, I received the following replies from a reliable source: *Query.* "What other relief was given during the Government works by private charity, committees, etc.?" *Answer.* "There was considerable relief given by charitable committees." *Query.* "What did the wealthy resident landlords give?" *Answer.* "Considerable." *Query.* "What did the wealthy non-resident landlords give?" Again the answer was, "Considerable." But I am sorry to add that the two latter queries were almost uniformly answered from various parts of the country by the expressive words, "Nothing whatever." The same correspondent said, in reply to another query, that the aged and infirm did not live more than a day or two after being sent to hospital. They died of dysentery. The two following anecdotes are given on the best authority: a family, consisting of father, mother, and daughter, were starving; they were devotedly attached to each other; the daughter was young and comely. Offers of relief were made by a wealthy person, but they were accompanied by a dishonourable condition, and they were therefore indignantly spurned. Fond as I am of my life, said the starving girl, and much as I love my father and mother, for whose relief I would endure any earthly toil, I will suffer them as well as myself to die, rather than get them relief at the price of my virtue. A Roscommon man thus writes in the query sheet sent to him: "Years after the Famine, and when in another part of the country, I was obliged, on my way to my house, to pass the house of a poor blacksmith; and often at night, as I passed, I heard him and his family reciting the Rosary. I told him one day how much edified I was at this. The poor fellow replied with great earnestness: 'Sir, as long as I have life in me I'll say the Rosary, and I'll tell you why. In the Famine times, my family and myself were starving. One night the children were crying with the hunger, and there was no food to give them. By way of stopping their cries they were put to bed, but, after a short sleep, they awoke with louder cries for food. At length, I recommended that all of us, young and old, should join in saying the Rosary. We did; and before it was ended a woman came in, whose occupation was to deal in bread, and she had a basketful with her. I explained our condition to her, and asked her to give me some bread on credit. She did so, and from that day to this we never felt hunger or starvation; and from that day to this I continue to say the Rosary, and will, please God, to the end of my life.'"

The news came from Sligo, through the public journals, that the Famine was carrying off hundreds and thousands there, and that the work left undone by the Famine would be finished by pestilence. The Workhouse was described as a pesthouse, and the guardians in terror had abandoned it. The following short note will give a better idea of the state of this part of the country than any lengthened description:—

"Riverston, 8th Feb.

"SIR,—*Half-a-dozen* starvation deaths have been reported to Mr. Grant this evening, and he directs me to write to you to request you will attend here early to-morrow morning to hold inquests.

"JAMES HAY, *Head Constable.*
"Alexander Burrows, Esq."

But things were much worse than was revealed by this note. Mr. Burrows was quite unequal to the work he had to do. In one day, although he tired three horses, he succeeded in holding only five inquests. Poor progress indeed, inasmuch as there were FORTY dead bodies in the district of Managharrow alone, awaiting him! One of the cases, that of Owen Mulrooney, was a moving one. He was a young, muscular man, in the prime of life. He had a wife and five young children. Here is the substance of his wife's depositions at the inquest held upon his remains. She sold all her little furniture for ten shillings, and with this sum she and her five children left home to make her way to England, as she thought her husband would be able to support himself, if unencumbered by her and the family. The weather became cold and rainy; and when she had got as far as Enniskillen, the children took cramps, and she had to retrace her steps by slow degrees, and seek again her desolate home. Meantime, the public works, upon which her husband had been employed, were stopped, and he was at once reduced to starvation. A neighbour gave him one meal of food and a night's lodging. He was revived by the food, and had strength enough to make up two loads of turf, which he sold, and bought an ass, which he killed, and tried to cook and eat. He partook of some portion of the ass's flesh twice or thrice, but his stomach refused the food, as it always brought on great retching. When his wife and children returned he was dying, and she was only in time to see him, and give the above sorrowful evidence. We select this case, said the local journal, out of dozens; because it has some remarkable features in it. Many, it further adds, who were sent to purchase food, died of starvation on the journey. The family of Mary Costello were in a state of starvation for three weeks, and she herself had not had food for two days. Previous to her death, one of her brothers procured the price of half-a-stone of meal, for which she was sent to town; and on the following morning she was found dead by the roadside, with the little bag of meal grasped tightly in her hand.

Although it is notorious that some districts in the South, especially Skibbereen, were the first to attract a large share of public attention, the county Mayo, so populous, so large, so poor, was from the beginning marked out for suffering; but it lacked an organ so faithful and eloquent as the *Southern Reporter*, through whose columns Skibbereen and Bantry and Skull became as well known to the Empire as Dublin, Paris, or London. Poor Mayo suffered intensely from end to end, although it suffered in comparative silence. In the beginning of January, what may be termed a monster meeting of the county was held in Westport. Forty thousand persons were said to have assembled on the occasion. The Very Rev. Dean Burke, who presided, complained that, as far back as September, a presentment of £80,000 was passed for the county, £12,000 of which was allotted to their barony, Murrisk; but from that time to the period of the meeting only £7,000 had been expended. Resolutions were passed, calling for a liberal grant of money to save the people from death; expressive of deep regret at the uncultured state of the corn lands of the county; calling for the establishment of food depôts in the remote districts; and recommending the completion of the roads then in progress. More than one speaker hinted that there existed an under current for preventing the employment of the people, and that this under current emanated from the landlords, who were opposed to the taxing of their properties for such a purpose. At the close of the meeting, one of the gentlemen present, Mr. John C. Garvey, made the following observations:—"It has been said that an under current exists to prevent the employment of the people. In my opinion the landlords would be working against their own interest in preventing the employment of the poor. (Cries of No, no.) Well, I, as one of the landlords, do declare most solemnly, before my God, that I have not only in public, but in private, done everything that I could do to extend the employment of the people (loud cheers); and I now brand every landlord that does not come forward and clear himself of the imputation."

A great number of coroners' inquests were reported from Mayo, but those inquests were no real indication of the number of deaths which occurred there from starvation; there were not coroners enough to hold inquests, and four-fifths of those that were held were not reported. Besides, inquests were not, and could not be held unless in cases where the death was somewhat sudden, or had some specialty about it. The effects of the Famine were not usually very sudden. People dragged on life for weeks, partly through that tenacity of life which is one of the characteristics of human nature; partly through chance scraps of food obtained from time to time, and in various ways. Families have gone on for many weeks on boiled turnips, with a little oatmeal sprinkled over them; often on green rape, and even the wild herbs of the fields and seaweed; such things kept prolonging life whilst they were destroying it. After a while they brought on dysentery: dysentery—death. But no one thought of a coroner in such cases, which were by far the most numerous class of cases until fever became prevalent, and even then dysentery commonly came in to close the scene.

"During that period," writes Mr. James H. Tuke, "the roads in many places became as charnel-houses, and several car and coach drivers have assured me that they rarely drove anywhere without seeing dead bodies strewn along the road side, and that, in the dark, they had even gone over them. A gentleman told me that in the neighbourhood of Clifden one Inspector of roads had caused no less than 140 bodies to be buried, which he found scattered along the highway. In some cases it is well known that where all other members of a family have perished, the last survivor has earthed up the door of his miserable cabin to prevent the ingress of pigs and dogs, and then laid himself down to die in this fearful family vault."[223]

In January, 1847, a Protestant gentleman, now a colonial judge, well known for his ability and integrity, gave, through the columns of a Dublin newspaper, an account of the state of Mayo as he saw it. He found great dissatisfaction—in fact indignation, existing with regard to the unaccountable delay of the public works, which had been presented for in that county; and this not merely amongst the starving people, but amongst the most respectable and intelligent persons with whom he conversed. He—a man not likely to take a narrow or prejudiced view of any subject—was of opinion that those complaints were not groundless. The officials, he says, instead of extending the works in Mayo, and feeding the people, "are employed in diverting public attention by prating of subscriptions, paltering about Queen's letters and English poor-boxes, and frittering away the strength of public opinion and the efficiency of all public action, by engaging private charity in a task that can be met only by the Herculean efforts of a whole nation, knit into a single power, and bound into concentrated exertion by all the constraining forces that the constitution of political society affords."[224] And then the starving people are blamed for finding fault, and for being suspicious. What else, he asks, can they be? How can a man dying of starvation have patience?

The chief places he visited were Balla, Claremorris, Ballyhaunis, and Hollymount. The scenes he witnessed were, he says, scarcely if at all less harrowing than those which had been reported from the locality of Skibbereen. This writer, a Protestant, conversed, amongst others, with the priests of the districts which he visited, and of them he says: "The Catholic clergy are the only persons who can form a tolerably correct estimate of the numbers of persons who are now dying of starvation. The Catholic clergy know all the people of their respective parishes—*no one else does*; the Catholic priest knows them as the shepherd does his sheep; he knows them individually; he knows not only every lineament of every individual face, but he knows, too, every ailment of body—every care of mind—every necessity of circumstance from which he is suffering. The Catholic clergy of the West attend every death-bed: the poor there are all Catholics. The Catholic clergy know, then, to what it is that the extraordinary mortality now prevalent is owing—*and they set it down as the immediate consequence of want and starvation.*"[225]

One of the priests of whom W.G. asked information told him his whole time, and that of his assistant, was unceasingly occupied in administering the last comforts of religion to the victims of starvation. It would, he said, be an endless task, and he feared a useless one, to record his sad experiences.

People died in Connaught whilst in full employment on the public works, just as they did in Munster. Of such cases, the following is one of which W.G. collected some particulars:—James Byrne, of Barnabriggan, Brize, parish of Balla, was employed up to his death on the public works. The last food of which he had partaken was obtained by his wife pledging her cloak. There was an inquest upon this poor man's remains, at which his wife deposed that up to the time of his death he was employed on the public works, and as they had no food she was obliged to pledge her cloak for one stone of meal. Deceased often said he would do well if he had food or nourishment. Deponent states to the best of her belief that her husband died for the want of food. She and her four children are now living on rape, which she is allowed to gather in a farmer's field. James Browne, Esq., M.D., being sworn, said he found, on examination, all the internal organs of the deceased sound. There was no food whatever in his stomach, or in any part of the alimentary canal. There was a small quantity of thin faeces in the lower portion of the large intestine. Is of opinion that deceased came by his death from inanition, or want of food. Verdict: "James Byrne came by his death in consequence of having no food for some days; and died of starvation."

"With every disposition," writes W.G., "to make allowances for the difficulties of their position, let me ask, Sir, how have the gentry acted?

They have seemed to think that the whole relief question just split itself into two sides, one of which belonged exclusively to the Government, the other exclusively to them. One side comprised the duty of providing for the lives of the people, and this was left to the Government; the other, the duty of providing for the safety of the estates, and this the gentry took upon themselves." "They [the landlords] have complained much of the character of the works; they have strongly urged the Government to undertake something else; *at all events to give up what they were doing at the moment*; but when did their indignation take the shape of complaining that what the Government was doing was inadequate for coping with the starvation that was abroad?"

The penetrating mind of W.G. led him to forecast tremendous results from the potato failure, exclusive of its immediate effect—death by starvation. Having expressed his opinion that the extent of the destitution was fearful, he makes the following observations, which time has completely verified. "As regards the effect," says he, "of the present calamity upon the relations of landlord and tenant, believe me, that terrible as are the immediate and direct effects of the calamity, you will find a set of collateral results springing out of it, tending to the EXTERMINATION of the smaller tenantry by the landlords, that may lead you, ere many months, to regard the secondary stage of this scourge as scarcely less terrible to our unhappy peasantry than the first." And again: "Symptoms of a WIDE-SPREAD SYSTEMATIC EXTERMINATION are just beginning to exhibit themselves. I am not speaking under the influence of any prejudice against the landlord class. Let none of your readers set down to the account of such a feeling my present warning as to the wholesale system of ejectment that is now in preparation." "The potato cultivation being extinguished, at least for a time, the peasant cultivators can pay no rents; sheep and horned cattle *can* pay rents, and smart rents too; therefore the sheep and cattle shall have the lands, and the peasants shall be ousted from them; a very simple and most inevitable conclusion, as you see." "I repeat it, a universal system of ousting the peasantry is about to set in. Whether this results from the fault or from the necessities of the landlords it matters not." The following extract from the *Roscommon Journal* is emphatically cited by W.G. in support of his views. *"The number of civil bills served by landlords for the approaching sessions of this town* WILL TREBLE THOSE EVER SENT OUT FOR THE LAST TEN YEARS."[226]

More than twenty years after W.G. wrote those letters, I had a conversation relative to the Famine with a gentleman who knew the Midland Counties and portions of the West well. I asked him what was the effect of the Famine in his district. "My district," he answered, "was by no means regarded as a poor one, but the Famine swept away more than half its population. The census of '41 gave the families residing in it as 2,200; the census of '51 gave them at 1,000." Did the landlords, I enquired, come forward liberally to save the lives of the people? "Only one landlord," he replied, "in the whole locality with which I am connected did anything to save the people, F—O'B—. He asked no rent for two years, and he never afterwards insisted on the rent of those two years; although I must say he was paid it by many of his tenants, of their own free will; but, for the rest, he cancelled those two years' rent and opened a new account with them, as with men owing him nothing." And what, I further asked, were the feelings of the landlords with regard to their tenants dying of starvation? He answered with solemn emphasis— "DELIGHTED TO BE RID OF THEM."

The present leader of the Conservative party seems to entertain feelings akin to this; for, some years ago, addressing his constituents, and speaking of some results of the Irish Famine, he said significantly— "there are worse things than a famine."

"I shall never forget," said Rev. Mr. F—to W.G., "the impression made on my mind a few days ago by a most heartrending case of starvation. It was this: The poor mother of five children, putting them to bed one night, almost lifeless from hunger, and despairing of ever again seeing them alive, took her last look at them, and bade them her last farewell.

She rose early in the morning, and her first act was to steal on tiptoe to where they lay. She would not awake them, but she must know the truth—are they alive or dead? and she softly touched the lips of each, to try and discover if there was any warmth in them, and she eagerly watched to see if the breath of life still came from their nostrils. Her apprehensions were but too well founded, she had lost some of her dear ones during the night."

The mournful poetry of this simple narrative must touch every heart.

Ass and horse flesh were anxiously sought for, even when the animals died of disease or starvation. In the middle of January it was recorded that a horse belonging to a man near Claremorris, having died, was flayed, and the carcass left for dogs and birds to feed upon; but, says the narrative, before much of it was consumed, it was discovered by a poor family (whose name and residence are given), and by them used as food. Father, mother and six children prolonged life for a week upon this disgusting carrion, and even regretted the loss of it, when the supply failed; and the poor mother said to the person who made the fact public, "the Lord only knows what I will now do for my starving children, since it is gone!" A fortnight earlier a most circumstantial account of the eating of ass flesh is given by a commercial gentleman in a letter addressed to the Premier, Lord John Russell, and dated "Ballina, Christmas-eve." (!) In this case the poor man killed his ass for food, the skin being sold to a skin dealer for 8d. The writer of the letter visited the skin dealer's house, in order to make sure of the fact. It was quite true, and the skin dealer's wife told him this could not be a solitary case, "as she never remembered so many asses' skins coming for sale as within the month just past."[227]

Mr. Forster, in his report to the Society of Friends, says of the condition of Westport in January, 1847, that it was a strange and fearful sight, like what we read of beleaguered cities; its streets crowded with gaunt wanderers, sauntering to and fro, with hopeless air and hunger-struck look; a mob of starved, almost naked women were around the poorhouse, clamouring for soup-tickets; our inn, the head-quarters of the road engineer and pay clerks, was beset by a crowd of beggars for work.[228] The agent of the British Association, Count Strezelecki, writing from Westport at this time, says, no pen could describe the distress by which he was surrounded; it had reached such an extreme degree of intensity that it was above the power of exaggeration. You may, he adds, believe anything which you hear and read, because what I actually see surpasses what I ever read of past and present calamities.[229]

The weather in March became mild, and even warm and sunny; some little comfort, one would suppose, to those without food or fuel. But no; they were so starved and weakened and broken down, that it had an injurious effect upon them, and hurried them rapidly to their end. A week after the passage quoted above was written, Count Strezelecki again writes, and says he is sorry to report that the distress had increased; a thing which could be hardly believed as possible. Melancholy cases of death on the public roads and in the streets had become more frequent. The sudden warmth of the weather, and the rays of a bright sun, accelerate prodigiously the forthcoming end of those whose constitutions are undermined by famine or sickness. "Yesterday," he writes, "a countrywoman, between this and the harbour (one mile distance), walking with four children, squatted against a wall, on which the heat and light reflected powerfully; some hours after two of her children were corpses, and she and the two remaining ones taken lifeless to the barracks. To-day, in Westport, similar melancholy occurrences took place."[230]

Some years ago, during a visit to Westport, I received sad corroboration of the truth of these statements. I met several persons who had witnessed the Famine in that town and its neighbourhood, and their relation of the scenes which fell under their notice not only sustained, but surpassed, if possible, the facts given in the above communications. A priest who was stationed at Westport during the Famine, was still there at the period of my visit. During that dreadful time, the people, he told me, who wandered about the country in search of food, frequently took possession of empty houses, which they easily found; the inmates having died, or having gone to the Workhouse, where such existed. A brother and sister, not quite grown up, took possession of a house in this way, in the Parish of Westport. One of them became ill; the other continued to go for the relief where it was given out, but this one soon fell ill also. No person heeded them. Everyone had too much to do for himself. They died. Their dead bodies were only discovered by the offensive odour which issued from the house in which they died, and in which they had become putrefied. It was found necessary to make an aperture for ventilation on the roof before anyone would venture in. The neighbours dug a hole in the hard floor of the cabin with a crowbar to receive their remains. And this was their coffinless grave!

This same priest administered in one day the last Sacrament to thirty-three young persons in the Workhouse of Westport; and of these there were not more than two or three alive next morning.

Mr. Egan, who at the date of my visit was Clerk of the Union, held the same office during the Famine. The Workhouse was built to accommodate one thousand persons. There were two days a-week for admissions. With the house crowded far beyond its capacity, he had repeatedly seen as many as three thousand persons seeking admission on a single day. Knowing, as we do, the utter dislike the Irish peasantry had in those times to enter the Workhouse, this is a terrible revelation of the Famine; for it is a recorded fact that many of the people died of want in their cabins, and suffered their children to die, rather than go there. Those who were not admitted—and they were, of course, the great majority—having no homes to return to, lay down and died in Westport and its suburbs. Mr. Egan, pointing to the wall opposite the Workhouse gate, said: "There is where they sat down, never to rise again. I have seen there of a morning as many as eight corpses of those miserable beings, who had died during the night. Father G—(then in Westport) used to be anointing them as they lay exhausted along the walls and streets, dying of hunger and fever."[231]

The principal aim of the Society of Friends was to establish soup-kitchens, and give employment to the women in knitting. As soon as their committee was in working order, they sent members of their body to various parts of the country—more especially to the West—to make inquiries, and to see things with their own eyes. Their reports, made in a quiet, unexaggerated form, are amongst the most valuable testimonies extant, as to the effects and extent of the Famine. The delegate who was the first to explore portions of the West writes that, at Boyle (a prosperous and important town), the persons who sought admission to the Workhouse were in a most emaciated state, many of them declaring that they had not tasted food of any kind for forty-eight hours; and he learned that numbers of them had been living upon turnips and cabbage-leaves for weeks. The truth of these statements was but too well supported by the dreadfully reduced state in which they presented themselves, the children especially being emaciated with starvation, and ravenous with hunger. At Carrick-on-Shannon he witnessed what he calls a most painful and heartrending scene—poor wretches in the last stage of famine begging to be received into the house; women, who had six or seven children, imploring that even two or three of them might be taken in, *as their husbands were earning but 8d. a-day*, which, at the existing high price of provisions, was totally inadequate to feed them. Some of those children were worn to skeletons; their features sharpened with hunger, and their limbs wasted almost to the bone. Of course, he says, among so many applicants (one hundred and ten), a great number were necessarily refused admittance, as there were but thirty vacancies in the house. Although the guardians exercised the best discrimination they could, it was believed that some of those rejected were so far spent, that it was doubtful if they could reach their homes alive—those homes, such as they were, being in many cases five or six Irish miles away. This kind-hearted gentleman, having expressed a wish to distribute bread to those poor creatures, that they might not, as he said, "go quite empty-handed," forty pounds of bread were procured, all that could be purchased in the town of Carrick-on-Shannon. They devoured it with a voracity which nothing but famine could produce. One woman, he says, was observed to eat but a very small portion of her bread; and being asked the reason, said she had four children at home, to whom she was taking it, as without it there would not be a morsel of food in her cabin that night. What struck him and his fellow-traveller in a special manner was the effects of famine on the children; their faces were so wan and haggard that they looked like old men and women; their sprightliness was all gone; they sat in groups at their cabin doors, making no attempt to play. Another indication of the Famine noticed by them was, that the pigs and poultry had entirely disappeared. To numberless testimonies, as to the spirit in which the poor people bore their unexampled privations, this good man adds his: "To do the poor justice," he writes, "they are bearing their privations with a remarkable degree of patience and fortitude, and very little clamorous begging is to be met with upon the roads—at least, not more than has been the case in Ireland for many years. William Forster," (his fellow-traveller), he adds, "has completely formed the opinion that the statements in the public newspapers are by no means exaggerated."[232]

Although Donegal is in the Ulster division of the kingdom, in the famine time it partook more of the character of a Connaught than an Ulster county. A gentleman was deputed by the Society of Friends to explore it, who has given his views upon the Irish Famine with a spirit and feeling which do him honour as a man and a Christian. Writing from Stranorlar he says: "This county, like most others in Ireland, belongs to a few large proprietors, some of them, unhappily, absentees, whose large domains sometimes extend over whole parishes and baronies, and contain a population of 8,000 to 12,000. Such, for instance, is the parish of Templecrone, with a population of 10,000 inhabitants; in which the only residents above small farmers are, the agent, the protestant clergyman, the parish priest, a medical man, and perhaps a resident magistrate, with the superintendent of police and a few small dealers.[233] Writing from Dunfanaghy in the midst of snow, he says: "A portion of the district through which we passed this day, as well as the adjoining one, is, with one exception, the poorest and most destitute in Donegal. Nothing, indeed, can describe too strongly the dreadful condition of the people. Many families were living on a single meal of cabbage, and some even, as we were assured, upon a little seaweed." A highly respectable merchant of the town called upon this gentleman and assured him that the small farmers and cottiers had parted with all their pigs and their fowl; and even their bed clothes and fishing nets had gone for the same object, the supply of food. He stated that he knew many families of five to eight persons, who subsisted on 2½ lbs. of oatmeal per day, made into thin water gruel—about 6 oz. of meal for each! Dunfanaghy is a little fishing town situated on a bay remarkably adapted for a fishing population; the sea is teeming with fish of the finest description, waiting, we might say, to be caught. Many of the inhabitants gain a portion of their living by this means, but so rude is their tackle, and so fragile and liable to be upset are their primitive boats or *coracles*, made of wicker-work, over which sailcloth is stretched, that they can only venture to sea in fine weather; and thus with food almost in sight, the people starve, because they have no one to teach them to build boats more adapted to this rocky coast than those used by their ancestors many centuries ago.[234] This is but one among many instances of the wasted industrial resources of this country which, whether in connection with the water or the land, strike the eye of the stranger at every step."[235]

To Glenties Mr. Tuke and his companions made their journey through a succession of wild mountain passes, rendered still wilder by the deep snow which covered everything. They put up at Lord George Hill's Gweedore hotel, and endorse all they had previously heard about the admirable zeal and enlightened benevolence of that nobleman, who had effected great improvements both in the land and in the condition of the inhabitants of one of the wildest portions of Donegal. "We started at daybreak," he writes, "for Glenties, thirty miles distant, over the mountains; and after leaving the improved cottages and farms on the

Gweedore estate, soon came upon the domain of an absentee proprietor, the extent of which may be judged by the fact, that our road lay for more than twenty miles through it. This is the poorest parish in Donegal, and no statement can be too strong with respect to the wretched condition, the positive misery and starvation in which the cottiers and small farmers on this immense domain are found. We baited at Dungloe. A more miserable and dilapidated village or town I never saw. What a contrast did its dirty little inn present to the hotel at Gweedore." There was not a single pound of meal, Indian or oat, to be purchased in this miserable place, whilst thousands were depending on it for their supplies. It was crowded with poor people from the surrounding country and from the island of Arranmore, who were crying with hunger and cold; the next market town was thirty miles from them, and the nearest place where food could be obtained was Lord George Hill's store at Bunbeg, some twenty miles distant. Surely this extreme wretchedness and neglect must be, to a great extent, attributed to the want of a resident proprietor.

"Leaving Dungloe," says Mr. Tuke, "we proceeded to Glenties, still on the same property; and throughout our journey met with the most squalid scenes of misery which the imagination can well conceive. Whilst thousands of acres of reclaimable land lies entirely neglected and uncultivated, there are thousands of men both willing and anxious to obtain work, but unable to procure it. On the following morning, William Forster had an interview with the resident magistrate, as well as with the rector of the parish and some other gentlemen, who gave distressing accounts of the poverty existing around them. Their attention was directed to the necessity for the immediate establishment of soup-kitchens, the employment of women in knitting, and the formation of local committees for their relief, extending over several parishes. We visited the poorhouse at Glenties, which is in a dreadful state; the people were in fact half starved and only half clothed. The day before, they had but one meal of oatmeal and water; and at the time of our visit had not sufficient food in the house for the day's supply. The people complained bitterly, as

399

well they might, and begged us to give them tickets for work, to enable them to leave the place and work on the roads. Some were leaving the house, preferring to die in their own hovels rather than in the Poorhouse. Their bedding consisted of dirty straw, in which they were laid in rows on the floor; even as many as six persons being crowded under one rug; and we did not see a blanket at all. The rooms were hardly bearable for filth. The living and the dying were stretched side by side beneath the same miserable covering! No wonder that disease and pestilence were filling the infirmary, and that the pale haggard countenances of the poor boys and girls told of sufferings which it was impossible to contemplate without the deepest commiseration and pity."

The carelessness and neglect of their duty by Irish landlords have so often come before us during the progress of the Famine, that it is a pleasure to meet with something worth quoting on the other side. "Throughout Donegal we found," says Mr. Tuke, "the resident proprietors doing much for their suffering tenantry; in many cases, all that landlords could do for their relief and assistance. Several of them had obtained loans under the late Drainage Act, and with this or private resources are employing large numbers of labourers for the improvement of their estates. We met with several who had one hundred men employed in this manner. Many of these landlords, as well as the clergy, are most assiduously working in all ways in their power. They have imported large quantities of meal and rice, which they sell at prime cost, there being in many districts no dealers to supply those articles; and are making soup at their own houses, and dispensing daily to their famishing neighbours."[236]

In the South, after Skibbereen, Skull, its neighbour, seems to have suffered most. To cross from Cape Clear to Skull—partly rowing, partly sailing—in a stiff breeze is very exciting, and might well cause apprehension, but for the crew of athletic Cape men, or Capers, as the people of the mainland call them, in whose hands you have placed your safety. With them you are perfectly secure. Those hardy, simple-minded people are as used to the sea as a herdsman is to green fields. Even when they are not actually upon its stormy bosom, they are usually to be seen in groups about the little harbour, leaning against the rocks, quietly smoking their pipes, watching the tide and the weather, and discussing the proper moment for "going out." It is some five miles from Cape Clear to the town of Skull. The distance is not long, but without skill and local knowledge the passage is dangerous, for what seems only a light gale elsewhere makes the sea almost tempestuous among the bluffs and rocky islands of this wild coast, where many a foundering barque has been rescued from destruction by the brave and trusty oarsmen of Cape Clear. Leaving Roaring-water bay to the north-east, and getting in shelter of the land, a church tower, humble in design and proportions, rises in the midst of a graveyard, crowded in one part with tombstones, and almost entirely devoid of them in the other. There rest the mortal remains of many generations of the people of Skull; but it is especially worthy of notice as the burial-ground which had to be doubled in size in order to receive upwards of half the population within its bosom in a single year; and yet all were not interred there: many found a grave in the fields nearest to which they died; many others, among the ruins of their dismantled cabins. This graveyard, looking out upon the restless waters from its quiet elevation, must remain for ages the most historic spot in the locality, although Skull is not without a history and historic remains. Many a castle and stronghold have the O'Mahonys and O'Donovans built among the crags of the rocky islands, which are grouped in such variety to seaward, the ruins of which are to-day full of interest and beauty for the tourist. But surely the day will come when those crumbling ruins shall be once again a portion of the common soil, nameless and forgotten; but distant though that day may be, Skull and Skibbereen, those two famine-slain sisters of the South, must still be found on the page of Irish history, illustrating the Great Famine of 1847.

The parish of Skull is situated in the barony of West Carberry, county of Cork, and is very large, containing no less than 84,000 acres. The town, a small one, is on the shore in the portion of the parish called East

Skull; West Skull runs inland towards Skibbereen, and in this division is the village of Ballydehob. The town of Skull is built upon a piece of low level ground, a short distance from which, in the direction of Ballydehob, there is a chain of hills, the highest of which, Mount Gabriel, rises 1,300 feet above the sea level. Nothing can be happier or more accurate than the poet's description of this scenery, when he writes:—

The summer sun is falling soft on Carbery's hundred isles,
The summer sun is gleaming still through Gabriel's rough defiles."[237]

A correspondent of the *Southern Reporter*, writing from Ballydehob during the first days of January, gives the most piteous account of that village; every house he entered exhibited the same characteristics,—no clothing, no food, starvation in the looks of young and old. In a tumble-down cabin resembling a deserted forge, he found a miserable man seated at a few embers, with a starved-looking dog beside him, that was not able to crawl. The visitor asked him if he were sick; he answered that he was not, but having got swelled legs working on the roads, he had to give up; he had not tasted food for two days; his family had gone begging about the country, and he had no hope of ever seeing them again. Efforts were still being made at this place to get coffins for the dead, but with indifferent success. There were not coffins for half the people; many were tied up in straw, and so interred. This writer mentions what he seems to have regarded as an ingenious contrivance of the Galeen relief committee, namely, the use of the coffin with the slide or hinged bottom, but such coffins had been, previously used in other places. He relates a touching incident which occurred at Ballydehob, at the time of his visit. Two children, the elder only six years, went into a neighbour's house in search of food. They were asked where their father was, and they replied that he was asleep for the last two days. The people became alarmed, and went to his cabin, where they found him quite dead, and the merest skeleton. The mother of those children had died some weeks before, and their poor devoted father sacrificed his life for them, as the neighbours found some Indian meal in the place, which he was evidently reserving for his infant children, whilst he suffered himself to die of starvation.

But a common effect of the Famine was to harden the hearts of the people, and blunt their natural feelings. Hundreds, remarks this correspondent, are daily expiring in their cabins in the three parishes of this neighbourhood, and the people are becoming so accustomed to death that they have lost all those kindly sympathies for the relatives of the departed, which formerly characterized their natures. Want and destitution have so changed them, that a sordid avarice, and a greediness of disposition to grasp at everything in the shape of food, has seized hold of the souls of those who were considered the most generous and hospitable race on the face of the earth. As happened in other places, no persons attended the funerals; those who were still alive were so exhausted that they were unable to inter the dead, and the duty of doing so was frequently left to casual passers-by.

About the middle of February, Commander Caffin, of Her Majesty's ship "Scourge," visited Skull, in company with the rector, the Rev. Robert Traill Hall. After having entered a few houses, the Commander said to the Revd. gentleman, "My pre-conceived ideas of your misery seem as a dream to me compared with the reality." And yet Captain Caffin had only time to see the cabins on the roadside, in which the famine was not so terrible as it was up among the hills and fastnesses, where, in one wretched hovel, whose two windows were stuffed with straw, the Rev. Mr. Hall found huddled together sixteen human beings. They did not, however, belong to one family—three wretched households were congregated into this miserable abode. Out of the sixteen, two only could be said to be able to work; and on the exertions of those "two poor pallid objects" had the rest to depend. Eight of the others were crowded into one pallet,—it could not be called a bed, being formed of a little straw, which scarcely kept them from the cold mud floor. A poor father was still able to sit up, but his legs were dreadfully swollen, and he was dead in two or three days after the Rev. Mr. Hall's visit. Beside him lay his sister, and at his feet two children—all hastening to eternity.

Captain Caffin wrote to a friend an account of his visit to Skull, and his letter was published in many of the public journals. "In the village of Skull," he says, "three-fourths of the inhabitants you meet carry the tale of woe in their features and persons, as they are reduced to mere skeletons, the men in particular, all their physical power wasted away; they have all become beggars. Having a great desire to see with my own eyes some of the misery which was said to exist, Dr. Traill, the rector of Skull, offered to drive me to a portion of his parish. I found there was no need to take me beyond the village, to show me the horrors of famine in its worst features. I had read in the papers letters and accounts of this state of things, but I thought they must be highly coloured to attract sympathy; but I there saw the reality of the whole—no exaggeration, for it does not admit of it—famine exists to a fearful degree, with all its horrors. Fever has sprung up consequent upon the wretchedness; and swellings of limbs and body, and diarrhoea, from the want of nourishment, are everywhere to be found." Again: "In no house that I entered was there not to be found the dead or dying; in particularizing two or three they may be taken as the picture of the whole—there was no picking or choosing, but we took them just as they came." A cabin which he entered had, he says, the appearance of wretchedness without, but its interior was misery. The Rev. Mr. Hall, on putting his head inside the hole which answered for a door, said: "Well, Phillis, how is your mother to-day?" Phillis answered, "O Sir, is it you? Mother is dead." Captain Caffin adds—"And there—fearful reality—was the daughter, a skeleton herself, crouched and crying over the lifeless body of her mother, which was on the floor, cramped up as she had died, with her rags and her cloak about her, by the side of a few embers of peat." They came to the cabin of a poor old woman, the door of which was stopped up with dung. She roused up, evidently astonished. They had taken her by surprise. She burst into tears, and said she had not been able to sleep *since the corpse of the woman had lain in her bed.* The circumstance which destroyed her rest happened in this way:— Some short time before, a poor miserable woman entered the cabin, and asked leave to rest herself for a few moments. She got permission to do so. She lay down, but never rose again. She died in an hour, and in this miserable hovel of six feet square, the body remained four days before the wretched occupant could get any person to remove it. It is not much to be wondered at that she had lost her rest.

"I could," says Captain Caffin, "in this manner take you through thirty or more cottages that we visited, but they, without exception, were all alike—the dead and the dying in each; and I could tell you more of the truth of the heartrending scene, were I to mention the lamentations and bitter cries of each of those poor creatures, on the threshold of death. Never in my life have I seen such wholesale misery, nor could I have thought it so complete. All that I have stated above," he concludes, "I have seen with my own eyes, and can vouch for the truth of. And I feel I cannot convey by words the impression left on my mind of this awful state of things. I could tell you also of that which I could vouch for the truth of, but which I did not see myself, such as bodies half eaten by the rats; of two dogs last Wednesday being shot by Mr. O'Callaghan whilst tearing a body to pieces; of his mother-in-law stopping a poor woman and asking her what she had on her back, and being replied it was her son, telling her she would smother it; but the poor emaciated woman said it was dead already, and she was going to dig a hole in the churchyard for it. These are things which are of every-day occurrence."[238]

Taking Ballydehob as a centre, there were, at this time, in a radius of ten or twelve miles around it, twenty-six soup kitchens—namely, at Skibbereen, Baltimore, Shirken, and Cape Clear (three); Creagh, Castlehaven (two); Union Hall, Aghadown (two); Kilcoe (three); Skull (two); Dunmanus, Crookhaven (two); Cahiragh (two); Durrus, Drimoleague, Drenagh, Bantry, Glengariff, Adrigoole, Castletown, Berehaven, and Ballydehob. They were making and distributing daily about seventeen thousand pints of good meat soup. They did great good, but it was of a very partial nature. Mr. Commissary Bishop tells us "they were but a drop in the ocean." Hundreds, he says, are relieved, but thousands still want. And he adds, that soup kitchens have their attendant evils: an important one in this instance was, that the poor small farmers were selling all their cows to the soup kitchens, leaving themselves and their children without milk or butter.

There seems to have been an understanding among the *employes*, that the true state of things, in its naked reality, was not to be given in their communications to Government. It was to be toned down and modified. Hence the studied avoidance of the word Famine in almost every official document of the time. Captain Caffin's letter was written to a friend and marked "private;" but having got into the newspapers, it must, of course, be taken notice of by the Government. Mr. Trevelyan lost no time, but at once wrote, enclosing it to Sir John Burgoyne. To use his own words on the occasion, the receipt, from the Commander of the Scourge, of "the awful letter, describing the result of his personal observations in the immediate neighbourhood of Skull," led him (Mr. Trevelyan) to make two proposals on the part of the Treasury. And indeed, it must be said, well meant and practical they were. The first was, to send two half-pay medical officers to Skull, to try and do something for the sick, many of whom were dying for want of the commonest care; and also to combine with that arrangement, the means of securing the decent interment of the dead. The second proposal was to provide carts, for the conveyance of soup to the sick in their houses in and around Skull; a most necessary provision, inasmuch as the starving people were, in numerous cases, unable to walk from their dwellings to the soup kitchen; besides which, in many houses the whole family were struck down by a combination of fever, starvation and dysentery. Sir John Burgoyne, as might be expected, picked holes in both proposals. In the carriage of soup to the sick Sir John sees difficulty on account of the scarcity of horses, which are, he says, diminishing fast. And he adds, that several, if not all of the judges, who were then proceeding on circuit, were obliged to take the same horses from Dublin throughout, as they would have no chance of changing them as usual. Then with regard to the decent burial of the dead, Sir John thought there were legal difficulties in the way, and that legislation was necessary before it could be done. He failed to produce any objection against the appointment of the medical officers. In a fortnight after, a Treasury Minute was issued to the effect that Relief Committees should be required to employ proper persons to bury, with as much attention to the feelings of the survivors as circumstances would admit, the dead bodies which could not be buried by any other means. How urgently such an order was called for appears from the fact, that at that time in the neighbourhood of Skull, none but strangers, hired by the clergy, could be found to take any part in a burial.[239]

The incumbent of Skull, the Key. Robert Traill Hall,[240] a month after Captain Caffin's letter was published, says, "the distress was nothing in Captain Caffin's time compared with what it is now." On reading Captain Caffin's letter, one would suppose, that destitution could not reach a higher point than the one at which he saw it. That letter fixed the attention of the Government upon Skull, and yet, strange result, after a month of such attention, the Famine is intensified there, instead of being alleviated.

Mr. Commissary Bishop had charge of the most famine-visited portion of the Co. Cork (Skibbereen always excepted), including West Carbery, Bantry and Bere. He seems to have been an active, intelligent officer, and a kind-hearted man; yet his communications, somehow, must have misled the Government, for Mr. Trevelyan starts at Captain Caffin's letter, as if suddenly awakened from a dream. Its contents appeared to be quite new, and almost incredible to him. No wonder, perhaps. On the 29th of January, a fortnight before the publication of Captain Caffin's letter, Mr. Bishop writes to Mr. Trevelyan: "The floating depôt for Skull arrived yesterday, and has commenced issues; *this removes all anxiety for that quarter.*" On the day before Captain Caffin's letter was written, Mr. Bishop says: "At Skull, in both east and west division, I found the distress, or rather the mortality had pretty well increased." And this, notwithstanding the floating depôt. Yet in the midst of the famine-slaughter described by Captain Caffin, Mr. Bishop is still hopeful, for he says: "The Relief Committees at Skull and Crookhaven exert themselves greatly to benefit the poor. There is an ample supply of provisions at each place."[241] How did they manage to die of starvation at Skull?—one is tempted to ask. Yet they did, and at Ballydehob too, the other town of the parish; for, three weeks after the announcement of the "ample supply of provisions," the following news reaches us from the latter place, on the most reliable authority. A naval officer, Mr. Scarlet, who was with the "Mercury" and "Gipsey" delivering provisions in the neighbourhood of Skull, on his return to Cork, writes, on the 8th of March, to his admiral, Sir Hugh Pigot, in these terms: "After discharging our cargoes in the boats to Ballydehob, we went on shore, and on passing through the town we went into the ruins of a house, and there were two women lying dead, and two, all but dead, lying along with them. When we enquired how it was that they did not bury them, a woman told us that they did not know, and that one of them had been dead for five days. As we were coming down to the boat, we told the boat's crew if they wanted to see a sight, to go up the street. When they went, there were four men with hand-barrows there, and the men belonging to the boats helped to carry the corpses to the burial ground, where they dug holes, and put them in without coffins."

At this period of the Famine, things had come to such a pass, that individual cases of death from starvation were seldom reported, and when they were they failed to attract much attention, deaths by wholesale had become so common. To be sure, when Dr. Crowley wrote from Skibbereen that himself and Dr. Donovan had interred, in a kitchen garden, the corpse of a person eleven days dead, the case, being somewhat peculiar, had interest enough to be made public; but an ordinary death from hunger would be deemed a very ordinary affair indeed. I will here give a specimen or two, of the way in which the progress of the Famine was chronicled at the close of 1846, and through the winter and spring of 1847. The correspondent of the *Kerry Examiner*, writing from Dingle under date of February the 8th says: "The state of the people of this locality is horrifying. Fever, famine and dysentery are daily increasing, deaths from hunger daily occurring, averaging weekly twenty—men, women and children thrown into the graves without a coffin—dead bodies in all parts of the country, being several days dead before discovered—no inquests to inquire how they came by their death, as hunger has hardened the hearts of the people. Those who survive cannot long remain so—the naked wife and children of the deceased, staring them in the face—their bones penetrating through the skin—not a morsel of flesh to be seen on their bodies—and not a morsel of food can they procure to eat. From all parts of the country they crowd into the town for relief, and not a pound of meal is to be had in the wretched town for any price."

"This parish (Keantra, Dingle) contained, six months since, three thousand souls; over five hundred of these have perished, and three-fourths of them interred coffinless. They were carried to the churchyard, some on lids and ladders, more in baskets—aye, and scores of them thrown beside the nearest ditch, and there left to the mercy of the dogs, which have nothing else to feed on. On the 12th instant I went through the parish, to give a little assistance to some poor orphans and widows. I entered a hut, and there were the poor father and his three children dead beside him, and in such a state of decomposition that I had to get baskets, and have their remains carried in them."[242]

A hearse piled with coffins—or rather rough, undressed boards slightly nailed together—each containing a corpse, passed through the streets of Cork, unaccompanied by a single human being, save the driver of the vehicle. Three families from the country, consisting of fourteen persons, took up their residence in a place called Peacock Lane, in the same city. After one week the household stood thus: Seven dead, six in fever, one still able to be up.

The apostle of temperance, the Rev. Theobald Mathew, gave the following evidence before a Committee of the House of Lords on "Colonization from Ireland":—

Question 2,359. "You have spoken of the state of things [the Famine] as leading to a very great influx of wretchedness and pauperism into the City of Cork. Will you yourself describe what you have seen and known?"

"No tongue," he answers, "can describe—no understanding can conceive—the misery and wretchedness that flowed into Cork from the western parts of the county; the streets were impassable with crowds of country persons. At the commencement they obtained lodgings, and the sympathies of the citizens were awakened; but when fever began to spread in Cork they became alarmed for themselves, and they were anxious at any risk to get rid of those wretched creatures. The lodging-house keepers always turned them out when they got sick. We had no additional fever hospitals; the Workhouse was over full, and those poor creatures perished miserably in the streets and alleys. Every morning a number were found dead in the streets; they were thrown out by the poor creatures in whose houses they lodged. Many of them perished in rooms and cellars, without its being known, and without their receiving any aid from those outside. It may appear as if the citizens of Cork and the clergy of Cork had neglected their duty; but they did not. The calamity was so great and so overwhelming, that it was impossible to prevent those calamities. As one instance, I may mention that one Sunday morning I brought Captain Forbes, who came over with the 'Jamestown,' United States' frigate, and Mr. William Rathbone, and several other persons, to show the state of the neighbourhood in which I resided, and to show them the thousands whom we were feeding at the depôt, While we were going round a person told me, 'There is a house that has been locked up two or three days.' It was a cabin in a narrow alley. We went in, and we saw seventeen persons lying on the floor, all with fever, and no one to give them assistance. Captain Forbes was struck with horror; he never

410

thought there could be in any part of the world such misery. That was in the south suburbs. A poor, wretched widow woman resided there; she let it out for lodgings, and received those people as lodgers, who all got the fever. We three gave what relief we could, and got them conveyed to the hospitals; but they all died."

Question 2,365. "Can you form any judgment what proportion of the population, which is thus added at present, bears to the ordinary population of the City of Cork?"

Answer. "Those poor creatures, the country poor, are now houseless and without lodgings; no one will take them in; they sleep out at night. The citizens of Cork have adopted what I consider a very unchristian and inhuman line of conduct. They have determined to get rid of them. Under the authority of an Act of Parliament, they take them up as sturdy beggars and vagrants, and confine them at night in a market-place, and the next morning send them out in a cart five miles from the town; and there they are left, and a great part of them perish, for they have no home to go to. When they fled from the country, their houses were thrown down or consumed for fuel by the neighbours who remained, and those poor creatures have no place to lay their heads."[243]

It would be a useless and a harrowing task to continue such terrible details, I therefore close this chapter with some account of Bantry, that town having had the misfortune to be the rival of Skull, Skibbereen, and Mayo during the Famine-slaughter.

The deaths at Bantry had become fearfully numerous before it attracted any great share of public sympathy, or even, it would seem, of Government attention. The *Southern Reporter* of January the 5th publishes this curt announcement from that town: "Five inquests to-day. Verdict—Death by starvation." The jury having given in its verdict, the foreman, on their part, proceeded to say that they felt it to be their duty to state, under the correction of the court, that it was their opinion that if the Government of the country should persevere in its determination of refusing to use the means available to it, for the purpose of lowering the price of food, so as to place it within the reach of the labouring poor, the result would be a sacrifice of human life from starvation to a fearful extent, and endangerment of property and the public peace. This remonstrance was committed to writing, and signed E. O'Sullivan, foreman; Samuel Hutchins, J.P.; Richard White, J.P.

One of the five cases was that of Catherine Sheehan, a child two years old. She had been a strong healthy child, never having complained of any sickness till she began to pine away for want of food. Her father was employed on the public works, and earned ninepence a day, which was barely enough to purchase food for himself, to enable him to continue at work. This child had had no food for four days before her death, except a small morsel of bread and seaweed. She died on the evening of Christmas day.

The case of Richard Finn was another of the five. He went into a house where they were making oatmeal gruel. He begged so hard for a little, that the woman of the house took up some of it for him, when it was about half boiled. The food disagreed with him, and he was able to take only a small portion of it. He soon got into a fainting state, and was lifted into a car by four men, in order to be carried to the Workhouse. One of the priests, Rev. Mr. Barry, P.P., was sent for. He was at the Relief Committee, but left immediately to attend Finn. In his examination before the coroner, he said he found him in a dying state, but quite in his senses. He would not delay hearing his confession till he reached the Workhouse, but heard it in the car. Finn was then removed to the House, and laid on a bed in his clothes, where he received the sacrament of Extreme Unction. "I feared," said the Rev. Mr. Barry, "the delay of stripping him." And the rev. gentleman was right, for he had scarcely concluded his ministrations when Finn expired.

Every Catholic will understand how severely the physical and mental energies of priests are taxed during times of fever, cholera, small pox, and the like; but all such epidemics combined could scarcely cause them such ceaseless work and sleepless anxiety as the Famine did, more especially in its chief centres. To those who are not Catholics, I may say that every priest feels bound, under the most solemn obligations, to administer the last sacraments to every individual committed to his care, who has come to the use of reason. What, then, must their lives have been during the Famine? Not only had they to attend the dying, but they were expected, and they felt it to be their duty, to be present at Relief Committees, to wait on officials, write letters, and do everything they thought could in any manner aid them in saving the lives of the people. Their starving flocks looked to them for temporal as well as spiritual help, and, in the Famine, they were continually in crowds about their dwellings, looking for food and consolation. The priest was often without food for himself, and had not the heart to meet his people when he had nothing to give them. An instance of this occurred in a severely visited parish of the West. The priest one day saw before his door a crowd—hundreds, he thought—of his parishioners seeking relief. He had become so prostrate and hopeless at their present sufferings and future prospects, that, taking his Breviary, he left the house by a private way, and bent his steps to a neighbouring wood. On reaching it, he knelt down and began to recite his office aloud, to implore Almighty God to have mercy on his people and himself. He did not expect to leave that wood alive. After a time he heard a voice not far off; he became alarmed, fearing his retreat had been discovered. Strange as the coincidence seems, it is perfectly true; the voice he heard was that of a neighbouring priest, a friend of his, who had taken the very same course, and for the same reason. Gaining strength and consolation from having met, and giving each other courage, they returned to their homes, resolving to face the worst.

A physician, an excellent, kind-hearted man, who had been sent on duty to Bantry in the later stages of the Famine, said one day to a priest there—"Well, Father—, how are you getting on these times?" "Badly," was the reply, "for I often remain late in bed in the morning, not knowing where to look for my breakfast when I get up."[244]

At this same time, there was a charitable lady in or near Bantry, who had discovered that another of the priests was not unfrequently dinnerless; so she insisted on being permitted to send him that important meal, ready-cooked, at a certain hour every day, begging of him to be at home, if possible, at the hour fixed. This arrangement went on for a while to her great satisfaction, but news reached her one day that Father—seldom partook of her dinner. Such dreadful cases of starvation came to his door, that he frequently gave the good lady's dinner away. She determined that he must not sink and die; and to carry out her view she hit upon an ingenious plan. She gave the servant, who took the dinner to Father—, strict orders not to leave the house until he had dined; the reason to be given to him for this was, that her mistress wished her to bring back the things in which the dinner had been carried to him. That priest, I am glad to say, is still among us, and should these lines meet his eye, he will remember the circumstance, and the honest and true authority on which it is related.

A short time after the five inquests above referred to were held, the *Cork Examiner* published the following extract from a private letter: "Each day brings with it its own horrors. The mind recoils from the contemplation of the scenes we are compelled to witness every hour. Ten inquests in Bantry—there should have been at least *two hundred inquests*. Every day, every hour produces its own victims—holocausts offered at the shrine of political economy. Famine and pestilence are sweeping away hundreds, but they have now *no* terrors for the people. Their only regret seems to be, that they are not relieved from their sufferings by some process more speedy and less painful. *Since the inquests were held here on Monday, there have been twenty-four deaths from starvation*; and, if we can judge from appearances, before the termination of another week the number will be incredible. As to holding any more inquests, it is mere nonsense; *the number of deaths is beyond counting*. Nineteen out of every twenty deaths that have occurred in this parish, for the last two months, were caused by starvation. I have known children in the remote districts of the parish, and in the neighbourhood of the town, too, live, some of them for two, some three, and some of them for *four days on water*! On the sea shore, or convenient to it, the people are more fortunate, as they can get *seaweed*, which, when boiled and mixed with a little Indian corn, or wheaten meal, they eat, and thank Providence for providing them with even that, to allay the cravings of hunger."

Although the writer of the above letter says, and with reason it would seem, that the holding of any more inquests at Bantry was useless; the very week after it was written, a batch of inquests were held there, one of which bids fair to be, for a long time, famous, on account of the verdict returned. There were forty deaths, but from some cause, perhaps for want of time, there were only fifteen inquests. A respectable jury having been sworn, the first of these was upon a man named John Sullivan. One of the witnesses in the case said a messenger came and announced to him that a man was lying on the old road in a bad state. Witness proceeded to the place, but, in the first instance, alone; finding the man still alive, he returned for help to remove him. He got a servant boy and a cart; but on going again to where Sullivan was lying, he found life was extinct. The jury having consulted, the foreman announced their verdict in these terms: "From the multitude of deaths which have taken place in the locality, and the number of inquests which have already been held, without any good resulting, he thought, with his fellow-jurors, that they ought to bring in a general verdict, inculpating Lord John Russell, as the head of the Government. That Minister had the power of keeping the people alive, and he would not do so. Notwithstanding the fatal consequences which had attended his policy, he had expressed his determination to persevere in the same course, and therefore he (the foreman) thought that he was guilty of this death and of the rest. He would bring in no other verdict but one of *wilful murder* against Lord John Russell." The Rev. Mr. Barry suggested that the verdict should simply record the immediate cause of death—starvation; and the jury might append their opinion as to how far it was attributable to the neglect of Lord John Russell in yielding to the interests of a class of greedy monopolists. The foreman said he wished it should be remembered that the opinion which he had expressed with reference to the conduct of the Government was that of men upon their oaths. A verdict was ultimately given of death from starvation, with the addition mentioned.

The inquest was held in the Court-house, in presence of three magistrates, assisted by the Catholic clergy of the town, and the officers of the Constabulary.

Other verdicts of the same tendency, although not so decided in tone as this one, were recorded in different parts of the country. At Lismore an inquest was held on a man, also named Sullivan, and the jury found that his death was caused by the neglect of the Government in not sending food into the country *in due time*. In this town fourteen horses died of starvation in one week.

Whilst Bantry was in the condition described above, Dr. Stephens was sent by the Board of Health to examine the Workhouse there. He found it simply dreadful. Here is an extract from his report, which duty compels me, however unwillingly, to quote: "Language," he says, "would fail to give an adequate idea of the state of the fever hospital. *Such an appalling, awful, and heart-sickening condition* as it presented I never witnessed, or could think possible to exist in a civilized or Christian community. As I entered the house, the stench that proceeded from it was most dreadful and noisome; but, oh! what scenes presented themselves to my view as I proceeded through the wards and passages: patients lying on straw, naked, and in their excrements, a light covering over them—in two beds living beings beside the dead, in the same bed with them, and dead since the night before." There was no medicine—no drink—no fire. The wretched creatures, dying from thirst, were constantly crying "Water, water," but there was no Christian hand to give them even a cup of cold water for the love of God.

Towards the end of April, the Rev. Mr. Barry estimated the deaths from famine, in Bantry alone, at four thousand.

Some time ago, speaking with a gentleman, a distinguished public man, about the hinged coffin, he said: "At the time of the Famine I was a boy, residing not far from Bantry. I have seen one of those hinged coffins, which had borne more than three hundred corpses to the grave. I have seen men go along the roads with it, to collect dead bodies as they met them."

Good God! picking up human forms, made to Thy image and likeness, and lately the tenements of immortal souls, as fishermen may sometimes be seen on the seashore, gathering the *debris* of a wreck after a storm!

With such specimens of the Irish Famine before us, we cannot but feel the justice, as well as the eloquence, of the following passage: "I do not think it possible," writes Mr. A. Shafto Adair, "for an English reader, however powerful his imagination, to conceive the state of Ireland during the past winter, or its present condition. Famines and plagues will suggest themselves, with their ghastly and repulsive incidents—the dead mother—the dying infant—the feast of cannibals—Athens—Jerusalem—Marseilles. But these awful facts stand forth as dark spots in the illuminated chronicles of time; episodes, it may be, of some magnificent epoch in a nation's history—tragedies acted in remote times, or in distant regions—the actors, the inhabitants of beleaguered cities, or the citizens of a narrow territory. But here the tragedy is enacted with no narrower limits than the boundaries of a kingdom, the victims—an entire people,—within our own days, at our own thresholds."[245]

FOOTNOTES:

213.   Letter from Captain Wynne, Government District Inspector to Lieutenant-Colonel Jones.—*Commissariat Series, part 1, p.* 438.—The italics are Captain Wynne's.

214.   Report of Central Relief Committee of the Society of Friends, pp. 180-2.

215.   Census of Ireland for the Year 1851. Report on tables of deaths.

216.   The circumlocutions had recourse to by relief committees and Government officials to avoid using the word *Famine* were so many and so remarkable,

that at one time I was inclined to attempt making a complete list of them. Here are a few: "Distress," "Destitution," "Dearth of provisions," "Severe destitution," "Severe suffering," "Extreme distress," as above; "Extreme misery," "Extreme destitution," etc., etc. The Society of Friends, with honest plainspeaking, almost invariably used the word "Famine;" and they named their report, "Transactions during the Famine in Ireland."

217.   Commissariat Series, part I, p. 409.

218.   Commissariat Series, part I, p. 382.

219.   *Ib.* p. 442.

220.   Appendix to Report of British Association, p. 181.

221.   Report of Central Relief Committee of Society of Friends, p. 168.

222.   This Workhouse was built to accommodate 900 persons. The Fever Hospital and sheds had room for only 250.

223.   *A Visit to Connaught in the Autumn of* 1847: by James H. Tuke, in a letter to the Central Committee of the Society of Friends, Dublin, p. 8.

At the end of February there was a meeting of coroners in Cork, at which they came to the determination of holding no more starvation inquests.

224.   Letters from Mayo to the Dublin *Freeman's Journal*, signed W.G.

225.   The italics in the above quotation are W.G.'s.

226.   It is not to be inferred from this, that evictions were rare in Ireland immediately preceding the Famine. A writer has taken the trouble of recording in a pamphlet Irish evictions, from 1840 to the 3rd of March, 1846; a period of about five years. Up to March, 1846, evictions *arising from the Famine* had not really begun, although preparations were being made for them; so that those recorded in the pamphlet were carried out under no special pressure of circumstances whatever. The writer premises that he regards his list as far from complete, inasmuch as it was compiled chiefly from the public journals, and every evicting landlord uses all his power and precaution to keep his evictions as secret as possible; still, it was found on record, that there were over 8,000 individuals evicted in Ireland during those five years, many of the evictions being attended with much hardship and suffering, such as the removal of sick and dying persons in order to take possession. In one case a dead body was actually carried out. In two instances, comprising the dispossession of 385 individuals, the evictions took place avowedly for the purpose of bringing in Protestant tenants; in a third, 1175 persons were evicted by a noble lord, and although he did not give his reason, his name

and his whole career abundantly justify the conclusion that this vast clearance was effected to make way for a Protestant colony.

227.   Letter of Mr. Joseph M. M'Kenna to Lord John Russell. Mr. M'Kenna gives the names of all the parties. Yet still more dreadful is the case we read of as having occurred in Galway. A man having been sentenced for sheep-stealing in that city, it was stated to the bench by the resident magistrate "that the prisoner and his family were starving; one of his children died, and he was, he said, credibly informed that the mother ate part of its legs and feet. After its death he had the body exhumed, and found that nothing but the bones remained of the legs and feet."—*Freeman's Journal, April, 1848.*

228.   Letter dated from Killybegs, 18th of 12th month, 1846. Report, p. 151.

229.   Count Strezelecki's Report to the British Association, p. 97. "In addition to the Government aid, large sums were distributed by the British Association, through the agency of the generous and never-to-be-forgotten Count Strezelecki."—*MS. letter from a Mayo gentleman, in author's possession.*

230.   Report, p. 97.

231.   MS. notes taken down from Mr. Egan.

232.   Joseph Crosfield's Report to the Society of Friends, p. 145.

233.   James H. Tuke's report to the same Committee, p. 147.

234.   In Irish *corrac*, pr. *corrach* or *currach*. This primitive boat was made of a slight frame work of timber and covered with skins, whence its name. In early times *corrachs* were used in all the British islands. They are mentioned by many Latin authors, especially by Cæsar, who had several of them made after the British model.

235.   Mr. Tuke's report, p. 148.

236.   Letter dated from Killybegs, 18th of 12th month, 1846. Report, p. 151.

237.   *The Sack of Baltimore*, by Thomas Davis. A ballad, one of whose many beauties is the striking correctness of its topography.

238.   Letter of Commander J. Cruford Caffin, R.N., of Her Majesty's steam sloop "Scourge," dated 15th February, 1847, written to Captain Hamilton.

239.   Assistant-Commissary Bishop's letter of 14th Feb., 1847.

240.   So he always signed himself, although Captain Caffin calls him Dr. Traill.

241.   Letter to Mr. Trevelyan of 14th Feb., 1847.

242.   Correspondent of Dublin *Freeman's Journal.*

243. "Report: Colonization from Ireland." Brought from House of Lords 23rd July, 1847; ordered by the House of Commons to be printed 23rd July, 1847; pp. 243 and 244.

244. This physician had three large crosses made from the timber of a sliding or hinged coffin. One of these he kindly presented to the author, which is now in his possession. It is two feet three inches long, by one foot one inch across the arms. It bears the following inscription:—

"During the frightful famine-plague, which devastated a large proportion of Ireland in the years 1846-47, that monstrous and unchristian machine, a "sliding coffin," was, from necessity, used in Bantry Union for the conveyance of the victims to one common grave. The material of this cross, the symbol of our Redemption, is a portion of one of the machines, which enclosed the remains of several hundreds of our countrymen, during their passage from the wretched huts or waysides, where they died, to the pit into which their remains were thrown.—T.W."

245. *The Winter of 1846-7 in Antrim, with Remarks on Out-door Relief and Colonization.* By A. Shafto Adair, F.R.S. London: Ridgway, 1847. Haliday Pamphlets, Royal Irish Academy, vol. 1,992. Mr. Adair is a landlord of large possessions in the County Antrim, who exerted himself very much to alleviate the sufferings of the people during the Famine.—He was raised to the Peerage in 1873 as Baron Waveney.

* * * * *

CHAPTER XIII.

The Irish Relief Act, 10th Vic., c.7—Rapid expansion of Public Works—
They fail to sustain the people—Clauses of the new Relief Act—Relief
Committees—Their duties—Union rating—Principal clergy members
of Relief Committees—Duties of Government Inspectors—Finance
Committees—Numbers on Public Works in February, 1847—Monthly
outlay—Parliament gives authority to borrow £8,000,000—Reduction of
labourers on Public Works—Task work condemned—Rules drawn up by
new Relief Commissioners—Rations to be allowed—Definition of soup—
First Report of Commissioners—Remonstrances—Quantity of stationery
used—Cooked food recommended—Monsieur Soyer comes to Ireland—His
coming heralded by the London Journals—His soup—Jealousy—M. Jaquet
on Soyer—The *Lancet* on the subject—Professor Aldridge, M.D., on Soyer's
soup—Sir Henry Marsh on it—M. Soyer's model soup kitchen—A "gala
day"—Ireland M. Soyer's "difficulty"—Last appearance!—Description of
his "Model Soup Kitchen" (*Note*).—Reclamation of waste lands—Quantity
reclaimable—Sir Robert Kane's view—Mr. Fagan on Reclamation—Mr.
Poulette Scrope on the Irish question—Unreclaimed land in Mayo—The
Dean of Killala—Commissary-General Hewetson on reclamation and over-
population—Opposition to reclamation—No reason given for it—Sir R.
Griffith on it—Mr. Fetherstone a reclaimer of bog—Reclamation of bog
in England—Second Report of Relief Commissioners—Relief Works
closed too rapidly—The twenty per cent. rule—M. Labouchere's reply to
Smith O'Brien—Letter from Colonel Jones—The Premier's promise—
The Claremorris deanery—Effect of the dismissals in various parts

of the country—Soup kitchens attacked—Third Report of the Relief Commissioners—Questions from Inspectors—O'Connell's last illness—His attempt to reach Rome—His death—His character—Remaining reports of the Relief Commissioners—The Accountant's department—Number of rations—Money spent.

The expansion of the system of Public Works, under the Labour-rate Act, was as unparalleled as it was unexpected by the Government. The number of persons employed rose, in less than three months, from 20,000 to four hundred thousand; the return for the week ending on the 5th of October was just 20,000; for the week ending on the 26th of December, 398,000! there being at the latter period at least one hundred and fifty thousand on the books of the officers of the works, who either would not or could not be employed; the famine-stricken were, meantime, hastening to their shroudless and coffinless graves by the thousand. During its progress the terrible scourge was checked more or less by the various means made use of, but it was never stayed. The Government were not only astonished—they were profoundly alarmed at the magnitude to which the public works had grown. Almost the sole object of those works was *to apply a labour test to destitution*; but the authorities now felt that they must dismiss that pet theory of theirs and try to feed the people in the most direct way possible.

At the opening of Parliament the Prime Minister brought forward, as we have seen, a new Irish Relief Act, the 10th Vic., c. 7. It was called an Act for the temporary relief of destitute persons in Ireland. It was framed according to the views expressed by the Prime Minister in his speech of January the 25th, and became law on the 26th of February.

The first clause acknowledged that the Labour-rate Act failed to meet the exigency, for it recites that "by reason of the great increase of destitution in Ireland, sufficient relief could not be given according to the provisions of the Labour-rate Act;" the Lord Lieutenant was, therefore, empowered to appoint Commissioners for the relief of destitution in that country, with full authority to carry out all arrangements under the Act. Its chief provisions were: That Relief Committees should be formed by order of the Lord Lieutenant, and their powers were to extend to the 1st of November, 1847, on which day they were to cease. Those Committees were to consist of the Justices of the district, the Poorlaw Guardians, and one of the Inspectors appointed by the Relief Commissioners. A Finance Committee was to be selected from the General Committee, but the Lord Lieutenant was empowered to add others to it. A chief duty of Relief Committees was to make out lists of persons requiring relief, but the Finance Committees had authority to examine such lists, and correct them if necessary. The money required for this new system of relief was to be levied and collected as a poor-rate; and the guardians of any Union who refused to do this could be dissolved by the Poorlaw Commissioners, who were also empowered to appoint paid Guardians in their place. The Treasury, on being applied to by the Relief Commissioners, was authorized to make advances to enable them to grant loans in aid of rates, but no such grant or loan was to be made after the 1st of October, 1847.

There is a clause in this Act which is not without its interest at the present time. It is the thirteenth. It recites that "the Relief Commissioners, with the sanction of the Lord Lieutenant, are empowered to direct, whether the whole or any part of the sum mentioned . . . shall be borne by and charged exclusively against the Electoral Division, or whether the whole or any part thereof shall be borne by and charged against the whole Union; and the Guardians shall charge the whole Union, and the several Electoral Divisions accordingly."

Here is Union-rating in 1847.

Immediate preparations were made to carry this Act into effect. Commissioners were appointed; a General Order was issued by the Lord Lieutenant, and in due time that most potential of documents, a Treasury Minute, was published.[246]

In virtue of the powers conferred on him, his Excellency, in his General Order, declared that besides the justices, Poorlaw Guardians and Relief Inspector; archbishops and bishops of every denomination, the principal officiating clergy of the three denominations, and the three highest ratepayers of the district should be members of Relief Committees. Some further regulations were made to meet such special difficulties as might arise. In the next place his Excellency defined the duties of Government Inspectors. They were: 1. To direct and stimulate the Committees within their districts; 2. They were to exercise vigilance in order that relief should be given only to persons really in need of it; 3. And they were commanded to interfere as little as possible with Committees that were performing their duties well, whilst, at the same time, it was laid down as their duty to interfere with, and address Committees whose proceedings were of an injurious kind.

As to Finance Committees, the Lord Lieutenant explained that they were to be composed of the resident gentlemen, who had the greatest interest in the welfare of the districts. The legislature intended, he said, that they were to be the superintending controlling bodies over the proceedings of the Committees of Electoral Divisions, inasmuch as it was to them the country had to look for the carrying out of the provisions of the Act, with the least injury to the great interests concerned. There is no doubt that in this matter the Lord Lieutenant used the powers vested in him with a good deal of freedom as to the appointment of the Finance Committees. The clause of the Act referring to them (the 6th) runs thus: "And be it enacted, that it shall be lawful for the Lord Lieutenant of Ireland, in every case in which it shall appear to him expedient, to appoint in every Union in which this Act shall be in force, a Finance Committee, which shall consist of the Inspector, to be appointed as aforesaid by the Relief Commissioners for such Union, and of such justices resident in the Union, or such other persons as the Lord Lieutenant should think fit, not being less than two and not more than four persons in addition to such Inspector."

The Treasury Minute repeats the numbers on the public works during the month of February. They were, in the

Week ending on the 6th,	615,055
Week ending on the 13th,	605,715
Week ending on the 20th,	668,749
Week ending on the 27th,	708,228

It also gives the outlay for three months, not including the expenses of the Commissariat Department, which were by no means inconsiderable.

It was for	December,	545,054
	January, 1847,	736,125
	February,	944,141

being nearly a million of money for that month. Besides excluding the expenditure of the Commissariat, this account did not, of course, take in the very large sums disbursed by charitable bodies and by private individuals.

The new Relief Act came into force on the 27th of February, and the Government obtained, without any difficulty, the permission of Parliament to borrow £8,000,000, to carry out its provisions. As this Act was to supersede the Public Works, it was decreed by the Treasury Minute that on Saturday the 20th of March the labourers on those works should be reduced by not less than twenty per cent. The remainder were to be dismissed by successive reductions, at such times and in such proportions as would be determined by the Board. The order in which dismissals wore to be carried out was, that persons holding ten acres of land and upwards, were to be discharged on the 20th of March, *even if they should exceed the twenty per cent.*; if they fell below it, the persons holding the next largest quantity of land should be discharged in order that the full twenty per cent. should be dismissed. In districts where rations of soup could be supplied by the Relief Committees, the Relief Works were to be entirely suspended.

It was added in the Minute, that as the Commissioners of Public Works were of opinion that, in existing circumstances, the mode of employing persons by task work did not answer the expectations that were formed of it, there should be a recurrence to daily pay, at such rates as might be fixed with the sanction of the Lord Lieutenant.

As soon as the Relief Commissioners entered upon their duties, they drew up a code of rules for the information and guidance of Relief Committees.

The following are the principal:

1. Relief Committees to be under the regulating control of a Finance Committee for each Union.
2. As to funds:—local or other subscriptions, with donations from Government and moneys in hand of Poorlaw Guardians, to be regarded as appropriated rates on electoral divisions, where needed.
3. The funds in hands of existing Relief Committees were to be generally available for Committees under the new Act.
4. Relief to be given exclusively in food; gratuitously to the absolutely desolate; by reasonable prices to such, as were in employment, or had the means of purchasing.
5. There was to be a Government Inspector of every Union, who was to be an *ex-officio* member of every Committee under the Act in the Union.
9. Persons requiring relief were to be classed under *four* heads, namely: (1) Those who were destitute, helpless or impotent; (2) Destitute able-bodied persons not holding land; (3) Destitute able-bodied persons who were holders of small portions of land; (4) The able-bodied employed at wages insufficient for their support, when the price of food was very high.
10. The first three classes to get gratuitous relief, but the fourth to be relieved by the sale of food of a cheap description: and it was specially laid down that there were to be "no gratuitous supplies of food to

them." "This," say the Instructions, "is to be a fixed rule." Yet it was afterwards modified with regard to class 4: the clause saying "they were to be relieved by the sale of food of a cheap description" did not, it would seem, mean that such food was to be sold under its value. This was represented as a hardship, and on the 11th of May the Relief Commissioners ruled, that with regard to the price of food to class 4, "any food cooked in a boiler might be sold under first cost."

12. Persons receiving wages, or refusing hire, to be excluded from gratuitous relief.

15. To entitle holders of land to gratuitous relief, it should be absolutely required of them to proceed with the cultivation of their land.

The relief lists were to be revised every fortnight; the food best suited to each district, and the most easily obtained *there*, to be at once taken into consideration.

As to rations, it was considered that the most nourishing and economical food was soup made after some of the approved receipts, with a portion of bread, meal, or biscuit.

The 26th rule fixed the quantity and quality of a ration.

It was to consist of

1½ lbs. of bread; or
1 lb. of biscuit; or
1 lb. of meal or flour of any grain; or
1 quart of soup thickened with a portion of meal, according to the known receipts, and one quarter ration of bread, biscuit or meal, in addition.

Persons above nine years of age to have one full ration; those under that age half a ration.

These rules were promulgated from the Relief Commission Office, in Dublin Castle, on the 8th of March.

A difficulty having arisen as to what could be strictly considered "soup," the following definition of it was issued by the Relief Commissioners to the Inspecting officers of each Union.

"Sir, As the term 'Soup' in the Instructions seems to have created an impression with many parties, that only the liquid ordinarily so called is meant, and that meat must necessarily form an ingredient, the Relief Commissioners beg that the general term 'soup,' in their Instructions, may be understood to include any food cooked in a boiler, and distributed in a liquid state, thick or thin, and whether composed of meat, fish, vegetables, grain or meal."

The Commissioners published their first report on the 10th of March, eleven days after the Relief Act came into force; an exceedingly short time for them in which to have done anything worth reporting; but this is explained by the fact, that they and their officers had been set to work a considerable time before the Relief Act had become law; the Government assuming that it would meet with no real opposition in its passage through Parliament.

From this Report we learn that there were, at the time, 2049 electoral divisions in Ireland; and from a later one, that Blackrock, near Dublin, was the smallest electoral division, consisting only of 257 acres; that the largest was Belmullet, in the County of Mayo, which contained 145,598 acres. The extremes in the valuation of electoral divisions were,—Mullaghderg, in Glenties Union, £331 10s. 0d.; South Dublin, £402,516 3s. 4d. So that a shilling rate levied off Mullaghderg would produce just £16 12s. 6d., which in all probability would not pay for the time necessary to collect it.[247]

The Commissioners report, that two conditions laid down by them had called forth several remonstrances, namely, (1) The prohibition of administering relief under the Act *in aid of wages*; and (2) The restriction to the sale of food under cost price, with the exception of soup.

The quantity of stationery necessary for the carrying out of the Relief Act is certainly worth noting. In the mere preparation for their work, the Commissioners had delivered to them upwards of 10,000 books, 80,000 sheets, and 3,000,000 of card tickets; the gross weight of all not being less than fourteen tons! Two Inspectors, Major Parker and Captain Drury, having caught fever at Skibbereen and Kinsale respectively, fell victims to it.

Lest they should be suspected of not being true believers in Political Economy, the Commissioners thus conclude their first report: "Your Lordships are aware that the relief that we are now administering is not only of a temporary character, but necessarily of a nature contrary to all sound principles of policy."

The determination of the authorities to supply, as far as possible, the starving people with cooked food, especially soup, made the question of preparing it for millions one of vast importance. To produce the greatest quantity of cooked food in a palatable form, at the minimum of cost, and with the maximum of nutrition, might save the country half a million of money, and many thousands of lives besides. With this object the Government fixed upon Monsieur Soyer of the Reform Club, and appointed him Head Cook to the people of Ireland. His elevation to this unique office was announced with considerable flourish. "We learn," says one of the London journals, "that the Government have resolved forthwith to despatch M. Soyer, the *chef de cuisine* of the Reform Club, to Ireland, with ample instructions to provide his soups for the starving millions of Irish people." And this journal further informs us that artizans were busy day and night constructing kitchens, apparatus, etc., with which M. Soyer was to start for Dublin, "direct to the Lord Lieutenant." His plans had been examined and approved of. The soup had been served to several of the best judges "of the noble art of gastronomy in the Reform Club, not as soup for the poor, but as soup furnished for the day, in the *carte.*" It was declared excellent. He undertook to supply the whole poor of Ireland, at one meal for each person each day. This meal with a biscuit, he assured the Executive, would be more than sufficient to sustain the strength of a strong and healthy man. One hundred gallons of the soup was to be produced for £1. And M. Soyer had satisfied the Government, that he would furnish enough and to spare of most nourishing food "for the poor of these realms;" and it was confidently anticipated that there would be no more deaths from starvation in Ireland.[248]

M. Soyer arrived in Dublin on the 1st of March, bringing with him his model kitchen and apparatus, and a building to receive them was erected on the ground in front of the Royal Barracks, and not far from the principal entrance to the Phoenix Park. Before leaving London he had published some of the receipts according to which he intended to make various kinds of soups for the starving Irish. Objections were raised in the columns of the *Times* against the small quantity of meat he used in making some of those soups. "A brother *artiste*," as M. Soyer calls him, maintained that a quarter of a pound of meat, allowed in making two gallons of his soup No. 1, was not at all enough. M. Soyer rather jauntily replies that he had made two gallons of excellent soup without any meat, and that he had, at the moment, three soups "on taste," two with meat and one without, and he defied the "scientific palate" of his brother *artiste* "to tell which was which." "The meat," says M. Soyer, "I consider of no more value than the other ingredients, but to give a flavour by properly blending the gelatine and the osmazome, for," he adds with complacent self-reliance, "in compounding the richest soup, the balance of it is the great art."

His brother *artiste*, M. Jaquet, of Johnson's tavern, Clare Court, rejoins that he never questioned M. Soyer's ability to make a palatable and pleasing soup with little or no meat, but that he himself had not acquired the valuable art of making nutritious and useful soup without meat, and that he would not like to make the experiment of doing so, "for the use of the destitute poor." He expressed the hope that receipt No. 1 might be analyzed, and if it had all things necessary for nourishment, he, of course, was silenced.

430

M. Jaquet had his wish. Scientific people took up M. Soyer's receipts, and dealt with them,—correctly and justly, no doubt, but in a manner that must have been anything but agreeable to the great *artiste* of the Reform Club, who seems to have had very exalted ideas of the importance of the mission on which he was sent to Ireland.

Thus wrote the *Lancet* on the subject: "The mass of the poor population of Ireland is in a state of starvation. Gaunt famine, with raging fever at her heels, are marching through the length and breadth of the sister island, and they threaten to extend their fury to this Country. The British public, under the form of clubs, committees, and relief associations, are actively engaged in sending food to the famine districts. All this is done without boasting or ostentation. But parliament and the executive, in the midst of the best intentions, seems to be agitated by a spasmodic feeling of benevolence; at one time adopting public works, at another preaching a poorlaw—now considering the propriety of granting sixteen millions for railways, and then descending to M. Soyer, the chief cook of the Reform Club, with his ubiquitous kitchens and soups, at some three farthings the quart, which is to feed all hungry Ireland.

"As this soup quackery (for it is no less) seems to be taken by the rich as a salve for their consciences, and with a belief that famine and fever may be kept at bay by M. Soyer and his kettles, it is right to look at the constitution of this soup of pretence, and the estimate formed of it by the talented but eccentric self-deceived originator.

"M. Soyer proposes to make soup of the following proportions:— Leg of beef, four ounces; dripping fat, two ounces; flour, eight ounces; brown sugar, half an ounce; water, *two gallons*.

"These items are exclusive of the onions, a few turnip parings, celery-tops, and a little salt, which can hardly be considered under the head of food. The above proportions give less than three ounces of solid nutriment to each quart of soup a la Soyer. Of this its inventor is reported to have said to the Government 'that a bellyful once a day, with a biscuit, (we quote from the *Observer,*) will be more than sufficient to maintain the strength of a strong healthy man.'

"To bring this to the test. Organic chemistry proves to us that the excretæ from the body of a healthy subject by the eliminatory organs must at least amount to twelve or fourteen ounces; and organic chemistry will not, we fear, bend to the most inspired receipts of the most miraculous cookery book, to supply the number of ounces without which the organic chemistry of the human body will no more go on than will the steam-engine without fuel. M. Soyer, supposing each meal of his soup for the poor to amount to a quart, supplies less than three ounces, or less than a quarter the required amount, and of that only one solitary half ounce of animal aliment, diluted, or rather dissolved in a bellyful of water. Bulk of water, the gastronomic may depend, will not make up for the deficiency of solid convertible aliment. No culinary digesting, or stewing, or boiling, can convert four ounces into twelve, unless, indeed, the laws of animal physiology can be unwritten, and some magical power be made to reside in the cap and apron of the cook for substituting fluids in the place of solids, and *aqua pura* in place of solids in the animal economy.

"It seems necessary to bring forward these facts, as M. Soyer's soup has inspired the public mind with much satisfaction—a satisfaction which, we venture to say, will never reach the public stomach.

"Marquises and lords and ladies may taste the meagre liquid, and pronounce it agreeable to their gustative inclinations; but something more than an agreeable titilation of the palate is required to keep up that manufactory of blood, bone, and muscle which constitutes the 'strong healthy man.'"

During M. Soyer's visit to Ireland, a Dublin chemist read, before the Royal Dublin Society, a paper upon the nutritive and pecuniary value of various kinds of cooked food. He had previously put himself in communication with M. Soyer, who showed him over his model kitchen, and allowed him to analyze his soups. The result of this analysis was remarkable, for he found that M. Soyer's dearest soup was the least nutritive, whilst his cheapest soup was the most so: a proportion which held through all the soups analyzed; their nutritive qualities being in an inverse ratio to their prices. In his calculation the chemist takes a child of four stones weight, as the average of persons who required food relief, and he found that—

160 gallons of Soyer's soup No. 2 would give sufficient nutriment to 213 such children for one day. Its price was 2-3/4d. the gallon.

160 gallons of Soyer's soup No. 4 would give sufficient nutriment to 420 such children for one day. Its price was 2-1/4d. the gallon.

160 gallons of his soup No. 5 would give sufficient nutriment to 385 such children for one day. Its price was 2-1/2d. the gallon.

160 gallons of his soup No. 6 (a fish soup) would give sufficient nutriment to 700 such children for one day. Its price was only 1-3/4d. the gallon.[249]

So that the famous cook of the Reform Club did not know the comparative nutritive qualities of his own soups.

But a still greater came on the scene in the person of Sir Henry Marsh, the Queen's physician, and long at the head of his profession in this country. He published a pamphlet of some ten pages, not for the purpose of finding fault with M. Soyer or his soups, but evidently to set the public right on the question of food, as they seemed to have taken up the idea that there resided some hidden power in the cook's receipt, distinct from the ingredients he used. Sir Henry thus deals with soup food:—

"A soft semi-liquid diet will maintain the life and health of children, and in times of scarcity will be sufficient for those adults whose occupations are sedentary, and is best suited to those who are reduced by and recovering from a wasting disease. Such persons stand in no need of the more abundant and more substantial nutriment which is essential to those who are daily engaged in occupations exacting much muscular labour. In the preparation and distribution of food, this I believe to be an important point, and one which should be held steadily in view. For the labourer the food must be in part solid, requiring mastication and insalivation, and not rapid of digestion. Food, however nutritious, which is too quickly digested, is soon followed by a sense of hunger and emptiness, and consequent sinking and debility. Food of this description is unsuited to the labourer. It will not maintain strength, nor will it maintain health, and, if long persevered in, it will be followed by some one or other of the prevailing diseases which result immediately from deficient, imperfect, and impoverished blood."

Again:—

"Our attention must not be too exclusively directed to soups and other semi-liquid articles of food. These pass away too rapidly from the stomach, are swallowed too hastily, and violate a natural law in superseding the necessity of mastication, and a proper admixture with the salivary secretion. Restricted to such food the carnivora cannot maintain life; nor can man, being half carnivorous, if laboriously employed, long preserve health and strength on food of such character ... Food, to be at once sustaining to the labourer, and preventive of disease, must have bulk— must possess solidity—must not be rapidly digestible, and must contain, in varied proportions, all the staminal ingredients of nutriment."

Sir Henry Marsh, said one of the morning journals, did not attack M. Soyer, but he demolished the soup kitchen as effectively as if he did.

As soon as M. Soyer's model soup depôt was completed, he resolved to open it for public inspection with a good deal of ceremony. On the 5th of April, therefore, the opening day, the space in front of the Royal Barracks presented a very animated scene; flags floated gaily in the breeze; the rich dresses of ladies of birth and fashion contrasted pleasingly with the costly and superb military uniforms among which they moved; and

434

M. Soyer was all politeness in explaining to his distinguished visitors the arrangements and perfections of his soup kitchen. In a famine-stricken land, the good taste of this exhibition was doubtful enough: at any rate it was criticised with no sparing hand.

When I got a card of invitation, writes one, I thought I was to see M. Soyer's peculiar appliances for making soup for the poor; but no— it was a "gala day:" drums beating, flags flying. Then the writer grows political, and says bitterly, that he "envied not the Union flag the position it occupied as it flaunted in triumph from the chimney top of the soup kitchen; it was its natural and most meet position; the rule of which it is the emblem has brought our country to require soup kitchens,—and no more fitting ornament could adorn their tops." All the parade he could, he says, have borne, but what he considered indefensible was the exhibition of some hundreds of Irish beggars "to demonstrate what ravening hunger will make the image of God submit to."[250] "His Excellency the Lord Lieutenant was there," wrote the *Evening Packet* (a Conservative journal); "the ladies Ponsonby and many other fair and delicate creatures assembled; there were earls and countesses, and lords and generals, and colonels and commissioners, and clergymen and doctors; for, reader, it was a *gala day*,—a *grand gala*." The provincial press dealt with the proceedings in the same spirit.

Like many other great men, M. Soyer, in a short time, found that Ireland was his "difficulty;" so he resolved, somewhat suddenly, it would appear, to return to the more congenial atmosphere of the Reform Club. His resolution was thus announced in one of the Dublin morning journals: "SOYER'S MODEL KITCHEN.—By the special desire of several charitable ladies, who have visited and paid particular attention to the working of the model kitchen, it will be opened again on Saturday next, from two to six, on which day those ladies, under the direction of Mrs. L—, will attend and serve the poor. The admission for the view on that day will be five shillings each, to be distributed by the Lord Mayor in charity; after which the kitchen will be closed, M. Soyer being obliged

435

to leave for the Reform Club, London." This smacked very much of a "positively last appearance." Referring to it, a Dublin journal exclaims—"Five shillings each to see paupers feed! Five shillings each to watch the burning blush of shame chasing pallidness from poverty's wan cheek! Five shillings each! When the animals in the Zoological Gardens can be inspected at feeding time for *sixpence*!"[251]

A few gentlemen gave M. Soyer a dinner and a snuff box before he left, and so his Irish mission was brought to a close; but his name was not forgotten, for *Sawyer's soup* was long a standing joke with a certain class of the Dublin people. Had the word come into popular use at the time, there is little doubt that M. Soyer's undertaking to feed the starving Irish would have been called a *fiasco*.[252]

Philanthropists of a stamp different from M. Soyer brought forward schemes for the good of Ireland at this time. They related chiefly to the reclamation of her waste lands. At the opening of Parliament in 1847, Lord John Russell, as we have seen, proposed to introduce a Bill on this subject, one million being the first grant to be made for the purpose. The plan on which the reclamation was to be carried out is given in the resumè of Lord John's speech at the opening of the session. It was the very best of the Premier's measures for the permanent improvement of Ireland; but, according to Mr. D'Israeli, it was faintly proposed, and finally abandoned in deference to the expressed opinion of Sir Robert Peel, who, at the time, governed from the Opposition benches.

This question of the reclamation of our waste lands had been often before Parliament and the public previous to 1847. The committee relating to the poor of Ireland in the year 1830 refer in their report to no less than twelve preceding sessions in which the importance of reclaiming the Irish wastes was strongly recommended, but the publication of the "Industrial Resources of Ireland," by Dr. (now Sir Robert) Kane, a short time before the Famine, directed public attention anew to the subject.

The area of Ireland is 20,808,271 statute acres. Of these it is commonly admitted that 18,600,000, or thereabouts, are susceptible of cultivation. In

1845, somewhat over 13,000,000 of acres were in cultivation, whilst nearly 5,000,000, which could be brought under culture, lay barren. Referring to the estimate of those writers who held that Ireland contained 4,600,000 acres of waste, which could be made arable, Dr. Kane said he did not think the estimate too high; and this opinion was quoted approvingly by Lord John Russell.[253]

But the question might still remain,—could those four and a-half millions of acres he profitably cultivated? Would their cultivation give remunerative interest on the capital expended? That is the purely commercial view of the matter; but there is another which should not be overlooked: Would it not be wise policy to increase the resources of a country,—to increase its area of cultivation,—to extend the means of employing and feeding its population, even though the work did not actually make a very remunerative commercial return? English capital has gone to make canals and railroads and harbours, and open mines for the antipodes, often with little or no return; not unfrequently with total loss; surely as much risk ought to be taken for home improvements, in which patriotism should come to the aid of commercial enterprise. The Chinese have, after their own fashion, devoted themselves to this kind of improvement for centuries; so have the enlightened Dutch, the most recent example of which is that noble engineering achievement, the draining of the lake of Haarlem; and although the sale of the drained land did not recoup the Government for the outlay, yet they felt the work was a great national benefit, inasmuch as it added forty-three thousand acres to the arable soil of Holland. So pleased indeed are they with the result, that they have at present under consideration another undertaking of the same kind, and of far greater extent, namely, the draining of the Zuider Zee.

It would seem, then, to be a question well worthy the consideration of statesmen, whether or not, in the reclamation of wastes, it would be the true and enlightened policy to act upon the commercial idea alone.

Mr. Fagan, a commercial man of sound practical ability, who sat in the House of Commons for the County Wexford, put forward, in the famine period, a scheme for the reclamation of the waste lands.[254] It was mainly based upon the principle, that the men whose labour reclaimed those lands should have a beneficial interest in them. The wealth—the capital of the poor man, he said, lie in the health and strength with which God has endowed him, and if he be denied the means of employing this capital profitably, what matters it to him that the harvest is bountiful—that the corn stores are full? Mr. Fagan discusses several plans according to which Irish waste lands might be reclaimed. 1. Individual exertion. This, in his opinion, would not answer, because it would be too slow, too isolated, to do the work in a broad, comprehensive manner, and within a reasonable time. 2. The next plan which he passes in review is what he terms joint-stock enterprise. This he also rejects, as being expensive in management, and therefore unremunerative. 3. Reclamation by the Government, so commonly advocated, he also rejects, because he did not think such an undertaking within the legitimate sphere of the Government, and that it would be inconsistent with sound policy.

Having set aside these three modes of reclamation, he puts forward his own.

1.   He was of opinion that the principle of *individual* industry should be applied to the reclamation of the waste lands, and that a reasonable share of the fruits of the industry of the reclaimer should be secured to him. Where enlightened proprietors have done this, their wastes, he says, became fertile, and agrarian outrages were unknown. Give, in a word, the Irish peasant the same interest in reclaiming the waste at home, that he gets in reclaiming the waste abroad, and the same beneficial results will follow.

2.   For the right working of this principle, the waste lands should be resumed by the State. This he regarded as an indispensable preliminary. Pay the proprietors fully for them, let the ground be

valued as it is valued for railways; paid for at its present, not its prospective value, and let it be vested in Commissioners. Lots of convenient size should be made, and sold, when reclaimed; but at no higher price than twenty-four years' purchase. The State should also empower the Commissioner to sell waste, in lots of not less than ten acres; ten acres to be the minimum of reclaimed lots also. Existing proprietors should have the option of reclaiming or selling; but in the former case security should be given that the work would be immediately proceeded with.

Mr. Fagan would ask no pecuniary aid from the Government to carry out his plan; he would meet the expenses of it by an agency tax, that is, a tax upon house and land agencies, and upon all agencies. In saying this he must have meant, that he would not ask money out of the Consolidated Fund; for he could not but have seen that in carrying it out by a tax of any kind, he would be doing so by the aid of the Government. The effect of Mr. Fagan's plan would have been, to create, to a certain extent, a peasant proprietary.

Mr. Poulett Scrope, then representing the borough of Stroud in Parliament, took much interest in Irish questions, more especially during the Famine; at which time he, in a series of letters addressed to Lord John Russell, put forward his views on the legislation which he considered necessary under the existing circumstances of this country. Three Bills in his opinion, should have been at once proceeded with in Parliament; one to facilitate the sale of encumbered estates; one to improve the relations between landlord and tenant; and the third for commencing without delay the reclamation of the waste lands. This last he considered as of the most pressing urgency. Strange enough, that since Mr. Scrope wrote, laws have been passed on the two former subjects, whilst the one considered by him the most necessary, still remains unlegislated on. His great object was, he said, to create employment, and to create it in the production of food, if possible. Surely, says Mr. Scrope, if this can be created for the people at home, it is much better, for a thousand reasons, than to attempt to find it for them in America. "I cannot refrain," he writes, "from expressing astonishment at the degree to which the almost inexhaustible resources offered by the waste lands of Ireland for the production of employment of the wretched and unwillingly idle labourers of that country, have been overlooked and neglected, no less by statesmen than individual proprietors."[255]

From whatever cause, Irish landowners did not, to any considerable extent, take up, in earnest, the question of the reclamation of waste lands. Roused by the pressure of the times and the impending poor-rate, the majority of them looked, says Mr. Scrope, "for salvation" to other means—to the eviction of their numerous tenantry—the clearing of their estates from the seemingly superfluous population by emigration or ejectment. "Yet," he continues, "nothing can be more true or more capable of demonstration than the assertion that there is no real redundancy of population in Ireland. Nay, that even in the most distressed and apparently overcrowded districts, a wise and prudent management of their natural resources might find profitable employment for all, to the great advantage of the proprietors themselves, and the still greater benefit of the people and the public, which is so deeply interested in the result."[256]

The readers of these pages cannot forget that Mayo suffered as much as, if not more than, any other county, during the Famine; yet here was the state of its surface at the time of that dreadful visitation: entire area of the County Mayo, 1,300,000 acres; of these only 500,000 acres were under cultivation, 800,000 acres being unreclaimed; of which 800,000 acres, Griffith says, nearly 500,000 could be reclaimed with profit;—that is, just half the county was cultivated. The Dean of Killala gave the following evidence about the same county before the Devon Commission: *Quest. 73.* "Is there sufficient employment for the people in the cultivation of the arable land?" *Answ.* "No; it does not employ them half the year." *Quest. 74.* "But there would be employment for them in reclaiming the waste?" *Answ.* "Yes; more than ample, if there was encouragement given. Where

I reside there are many thousands of acres waste, because it would not be let at a moderate rent." *Quest.* 75. "Is the land with you termed waste, capable of being made productive?" *Answ.* "Yes; every acre of it."

On this same question of the reclamation of Irish waste lands and redundant population, Commissary-General Hewetson, one of the principal assistants of Sir Randal Routh, writes, in the height of the Famine: "The transition from potatoes to grain requires tillage in the proportion of *three* to *one*. It is useless, then, to talk of emigration, *when so much extra labour* is indispensable to supply the extra food. Let that labour be first applied, and it will be seen whether there is any surplus population. *If the waste lands are taken into cultivation*, and industrious habits established, it is very doubtful whether there will be any surplus population, *or even* whether it would be equal to the demand." "Providence," he adds, "has given everything needful, and nothing is wanting but industry to apply it." "Yes!" to use the words of Mr. Scrope, "there are two things more wanted—namely, that Irish industry should have leave to apply itself to the improvement of the Irish soil, and be assured of reaping the undivided fruits of such application."[257]

From causes which can be only guessed at, there seems to have been always a passive but most influential opposition to the reclamation of the waste lands of Ireland. Its opponents never met the question in the field of logical argument, yet, somehow, they had power enough to prevent its being carried into effect. When Lord John Russell proposed the million grant to begin the work, Sir Robert Peel said he thought some more useful employment could be found for that sum, but he did not even hint at what it was. A writer, who published in 1847 a work on Ireland "Historical and Statistical," thus deals with the reclamation question: "The Irish waste lands being of considerable extent have long attracted the notice of speculators and improvers. They are about to receive the attention of her Majesty's Government, and a sum of one million is promised to the Irish landlords as an aid towards their reclamation. But there is much room to doubt the policy of such a proceeding at any time,

441

and especially at the present time."[258] Here is a pretty decided opinion against reclamation, but there is no reason whatever vouchsafed for it.

On the other hand those who were favourable to the reclamation of our waste lands were rich in facts and arguments. In the Parliamentary Session of 1835, a Committee of the House of Commons on public works reported that "no experiment was necessary to persuade any scientific man of the possibility of carrying into effect the reclamation of bogs." Nor is this strongly expressed opinion to be wondered at, founded, as it was, upon such evidence as the following:—

Mr. Griffith deposed that—

"The mountain bog of the south of Ireland—the moory bog—varies in depth from nine inches to three feet, below which there is a clayey or sandy subsoil. On the average, about £4 per statute acre is required to bring it from a state of nature to one of cultivation, and then it will fetch a rent of from 5s. to 10s. per English acre."

Again:

"£1 4s. an acre is the highest estimate for the draining of this land in covered drains; the remainder of the expense consists in the trenching up the surface, turning up the subsoil, and mixing it with the bog; no manure is wanted, a portion of the bog being burned for that purpose."

With regard to deep bogs, his testimony was as follows:

"The expense of reclaiming deep bogs per acre may be estimated thus:—Drainage of an English acre, in the most perfect way, about £1 4s., which is about 40s. the Irish acre; that includes the under drain: the levelling and digging comes to about £1 10s.; and afterwards the claying comes to about £6 12s. per statute acre."

Finally, he said:

"The reclamation of mountain land is very profitable, and easily effected; but the reclamation of deep bog land is attended with a much greater expense, and requires both care and judgment. But both are certainly reclaimable, and would give a successful return when judiciously treated."

442

Mr. Featherstone, a practical and successful farmer, told the Committee that he had reclaimed the worst sort of bog land for £13 an acre, and some cushbog land for, £6 an acre: the former, when reclaimed, was worth £1 an acre, and the latter £2 an acre. "It took me," he said, "£13 an acre to reclaim the first red bog I tried my hand on: and it would take to reclaim, on the average, the red bog of Ireland, £10 an acre."

The soundness of the views put forward by Sir Richard Griffith and Mr. Featherstone is proved by the reclamation of similar wastes in England. With regard to Chat-moss, on the Liverpool and Manchester railway, Mr. Baines writes from Barton Grange, in Lancashire, which he calls "a house standing in the midst of a tract of 2,000 acres of peat moss, within a few years past as wet and barren as any morass in Ireland, but now covered with luxuriant crops." He averages the sum expended in reclaiming the Lancashire mosses at £10 an acre, *all spent in* manual labour.[259] One thousand acres of Rawcliffe-moss in Lancashire was reclaimed for £9,000, although high wages were paid to the labourers. It pays, says Mr. Scrope, ten per cent. on the outlay, and now gives constant employment to seventy labourers. In Ireland, he adds, private enterprise cannot do such work. There is no capital. With regard to reclamations made on the estate of Sir Charles Styles, in the county Donegal, Captain Kennedy, the manager, testified before the Devon Commission that the original cost of reclamation was refunded in three years. And he further expressed his conviction that an outlay of £5 an acre would pay ten per cent. on those lands.

What grave mysterious reasons of State, then, have prevented the Irish wastes from being reclaimed? In the Famine, our roads were torn up and made impassable to apply a labour test to destitution; food was next served out without any such test; M Soyer was sent over to make cheap soup for the million; the bone and sinew of the country were shipped off to spend themselves in trying to subdue the wildernesses of another hemisphere, or die *in transitu*, or on Grosse Isle and such charnel-houses, whilst nearly five millions of reclaimable acres in their own fertile load were still left as nature had left them.

The second report of the Relief Commissioners bears date the 15th of May. For practical purposes it may be looked upon as the first report, the one called the first being merely preliminary. We learn from it that only 1,248 electoral divisions had come under the operation of the Act up to that date, a state of things with which the Commissioners expressed themselves dissatisfied, for they say the Act should have been, at the time of their report, in full operation over the whole country. They found a difficulty in establishing soup kitchens, because dry meal was universally preferred; and they further say that relief by food instead of by public works was extremely unpopular with every class. All works, they announce, had been stopped on the first of May. To this general stoppage, some exceptions, it would seem, were permitted. Memorandum No. 12 of the Relief Department (marked "confidential") vests certain relief officers with a discretionary power to continue the works in those baronies where it would be dangerous to stop them, either because the new measures of relief had not come into operation, or on account of the absence of employment, either public or private, in such baronies. From the general outcry at the stoppage of the works, it would appear that this memorandum was very little, if at all, acted upon.

The second report of the Relief Commissioners, embracing a most trying period of over two months, is very curt and unsatisfactory. The dismissal, within six weeks, of nearly three quarters of a million of workmen, representing more than three millions of people, could scarcely be effected without the infliction of considerable suffering. The Government were right in compelling labour to apply itself to the production of food by the cultivation of the land, and they began this movement in the Spring, the proper time for it, but they began too late. The 20th of March was far too late for the fast dismissal of twenty per cent., for much of the Spring work ought to have been done then. They should have begun a month earlier at least, which arrangement would have had the further advantage of enabling them, to make the dismissals more gradually, and therefore with less inconvenience to the people.[260]

It was either great negligence or a very grave error on the part of the Government, that they began to close the public works against the people before any other means of getting food was open to them. The Relief Act, 10 Vic. c. 7, was intended to take the place of the public works, *and that immediately on their cessation*; but this was far from being the case,—a point upon which this second report is not at all satisfactory. In it the Commissioners express their regret that on the 15th of May there were only 1,248 electoral divisions under the operation of the Act, whilst all relief works had ceased on the first of May. That was bad enough; but what the report makes no mention of is that the Act was not in operation in any part of Ireland on the 20th of March, the day on which twenty per cent—146,000 individuals—of those who were employed on the public works were dismissed. On introducing that Act in Parliament, both the Prime Minister and the Irish Secretary promised that employment on the public works should be continued until the new system of relief would be in full operation, whilst this report tells us that on the 15th of May, a full fortnight after *all* public works had been stopped, out of 2,049 electoral divisions only 1,248 were under the operation of the Act. Besides, "under the operation of the Act" is itself a doubtful phrase: How long were they under it? How far was their machinery complete and efficient? Did the Act, to the full extent, supply the place of the public works, where it had come into operation? These are questions to which we have no answers from the Commissioners. On the 23rd of March, three days after the twenty per cent were dismissed, a Dublin newspaper said, with regard to the new Relief Act:—"It is not in operation in any district of Ireland. Even in Dublin—the head quarters of the Relief Commissioners—the residence of the official printer—the requisite forms for arranging the preliminaries could not be supplied to the relief committees yesterday, they not having been as yet printed."[261]

On the 25th of March, some of the Irish members appealed, in the House of Commons, to the Irish Secretary not to allow the labourers on the public works to be dismissed until provision could be made for their support under the new Act. It was understood by both sides of the House, Mr. Smith O'Brien said, that the Government had given instructions against any dismissals taking place until other means had been provided to enable the people to procure subsistence. Unless this were done, he said, the greatest confusion must follow the putting in force of the order for dismissing persons from the public works, which was to come into operation on the 20th inst. Seven weeks had elapsed since the temporary relief bill had become law, and he could not conceive why relief committees had not been constituted. Mr. Labouchere said in reply that the greatest caution was necessary in removing the labourers from the works, and that although twenty per cent. of them were ordered to be struck off on the 20th instant, that did not mean that twenty per cent. of the people employed in every district on public works should be dismissed, but that in the aggregate twenty per cent. of those employed should be put off, leaving to the Irish Government to decide upon the proportion to be removed from each district. It would be necessary and proper to make a general reduction, but the Irish Government was left to the exercise of its discretion in making the several reductions by districts, as the executive in Ireland could best decide where it might be dangerous or improper to make any change, and where a change might be made with propriety and safety.

Four days later, on the question that the Irish Poor Relief Bill should be re-committed, Mr. O'Brien again adverted to the discharge of the labourers from the public works. He repeated, that the House and others had been led to believe, that the dismissal would not take place until new measures for temporary relief should come into operation; that, nevertheless, in various parts of Ireland labourers had been dismissed before any other relief had been provided; and he had, he said, received from a part of the county he represented a letter from a Protestant clergyman, stating that not only twenty per cent., but many more labourers had been dismissed, and were, therefore, on the verge of starvation. No one, he admitted, could justly object to the general proposition of the gradual withdrawal of the people from the public works; but it appeared to him that such withdrawal, until some other mode of subsistence was ready for them, was nothing short of sentencing the people to death from starvation.

To Smith O'Brien's remarks, Mr. Labouchere gave the following reply, a more formal and elaborate one than the above. He said:—"Her Majesty's Government were satisfied, after the best inquiry they were able to make upon the subject, that it was expedient and proper that on a certain day the number of persons employed on the public works throughout Ireland should be reduced by twenty per cent. They thought that was a step which, upon their responsibility, they were bound to adopt, and in that respect they left no discretion whatever with any one connected with the Irish Government; but the rule laid down was this— they required that twenty per cent. should be reduced on the aggregate number of the persons employed throughout the whole of Ireland, leaving to the Board of Works in Ireland a discretion as to whether, in each particular instance, that precise number should be the proportion to be reduced or not. The Board of Works in Ireland thought they should best meet the views of the Government, by striking off twenty per cent. from the number of persons employed in each district, but it was not the case that the rule had been applied strictly and invariably on every public work in Ireland; and as a proof that such was the case, he read the following extract from a report which had been received from Captain O'Brien, the inspecting officer for Clare, and which was dated the 20th of March, inst.:—'As in some districts the numbers hitherto employed are much less than in others, it would be unjust to strike off the same percentage from all. I have, therefore, directed that the number in each district shall be reduced to a certain proportion of the population, so that at least twenty per cent, of the population will be reduced on the whole.' With regard to the alleged promise of the Government that there should be no dismissals from the public works until the new Relief Act was in operation, Mr. Labouchere said 'he believed if the Government had made any such statement, they would have acted very improperly. They could not disguise from themselves the fact, that in most parts of Ireland a great preference was shown for the public works over the new relief system, and if her Majesty's Government had made such an announcement as that attributed to them by the honourable gentleman, the greatest delay would assuredly have taken place in bringing the new Act into operation.' He also read a letter that had been received that day, addressed from Colonel Jones, the chairman of the Board of Works, to Mr. Trevelyan:—'Upon reading the Dublin journals,' writes Colonel Jones, 'it would be supposed that the men discharged from the works had been deprived in an instant of their daily food; the fact is, that they were not entitled to be paid until the Tuesday or Wednesday following, and the payments so made were to be the means of procuring subsistence for another week, so that with the time between the publishing of the order and the moment when the money would be expended, ample time was afforded for procuring other employment, or for the electoral division committees to have made the necessary preparations for supplying the destitute with food.' He (Mr. Labouchere) trusted the House would be satisfied that as much consideration had been shown for the people as it was in their power to bestow, and he had the satisfaction to think that on the whole this great reduction had been carried into effect with as little temporary suffering and embarrassment as possible."

The first thing that strikes one with regard to the above reply is, that the Board of Works used the discretion given to them with reference to the dismissals, in opposition to what Mr. Labouchere says was the intention of the Government. Government wished the dismissals to be twenty per cent, in the aggregate, which means ten or fifteen per cent. of a reduction in one district, and twenty-five or thirty per cent. in another, according to circumstances. But the Secretary *naively* adds, that the Board of Works thought they should best meet the views of the Government by striking off twenty per cent, of those employed *in each district.* Probably the Government and the Board of Works understood each other well enough on this point. Even assuming the extract from Captain O'Brien's report to have the meaning attached to it by Mr. Labouchere, as it is the only case of the kind he brings forward, we must receive it as the exception which proves the rule. The Secretary next tells us that employment on the public works was far more popular with the people than the new system of relief. This he asserted in the House of Commons on the 29th of March. We know the official printed forms for putting the new Relief Act into operation were not ready for delivery, even in Dublin, on the 22nd of March, just one week before. How, in that one week they were got ready, and sent by tons and hundreds weight to all parts of the country; how the new committees were organized; how the boilers were set up, the fires lighted, and the soup made and distributed to three quarters of a million of people; how those people discussed its flavour and qualities, and how they had had time to give expression to their views, and how those views reached the Irish Secretary in London before the 29th of March, are things which could be only explained by the Irish Secretary himself. This fact, however, was known to the general public, that on the 23rd of March there was not a quart of the new relief-system soup yet made in Ireland; and that on the 29th, at the moment the Secretary was answering Smith O'Brien, it is more than probable that the fact was still the same.

The promise which Mr. O'Brien said the Government was understood to have made, and which Mr. Labouchere treats so cavalierly in his reply, was contained in the following words, spoken by the First Minister on bringing forward the new Relief Bill:—"We must take care—and the Lord Lieutenant is prepared to take care—that the substitution of this system for public works shall be made as easy in the transition as possible. There will be no rude dismissal of the people at once, who otherwise might find great difficulty in obtaining subsistence; but when the arrangements are made for carrying the scheme I have described into effect, it will be provided that no further presentments shall be made, and no new public works undertaken."[262] These are strong words, and were certainly meant to convey that there was to be no interregnum in which the people would be left to starve between the cessation of the public works and the establishment of the new system of relief.

But the most curious part of Mr. Labouchere's explanation is the extract from Colonel Jones's letter. In the Colonel's opinion it was a great mistake of the Dublin press to assume that the men discharged from the works had been deprived, in an instant, of their daily food. No such, thing: it was gross ignorance or wilful calumny to assert it. The dismissed labourers, Colonel Jones tells us, had no right to claim their wages till Tuesday or Wednesday, yet he generously pays them on the Saturday— two or three days before! But did he pay them for the Monday and the Tuesday?—not a word about that. Then where was the generosity? The order was that the men were to be dismissed on Saturday, the 20th of March, and Colonel Jones's vast bounty consisted in paying them the day he dismissed them, instead of compelling them to loiter about two or three days waiting to be paid. It well became Colonel Jones, indeed, to brag of such an act, in face of the many inquests at which such verdicts as this were returned:—"Died of hunger, in consequence of not being paid by the Board of Works, a fortnight's wages being due at the time of death."

Some time previous to this, the Irish Secretary said in the House of Commons that there was an organized combination amongst the people not to till their farms. Such a combination could hardly exist to any considerable extent, but there can be little doubt that a strong feeling had sprung up in the minds of the people against tilling their farms, not because they were opposed to tillage, but for quite another reason: they felt that whatever labour they might expend upon their farms would be thrown away, as far as they were concerned, because they knew full well that the landlords would seize the produce of their farms for rent, so that after expending their labour they would be still left to starve,—in fact, that they would be tilling the land for others instead of for themselves. Rents at the time were, of course, over due, and the landlords' power to seize was unlimited. At a meeting of the Claremorris deanery it was declared, that the assertion in the House of Commons, that there was a systematic combination not to till the ground, was a great calumny; and further, that there should be legal security that the people would get the fruit of their labour in autumn. A petition to Parliament from Ballinrobe says:—"Your petitioners have read with the utmost alarm the letter of the Secretary of the Board of Works, directing that twenty out of every hundred should be put out of employment on Saturday, the 20th inst., as we are convinced that death by starvation to thousands will be the result of such a fatal measure. That we pray your honourable House, to direct the Board of Works to have the persons now employed on the public works transferred to labour on their own holdings, at the same rate of wages as if on the public works, from the 25th of March, inst., to the 1st of May next, enabling them, at the same time, to have seed on reasonable terms sufficient to sow their little farms, to prevent the recurrence of famine next year."

The effect of the dismissals soon began to manifest itself in complaints and remonstrances. Of Balla, in the county of Mayo, we read that the order was rigidly enforced there, that the people had no seed to sow their land, and that there was no provision for supplying them with food. All remonstrance with the inspecting officer, writes a correspondent from Ballyglass, in the same county, is useless; he said the Government orders were peremptory. No seed. No food.

Ballnigh, Co. Cavan: Twenty per cent. dismissed, no provision whatever having been made for their support.

Enniscorthy, Co. Wexford: No provision made to supply food to the dismissed labourers.

Clones, Co. Monaghan: No provision.

Maryborough, Queen's Co.: No means of support.

Clonmel, Tipperary: No provision. The relief committee under the new Act is in course of organization, but some time must elapse before it can afford relief.

From persons who were in possession of some land, the first twenty per cent., as we have seen, were to be selected for dismissal, but in Kilnaleck, in the County of Cavan, all those employed on the public works were about equally destitute, so that the twenty per cent. with land could not be furnished: lots had to be cast, and those on whom the lot for dismissal fell received it like a sentence of death. Of course the Board of Works felt they were best carrying out the intentions of Government by dismissing the full twenty per cent. at Kilnaleck.

The state of things in Cashel was this: the twenty per cent. were dismissed before the committee had any preparation made, or was, in fact, appointed. The old committee had emphatically protested against the dismissal, and published a resolution condemnatory of it, as an inexcusable cruelty. Although twenty per cent. of the labouring population were turned adrift in that locality, not one supernumerary was disemployed. No pay-clerk lost his salary, though his labour was diminished by one-fifth; no check-clerk was dismissed, though there were twenty per cent. fewer to check; no steward or under-steward was displaced. Such are specimens of the accounts from nearly every part of the country.

Threatening meetings of the disemployed began to be held. Towards the end of April we read of vast crowds assembling in the neighbourhood of Drone, county Tipperary, crying aloud for food and employment. They consisted chiefly of the dismissed labourers. Their wretched emaciated children were clinging to them for sustenance, but they had not wherewith to satisfy their hunger. Large numbers also assembled near Thurles, crying out for bread and employment; they proceeded to that town, and had an interview with the head officer under the Board of Works.[263]

The news from Galway was, that the funds of the old relief committee were completely exhausted, and although it was the 5th of May, the new one had not completed the lists, so as to procure food for distribution to the unemployed destitute. Some of the public works were stopped for want of money; the labourers on the others were dismissed, with a very few exceptions. The labourers paraded the streets with a white flag bearing the inscription, "We are starving;" "Bread or employment." They conducted themselves with the utmost order.

About four hundred men who had been employed on the public works near Ballygarvan assembled and marched in procession into Cork. Having drawn up before the door of the Board of Works' office, they sent a deputation to confer with Captain Broughton, to state the distress they were suffering, in consequence of being suddenly dismissed off the works. He assured them he could do nothing for them.

The *Limerick Reporter* says: "On Monday morning the people of Meelick and its neighbourhood, who had been lately discharged from the public works, assembled at Ahernan Cross, to the number of two hundred, and afterwards proceeded to the residence of Mr. Delmege, J.P., of Castle Park, with whom they had an interview, declaring that they should get work; that they were ready and willing to work, but that they would not put up with nor endure the use of soup or porridge; that they could not, nor would they live upon one pound of meal in the twenty-four hours." They proceeded to the soup-kitchen of the parish, broke the boiler and all utensils belonging to the kitchen, and tore the books which contained the names of those to be relieved. Their numbers increased to about six hundred, when they proceeded to demolish the soup-kitchen at Ardnacrusha, quite close to the police barrack. The police succeeded in taking a man named Pat Griffin in the act of breaking the boiler with a large stone hammer, and succeeded in getting him into the barracks. The crowd attempted to rescue him. They broke the windows, and were demolishing the doors, when the police began to fire from within. Two men were severely wounded. The police discharged forty rounds before the people dispersed. Griffin stated that neither himself, nor many of the people assembled, had eaten any food for two or three days.

In several other places the soup-kitchens were attacked, and the boilers broken or attempted to be broken. At Kilfenora, the people carried off the boiler and threw it into a lough. So that in the matter of the new relief system, the Government were not only very slow in getting it into operation, but when they did so, it was distasteful to the people in various places. How slow they were appears from an answer given to a question asked by Lord Fitzwilliam in the House of Lords, so late as the 11th of May. On that day he asked the Government to what extent the new Act—commonly known as the Soup-kitchen Act— had been brought into operation. Lord Lansdowne, in reply, said that "there had been preparations in various places under the auspices of the relief committees, and with the aid of voluntary contributions they were putting the Act into operation; but *the Act had been so recently passed*, the Government had no exact information upon the subject; inquiries, however, should be instituted." The Act had become law on the 26th of February, nearly three months before; besides which, the Government were, or said they were, organizing beforehand the machinery by which it was to be carried out, and it was specially intended to take the place of the relief works, all of which had ceased on the 1st of May, so that Lord Lansdowne's reply was a very cool one under the circumstances.

Although the spring work must have absorbed a very considerable portion of the dismissed labourers, it did not absorb them all, nor anything near it; whilst those who failed to get employment, or were unfit for it, had not the new relief to turn to. The poorhouses became dangerously crowded. The poorlaw statistics of 1847 show this in a striking manner: in the beginning of the year—that is in mid-winter, a time when there is scarcely any employment—the total number receiving relief in the Irish workhouses was 52,626. One month after the dismissals of the 20th of March—namely, on the 17th of April, perhaps the very busiest period in the farmer's year—the number in the workhouses had doubled; the figure standing on that day at 104,200; being about 11,000 more than they were built to accommodate; nor did this suffer any notable diminution until the harvest came in.

The Relief Commissioners published their third report on the 17th of June, at which time 1677 electoral divisions were under the operation of the Relief Act; being 429 more than at the date of the second report, the 15th of May. They were then distributing 1,923,361 rations per day gratuitously, at an average cost of 2-1/2d. per ration; and 92,326 rations were sold, making in all 2,015,687 rations. Of the 1677 electoral divisions under the Act, 1479 had received loans or grants, 198 had not applied for any advances, and 312 had not sent in any return up to the time the report was published. The Commissioners make this calculation: If, they say, the number of rations necessary for the returns still to be received shall be in proportion to those of which we have already cognizance, the entire number of rations will be 2,388,475; and if the ordinary proportion for children at half rations be added, the number of persons to receive relief will be 2,729,684, of whom 2,622,684 will receive relief gratuitously.

The springing up of abuses under such an extensive system of relief was unavoidable, some of which the Commissioners mention in their third report. Cases occurred in which more rations were demanded than there were individuals in the whole district. Hundreds of names were struck off by the inspecting officers, including servants and men in the constant employ of persons of station and property; these latter were frequently themselves members of the committees; and in some cases the very chairmen, being magistrates, have sanctioned the issue of rations to tenants of their own of considerable holdings, possessed of live stock, and who, it was found, had paid up their last half year's rent. The intimidation attempted in various places, say the Commissioners, was generally successfully resisted, although to this there were exceptions deserving of notice. It was reported to them that the introduction of cooked food had produced the best effects on the health and appearance of the people.

An inspector asks this question: "Is a man who owns a horse, or a cow, or such things, destitute?" The Commissioners answer: "No, in the abstract; but better give him relief than to drive him to permanent destitution." On the 27th of May an inspector, who appears to have been in a state of worry and excitement, writes to head-quarters:—"Entirely deserted by the landlords and their representatives; the working of the Committee [he names a particular committee] has fallen into the hands of a class who insist on '*Universal Relief*,' who will not think of scrutinizing lists to prevent fraud, and who are eager to have brothers, cousins, and dependants employed in the distribution." Alluding to the violence on the part of the people, another inspector writes: "I have spoken to the Roman Catholic Clergymen on this subject, and take this opportunity of stating that I have received great assistance from those gentlemen." Another says: "The people who ought to have an interest in checking abuses are mostly absentees, and the few who are living in the country try all they can to provide for their own tenants." Another: "All jobbing and intrigue here." Another: "A day or two since I found the wife of a coachman of a magistrate of £2,000 a year on the relief list." The Commissioners, however, were strongly of opinion that the introduction of cooked food was a great means of checking fraud.

Up to the 17th of June there were 570 electoral divisions which had received neither grant nor loan; some of these were the richest, and some were the poorest in the country. Perhaps, says the Report, the rich ones had other means, and the poor ones could not get the loan, and may have had the remains of subscriptions. The Commissioners had much difficulty in getting the accounts from committees; the clerks in rural districts were, for the most part, totally inefficient, and the weekly stipend of twenty-one shillings was not sufficient to induce any person accustomed to keep accounts to quit the towns and undertake such duties.

Ireland, it would seem, was destined at this time to have sorrow upon sorrow; her great Liberator, O'Connell, died in May, 1847. For some time his powers had been evidently failing, and no wonder, after the life of hard work he had gone through. Besides, he was in his seventy-second year. Many members of his family lived to be much older, and he used to say, good-humouredly, that they had a trick of living till ninety. But they did not labour as he did. The writer heard him in Conciliation Hall, shortly before he went to England for the last time, and his feebleness was painful, especially to any one who remembered his proud, defiant energy in earlier years. The quarrels and dissensions, which had arisen amongst the national party teased, and depressed him, and must have affected his health. It was observed, too, by his friends, and indeed by all, that his imprisonment in Richmond told considerably upon him; his speeches, after his liberation, lacking that buoyant pleasantry for which they were wont to be remarkable. The famine also weighed heavily upon his spirits; every question, he frequently said, must be postponed but the one of saving the lives of the people. We need not, however, go in search of causes for his death; he had done the work of a host of men, he was seventy-two, and it was natural he should die; but the Irish people were not at all prepared for his death: no, in their affection for him, they had made up their minds that their Liberator was to live up to that ninety, which he had so often promised them,—and, with the vigour of forty-five.

In the last days of March, 1847, O'Connell left Dublin for London, to attend his parliamentary duties. He presented some petitions on the 1st of February, and spoke at some length about the Famine on the 8th; his speech, the last he ever made, occupying about one hundred lines of a newspaper column. He was imperfectly heard. One report says, "Mr. O'Connell rose, but spoke very indistinctly, and directed his voice very much to the lower part of the house." The opening remark in Hansard is,—"Mr. O'Connell was *understood to* say." He was very kindly received by the house; hears and cheers are thickly strewn through his speech as reported. This was in part, no doubt, the kindness of pity for the great old man, in the hour of his feebleness and humiliation. For he, who in the day of his might, had hurled "his high and haughty defiance" at them all, was there to crave bread, to save the lives of those millions with whom he had so often threatened them. His last words were an appeal to their charity; they also contained a prophecy, which was, alas! but too strictly verified. "She is in your hands," he said, "she is in your power. If you don't save her, she can't save herself; and I solemnly call upon you to recollect that I predict, with the sincerest conviction, that one-fourth of her population will perish, unless you come to her relief. (Cheers from both sides)."

So ended the public career of the great leader of the Irish nation, to be followed in two short months by his death. Two days after he had spoken in the House of Commons, the rumour reached the Clubs that he was dangerously ill. This was contradicted, and a letter from himself to the Repeal Association, which was read at their next meeting, reassured the public. Next, the news came that writing fatigued him, and that his physicians forbade it; so, for the future his son John wrote, in his own name, to the Association, always, as might be expected, taking the sanguine view of his father's health. A month passed. His physicians ordered him to Hastings, and after spending a fortnight there he sailed for France. His intention was to go to Rome. At Lyons, he felt so poorly that he was obliged to refuse audiences to the various deputations of that Catholic city, which crowded to his hotel to do him honour. He arrived at Genoa, his final stage, on the 6th of May, and breathed his last in that city on the evening of the 15th, with the tranquillity of a child. His faithful friend, the Rev. Dr. Miley, and several of the principal clergy of the place were kneeling in prayer around his bed when he expired.

O'Connell's character has been traced by many eloquent pens, some friendly, some the reverse, but all are forced to admit that the powers with which he was gifted were of the highest order. He first became distinguished as a lawyer; soon after being called, he distanced those of his own standing, and in time, his legal opinion was regarded as oracular. Crown lawyers, and even judges feared him, as well they might, for he never spared them when they were wrong. In the early part of his career, his admiring countrymen loved to call him, "the counsellor," and it was their highest delight to hear him cross-examine a witness. Anecdotes of his wit, humour, and keen penetration whilst so engaged, are very numerous, very amusing, and full of character. As a cross-examiner he had no rival at all; lawyers of his time there were, who might dispute the palm with him for profound knowledge of the laws and constitution of the country, yet some how or other it came to be admitted, openly or tacitly, that no other lawyer could see so far into an Act of Parliament as Dan, nor drive a coach and six through it so triumphantly.

But it was in the political arena he made his enduring fame. When he entered public life, the Catholics of Ireland were a despised, enslaved race: not only were they enslaved, but through custom, or by tradition, they thought, and spoke, and acted, like slaves. Their leaders were the few Catholic peers that Ireland possessed, and the heads of those old Catholic families, who, by some means, managed to retain a portion of their property. These were called "the natural leaders of the people." They were not remarkable for talents; they were timid; they were prostrate in the dust, and they half accepted the situation. They had been so long regarding the Protestants as a superior race, that they came to believe it at last, and, hence, in the presence of Protestants, they always bore themselves with the humble downcast manner which became inferiors. The young counsellor, fresh from the Kerry Mountains—an athlete in mind and body—had no notion to submit so such degradation from men who were his inferiors in every respect, and, consequently, his language was full of manly independence. His high spirit appeared in his whole manner, and as he walked through Dame Street, Parliament Street, and along the quays to the Four Courts, he looked the noblest and proudest man in Dublin—a very king of men.

In attack and denunciation he was terrible. What he said of Peel, when Irish Secretary, is an example of this. At an aggregate meeting in 1815, he alluded to him, as the worthy champion of Orangeism. At the mention of Mr. Peel's name, says the report, there was much laughing.

"You mistake me, said Mr. O'Connell. I do not—indeed I do not intend, this day, to enter into the merits of that celebrated statesman. All I shall say of him, by way of parenthesis, is, that I am told he has, in my absence, and in a place where he was privileged from any account, grossly traduced me. I said, at the last meeting, in the presence of the notetakers of the police, who are paid by him, that he was too prudent to attack me in my presence. I see the same police informers here now, and I authorize them carefully to report these my words, that Mr. Peel would not DARE, in my presence, or in any place where he was liable to personal account, use a single expression derogatory to my interest, or my honour."

This passage led to the affair of honour between himself and Peel. No hostile meeting, however, took place.

His best friends thought his propensity of arraigning and denouncing those who differed from him, was often carried to excess, but he refused to give it up or modify it. The defence he once made for it was, that it was not *irritation*, it was *calculation* that made him adopt that style of animadversion.[264] The Catholic aristocracy and the older leaders of the Catholics were offended with it, and soon retired from any active part in Catholic affairs. This may have been one of O'Connell's calculations. Although his aggressive propensities were sometimes indulged to an extreme degree, he was right in the main, for, the "whispering humbleness" of the older Catholic leaders would have never won emancipation; and this was handsomely and honourably confessed to Mr. P.V. Fitzpatrick by Lord Fingal, shortly before his death. Lord Fingal having sent for Mr. Fitzpatrick, that gentleman repaired immediately to his lordship's residence, and having been shown into the library, where the dying nobleman was reclining in an easy chair, feeble in body, but bright and vigorous in mind, his lordship addressed him as follows: "Mr. Fitzpatrick, I have been for some time thinking whom I should pitch upon, to discharge my conscience of a heavy debt, and I have fixed upon you, as the most appropriate person, because you not only know me and Mr. O'Connell, but you knew us all who were connected with Catholic politics for years, and well. You know, too, that I went forward to an extent, that caused me to be sometimes snubbed by those of my own order in that body; but, notwithstanding, I, like them was criminally cowardly. We never understood that we had a nation behind us—O'Connell alone comprehended that properly, and used his knowledge fitly. It was by him the gates of the Constitution were broken open for us; we owe everything to his rough work, and, to effect further services for Ireland, there must be more of it. I never understood this properly until they made me a peer of parliament, and I feel myself bound to make the avowal under the circumstances in which you now see me, preparatory to my passing into another world. You will communicate this to O'Connell, and my most earnest wish, that he will receive the avowal as an atonement for my not having always supported him, as I now feel he should have been supported."[265]

O'Connell, as an orator, aimed at being what he was called for many years, "The Man of the People." In some of his earlier speeches there are marks of care and preparation, but during three-fourths of his career, his only preparation was to master his subject; words of the best and most effective kind never failed him. There is little doubt, that elaborate preparation would have marred the effect of O'Connell's oratory. He, like all great men, had a quick, intuitive mind—one, in fact, that could scarcely bear the tedium of careful preparation, and the true character of which came out in cross-examining and in reply; for although great and lucid in statement, he was still more powerful in reply. Woe to the man who provoked the lion to anger,—he pawed him to death. His gesture was not very demonstrative, but it was sometimes very energetic, and when he wanted a cheer for a man or a principle, he called for it, by a bold flourish of his hand above his head. But O'Connell stood in little need of the aids which gesture commonly gives the public speaker; his fine presence and unrivalled voice did everything for him. It is said he had no ear for music, but his voice when speaking in public, was the most musical that could be heard: great in power and compass, rich in tone, ever fresh in the variety of its cadences, it was as unique and striking as the great man to whom it belonged; nor was the charming brogue which accompanied it, the least of its attractions. Another advantage possessed by him has not been so much remarked upon—the rapid, changeful expression of his features. By observing O'Connell's face, as he spoke, one could be sure of the tone and temper of what was coming. Was he about to make an adversary ridiculous by an anecdote or a witticism? His eyes, his lips, his whole face suddenly became expressive of humour. Did he intend to turn from pleasantries to solemn warning, or fierce denunciation? (a usual habit of his); the dark cloud was sure to cast its shadow across his manly features, before the thunder came forth.

His style was simple and forcible. He very seldom quoted the classics, although he was fond of giving passages from the English poets, more especially from Moore; but the lines which expressed the guiding principle of his life were taken from Byron:

"Hereditary bondsmen, know ye not
Who would be free themselves must strike the blow."

The moment I read that passage, he once said, I saw it was the motto for Ireland; and up to 1829, the year of Emancipation, he seldom spoke without quoting it. He avoided figurative language. He amused his audience with stories and old sayings which they understood and appreciated. He brought the shrewd apothegms, familiar at their own firesides, to bear upon the principles he was inculcating, but flowers of rhetoric he knew would be feeble weapons for the warfare in which he was engaged. He once indeed complimented Sheil, by calling him "the brightest star that ever rose in the murky horizon of his afflicted country;" but that suited the man and the occasion.

He had a true conception of what a great teacher ought to be; and for this reason he kept repeating his principles and his arguments in the same or almost the same words. Many an admirer of his thought he dosed his countrymen far too much with, "first flower of the earth," and "Hereditary bondsmen;" but, as he said about his attacks on men, it was *calculation* made him do it, and he proclaimed this so late as 1846, at the Repeal Association, in the following words: "I have often said, and repeated it over and over again, that I had found, that it was not sufficient in politics to enunciate a new proposition, one, or two, or three times. I continue to repeat it, until it comes back like an echo from the different parts of the country; then I know it is understood, and I leave it to its fate." The lesson had been learned.

Physically, O'Connell was a very powerful man. He was taller than he seemed, his muscular frame taking away, in appearance, from his height. The earliest portraits of him make him a soft-faced athletic young man, very likely to be a dangerous antagonist in the prize ring, but his features, as given at the time, bear scarcely any resemblance to later portraits of him. His shoulders were broad, and in walking he pushed them forward alternately in a rather remarkable manner. This peculiarity, arising more from physical necessity than from choice, gave him a sort of slinging gait, which caused a Tory print to call him, derisively, "Swaggering Dan." This nickname of their favourite did not offend the people, they even thought it appropriate, there was such a dashing independence in his whole manner; and Shiel never wrote anything more felicitously true, than when he said of him—"He shoulders his umbrella like a pike, and throws out his legs, as if he were kicking Protestant ascendancy before him."

O'Connell was a liberal in the highest sense; he loved toleration; but he was also a Catholic to the heart's core—thorough, uncompromising: proud of the down-trodden Church to which he belonged, with—at first, perhaps, an intuitive feeling; later on, the proud consciousness, that his name would be linked with her struggles and her triumphs.

"One of my earliest aspirations," he more than once said, "was to do something for the good of my country, and write my name on the page of her history." He was fervently devoted to the holy practices of the Catholic Church. The fatal result of his duel with Captain D'Esterre, seems to have exercised a marked influence upon his whole life, and he frequently alluded to it in terms of the profoundest regret. It was a sight not to be forgotten, to see him attend Mass and receive Holy Communion in Clarendon Street. When he was at home, his habit was to walk from Merrion Square to that, his favourite chapel, to eight o'clock Mass. On those occasions he usually wore a very ample cloak, the collar of which concealed the lower half of his face. Thus enveloped, he entered the sanctuary with an expression of recollection so profound, that it might have been a Trappist who had entered. So it was during the hour he remained: he seemed perfectly unconscious of any human creature being in the place, except the priest at the altar before him. He seldom used a prayer-book, and his eyes were never once raised during the whole time. Buried in his great cloak, he moved noiselessly out, as he had entered—a bright example,—a very model,—to the whole congregation.

The remaining reports of the Relief Commissioners do not call for any very lengthened notice. The fourth of the series was published on the 19th of July, at which time 1,823 electoral divisions were receiving relief under the Act. They say: "By an arrangement with the Commissary General, we are clearing out the Government depôts of provisions, by orders on them in lieu of so much money. These depôts were established at an anxious period of a prospect of great deficiency of supplies, which no longer exists." It is needless to repeat here what has been abundantly proved before, that the people died of starvation within the shadow of those sealed up depôts, and they would not be opened;—they were opened when the supplies they contained were not required, there being plenty in the market.

From the accountant's department we learn that 2,643,128 rations were being daily issued, which it was hoped would be the maximum relief that the Commissioners would be called on to administer; 79,636 of these were sold. This shows an increase of daily rations from last report of 291,028. The fall in provisions had reduced the price of each ration from 2-1/2d. to 2d. The amount given in loans and grants was now reduced by about £3,000 a day, the expenditure in that way being then about £20,000 a day. The aggregate amount of money issued up to the 19th of July was £1,010,184 7s. 10d. to 1,803 electoral divisions. The cost of the Government staff for superintending the issuing of relief, is set down at two and a half per cent.—6d. in the pound,—a low figure, indeed, but it must be taken into account that they only *superintended*; the committees did the actual work of giving out the relief. The issue of cooked food was opposed by the people in some places, and this opposition was punished, by a reduction being made in the quantity of rations issued in such places. In a fortnight, about 8,000 tons of the food in the Government depôts were given in lieu of money, the money value of which was £98,728, the daily market price being that charged by the Commissary General. The arrangement was carried out in this way: There was issued on the 1st of June a circular to the inspecting officer of each Union, by virtue of which an order on the Government depôt was given to the Finance Committee of the Union, instead of the amount (in cash) of the fortnightly estimate sent in of the sum required for each electoral division of that Union; but the whole fortnightly estimate was not usually supplied in meal only, to any one electoral division; it was given partly in meal and partly in money.

At this time there were thirty-three Commissariat depôts, and sixteen British Association depôts.

By circular No. 58 it was announced that after the 15th of August the support of destitute persons was to be provided for under the new Poor Law, 10 Vic., c. 31. All relief committees were warned to be prepared to close their arrangements for the issue of rations, when the funds provided for the estimates, ending on the 13th of August, would be expended.

The hope expressed in the fourth report, that the Commissioners had arrived at the maximum daily relief which the country required, was not verified by fact. The fifth report was published on the 17th of August. At that date there were 1,826 electoral divisions under the Act. The maximum relief within the period embraced in the report was: Gratuitous rations per day, 2,920,792; sold, 99,920; total, 3,020,712 rations daily![266] Thus, considerably more than one-third of the whole population was living on what may be termed out-door relief. This, the highest point, was reached on the 3rd of July; the daily rations had, on the 1st of August, come down to 2,467,989 gratuitous, and 52,387 sold rations, being a total of 2,520,376 rations.

The absolute termination of advances on account of temporary relief was fixed by the Act of Parliament for the end of September. The number of temporary fever hospitals established under the Act 10 Vic., c. 22, amounted at the date of the fifth report to 326.

The Relief Commissioners published their sixth report on the 11th of September. It was a hopeful one. The crops were abundant, and a rapid decrease in the number of rations issued was the result, more especially from the middle of August. Out of 127 Unions, which were under the Act, fifty-five had had no advances made to them, on estimate, for any period after the 15th of August; twenty-six more ceased to call for advances on the 29th of August; and the remainder were to cease on the 12th of September, with the exception of the advances to the fever hospitals, which were continued to the 30th of September.

The Commissioners expressed the opinion that the discontinuance of relief had not been attended by the suffering which might have been apprehended. They say the relief "was made a system of bonus rather than of necessity, which increased the expenditure in an enormous degree."

We learn from this sixth report that the Commissioners had expended a sum approaching £2,000.000 within a period of eight months, through the agency of upwards of two thousand committees, constituted by general regulation, and subject only to a very general control. Such being the case, the testimony borne by the inspecting officers to those committees, is highly creditable to them; the inspecting officers, says the report, "express their belief that there has been almost a total absence of misappropriation of *money* by committees."

On the 28th of August the number of daily rations issued was down to 967,575.

The seventh and last report of the Commissioners under the Relief Act, bears date the 15th of October. In it they say, they have the satisfaction of believing, that the Act was thoroughly successful in its primary object; and they did not consider the expenditure excessive in proportion to the object. The entire outlay under the Act was £1,676,268 11s. 7d.,[267] a part of which was a free gift from the State, the remainder a charge to be repaid by the Unions, by a percentage on the rateable property, which, in the opinion of the Commissioners, should in no case exceed three shillings in the pound. The summary of the accounts department informs us that the rations issued on the 11th of September, the day previous to the final stoppage of relief under the Act, were 442,739, being a decrease from the 28th of August of 599,816 daily rations.

The expenditure under the Act is thus detailed:—

To Sir R. Routh for provisions from depôts	£136,795 0 8
Money advanced fortnightly to the several electoral divisions for relief	£1,420,417 14 11
To fever hospitals	£119,055 16 0

The advances at one time exceeded £60,000 a-day, distributed over nearly two thousand accounts.

The sum given to Sir R. Routh for the food in the depôts shows there were about twelve thousand tons of provisions in them.

The sum set down to the fever hospitals includes the erection and furnishing of the fever sheds. In addition to this amount, £4,479 was expended in providing proper medical inspection and superintendance in localities in which great sickness prevailed, and £60,000 was advanced for the enlargement of the Workhouses, principally by the erection of fever wards.[268]

In the appendix to this, their last report, the Commissioners bear honourable testimony to the manner in which the people behaved. They say: "The order and good conduct of the peasantry, and of the people generally, notwithstanding the great influx of paupers into the towns, is highly to be commended. All admit, that the resignation and forbearance of the labouring classes was *astonishing*, when it is remembered with what rapidity the real famine encompassed them."

FOOTNOTES:

246.   The following were the Commissioners appointed under the Act: Sir John F. Burgoyne, Thomas N. Redington, Esq., Under Secretary; Edward T.B. Twistleton, Esq., Colonel Duncan M'Gregor, Commissary-General Sir Randolph J. Routh, and Colonel Harry D. Jones.

247.   The number of electoral divisions is, at present, 3,438, embraced within 163 Unions.

248.   *Sunday Observer*, which journal should, for the information of posterity, have placed upon record what, if any, were the other courses in the *carte* at the Reform Club, the day on which M. Soyer's Irish Soup No. 1 was so highly approved of.

249.   *The comparative nutritive and pecuniary value of various kinds of cooked food*, by John Aldridge, M.D., M.R.I.A., read at a meeting of the Royal Dublin Society on the 6th of April, 1847.

250.   *Freeman's Journal*, April 6th.

251.   *Evening Packet.*

252.   He did not even escape the shafts of ridicule. A writer in the Dublin *Nation*, imitating the Witches' scene in Macbeth, thus attacked him:—

　　　1st Cook—Round about the boiler go,
　　　　In twice fifty gallons throw—
　　　　Water that in noisome tank
　　　　Mossed with verdure rich and rank.
　　　2nd Cook—Shin of beef from skinny cow
　　　　In the boiler then you'll throw;

Onion sliced and turnip top,
Crumb of bread and cabbage chop.
3rd Cook—Scale of cod fish, spiders' tongues,
Tomtits' gizzards, head and lungs
Of a famished, French-fed frog,
Root of phaytee digged in bog, etc.

It is only just to M. Soyer to say that his soup kitchen was regarded by good judges as a clever and convenient contrivance for its purpose. The building in which it was placed was constructed of wood, and was about forty feet by twenty. It consisted of one apartment. In the centre was a large steam boiler mounted on wheels, and arranged around were a number of metallic box-shaped vessels, also mounted on wheels, in which the materials for the soup were placed. These were heated by steam conveyed by iron pipes from the central boiler, and by a slow digestive process the entire of the nutriment contained in the materials were supposed to be extracted without having its properties deteriorated. When the soup was ready, the recipients were admitted by a narrow entrance at one side of the house, one by one, each receiving a large bowl of soup, and, having drank it, five minutes was the time allowed for drinking it,. they received an allowance of bread or a biscuit, and were dismissed by another door in the rere of the building. In this manner M. Soyer calculated he would be able to give one meal every day to at least five thousand persons, from an establishment the size of the one at the Royal Barracks. At the entrance, in the centre, was the weighing machine. There was what was called a glaze-pan over the steam boiler capable of holding three hundred gallons, and, at the end, an oven to bake one hundred weight of bread at a time, and all heated by the same fire. Round the two supports of the roof were circular tin boxes for the condiments. Seven feet from the ground at each corner was placed a safe five feet square and seven feet high, with sides of wire for ventilation, which contained respectively meat, vegetables, grain, and condiments. At the same elevation as the safes were sixteen butts, containing *seventeen hundred and ninety-two gallons of water.*

253.   The Commission of 1809 on the reclamation of the bogs of Ireland returned as improvable:

1,576,000 acres of flat bog;
1,254,000 acres of mountain top bog;
2,070,000 acres of convertible mountain bog.

4,900,000 acres in all.

254. "Waste Lands of Ireland: Suggestions for their immediate reclamation, as a means of affording reproductive employment for the able-bodied destitute. By James Fagan, Esq., M.P. for the Co. Wexford." Dublin: James McGlashan, 1847. Halliday Pamphlets, vol. 1991.
255. Letters to Lord John Russell, p. 9.
256. *Ib.*, p. 12.
257. Commissariat Correspondence, p. 452. G.P. Scrope's letters to Lord John Russell, p. 58.
258. Ireland: Historical and Statistical. By George Lewis Smyth, vol. 2, p. 452.
259. "In the neighbourhood of Mullinahone I witnessed the daily painful sight of the perversion of the labour of this country to the most profitless ends. Roads, which are now more than ever necessary to be kept in order, are in the course of obstruction, whilst waterlogged lands, reclaimable bottoms, and mountain slopes stand out in damning evidence of the indolence, neglect, and folly of man."—*Letter of Lieut.-Colonel Douglas to Sir S. Routh, dated Clonmel, 28th January, 1847. Commissariat Series, part 2.* Strong language from a Government official.

"Some persons recommend emigration as a panacea for the distress in Ireland—that is, in plain English, to send the bone and sinew of our country to cultivate foreign lands, when countless acres are at their doors untilled, undrained, and therefore unremunerative."—*The Case of Ireland: in two letters to the Right Hon. Henry Labouchere, Chief Secretary for Ireland. By the Rev. Wm. Prior Moore, A.M., Cavan.* Dublin: Wm. Curry and Co., 1847.

260. The number of persons employed on the public works reached its highest point in March, 1847, viz., 734,000. But this was the average for the whole month. Before the Committee of the House of Lords on "Colonization from Ireland," Captain Larcom, one of the Commissioners of Public Works, said that the Commissioners expected the number employed on those works to rise to 900,000 in June and July, having risen to 740,000 when the first stoppage took place on the 20th of March, at which time they were increasing at the rate of 20,000 weekly.—*Answer to Question 2,547, p. 265.*

261.   *Freeman's Journal.*
262.   Hansard, vol. clv., p. 436.
263.   1847, March 11—Food riots occurred in the Highlands. May 19: Alarming food riots took place in various parts of England, at Taunton and in Jersey, and also in France and Spain.—*Census of Ireland for 1851, Tables of Deaths. Vol. 1. p. 289.*
264.   Fagan's "Life of O'Connell," vol. I, p. 111.
265.   Fagan's "Life of O'Connell", vol. I, p. 161.
266.   "At length, in seventh month, this system of relief reached its height. In that month, 3,020,712 persons received daily rations. Even under this gigantic system of relief, we found that our distribution could not be discontinued. There were several classes of persons whose claims we were bound to recognise, and in these cases relief was still afforded, though on a reduced scale, and with considerable caution."—*Transactions during the Famine in Ireland. By the Society of Friends.*
267.   This was up to the 16th of October only, but on the 31st of December, when the account was finally closed, Mr. Bromley, the head accountant, says,—Total expended to this day, £1,724,631 17s. 3d.
268.   Irish Crisis.

* * * * *

CHAPTER XIV.

The Fever Act—Central Board of Health—Fever Hospitals—Changes in the Act—Outdoor Attendance—Interment of the Dead—The Fever in 1846—Cork Workhouse—Clonmel—Tyrone—Newry—Sligo—Leitrim—Roscommon—Galway—Fever in 1847—Belfast—Death-rate in the Workhouses—Swinford—Cork—Dropsy—Carrick-on-Shannon—Macroom—Bantry Abbey—Dublin—Cork Street Hospital—Applications for Temporary Hospital accommodation—Relapse a remarkable feature—Number of cases received—Percentage of Mortality—Weekly Cost of Patients—Imperfect Returns—Scurvy—The cause of it—Emigration—Earlier Schemes of Emigration—Mr. Wilmot Horton—Present Stats of Peterborough *(Note)*—Various Parliamentary Committees on Emigration—Their Views—The Devon Commission—Its Views of Emigration—A Parliamentary Committee opposed to Emigration—Statistics of Emigration—Gigantic Emigration Scheme—Mr. Godley—Statement to the Premier—The Joint Stock Company for Emigration—£9,000,000 required—How to be applied—It was to be a Catholic Emigration—Mr. Godley's Scheme—Not accepted by the Government—Who signed it—Names *(Note)*—Dr. Maginn on the Emigration Scheme—Emigration to be left to itself—Statistics of Population—The Census of 1841—Deaths from the Famine—Deaths amongst Emigrants—Deaths amongst those who went to Canada—Emigration to the United States—Commission to protect Emigrants—Revelations—Mortality on board Emigrant Ships—Plunder of Emigrants—Committee of Inquiry—Its Report—Frauds about Passage Tickets—Evidence—How did any survive?—Remittances from Emigrants—Unprecedented—A proof of their industry and perseverance.

In anticipation of fever and other epidemics resulting from the Famine, a Fever Act was passed for Ireland in the early part of the Session of 1846, by which the Lord Lieutenant was empowered to appoint Commissioners of Health, not exceeding five in number, who were to act without salaries. They constituted what was called the Central Board of Health. He was further empowered to appoint medical officers for the Poor Law Unions, with salaries to be paid by the Treasury; such medical officers to be under the control of the guardians. The Board of Health was authorized to direct guardians to provide fever hospitals and dispensaries, together with medicines and all other necessaries for those hospitals. This Act was to cease in September, 1847, but in the April of that year an Act to amend and extend it to November, 1847, was passed. Eventually, it remained in its amended form in force until the end of the Parliamentary Session of 1850.

The changes made by this second or amended Fever Act were of a very extensive kind. By the previous one medical relief was to be given through the guardians of the poor; by the Act as amended, the Board of Health was empowered to certify to the Relief Commissioners, the necessity of medical relief being afforded, in *any electoral division* in which there was a Relief Committee. It was also to direct such Committees to provide fever hospitals, and every other thing necessary for the treatment of patients. And further: the Relief Commissioners, on the certificate of the Board of Health, were to issue their order to Relief Committees, to provide medical attendance, medicines, and *nutriment*, if necessary, for such patients as were not received into hospital, either because there was not accommodation for them, or because it might endanger their lives to remove them. The Board of Health acted as little as possible upon this clause; holding that, under existing circumstances, it was impossible to treat patients with advantage in their own houses. Those hospitals and dispensaries were managed by the Relief Committees, under the control of the Relief Commissioners, appointed to carry out the Act 10 Vic., cap. 7. By the 16th clause of the amended Fever Act, provision is made "for the proper and decent interment of the deceased destitute persons who shall die of fever or any other epidemic disease in any electoral division or district, for which any Relief Committee shall have been constituted."

Whilst this very extensive system of medical relief was established and carried out under the second Bill, the guardians of the poor continued to use the powers granted to them in the former Bill, of giving medical relief. The returns from these two sources give, respectively, the number of fever cases received into their hospitals, but we have no authentic means of determining the number of persons who died of fever in their own houses, or on the highways and byways, as they wandered about in search, of food. Such cases must have been very numerous.

Although fever or other epidemics did not arise to an alarming extent in 1846, still, that year showed a decided increase of them over previous years. The following summary, derived from circulars issued, shows the origin and progress of fever in 1846. "Fever began in Mitchelstown, County Cork. It attacked equally those in good and bad health; but in some instances, as in Innishannon and in Cove, many, in the best health; while in Mitchelstown, the majority had previously suffered from privation. Young persons appear to have been the subject of the epidemic, more than those of more advanced life. The pressure from without upon the city [of Cork] began to be felt in October; and in November and December, the influx of paupers from all parts of this vast county was so overwhelming, that, to prevent them from dying in the streets, the doors of the Workhouse were thrown open, and in one week, 500 persons were admitted without any provision, either of space or clothing, to meet so fearful an emergency. All these were suffering from famine, and most of them from malignant dysentery or fever. The fever was, in the first instance, undoubtedly confined to persons badly fed, or crowded into unwholesome habitations; and, as it originated with the vast migratory hordes of labourers and their families congregated upon the public roads, it commonly was termed 'the road fever.' In Cloughjordan, County Tipperary, the fever cases doubled in 1846 what they had been in the previous year. The disease commenced in Clonmel in November. The accounts from the Counties of Limerick and Kerry do not record any increased sickness during this year. The epidemic commenced in the County of Tyrone in the December of 1846. Young persons were those chiefly attacked there. The fever commenced at Loughgall, County Armagh, in the end of this year. The lower classes were chiefly attacked; the majority of those affected having been previously in bad health. The epidemic materially declined as the poor were better fed. The fever was frequently preceded by scurvy. Individuals at the age of puberty were chiefly attacked,—females more generally than males. In Newry, dysentery existed as an epidemic during the autumn of 1846, being very fatal among the old and infirm, who, if not carried off, were so debilitated by its effects, as to render them an easy prey to the fever which followed. In Dublin, although the great outbreak of the fever was in 1847, yet, cases were noticed to have occurred in the latter end of 1846, in a greater proportion than usual. Those first attacked were individuals who had been reduced by bad diet or insufficiency of food, and throughout the continuance of the epidemic, the lower classes were chiefly affected. In many cases, the fever set in immediately after recovering from the effects of starvation, and although scurvy preceded the disease, neither it nor purpura was noticed to have occurred as a concomitant symptom. In the Province of Connaught, the epidemic commenced in many places during the year 1846, especially in the Counties of Sligo and Leitrim; in the former locality the young were chiefly attacked; in the latter fever broke out so early as June, when upwards of two hundred cases were at one time in the Workhouse of Carrick-on-Shannon; while, in the remote northern hilly districts of the county, it did not appear until December, 1847; those attacked were, for the most part, reduced from want of food. In some

475

parts, the fever was preceded by aphthous ulcers on the tongue and gums; young persons were those chiefly attacked, and females more than males. In the County of Roscommon, the previous health of the population was much impaired; bowel complaints were frequent; the fever commenced in the end of 1846 or beginning of 1847, and was very prevalent. The Workhouse of Castlerea was one of the most severely afflicted during the epidemic, of any similar class of institution in Ireland—as many as fifty persons a week having died at one period subsequent to this—and, for a long time, all attempt at separate burial was found impossible. In the County Galway the epidemic of both dysentery and fever appeared at Ahascragh and Clifden, separate ends of the district, at the end of this year."[269]

As was anticipated, fever rose to a fearful height in 1847. And, say the Commissioners of Health, "the state of the medical institutions of Ireland was, unfortunately, such as peculiarly unfitted them to afford the required medical aid, on the breaking out of the epidemic. The county infirmaries had not provision for the accommodation of fever patients. The county fever hospitals were destitute of sufficient funds; and dispensaries, established for the purpose of affording only ordinary out-door medical relief, could, of course, afford no efficient attendance on the numbers of destitute persons, suffering from acute contagious diseases in their own miserable abodes, often scattered over districts several miles in extent."

In January, fever complicated with dysentery and small pox became very rife in Belfast, and accounts from various other places soon showed, that it had seized upon the whole country. The week ending the 3rd of April, the total number of inmates in Irish Workhouses was 104,455, of whom 9,000 were fever patients. The deaths in that week were 2,706, and the average of deaths in each week during the month was twenty-five per thousand of the entire inmates—a death rate which would have hurried to the grave, every man, woman, and child in the Workhouses of Ireland, in about nine months! but it gradually decreased, until in October it stood at five per thousand in the week.

On the 19th we read that, "the number suffering from fever in Swinford is beyond calculation." Some idea of the dreadful mortality now prevalent in Cork, may be found from the fact, that in one day thirty-six bodies were interred in the same grave; the deaths in the Workhouse there from the 27th of December, 1846, until the middle of April—less than four months—amounted to 2,130. At this period, dropsy, the result of starvation, became almost universal. On the 16th of April, there were upwards of three hundred cases of fever in the Carrick-on-Shannon Workhouse, and the weekly deaths amounted to fifty. Again: every avenue leading to the plague-stricken town of Macroom has a fever hospital; persons of all ages are dropping dead in the streets. In May, it is announced that fever continued to rage with unabated fury at Castlebar. "Sligo is a plague spot; disease in every street, and of the worst kind." "Fever is committing fearful ravages in Ballindine, Ballinrobe, Claremorris, Westport, Ballina, and Belmullet, all in the county of Mayo." From Roscommon the news came, that the increase of fever was truly awful; the hospitals were full, and applicants were daily refused admission; "no one can tell," says the writer, "what becomes of these unfortunate beings; they are brought away by their pauper friends, and no more is heard of them." "Seven bodies were found inside a hedge," in the parish of Kilglass; the dogs had the flesh almost eaten off. Under date of the 18th of May, I find this entry; "Small pox, added to fever and dysentery, is prevalent at Middleton, County Cork; and, near Bantry Abbey, 900 bodies were interred in a plot of ground forty feet square." From the autumn of 1846 to May, 1847, ten thousand persons were interred in Father Mathew's cemetery at Cork—he was obliged to close it. On the 12th of June, the number of fever patients in the hospitals of Belfast was 1,840. "Awful fever," "Fearful increase of fever," were the ordinary phrases, in which the spread of the disease was announced from every part of Ireland.[270]

"Of the extent of the epidemic in Dublin, it would not be easy to give any very correct idea. The hospital accommodation of the city amounted to about 2,500 beds, a greater amount by 1,000, I believe, than were opened in any previous epidemic. It may give some idea of the vast amount of sickness, to state, that, at the Cork Street hospital, nearly 12,000 cases applied during a period of about ten months. At one period there were upwards of 400 outstanding tickets; and as many as eighty applications for admission have been made in one day. Still it may be safely stated, that all this would give a very imperfect idea of the real amount; for all who had to go amongst the poor at their own houses, were well aware, that vast numbers remained there, who either could not be accommodated in hospital, or who never thought of applying. It was quite common to find three, four, and even five ill in a house, where application had been made but for one. I think the very lowest estimate which could be arrived at cannot make the numbers who sickened in Dublin short of 40,000. The greatest pressure on the hospital took place in the month of June, from which time the fever gradually declined, till the month of February, 1848, when the epidemic may be said to have ceased."[271]

In February, 1847, fourteen applications were made to the Board of Health, for providing temporary hospital accommodation; in March, they received fifty-one such applications; in April, fifty-three, in May, fifty-two; in June, twenty-two; in July, sixty; in August, forty-eight; in September the number was ten, and in October only eight. The applications to the Board of Health for temporary fever hospitals in 1847 were 343; the entire number of such applications up to 1850, when the Board closed its labours, were 576, of which 203 were refused.

Relapse was a remarkable feature of this famine-fever. "Relapses were so common," writes Dr. Freke from a western county, "as to appear characteristic of the epidemic; in several cases they have occurred so frequently as three, or even four times in the same individual." At Nohaval, Kinsale Union, out of 250 cases 240 relapsed.

The cases received into the permanent and temporary fever hospitals of Ireland in the year 1845, were 37,604; in 1846 they increased to 40,620; and in 1847 they rose to the enormous amount of 156,824 cases![272] of which, according to the Report of the Board of Health, 95,890 were admitted into temporary hospitals,[273] in which the percentage of deaths was ten two-fifths; more males dying than females, the percentage of deaths among males being eleven one-fifth, and among females nine six-tenths. But the mortality in the fever sheds sometimes rose to fifteen, twenty, twenty-five, and in a few instances to twenty-eight and twenty-nine per cent.; the cause being previous dysentery (on which cholera sometimes supervened) and starvation. In Eyrecourt, Ballinrobe Union, the death-rate rose to twenty-nine one-third per cent.; in West Skull to twenty; and in Parsonstown to twenty-nine five-eighths. The principal complications of this famine-fever, according to the Commissioners of Health, were dysentery, purpura, diarrhoea, and small-pox; and they further say of it that it was, perhaps, unparalleled for duration and severity.[274]

The average weekly cost of each patient in the temporary hospitals, including the salary of the medical officer, was four shillings and one halfpenny.

"Some approximation to the amount of the immense mortality that prevailed may be gleaned from the published tables, which show that within that calamitous period between the end of 1845 and the conclusion of the first quarter of 1851, as many as 61,260 persons died in the hospitals and sanitary institutions, exclusive of those who died in the Workhouses and auxiliary Workhouses. Taking the recorded deaths from fever alone, between the beginning of 1846 and the end of 1849, and assuming the mortality at one in ten, which is the very lowest calculation, and far below what we believe really did occur, above a million and a-half, or 1,595,040 persons, being one in 4.11 of the population in 1851, must have suffered from fever during that period. But no pen has recorded the numbers of the forlorn and starving who perished by the wayside or in the ditches, or of the mournful groups, sometimes of whole families, who lay down and died, one after another, upon the floor of their miserable cabins, and so remained uncoffined and unburied, till chance unveiled the appalling scene. No such amount of suffering and misery has been chronicled in Irish history since the days of Edward Bruce, and yet, through all, the forbearance of the Irish peasantry, and the calm submission with which they bore the deadliest ills that can fall on man, can scarcely be paralleled in the annals of any people."[275]

An unusual disease on land, scurvy, appeared during the Famine. The Commissioners of Health attribute its appearance (1) to the want of variety of food: the potato being gone, they say, the people did not understand the necessity for variety, and men, such as railway porters, who had wages enough to buy food, took scurvy for want of this variety, coffee and white bread being their common dietary. (2) Another cause was the eating of what was called "potato flour," got from rotten potatoes; it was not flour at all, and did not contain the elements of the potato, but consisted wholly of starch as foecula. (3) The use of raw or badly cooked food also brought on scurvy; and the Commissioners of Health, therefore, strongly recommended the giving of food in a cooked form.[276]

Emigration played a very leading part in the terrible drama of the Irish Famine of 1847; indeed, it was the potato failure of 1822, and the consequent famine of 1823, which first gave emigration official importance in this country. A Parliamentary Committee was appointed in the latter year, before which Mr. Wilmot Horton, the Under Secretary of State, explained in detail a plan of emigration from Ireland, then under the consideration of Government, and which was afterwards carried into effect. The emigrants were sent to Canada; and Peterborough, at the time a very insignificant place, was fixed upon as their head quarters. On two subsequent occasions, Mr. Horton stated this emigration to have been eminently successful, which was fully corroborated by the evidence of Captain Rubidge, before the Lords' Committee of 1847, on "Colonization from Ireland." But this emigration, as well as that of 1825, both of which were superintended by the Hon. Peter Robinson, was on a very limited scale. The number taken out to Canada in the first emigration was only 568 persons, men, women, and children. The Government supported them for eighteen months after their landing, which very much increased the expense; each of those emigrants having cost the country £22 before they were finally settled. In 1825 Mr. Robinson took out 2,024 emigrants under the same conditions, but in this instance the expense was slightly diminished, the cost of each person being £21 10s. These emigrants also prospered, but the money outlay in each case was so considerable, that the experiment could not be extended, nor, in fact, repeated.[277]

From this period, committees continued to sit on the subject of emigration, almost year after year; emigration from Ireland, even in the absence of famine, being considered of the highest importance— and why? Chiefly, because Irish labourers were lowering the rate of wages in the English labour market—so it is stated in the report of the Select Committee of 1826, in the following words:—"The question of emigration from Ireland is decided by the population itself; and that which remains for the legislature to decide is, whether it shall be turned to the improvement of the British North American colonies, or whether it shall be suffered and encouraged to take that which will be, and is, its inevitable course, *to deluge Great Britain with poverty and wretchedness*, and gradually, but certainly, to equalize the state of the English and Irish peasantry. Two different rates of wages, and two different conditions of the labouring classes, cannot permanently co-exist. One of two results appears to be inevitable; the Irish population must be raised towards the standard of the English, or the English depressed towards that of the Irish. The question, whether an extensive plan of emigration shall or shall not be adopted, appears to your Committee to resolve itself into the simple point, whether the wheat-fed population of Great Britain shall or shall not be supplanted by the potato-fed population of Ireland?"[278]

The same reasons are given by the same Committee in 1827, and they are again repeated in 1830, by another Committee, whose duty it was to inquire into the state of the Irish poor.

The famous Devon Land Commission, which was called into existence in 1842, presented its voluminous report to Parliament in 1845, which was founded on the examination of eleven hundred witnesses, whose evidence was taken on the spot in every county in Ireland; the Commissioners having visited more than ninety towns for the purpose;—that Commission recommended emigration from Ireland, but in a cautious and modified way. The Commissioners say:—"After considering the recommendations, thus repeatedly made by Committees of Parliament upon this subject, and the evidence of Mr. Godley, in which the different views of the subject are well given, we desire to express our own conviction, that a well-organized system of emigration may be of very great service, as one among the measures which the situation of the occupiers of land in Ireland, at present calls for. We cannot think that either emigration, or the extension of Public Works, or the reclamation or improvement of land can, singly, remove the existing evil. All these remedies must be provided concurrently, according to the circumstances of each case. In this view, and to this extent only, we wish to direct attention to the subject of emigration."[279]

A Select Committee of the House of Lords, on the operation of the Poor Law in Ireland, spoke approvingly of emigration as a relief to the labour market at home, and it therefore recommended, "that increased facilities for the emigration of poor persons should be afforded, with the cooperation of the Government."[280]

One Parliamentary Committee, at least, condemned emigration in terms both decided and remarkable; it was the Committee of Public Works appointed in 1835. In its second report this passage occurs:—"It may be doubted, whether the country does contain a sufficient quantity of labour to develope its resources; and while the empire is loaded with taxation to defray the charges of its wars, it appears most politic to use its internal resources for improving the condition of its population, by which the revenue of the exchequer must be increased, rather than encourage emigration, by which the revenue would suffer diminution, or than leave the labouring classes in their present state, by which poverty, crime, and the charges of Government must be inevitably extended."[281]

Previous to the Famine there was a large and steady emigration from Ireland for many years, independent of Government aid. The total colonial and foreign emigration between 1831 and 1841 amounted to 403,459, to which the returns add 25,012, for probable births, that item being calculated at one and a-half per cent. per annum; making a total of 428,471. These figures give a yearly average of nearly 43,000.[282] Of these, 214,047 embarked from Irish ports, 152,738 from Liverpool; and ten per cent. was added for imperfect returns. The largest number of those who went from Ireland *direct* to the colonies or foreign countries, from any one port, embarked at Belfast, viz., twenty per cent. of the whole. From Cork nearly the same. From the ports of Ulster there went 76,905. From the ports of Munster 70,046. From Leinster 34,977, and from Connaught only 32,119. Those emigrants who embarked from Irish ports proceeded as follows:—189,225 to British America, namely, 107,792 males and 81,233 females; to the United States of America 19,775, namely, 10,725 males, and 2,950 females; to the Australian colonies, there went 4,553, in the proportion of 2,300 males and 2,253 females; and 494 persons embarked for the West Indies—300 males and 194 females.[283]

Within the decade of years comprised between 1831 and 1841, emigration was at its minimum in 1838, the number that left our shores in that year being only 14,700; it rose to its maximum in 1841, namely, 71,392. It rose still higher in 1842, the emigrants of that year being set down at 89,686. The year 1843 was named by O'Connell the Repeal year; the people were filled with the hope of soon seeing a parliament in College Green, and to this fact may probably, be attributed the great falling off in emigration; the number for that year being only 37,509.

It increased in 1844 to 54,289; and in 1845—the eve of the Famine, to 74,969 persons.

In the year 1846, as might be expected, emigration from Ireland reached a height which it had never attained before in a single year; the number, as estimated by the Emigration Commissioners, being 105,955. Besides which between the 13th of January and the 1st of November, 278,005 immigrants arrived at Liverpool from Ireland; but the Irish labourers who, at that time, annually visited England, and who were variously estimated at from 10,000 to 30,000, are included in the number. For the protection of the emigrants, additional agents were appointed by the Government at Liverpool and some Irish ports; and the annual vote in aid of colonial funds, for the relief of sick and destitute emigrants from the United Kingdom, was increased from £1,000 to £10,000.[284]

In the spring of 1847, a gigantic emigration scheme was launched. It was said to have emanated from, and was certainly patronized by members of the so-called Irish party, which, with so few elements of cohesion, was inaugurated at the Rotundo meeting; but the father of the scheme seems to have been Mr. J.E. Godley. By it, two millions of Irish Catholics were to be transferred to Canada in three years; it being a leading feature in the scheme to send none but Catholics. It was, the promoters said, to be an Irish Catholic colony, with a distinct and well marked Irish nationality,—in fact, a New Ireland! There was a memorial on the subject which extended over fifty one pages of a pamphlet, and which was prepared by Mr. Godley with much ability. It went very fully into the whole scheme. This, accompanied by a short explanatory letter, was presented to the Prime Minister on the last day of March.

The memorialists assumed that the cultivation of the potato could not be persevered in, and that Ireland, in her existing condition, could not grow enough of corn food for six millions of people. Hence the necessity for an extensive emigration. They are not, they say, to be ranked among those who believe Ireland incapable of supporting its existing population in comfort, under other circumstances; far from it. On the contrary, they do not doubt that if "the social economy" of Ireland were made to resemble that of England, the population of Ireland might be larger than it then was. It was only under existing circumstances that the population of Ireland was redundant, and all they desired was a temporary decrease.

In the letter which accompanied the memorial to the Premier, the memorialists put their views, shortly, as follows:—1. The present condition of Ireland is such, that there must be, for some years, a vast increase of emigration, they, therefore, urge the necessity of what they call "systematic colonization," both for the advantage of the emigrants themselves, and the good of the colony to which they would emigrate. They think this colonization, "on a very large scale," ought to be made from Ireland to Canada, and that the State ought to lend its assistance to promote it. 2. In the second place they lay it down as an essential part of their scheme, that religious provision must be made for the emigrants. 3. They think there would be great advantage in enlisting private enterprise, in the form of agency, to carry out the plan. 4. Furthermore, there must be a willingness on the part of the nation to accept an income and property tax, for the purpose of defraying the cost of emigration: and, 5. To help the emigrants to settle on the land, "aids to location," as Mr. Godley called them, must be provided.

How was this vast scheme to be carried to a successful issue? A joint-stock company, to be called "The Irish Canadian Company," was to undertake the entire management of it. This Company was to be legalised by Act of Parliament, and recognised by the Canadian Government. It was to transmit to Canada and settle there a million and a half of the Irish people in three years, being at the rate of half a million a year. To do this, £9,000,000 was to be lent by the Government, at the rate of £3,000,000 each year, on the security of Irish property and an Irish income tax. This tax was to be one per cent. the first year, two per cent. the second year, three per cent. the third year, and to stand at three per cent. until the first instalment of the loan could be paid, and was, of course, to cease altogether when the last instalment was paid. Repayment was to be made at the rate of six and a half per cent., per annum, which would extinguish principal and interest in twenty two years.

The £9,000,000 so lent and to be so repaid, was to be expended in this manner: The passage money of each individual was computed at £3; of this the Government was to advance one pound, the emigrants themselves finding the other two in some way—to be given by friends—saved from wages—obtained from their landlords—however the £2 was to be found,—that sum was to be provided by the emigrant. One pound to each of one million and a-half of emigrants would absorb £1,500,000 of the £9,000,000. The joint-stock company that was to work the concern must, of course, have profits, and be paid for its labours; it was, therefore, to have a bonus of £5, or a sum of about that amount, for each emigrant it would prove to the satisfaction of Government that it had located in Canada. It was to have other profits. It was to be empowered to lend money to the district councils in Canada, to effect local improvements, and the interest of this money was to be a portion of its profits. All the emigrants were to be settled on the land in Canada; this would be bought in its rude state by the company, and resold at a profit, when it had improved it, and established upon it those "aids to location" enumerated further on. This bonus of £5 on each, emigrant would amount to £7,500,000, which, together with the £1,500,000 mentioned above, would absorb the £9,000,000.

As already stated, it was a marked characteristic of this systematic emigration, or colonization, that it was to be exclusively Catholic, and that a number of priests, proportioned to the number of emigrants, should be appointed to accompany them and settle down with them. This Mr. Godley held to be absolutely necessary. Before the Lords' Committee on Colonization he is asked: "Has any mode occurred to you by which a more compacted social organization might be given to emigration, carrying with it more of the characteristics and elements of improved civilization than at present exists?" He answers: "Yes. I have explained my views upon the subject at considerable length elsewhere. I think that the nucleus of an Irish Roman Catholic emigration must be ecclesiastical, I think they are debarred from going upon the land and settling socially, by the want of the ordinances of their church; I think that the first and most important element, in an Irish social settlement must be religious and ecclesiastical."[285] Again he is asked: "At the present moment, has it come within your knowledge, that the want of such spiritual care and assistance checks the progress of settlement among Irish emigrants, and, consequently, to a certain extent, discourages emigration?" "Certainly," Mr. Godley answers, "it prevents them from going upon the land all over America." "How does it," he is further asked, "prevent them from going upon the land?" "In this way," he replies, "they being too poor to take the priest with them to the wilderness, in order to partake of the ordinances of their church, and to enjoy spiritual advice and comfort, remain in the towns, where they are simply labourers, and are checked in going upon the land as rural settlers."[286] *Question* 1819: "How do you propose that the priests should be paid?" *Answer.* "By a grant from this country or from Ireland." *Question* 1820: "Do you mean simply the expense of their emigration, not as a permanent endowment in the colony?" *Answer.* "I never entered so exactly into the detail as to say in what manner I thought the endowment might be best effected, and, consequently, I do not consider myself as committed to any particular plan of endowment. The probability is, that the most effective way of endowing them would be, to a certain extent, in money, and to a certain extent by land in Canada; but that is a part of the plan which I did not consider necessary to draw out in detail." The following question and answer explains what Mr. Godley meant by "aids to location:"—*Question* 1848: "What is the practical mode in which you would set about the establishment of a colony?" *Answer.* "I would open the country by means of roads and bridges, build mills, endow a clergyman, and build a school. Those are the leading features of a social settlement to which I think a company, or any body that wanted to establish a settlement, ought to attend first."

The memorial to Lord John Russell, praying that the Government would give its sanction and support to Mr. Godley's scheme of colonization, was signed by one archbishop, four marquises, seven earls, three viscounts, thirteen barons, nine baronets, eighteen members of parliament, some honourables, and several deputy-lieutenants. The memorialists were, in all, eighty—that is, eighty of the leading peers, members of parliament, and landowners approached the First Minister, to beg that he would aid them in sending two millions of Irish Catholics to Canada, to reclaim the land in that colony. Everybody knows that the statement of Sir Robert Kane is accepted as a truth, that there are in Ireland four and a-half millions of barren acres, the greater portion of which would richly, and promptly, repay for their reclamation. Yet the Government Bill for beginning that reclamation was withdrawn by the Prime Minister, and no single voice was raised in favour of going on with it; moreover, he said his reason for withdrawing it was, the opposition which the House of Lords offered to it. Yes; they would have no reclamation of Irish lands, but they would submit to bear increased taxation in order to send the Celtic race by the million to delve in Canada!—yet, even for that it became the Irish people to be duly grateful, inasmuch as it was a decided improvement upon the older colonization scheme of "To h—or Connaught."[287]

The colonization scheme met with little or no support in Ireland. It was suspected. It was regarded as a plan for getting rid of the Celt by wholesale. A Protestant gentleman, Mr. Thomas Mulock, thus comments on the memorial: "And is it come to this, O ye lords and gentlemen! representatives of the Irish party, with prospective adhesions after the Easter holidays from the vast majority of Irish Protestant proprietors,— do you avow yourselves to be in the position of landowners, who stand in no relation of aristocracy or leadership, government or guidance, succour or solace to millions of the people, who famish on the territorial possessions from which you derive your titles, your importance, your influence, your wealth. Has confiscation been mellowed into the legal semblance of undisputed succession, only to bring about a state of

488

things which the most ruthless ravagers of nations never permanently perpetrated?"[288]

The memorial was extensively circulated. Amongst many others, one was sent to the Right Rev. Dr. Maginn, Coadjutor Bishop of Derry. He replied in terms scathing as they were indignant. The following is an extract from his letter:—"In sober earnestness, gentlemen, why send your circular to a Catholic bishop? Why have the bare-faced impudence to ask me to consent to the expatriation of millions of my co-religionists and fellow-countrymen? You, the hereditary oppressors of my race and my religion,—you, who reduced one of the noblest peoples under heaven to live in the most fertile island on earth on the worst species of a miserable exotic, which no humane man, having anything better, would constantly give to his swine or his horses;—you, who have made the most beautiful island under the sun a land of skulls, or of ghastly spectres;—you are anxious, I presume, to get a Catholic bishop to abet your wholesale system of extermination—to head in pontificals the convoy of your exiles, and thereby give the sanction of religion to your atrocious scheme. You never, gentlemen, laboured under a more egregious mistake than by imagining that we could give in our adhesion to your principles, or could have any, the least confidence, in anything proceeding from you. Is not the *ex-officio* clause in the Poor-law Bill your bantling, or that of your leader, Lord Stanley? Is not the quarter of an acre clause test for relief your creation? Were not the most conspicuous names on your committee the abettors of an amendment as iniquitous as it was selfish—viz., to remove the poor-rates from their own shoulders to that of their pauper tenantry? Are not they the same members who recently advocated, in the House of Commons, the continuation of the fag-end of the bloody penal code of the English statute book, by which our English brethren could be transported or hanged for professing the creed of their conscience, the most forward in this Catholic emigration plan? What good could we expect from such a Nazareth?"[289]

The Prime Minister did not take up the great colonization scheme. He said, in the House of Commons, on the 29th of April, that he declined, on the part of the Government, assuming the responsibility of providing for the absorption of the great excess of labour then existing in Ireland. "I deny," said Lord John, "on the part of the Government, the responsibility of completely, still less suddenly, resolving that question. What we can do, and what we, the Government, have endeavoured to do is, to mitigate present suffering."

The Government was of opinion that emigration, left to itself, would transfer the starving people to the United States and British America, as quickly as they could be provided for in those countries. This calculation turned out to be correct enough, as the following figures will show:— Emigration from Ireland in the year 1845 is set down at 74,969; it increased in 1846 to 105,955, although the Famine had not to the full extent turned the minds of the people to seek homes in the New World. The emigration of 1847 more than doubled that of 1846, being 215,444; ti fell in 1848 to 178,159, but in 1849 the emigration of 1847 was repeated, the emigrants of that year being 214,425, of which 2,219 were orphan girls from the Workhouses. The magnitude of the exodus was maintained in 1850, that year giving 209,054 voluntary exiles; but the emigration in 1851, which year closed the decade, quite outstripped that of any previous year, the figure in that year standing at 257,372.[290]

The census of 1841 shows the population of Ireland to have been in that year 8,175,124. Taking the usual ratio of births over deaths, it should have increased in 1851 to 9,018,799, instead of which it fell to 6,552,385; thus, being nearly two millions and a-half less than it should have been. These two millions and a-half disappeared in the Famine. They disappeared by death and emigration. The emigration during the ten years from 1842 to 1851, both inclusive, was 1,436,862. Subtracting this from the amount of decrease in the population, namely, 2,476,414, the remainder will be 1,039,552; which number of persons must have died of starvation and its concomitant epidemics; but even this number,

490

great as it is, must be supplemented by the deaths which occurred among Famine emigrants, in excess of the percentage of deaths among ordinary emigrants.

During the Famine-emigration period this excess became most remarkable and alarming. The deaths on the voyage to Canada rose from five in the thousand (the ordinary rate) to about sixty in the thousand; and the deaths whilst the ships were in quarantine rose from one to forty in the thousand. So that instead of six emigrants in the thousand dying on the voyage and during quarantine, one hundred died. Subtracting six from one hundred, we have ninety-four emigrants in the thousand dying of the Famine as certainly as if they had died at home. Furthermore, great numbers of those who were able to reach the interior died off almost immediately. Sir Charles Trevelyan, the Government official, from whose *Irish Crisis* I take the above figures, adds these remarkable words: "besides *still larger* numbers who died at Quebec, Montreal, and elsewhere in the interior."[291]

89,738 emigrants embarked for Canada in 1847. One in every three of those who arrived were received into hospital, and the deaths on the passage or soon after arriving were 15,330, or rather more than *seventeen* per cent. As the deaths amongst emigrants, in ordinary times, were about ¾ per cent., at least sixteen per cent. of those deaths may be set down as being occasioned by the Famine. But seventeen per cent., high as it seems, does not fully represent the mortality amongst the Famine emigrants. Speaking of those who went to Canada in 1847, Dr. Stratten says: "Up to the 1st of November, one emigrant in every seven had died; and during November and December there have been many deaths in the different emigrant hospitals; so that it is understating the mortality to say that one person in every five was dead by the end of the year."[292]

This would give us twenty per cent. of deaths up to the end of 1847; but the mortality consequent upon the Famine-emigration did not stop short at the end of December; it must have gone on through the remainder of the winter and spring, so that, everything considered, twenty-five per cent. does not seem too high a rate at which to fix it for that year. It is, however, to be taken into account, that the mortality amongst Irish emigrants in 1847 was exceptionally great, so, in an average for the six years from 1846 to 1851 we must strike below it. Seventeen per cent does not seem too high an average for those six years.

We have not such full information about those who emigrated to the United States as we have of those who went to Canada; the Canadian emigrants had certainly some advantages on their side; for, until the year 1847 there was no protection for emigrants who landed at New York. In that year the Legislature of the State of New York passed a law, establishing a permanent Commission for the relief and protection of emigrants, which, in due time, when it got into working order, did a world of good. Previous to this, private hospitals were established by the shipbrokers (the creatures of the shipowners), in the neighbourhood of New York. A Committee appointed by the Aldermen of New York in 1846 visited one of those institutions, and thus reported upon it: "The Committee discovered in one apartment, 50 feet square, 100 sick and dying emigrants lying on straw; and among them, in their midst, the bodies of two who had died four or five days before, but who had been left for that time without burial! They found in the course of their inquiry that decayed vegetables, bad flour, and putrid meat, were specially purchased and provided for the use of the strangers! Such as had strength to escape from these slaughter-houses fled from them as from a plague, and roamed through the city, exciting the compassion—perhaps the horror—of the passers by. Those who were too ill to escape had to take their chance— such chance as poisonous food, infected air, and bad treatment afforded them of ultimate recovery."[293]

It may be fairly assumed that the mortality amongst the emigrants who went to the United States was at least as great as amongst those who went to British America. The emigration from Ireland for the above six years was, as already stated, 1,180,409, seventeen per cent. of whom will give us 200,668, which, being added to 1,039,552, the calculated number of deaths at home, we have ONE MILLION, TWO HUNDRED AND FORTY THOUSAND DEATHS resulting directly from the Irish Famine, and the pestilence which followed in its track.

The mortality on board some of the emigrant ships was terrible; and, whatever the cause, the deaths in *British ships* enormously exceeded those in the ships of any other country.[294] The "Erin Queen" sailed with 493 passengers, of whom 136 died on the voyage. The scenes of misery on board of this vessel could hardly have been surpassed in a crowded and sickly slaver on the African coast. It appears, writes Dr. Stratten, that the "Avon," in 552 passengers, had 246 deaths; and the "Virginius," in 476, had 267 deaths.[295] An English gentleman, referring to a portion of Connaught in which he was stationed at the time, writes thus: "Hundreds, it is said, had been compelled to emigrate by ill-usage, and in one vessel containing 600 not *one hundred* survived!"[296]

Much sympathy was shown in Canada for the poor emigrants, and their orphans were, to a great extent, adopted by charitable families. The legislature of the State of New York, and many of its leading citizens, showed a laudable desire to aid and protect emigrants, in spite of which the most cruel and heartless villainies were practised upon the inexperienced strangers the moment they landed; in fact, before they landed the ship was surrounded by harpies, who seized their luggage and partly by violence, partly by wheedling and misrepresentation, led them where they pleased, and plundered then at will.

The legislature of the State of New York, in 1847, appointed a Committee to inquire into the frauds practised upon emigrants. It made its report in January 1848. In the fourth page of that Report these words occur: "Your Committee must confess, that they had no conception of, nor would they have believed the extent to which these frauds and outrages have been practised, until they came to investigate them." The first set of robbers into whose hands the emigrants fell were called "runners." They are described in the Report as a class who boarded the emigrant ship and brought the emigrants to their special lodging-houses in spite of them, and in spite of the authorities. They took charge of their luggage, pretending that nothing would be demanded for the storage of it, the price claimed for which afterwards was exorbitant, and the luggage was held until it was paid.

The frauds committed with regard to passage tickets were if possible more grievous than those practised by the runners. "The emigrant," says the Report, buys a ticket at an exorbitant price, with a picture on it representing a steam-boat, railway cars, and a canal packet drawn by three prancing horses, to bring him to some place beyond Albany. *He gets a steam-boat ticket to Albany.* Here his great ticket, with the pictures, is protested; he has to pay once more, and instead of railroad cars and a packet-boat, he is thrust into the steerage or hold of a line boat, which amongst other conveniences is furnished with false scales for weighing his luggage.

A few extracts from the testimony of some of the witnesses examined before the Committee will show how unexaggerated was the Report.

Henry Vail is examined: he testifies that he is employed by E. Mathews. His practice is to get all he can for tickets; he retains whatever is over the proper price and gets his monthly pay besides. The only exception to his getting all he can, is, he declares upon his oath, that he "*never shaves a lady that is travelling alone.* It is bad enough," in his opinion, "to shave a man."[297] Charles Cooke said, in his examination, that he had been employed by many offices. He heard Rieschmüller tell passengers to go to the d—l, they could not get less than twelve dollars as deck passengers on the lake, and he made them believe they must get their tickets from him, which they did. "Rieschmüller told me," said Cooke, "that all he was compelled to pay for a passenger to any port on the lakes was from two dollars to two and a-half. Wolfe told me that two dollars was the price, and all luggage free."[298] Mervyn L. Ray swore that he knew Mr. Adams to take twelve dollars for a passenger to Buffalo, when he (Ray) would have given him the same fare at two dollars.

One of the witnesses, T.R. Schoger enters into some details. 1. The first fraud, he says, practised on emigrants is this:—the moment the vessel arrives it is boarded by runners, whose first object appears to be to get emigrants to their respective public houses. Once there they are considered sure prey. There are, of course, rival establishments; each has agents (runners) and bullies. There is often bloodshed between them. The emigrant is bewildered. He is told he will get meals for sixpence a piece—he never gets one less than two shillings, and he is often charged a dollar a meal. 2. The next ordeal is called booking; that is, he is taken to the forwarding office, and told it is the *only* office, the proprietors being owners of boats, railways, etc. The runner gets one dollar for everyone booked. 3. The next imposition is at Albany; it is there the great fraud is perpetrated. If they find the emigrant has plenty of money they make him pay the whole passage over again,—repudiating all that was done at New York. 4. The next is the luggage. It is falsely weighed, and the emigrant is often made to pay five or six times more than the proper charge. "The emigrant," adds Mr. Schoger, "now thinks himself out of his difficulty, but finds himself greatly mistaken. The passengers are crowded like beasts into the canal boat, and are frequently compelled to pay their passage over again, or be thrown overboard by the captain."[299] The mates of the ships often took the property of emigrants; their locks were picked and their chests robbed; for none of which outrages was there the slightest redress.[300]

Before the legislature took any effective action in protecting the emigrants who landed at New York, many philanthropic and benevolent societies were formed for that purpose. Of those societies one Hiram Huested gave the following testimony on oath: "I am sure, there is as much iniquity amongst the emigrant societies as there is amongst the runners."[301]

What with shipwrecks, what with deaths from famine, from fever, from overcrowding; what with wholesale robbery, committed upon them at almost every step of their journey, it is matter for great surprise indeed, that even a remnant of the Famine-emigrants survived to locate themselves in that far West, to which they fled in terror and dismay, from their humble but loved and cherished homes, in the land of their fathers. The Irish race get but little credit for industry or perseverance; but in this they are most unjustly maligned, as many testimonies already cited from friend and foe, clearly demonstrate. If one more be wanting, I would point to a fact in the history of the worn-out remnant of our Famine-emigrants, who had tenacity of life enough to survive their endless hardships and journeyings. That fact is, the large sums of money which, year after year, they sent to their friends—every penny of which they earned by the sweat of their brow—by their industry and perseverance.

Thus write the Commissioners of Emigration, in their thirty-first General Report: "In 1870, as in former years, the amount sent home was large, being £727,408 from North America, and £12,804 from Australia and New Zealand. Of this sum there was remitted in prepaid passages to Liverpool, Glasgow, and Londonderry, £332,638; more than was sufficient to pay the passage money for all who emigrated that year! Imperfect as our accounts are," continue the Commissioners, "they show that, in the twenty three years from 1848 to 1870 inclusive, there has been sent home from North America, through banks and commercial houses, upwards of £16,334,000. Of what has been sent home through private channels we have no account."[302]

A public writer, reviewing the Commissioners' Report, says: "Even this vast sum does not represent more than the one half of the total sent home. Much was brought over by captains of ships, by relatives, friends, or by returning emigrants." No doubt, a great deal of money came through private channels, but it is hardly credible, that another sixteen or seventeen millions reached Ireland in that way. It is only guess-work, to be sure, but if we add one-fourth to the sum named in the Report, as the amount transmitted by private hand, it will probably bring us much nearer the truth. This addition gives us, in all, £20,417,500.

There, then, is the one more testimony, that the Irish race lack neither industry nor perseverance. For the lengthened period of three and twenty years, something like £1,000,000 a-year have been transmitted to their relatives and friends by the Irish in America. In three and twenty years, they have sent home over TWENTY MILLIONS OF MONEY. Examine it; weigh it; study it; in whatever way we look at this astounding fact— whether we regard the magnitude of the sum, or the intense, undying, all-pervading affection which it represents—it STANDS ALONE IN THE HISTORY OF THE WORLD.

FOOTNOTES:

269. Census of Ireland for the decade of years ending 1851. Tables of deaths, vol. I, p. 277. Quotation from *Dublin Quarterly Medical Journal.*
270. See "Census of Ireland, from 1841 to 1851." Tables of Deaths, vol. 1, p. 296.
271. Dr. H. Kennedy, in *Dublin Quarterly Journal.*
272. Census Returns.
273. Those admissions increased to 110,381 in 1848.
274. The percentage of deaths in the cholera, which succeeded to this fever in 1849, was forty-two one-fifth.
275. Census of Ireland for the year 1851. Report on tables of deaths.
276. Report of Commissioners of Health.
277. It is pleasant to know that the settlement at Peterborough has continued to flourish, as the following extract from the late John F. Maguire's "Irish in America" will show.—"The shanty, and the wigwam, and the log-hut have long since given place to the mansion of brick and stone; and the hand-sleigh and the rude cart to the strong waggon and the well-appointed carriage. Where there was but one miserable grist mill, there are now mills and factories of various kinds. And not only are there spacious schools under the control of those who erected and made use of them for their children, but the 'heavy grievance' which existed in 1825 has long since been a thing of the past. The little chapel of logs and shingle—18 feet by 20—in which the settlers of that day knelt in gratitude to God, has for many years been replaced by a noble stone church, through whose painted windows the Canadian sunlight

streams gloriously, and in which two thousand worshippers listen with the old Irish reverence to the words of their pastor. The tones of the pealing organs swell in solemn harmony, where the simple chaunt of the first settlers was raised in the midst of the wilderness; and for miles round may the voice of the great bell, swinging in its lofty tower, be heard in the calm of the Lord's day, summoning the children of Saint Patrick to worship in the faith of their fathers."—*The Irish in America*, by John F. Maguire, M.P. London, 1868, p. 110.

278.   Quoted in Report of Committee of the House of Lords on Colonization from Ireland in 1847, p. vii.

279.   Quoted in Report of Committee of the House of Lords on "Colonization from Ireland" in 1847, p. 10.

280.   Sessional Papers, 1846, No. 24.

281.   Sessional Papers, 1835.

282.   The Census Commissioners, whose Emigration Statistics I use, do not add the one and a-half per cent. for probable births; hence they state the number of emigrants between 1831 and 1841 at 403,459 only.

283.   Census Returns for 1851—Tables of Deaths, p. 227-8.

284.   Census of Ireland for the year 1851—Report on Table of Deaths, p. 278. Thorn's Directory for 1848, p. 126.

285.   *Question* 1790, and *Answer*.

286.   *Questions* and *Answers* 1797 and 1798.

287.   A million and a-half of emigrants was the number contemplated by Mr. Godley's scheme, but his opinion was that there would be "a parallel stream of half a million, drawn out by the attraction of the new Irish colony, which, would make the whole emigration two millions."

The following is a list of those who signed the memorial for colonization in Canada:—Archbishop Whately, the Marquis of Ormonde, the Marquis of Ely, the Marquis of Sligo, the Marquis of Headfort, the Earl of Devon, the Earl of Desart, the Earl of Rosse, the Earl of Lucan, the Earl Fitzwilliam (modified assent), the Earl of Glengall, the Earl of Limerick, Viscount Massareene, Viscount Adare, Viscount Castlemaine, Lord Farnham, Lord Jocelyn, Lord Dunally, Lord Rossmore, Lord Oranmore, Lord Blayney, Lord Clonbrock, Lord Wallscourt, Lord Courtney, Lord Gort, Lord Sydney Osborne, Lord George Hill, Lord Stuart de Decies, Sir Walter James, Bart., M.P., Rt. Hon. Sir A.J. Foster, Bart., Sir Charles Coote, Bart., M.P., Sir Vere de Vere, Bart.,

Sir Michael Bellew, Bart., Sir Thomas Staples, Bart., Sir Colman O'Loghlin, Bart., Sir Roger Palmer, Bart., Sir Ralph Howard, Bart., Col. Wyndham, M.P., E.J. Shirley, Esq., M.P., Lieut.-Colonel Taylor, M.P., D.S. Kerr, Esq., M.P., W. Hutt, Esq., M.P., Rt. Hon. Colonel D. Darner, M.P., Alex. M'Carthy, Esq., M.P., R.B. Osborne, Esq., M.P., Hon. James Maxwell, M.P., Major Layard, M.P., Jas. H. Hamilton, Esq., M.P., M.J. O'Connell, Esq., M.P., W.H. Gregory, Esq., M.P., W.V. Stuart, Esq., M.P., B.J. Chapman, Esq., M.P., D.R. Mangles, Esq., M.P., C.B. Adderley, Esq., M.P., W. Ormsby Gore, Esq., M.P., Hon. Stephen Spring Rice, Hon. Standish Vereker, Hon. James Hewitt, Thomas Fortescue, Esq., D.L., Major Blackball, D.L.; James Lendrum, Esq., D.L.; T.J. Fetherstone Haugh, D.L., Mervyn Pratt, Esq., D.L., E. Housley, Esq., D.L., Colonel A. Knox Gore, Lieut. Co. Sligo, George Vaughan Jackson, Esq., D.L., R.M. Fox, Esq., D.L., Edward Cane, Esq., Charles Hamilton, Esq., Charles S. Monck, Esq., William Monsell, Esq., Thomas S. Carter, Esq., Charles W. Hamilton, Esq., Richard Bourke, Esq., Fetherstone Haugh O'Neill, Esq., John Vernon, Esq., George Lendrum, Esq., Francis Latouche, Esq., Peter Latouche, Esq., John Robert Godley.—*Report of House of Lords on Colonization from Ireland, p. 168.*

288.   Public letter.

289.   Reply to M.J. O'Connell, Esq., M.P., W.H. Gregory, Esq., M.P., and John R. Godley, Esq., Secretaries to the Canadian Colonization Scheme; 9th of April, 1847.

290.   Taken from Thom's Almanack for 1853, p. 252. The census of 1851 only gives the emigration for the first three months of that year. The number of emigrants in 1852 was largely in excess of those of 1851.

291.   "At Quebec in particular, we read that 'the mortality is appalling;' it was denominated The Ship Fever."—*British American Journal.* "Upwards of £100,000 was expended in relieving the sick and destitute emigrants landed in Canada in 1847."—Nicholls' History of the Irish Poorlaw, p. 327—*note.*

292.   Dr. Stratten, in Edinburgh Medical and Surgical Journal, quoted by Census Commissioners for 1851 in p. 305 of their Report on Tables of Deaths.

293.   "The Irish in America," by John Francis Maguire, p. 186.

294.   "Report of Commissioners of Emigration for the State of New York," quoted by Mr. Maguire.

295.   Dr. Stratten in "Edinburgh Medical and Surgical Journal."

296.   Twelve months' residence in Ireland during the Famine and the Public Works: by William Henry Smith, C.E., late conducting engineer of Public Works, p. 92.

297.   Report p. 27. Halliday pamphlets, vol. 1990.

298.   Report, pp. 29, 30.

299.   Report, pp. 33, 34.

300.   *Ib.*, pp. 54, 55.

301.   *Ib.*, p. 73.

302.   The report of the Emigration Commissioners for 1873 just issued 28th October, 1874. gives the following facts. In the course of last year 310,612 emigrants sailed from the ports of the United Kingdom, being a larger number than in any year since 1854. Of these, 123,343 were English, 83,692 Irish, 21,310 Scotch, 72,198 Foreigners, who had merely touched at British ports, and 10,929 whose nationality was not ascertained. The remittances of Irish Emigrants to their friends at home were as usual very large, the total sum being, according to the information within reach of the Commissioners, £724,040. This includes the remittances of both the United States and Canada. Of this sum £341,722 came in the shape of prepaid passages, more than sufficient, says the Report, to defray the cost of steerage passages at £6 6s. each for the 83,692 Irish who emigrated within the year. *Thirty-first General Report of the Emigration Commissioners, p. 4.*

*   *   *   *   *

CHAPTER XV.

The Temporary Relief Act, popularly known as the Soup-kitchen Act,
was limited to the 1st of October, 1847. The Government determined
that after its expiration relief should be given through the Poorlaw system
only. In preparation for this arrangement, an Act (the 10th & 11th Vic.

cap. 31,) was passed in June, sanctioning outdoor relief. The harvest of 1847 was a good one, but so utterly prostrate was every interest in the country, that the outdoor relief system soon expanded into alarming proportions. In February, 1848, the cost of outdoor relief was £72,039, and in March it rose to £81,339. The numbers and cost were then both at their maximum, and according to the best estimate which can be formed, the number of outdoor poor relieved was 703,762, and of indoor 140,536, making an aggregate of 844,298 persons, irrespective of more than 200,000 school children, who were, as stated above, fed and in part clothed by "the British Association." So that the total number receiving relief in March, 1848, exceeded a million of persons; being about one out of every seven of the population.

The parliamentary papers issued from time to time, detailing the sums granted on account of the Irish Famine, are, for the most part, very perplexing; because, being usually printed on the motion of some member of parliament, they only give the precise information called for, and only up to the period at which it was called for; so, not only are they perplexing, but they are often misleading, although correct enough in themselves. Then again, it sometimes happens, that the sum voted by parliament is not entirely expended on the object for which it was granted. To give an instance of this: there is a parliamentary paper before me, ordered on the 2nd of December, 1847, which says, the amount voted under the Temporary Relief Act was £2,200,000, of which sum there was *expended* £1,676,000. Sir Charles Trevelyan gives the sum expended as £1,724,631. The only way of accounting for this seeming discrepancy is, that Sir Charles's statement was published later than the blue book, and that an outlay was still going on under the above Act, after the blue book had been published, which brought the expenditure up to the sum stated by him.

Here, besides the difference as to the actual sum expended, we have a considerable difference between the sum voted and the sum expended. But there is yet another thing connected with the Famine advances, which is very likely to mislead. The usual course was, that the money issued from the Treasury to meet the Famine, was in part a free grant, and in part a charge upon the land. It is only simple justice to state clearly how much of this money was a free grant, and how much of it was levied off Ireland, as a tax. The proportion is given in the Acts of Parliament, but it happens that the proportion eventually paid was less than what was levied: so that the proportions as given in the Acts of Parliament have to be altered to the extent of the remissions made.

In the short statement I am about to give, I follow Sir Charles Trevelyan's figures; being Secretary to the Treasury, he must have known the sums actually advanced by the Treasury, and the sums returned to it in payment of the loans granted.

	Amount advanced from the Treasury.			Amount finally charged under the Consolidated Annuities Act.		
	£	s.	d.	£	s.	d.
Under 9th Vict., cap. 1,	476,000	0	0	238,000	0	0
Under 9th and 10th Vict., cap. 107,"The Labour-rate Act,"	4,766,789	0	0	2,231,000	0	0
Under 10th Vict., cap. 7, "The Temporary Relief Act,"	1,724,631	0	0	953,355	0	0
Loans for building Workhouses,	1,420,780	0	0	122,707	0	0
Loans to pay debts of distressed Unions,	300,000	0	0	300,000	0	0

Grants by Parliament at various times: 1845, 1846, 1847, 1848, and 1849,	844,521	0	0	---		
	---------------	----	---	--------------	----	----
Total,	£9,532,721	0	0	4,845,062	0	0

During the years 1846, 1847, and 1848, the following sums were also expended by the Board of Works:

For arterial drainage,	470,617	10	3
Works under the Labouchere letter,	199,870	9	2
For land improvement.	520,700	0	0
	---------------	----	---
Total,	£10,723,908	19	5

In the above ten millions seven hundred thousand pounds, it may be fairly assumed, we have all the monies advanced by Government to mitigate the effects of the potato failure. Our next duty is to inquire how much of this sum was paid back by Ireland, and how much of it was a free gift from the Treasury.

The money advanced under the Labouchere letter for land improvement, and for arterial drainage cannot, of course, be regarded as a free gift towards staying the Famine; arterial drainage and land improvement go on still, through money advanced by Government.

504

The works under the Labouchere letter were, no doubt, intended to give reproductive employment during the Famine, but the cost of them was a charge upon the land and not a free gift.

The money spent on arterial drainage and land improvement, under the Labouchere letter and various drainage Acts, during the years 1846, 1847 and 1848, was, as given above, £1,191,187 19s. 5d., which being deducted from £10,723,908 19s>. 5d. leaves the sum of £9,532,721, of which there was finally charged to this country £4,845,062. Deducting this from the £9,532,721 we have £4,687,659 as the amount of money given by Government as a free gift to Ireland to sustain the people through the Great Famine. To this, however, there is to be added a sum of about £70,000 paid for freights. The American people, when they had collected those generous contributions of theirs, and when they had resolved to send them in the form of food to Ireland, began to make arrangements for paying the freights of their vessels, but all trouble and anxiety on this head was removed by the action of the English Government, which undertook to pay the freights of all vessels carrying to Ireland, food purchased by charitable contributions. Those freights finally reached about £70,000. The addition of this sum brings the whole of the Government free gift towards the Irish Famine to £4,757,659.

The amount collected and disbursed by charitable Associations can be only approximated to. There is a list of those subscriptions, as far as they could be ascertained, given in the Report of the Society of Friends. They amount to £1,107,466 13s., but the compiler of the Report was of opinion that the sums so collected and distributed could not have fallen far short of a million and a-half.

No effective means were taken to ascertain the moneys sent to Ireland by emigrants until the year 1848; however, Mr. Jacob Harvey, a member of the Society of Friends, from inquiries made by him in New York, Baltimore, and Philadelphia, computed the remittances from emigrants in 1847 at £200,000, but it is highly probable that the actual amount was far in excess of that; for we find in the next year, 1848, there came to Ireland through the banks and commercial houses alone, £460,180; which sum may also be regarded as a contribution towards the Irish Famine. I think we are justified in naming £300,000 for 1847, instead of £200,000, Mr. Harvey's estimate, these two sums make £760,180, which being added to the acknowledged amount of public subscriptions, we have a total of £1,867,646, 13s. as the amount voluntarily and charitably contributed to our Famine-stricken people. But if we take one million and a-half to represent *the actual charitable subscriptions*, as assumed by the Report of the Society of Friends, and add to it the money sent by emigrants in 1847 and 1848, we will have the enormous sum of £2,260,180.

The most important of all the Associations called into existence by the Famine was "The British Association for the Relief of extreme distress in Ireland and Scotland." There are about 5,550 distinct subscriptions printed in the Appendix to its report, but the number of individual subscriptions was far beyond this, for, many of the sums set down are the result of local subscriptions sent to the Association from various parts. This Association established about forty food depôts in various districts. They were, of course, most numerous in the South and West—most numerous of all in Cork, the wild and difficult coast of which county was marked by a line of them, from Kinsale Head to Dingle Bay.

Noblemen and gentlemen of high position volunteered their services to the Association, and laboured earnestly among the starving people. Amongst them may be named the Count Strezelecki, Lord R. Clinton, Lord James Butler, and Mr. M.J. Higgins, so well known on the London press by his *nom de plume* of "Jacob Omnium."

Besides the sums contributed directly to the Association, the Government gave it the distribution of the proceeds of two Queen's letters, amounting in the aggregate to £200,738 15s. 2d.[303] In August, 1847, when the Association was about to enter upon what it calls the second relief period, it found itself in possession of a clear cash balance of £160,000. It had to consider how this sum could be most beneficially applied during the ensuing winter. The Secretary of the Treasury, Mr.

Trevelyan, in that month wrote to the chairman, recommending the Association to select, through the Poorlaw Commissioners, a certain number of Unions, in which there was reason to believe the ratepayers would not be able to meet their liabilities, and that the Association should appropriate, from time to time, such sums as the Poorlaw Commissioners might recommend, for the purpose of assisting to give outdoor relief in certain districts of such Unions. After much deliberation the Association accepted this advice, and asked for the names of the most distressed Unions. A list of twenty-two was supplied to it in September. Some others were added later on. The grants of the Association were issued in food, and the Assistant Poorlaw Commissioners aided in the distribution of it. Under this arrangement the advances made by the Association from October to July amounted to £150,000.

A peculiar feature of this relief system, adopted and carried into effect by the advice of Count Strezelecki, was the giving of clothing and daily rations to children attending school. This was done in twenty-seven of the poorest Unions, and with the best results. By the first of January, 1848, the system was in full operation in thirteen Unions, and 58,000 children were on the relief roll of the Association. The numbers went on increasing until, in March, there were upwards of 200,000 children attending schools of all denominations, in twenty-seven Western Unions, participating in this relief. The total sum expended on food for the children amounted to £80,854, in addition to which £12,000 was expended on clothing for them.

On the 1st of November, 1848, £12,000 was still to the credit of the Association. By a resolution, it was handed over to the Poorlaw Commissioners for Ireland; and so closed the labours of the British Relief Association, so vast in its operations, so well managed, so creditable to all engaged in it, and such a lasting testimony to the generous charity of the subscribers.

Such frequent reference has been made in these pages to the "Transactions" of the Relief Committee of the Society of Friends, during the Famine, and so much use has been made of the information contained in that carefully compiled book, that I will only here repeat the amount of the charitable offerings confided to them for distribution. It was:—£198,326 15s. 5d.

The General Central Relief Committee for all Ireland, which met in College Green, received in contributions £83,934 17s. 11d., but of this, £20,000 was given by the British Association. The Marquis of Abercorn, the most Rev. Dr. Murray, Archbishop of Dublin, the Lord Mayor, the Provost of Trinity College, Lord Charlemont, O'Connell, the Dean of St. Patrick's, and several other noblemen and gentlemen were members of this Committee. The president was the present Duke of Leinster, then Marquis of Kildare. It remained in existence just one year, from December, 1846, to December, 1847.

"The chief source," says the "Transactions" of the Society of Friends," whence the means at our disposal were derived, was the munificent bounty of the citizens of the United States. The supplies sent from America to Ireland were on a scale unparalleled in history."

When authentic intelligence regarding the Irish Famine reached America, a general feeling of sympathy was at once excited. Beginning with Philadelphia, in all the great cities and towns throughout the Union, meetings were almost immediately held to devise the best and speediest means of relieving the starving people of this country. "All through the States an intense interest, and a noble generosity were shown. The railroads carried, free of charge, all packages marked 'Ireland.' Public carriers undertook the gratuitous delivery of any package intended for the relief of the destitute Irish. Storage to any extent was offered on the same terms. Ships of war approached our shores, eagerly seeking not to destroy life but to preserve it, their guns being taken out in order to afford more room for stowage."[304]

The total contributions received from America by the Central Relief Committee of the Society of Friends, were,—Money, £15,976 18s. 2d.— Provisions, 9,911 tons, valued at £133,847 7s. 7d. Six hundred and forty-two packages of clothing were also received, the precise value of which could not be exactly ascertained. The provisions were carried in ninety-one vessels, the united freights of which amounted to £33,017 5s. 7d.[305]

The total number of ships which carried provisions, the result of charitable contributions, to Ireland and Scotland in 1847, is set down at one hundred and eighteen; but as only four of these went to Scotland, one hundred and fourteen of them must have come here. The total freightage paid to those ships by Government, was £41,725 8s. 5-1/2d; but as I find in another part of the Blue book, that between £60,000 and £70 000 was paid by Government for freights on the cargoes of provisions consigned to the Society of Friends and to the British Association, and which I have above assumed to be £70,000, we may take it for granted that something like twenty thousand tons of provisions were consigned to both Societies, the money value of which was about £280,000.

Two American ships of war, the "Jamestown" and "Macedonian," carried cargoes of provisions to Ireland, for which no freight was charged.

The "Jamestown," a sloop of war lent by the government for the voyage, was freighted by the people of Massachusetts with 8,000 barrels of flour. She sailed from Boston on the 28th of March, 1847, and arrived at the Cove of Cork on the 12th of April, after a most prosperous voyage. The people of Cove immediately held a public meeting, and adopted an address to her Commander, Captain Forbes, which they presented to him on board. The citizens of Cork addressed him a few days later; and the members of the Temperance Institute gave him a *soiree*, at which the Rev. Theobald Mathew assisted.

The "Macedonian," another ship of war, arrived later on, conveying about 550 tons of provisions, a portion of which was landed in Scotland. Both ships were manned by volunteers.

On the appearance of the potato blight scientific men earnestly applied themselves to discover its cause, in the hope that a remedy might be found for it. Various theories was the result. There was the

509

Insect Theory; the Weather Theory; the Parasitical Theory; the Electrical Theory; the Fungus Theory; the Fog Theory. But whilst philosophers were maintaining their different views;—whilst Sir James Murray charged electricity with being the agent of destruction, and Mr. Cooper cast the blame upon the fogs; whilst Professors Lindley, Playfair, and Kane were busy with their tests, and retorts, and alembics; and whilst others again— microscope in hand—were in active pursuit of the *Aphis vastator*, or *Thrips minutissima*, a not inconsiderable class of persons, departing widely from all such speculations, discovered, beyond all doubt, that *Popery* was the true cause of the potato blight.

"As this predicted system" [popery], says a pamphleteer, "is an idolatrous one, any treaty with it must be opposed to God's will, and call down his wrath upon those nations who have commerce with it: more particularly upon nations wherein its hideous deformities are most signally manifested. Now, how have we seen in the first part of this work, that He has repeatedly punished? By famine and pestilence! Oh, beloved countrymen of every diversity of creed, in the heart-rending scenes around us do we witness punishment for national idolatry, systematic assassinations, performed occasionally with a refinement of cruelty worthy of incarnate devils."[306]

"This much is certain" writes a public journalist, "that our country is scourged with famine." Three causes are then given for the scourge; the second of which is, "Idolatry in the professing people of God, especially when sanctioned by the rulers of the country." After quoting examples from the Old Testament of the manner in which God punished idolatry, he proceeds: "It [idolatry] is just as true of the millions of Ireland as it was of the millions of Judah: 'They worship the work of their own hands, that which their own fingers have made.' And to complete the resemblance to apostate Israel, and fill the measure of our national guilt, the prevalent idolatry is countenanced and supported by our government. The Protestant members of the Houses of Lords and Commons have sworn before God and the country that Popery is idolatrous; our Queen, at her coronation, solemnly made a similar declaration,—yet, all have concurred in passing a Bill to endow a college for training priests to defend, and practise, and perpetuate, this corrupt and damnable worship in this realm. The ink wherewith the signification of royal assent was given to that iniquitous measure was hardly dry when *the fatal rot* commenced its work of destruction; and as the stroke was unheeded, and there was no repentant effort to retrace the daring step of the first iniquity, but rather a disposition to multiply transgression, we are now visited with a second and a severer stroke of judgment."[307]

The Rev. Hugh M'Neill preached a "Famine" sermon in St. Jude's, Liverpool, and published it under the title of "The Famine, a rod;" a rod that was meant to scourge England for tolerating Popery, of which he said: "That it is a sin against God's holy law to encourage the fables, deceits, false doctrines, and idolatrous worship of Romanism, no enlightened Christian—no consistent member of the church of England can deny."[308] "She [England] is fondly anticipating, as the result of generous concession, that she shall witness Roman Cooperation in general Liberty! Alas, for the Romans! With equal reason might she expect the Ethiopian to change his skin, or the leopard his spots. With the rich and responsible inheritance of an open Bible before her, and with free access to the illustrations of authentic history, this absurdity is England's sin, England's very great sin. There can be little doubt, that except repentance *and amendment* avert the stroke, this will prove England's plague, England's great plague, England's very great plague."[309]

It may be urged that the Rev. Hugh M'Neill is a man of extreme views. Be it so; but his extreme views seem rather to have advanced his interests than to have offended his superiors, for he is now Dean of Ripon.

Let us hear another and a very different stamp of man.

"I don't know whether I have mentioned before," writes Charles Dickens, "that in the valley of the Simplon, hard by here, where, (at the Bridge of St. Maurice over the Rhone), this Protestant canton ends and a Catholic canton begins, you might separate two perfectly distinct and different conditions of humanity, by drawing a line with your stick in the dust on the ground. On the Protestant side, neatness; cheerfulness; industry; education; continual aspiration, at least, after better things. On the Catholic side, dirt; disease; ignorance; squalor; and misery. I have so constantly observed the like of this, since I first came abroad, that *I have a sad misgiving*, that the religion of Ireland lies as deep at the root of all her sorrows even as English misgovernment and Tory villainy."[310]

Charles Dickens is looked upon not only as the strenuous denouncer of vice, but as the happy exponent of the higher and purer feelings of human nature also. For three-fourths of his life he wrote like a man who felt he had a mission to preach toleration, philanthropy—universal benevolence. He had travelled much. He had been over Belgium and France; he was through the Rhenish Provinces; in all which places the people are Catholics; they have received the highest praise from travellers and writers for their industry; their thrift; their cleanliness; Charles Dickens saw all this, but it never occurred to him to credit their religion with it. When the contrary occurs, and when fault is to be found, Popery, like a hack-block kept for such purposes, is made responsible, and receives a blow. He had, indeed, a sad misgiving that the religion of Ireland lay deep at the root of her sorrows. Surely this is enough to try one's patience. We have passed through and out-lived the terrible codes of Elizabeth and James and Anne and the two first Georges, under which, gallows-trees were erected on the hill side for our conversion or extinction; we have even survived the iron heels and ruthless sabres of Cromwell's sanctimonious troopers; and we can go back upon the history of those times calmly enough now. But this "sad misgiving" of Mr. Dickens; this patronizing condescension; this contemptuous pity, is more than provoking. It is probable he had not the time or inclination to read deeply into Irish history, but he must have had a general knowledge of it more than sufficient to inform him, that there were causes in superabundance to account for the poverty and degradation of our people, without going to their religion for them. Instead of doing so, he should have confessed with shame and humiliation, that his own countrymen, for a long series of years, did everything in their power to destroy the image of God in the native Irish, by driving them like beasts of chase into the mountains, and bogs, and fastnesses, and over the Shannon. Our people suffered these things and much more for conscience sake; inflicted, as they were, by Mr. Dickens's countrymen, in the name of religion; in the name of conscience; in advancing, as they pretended, the sacred cause of the right of private judgment. *He* makes Popery responsible for the results.

Those who held that Popery was the real cause of the potato-rot were influential, if not by their numbers, at least by their wealth; so they set about removing the fatal evil energetically. Large sums of money were collected, and a very active agency was established throughout the West of Ireland for this purpose; with, it would seem, very considerable success. But whilst those engaged in, the work, maintained, that the conversions were the result of instruction and enlightened investigation, others believed that most of the converts were like the poor woman mentioned by the late Dr. Whately, in a conversation with Mr. Senior.

In 1852, Mr. Nassau Wm. Senior was on a visit with the Archbishop, at his country house, near Stillorgan, five miles from Dublin. Mr. Senior asked him, to what cause the conversions made during the Famine were attributable. The Archbishop replied, that the causes must be numerous. Some, he said, believed, or professed to believe, that the conversions were purchased; this of course was the Catholic view. He then related the following anecdote on the subject:

"An old woman went to one of my clergy, and said, 'I'm come to surrender to your Reverence—and I want the leg of mutton and the blanket.' 'What mutton and blanket?' said the clergyman. I have scarcely enough of either for myself and my family, and certainly none to give. Who could have put such nonsense into your head?' 'Why, Sir,' she said, 'Father Sullivan told us, that the converts got each a leg of mutton and a blanket; and as I am famished, and starving with cold, I thought that *God would forgive* me for getting them.'"[311]

Dr. Whately was president of the "Society for protecting the Rights of Conscience," and he indignantly denied that any reward or indemnity had been held out, directly or indirectly, by that Society, to persons, to induce them to profess themselves converts; and he adds: "not only has no case been substantiated—no case has been even brought forward." This may be true of that particular Society, but to deny that neither money nor food were given, to induce persons to attend the Scripture classes and proselytizing schools, is to deny the very best proven facts.

In the *Tralee Chronicle* of the 19th of November, 1852, Archdeacon O'Sullivan, of Kenmare (lately deceased), published an abstract of a Report of one of those Missionary Societies which fell into his hands. The expenditure of a single Committee was £3557 1s. 6d. The salaries of clerical and lay agents are set down at £382 0s. 11d. What became of the remainder of the money?

But here is testimony that Dr. Whately himself would scarcely impugn:

Dr. Forbes, in his "Memorandums made in Ireland" in 1852, visited Connaught, and examined many of the proselytizing schools. He speaks without any doubt at all of the children who attended those schools receiving food and clothing. It did not seem to be denied on any side. Here is an extract: "I visited two of the Protestant Mission Schools at Clifden, one in the town, and the other about a mile and a-half beyond the town, on the road leading to the mouth of the bay. In the former, at the time of my visit, there were about 120 boys and 100 girls on the books, the average attendance being about 80. Out of the 80 girls there were no less than fifty-six orphans, *all of whom are fed and clothed out of the school funds, and a large proportion provided with lodgings also.* Only two of these girls were children of Protestant parents; and in the boy's school there was only one born of parents originally Protestant . . . At the probationary girls' school there were 76 on the books, at the time of my visit, their ages varying from eight to eighteen years. They are all Catholics, or children of Catholic parents; and out of the number no fewer than 40 *were orphans.*

All the children at this school receive daily rations of Indian meal; 45 of them one pound, and the remainder half that quantity. *Whether this is exclusive of the stirabout breakfast I saw preparing for them in the school*, I forgot to ask. All the children of these schools read the Scriptures and go to the Protestant Church, Catholic and Protestant alike."[312]

But I turn with pleasure from this uninviting and uncongenial subject, to one more elevating,—to the all but unlimited private charity which was called forth by the Irish Famine. I have already endeavoured to give some idea of it, but of course an imperfect one. The feelings evoked, and the almost unasked alms bestowed with a noble Christian generosity, during that awful time, can be only fully known to Almighty God; the Great Rewarder. The Merciful Rewarder has recorded them, and that is enough, at least for the givers. However, there were some amongst them who should not be passed over in silence. Baring, Brothers & Co.; Rothschild & Co.; Smith, Payne & Smith; Overend, Gurney & Co.; Truman, Hanbury & Co.; The Duke of Devonshire; Jones, Lloyd & Co.; an English friend (in two donations); and an Irish landlord (for Skibbereen) subscribed £1000 each.

Irish landlords did not contribute very munificently to the Famine-fund; but here is £1000 from one, and for a special locality. Who was the retiring but generous donor? The following extract of a letter will answer the question; and throw light upon another remarkable offering sent every month to Skibbereen for more than a year.

"The first case of death clearly established as arising from starvation," writes Mr. M'Carthy Downing, "occurred at South Reen, five miles from the town of Skibbereen. The case having been reported to me, as a member of the Relief Committee, I procured the attendance of Dr. Dore, and proceeded to the house where the body lay; the scene which presented itself will never be forgotten by me.

"The body was resting on a basket which had been turned up, the head on an old chair, the legs on the ground. All was wretchedness around. The wife, emaciated, was unable to move; and four children, more like spectres than living beings, were lying near the fire-place, in which apparently there had not been fire for some time. The doctor opened the stomach, and repugnant as it was to my feelings, I, at his solicitation, viewed its contents, which consisted solely of a few pieces of raw cabbage undigested.

"Having visited several other houses on the same townland, and finding the condition of the inmates therein little better than that of the wretched family whom I had just left, I summoned the Committee, and had a quantity of provisions sent there for distribution by one of the relieving officers; and then published in the Cork and Dublin papers a statement of what I had witnessed.

"Many subscriptions were sent to the Committee in consequence, and I received from an anonymous correspondent a monthly sum varying from £6 to £8, for a period of more than twelve months.

"One subscription of £1000 came from another anonymous donor, and for years the Committee knew not who those generous and really charitable parties were; but I had always a suspicion that the giver of the £1000 was Lord Dufferin. The grounds for my supposition were, that during the height of the sufferings of the people, I heard that two noblemen had been in the neighbourhood, visiting some of the localities. One was Lord Dufferin, then a very young man, who alluded subsequently in feeling terms to the wretchedness and suffering which he had witnessed; the other, I heard, was Lord John Manners.

"In some years after, I met at the house of Mr. Joshua Clarke, Q.C., in Dublin, Mr. Dowse, then a rising barrister, now a Baron of the Court of Exchequer, who addressed me, saying, 'We are old acquaintances;' to which I replied that I thought he was mistaken, as I had never the pleasure of meeting him before. He said 'That is quite true, but do you remember having received monthly remittances during the severe pressure of the Famine in Skibbereen?' I answered in the affirmative; and thereupon he said, 'I was your correspondent, I remitted the moneys to you, they were the offerings of a number of the students of Trinity College.'

516

"I need scarcely say that the incident created in me a feeling of esteem and regard for Mr. Dowse, which has continued to the present moment.

"During the passing of the Land Bill through the House of Commons, in the year 1870, I proposed several amendments, in consequence of which I received a letter from Lord Dufferin, asking for an interview, which subsequently took place at his house, and lasted more than three hours. When about to leave, I said that I had a question to put to his Lordship, which I hoped he would not refuse to answer; and having received his assent, I said,—Lord Dufferin, are you the anonymous donor of a subscription of £1000 to the Relief Committee at Skibbereen twenty-three years ago? And with a smile, he simply replied 'I am.'

"I left with feelings of high admiration for the man."[313]

To conclude. Every reader, will, doubtless, form his own views upon the facts given in this volume; upon the conduct of the people; the action of the landlords; the measures of the Government; those views may be widely different; but of the bright and copious fountains of living charity, which gushed forth over the Christian world, during the Great Irish Famine, history has but one record to make,—posterity can hold but one opinion.

FOOTNOTES:

303. The first Queen's letter produced £170,571 0s 10d.; the second only £30,167 14s. 4d.

304. Transactions of Society of Friends during the Famine in Ireland p. 49.

305. *Ibid.* Appendix vii, p. 334

306. The connection between Famine and Pestilence, and the Great Apostacy. By Nagnatus, p. 49. P.D. Hardy, Dublin, 1847. Halliday Pamphlets, Vol. 1990.

307. The Achill Missionary Herald for August, 1846, p. 88.

308. The Famine, a rod. By the Rev. Hugh M'Neill, p. 23.

309. The Famine, a rod, pp. 25, 26. The capitals and italics are Mr. M'Neill's.

310. Letter quoted in "Forster's Life of Dickens," written in the Autumn of 1846. Vol. II. p. 233.

311. "Journals, Conversations, and Essays relating to Ireland." by Nassau William Senior. Vol. II., Second Edition, p. 60.

312. "Memorandums made in Ireland in the Autumn of 1852." By John Forbes, M.D., F.R.S., Hon. D.C.L. Oxon., Physician to Her Majesty's Household. Vol. I. pp. 246 and 247. Dr. Forbes was afterwards knighted.

313. Letter of M'Carthy Downing, Esq., M.P., to the Author, dated Prospect House, Co. Cork, August 31st, 1874.

* * * * *

(NOTE A.)—
ABSENTEEISM: MR. M'CULLOGH's DEFENCE OF IT EXAMINED.

The question of Irish Absenteeism has, for a long time, been discussed by politicians and political economists; some maintaining it to be a great evil; some admitting its injurious effects, but in a modified way only; whilst others, with Mr. J.R. M'Culloch, maintain that, by the principles of economic science, Absenteeism is no evil at all.

Apart altogether from the views of political economists, there are certain evils which result from Absenteeism. 1. There is that estrangement between landlord and tenant, which must naturally exist in cases where the tenant seldom or never sees his landlord; has no intercourse with him; is unacquainted with the sound of his voice, from which no word of kindly encouragement ever reaches him; never hears of him, except when the agent demands, in his name, the rent, which is to be sent to England, or to whatever foreign country he may reside in. Even though the argument were true, that his living out of Ireland inflicts no real pecuniary loss upon Ireland, the impression on the tenant's mind is different, and helps to increase the estrangement between him and his landlord, which so generally exists, and which all must lament as an evil. 2. It is an old and a commonly accepted adage, that affairs thrive under the master's eye, and that those things which he neither sees nor takes an interest in exhibit the signs of neglect. As a resident landlord rides over his property, improvements will frequently suggest themselves to his mind; some of them often easily and inexpensively done, although important from their usefulness. He is sure, at any rate, to know the condition of his estate, and he can, with a just discernment, encourage the industrious, help the weak, urge forward the slow, and have a friendly word for all, whether he approves, or is obliged to find fault. The value of this mode of dealing with the people cannot be over estimated, especially in Ireland, where a kind word from a superior goes a great way.[314] An agent manages the property of an absentee. There are many such agents who are just and considerate, but the traditional character of an Irish land agent, resulting from long experience, is, that he is a haughty oppressive man, who has other interests to serve besides those of his employer; and who makes his employer's interests subservient to his own. Whether he thinks it a duty he owes his master, or that he believes it gives himself importance, an Irish land agent is frequently in the habit of acting in a proud, browbeating manner towards the tenants under him. I have seen a most respectable body of tenants, with their rent in their hands, stand with cowed and timid looks in the agent's office; they kept at as great a distance from him as space would allow; they were afraid to tender the rent, and yet they feared to hang back too long, as either course might bring down the ire of the great man upon them. His looks, his gestures, the few words he condescended to utter—even his manner of counting bank notes, which he thumped and turned over with a sort of insolent contempt,— all went to prove that those fears were not ill-founded. The scene forcibly reminded me of a group of children in the Zoological gardens, before the cage of one of the fiercer animals; they view him with awe, and, on account of his size and spots, with a certain admiration, but they are afraid of their lives to approach him. It is usual for a resident landlord to have an agent too, but he is subject to the personal observation, and under the immediate control of the landlord, who can be easily appealed to, if a misunderstanding should arise between him and any tenant. It is always a great satisfaction to the weaker party to have an opportunity of going, as they say, to the "fountain-head." It is bringing one's case before a higher tribunal when one feels he has not got justice in the court below.

520

3. Whether it is or is not the fact, that the landlord by living at home and spending his fortune amongst his people adds to the aggregate wealth of the nation, it is certain that his doing so is a partial and immediate good to the locality in which he resides. Often does the Irish peasant point to the decayed village, and the crumbling mansion, as evidences that the owner of the soil is an Absentee. 4. There is a special reason given by at least one English writer, why Irish landlords ought to be resident, and thus endeavour to gain the confidence of their tenants; and that is, because nine-tenths of the Irish estates have been confiscated from the native owners, and are held by men who differ from their tenants in country and religion; and their non-residence, and consequent want of sympathy with the people, perpetuates in the minds of those people the bitter traditions of rapine and conquest; so that, instead of feeling they are the tenants of kind, considerate landlords, they are apt to regard themselves, in some sort, as the despised slaves of conquerors, who, if they do not still look upon them as "Irish enemies," do not certainly entertain for them the feelings which ought to find a place in the breasts of landlords who look upon their tenants as something more than mere rent producers.

So much for the moral and social aspect of Absenteeism. Now, let us examine, a little, the ground taken up by Mr. J.R. M'Culloch, who maintains that, according to the accepted principles of political economy, the fact of Irish landed proprietors residing out of their country inflicts no injury upon it. For Mr. Prior's views on Absenteeism he manifests great contempt, but treats himself with a kind of respectful commiseration, as being, in spite of his ignorance of political economy, "a gentleman in other respect—of great candour and good sense." He quotes his assertion that the aggregate of the absentee rents, amounting then to £627,799 annually, was entirely sent to the Absentee landlords in treasure, "which," continues Mr. Prior, "is so great a burthen upon Ireland that I believe there is not in history an instance of any one country paying so large a yearly tribute (!) to another." The parenthetic note of astonishment is Mr.

M'Culloch's, who says, with regard to this passage, "it would really seem that in this, as in some other things, the universality and intensity of belief has been directly as the folly and falsehood of the thing believed."[315]

It was in his examination in 1825, before a Parliamentary Committee, that Mr. M'Culloch put forward his views on Irish Absenteeism. He was asked this question: "Supposing the largest export of Ireland were in live cattle, and that a considerable portion of rent had been remitted in that manner, does not such a mode of producing the means of paying rent, contribute less to the improvement of the poor than any extensive employment of them in labour would produce?" He replies: "Unless the means of paying rent are changed when the landlord goes home, his residence can have no effect whatever." "Would not," he is asked, "the population of the country be benefited by the expenditure among them of a certain portion of the rent, which (if he had been absent) would have been remitted (to England)?" "No," he replies, "I do not see how it could be benefited in the least. If you have a certain value laid out against Irish commodities in the one case, you will have a certain value laid out against them in the other. The cattle are either exported to England or they stay at home. If they are exported the landlord will obtain an equivalent for them in English commodities; it they are not he will obtain an equivalent for them in Irish commodities; so that in both cases the landlord lives on the cattle, or on the value of the cattle: and whether he lives in Ireland or England there is obviously just the very same amount of commodities for the people of Ireland to subsist upon."[316] Mr. Senior exposes this fallacy in the following words; "This reasoning assumes that the landlord, whilst resident in Ireland, himself personally devours all the cattle produced on his estates; for, on no other supposition can there be the very same amount of commodities for the people of Ireland to subsist upon, whether their cattle are retained in Ireland or exported."[317] It may be said with equal truth, that to assume, as Mr. M'Culloch assumes, the Irish absentee's residence in England to be of no advantage to the people there, is assuming that "himself personally" devours all the cattle

522

and corn sent to him in the shape of rent. But the landlord does not in either case devour all the beef and all the corn; by far the greater portion of those products go to house, and clothe, and feed the persons who minister to his various wants.

In the beginning of his Essay on Absenteeism Mr. M'Culloch, referring with apparent satisfaction to his evidence before the Committee, says, "it had been previously established, and is now universally conceded that the gentlemen who consume nothing in their families but what is brought from abroad are quite as good, as useful, and as meritorious subjects as they could be, if, they consume nothing but what is produced at home; and such being the case, it will require a sharper eye than has yet looked at this subject, to discover the great injury which is said to be done by their going abroad."[318]

With the greatest respect for Mr. M'Culloch's skill as a political economist, this proposition has neither been established nor conceded in the unlimited sense in which he here puts it forward. Enthusiastic men, who become enamoured of some favourite theory, are apt to attach too much importance to it—push it too far, and try to fit things into it which it will not contain, without being modified or enlarged. This has been the case with political economists to a remarkable extent; a fact which John Stuart Mill notices and complains of as injurious to the science.[319] The chief flaw in Mr. M'Culloch's apology for Absenteeism (as his essay may well be called) is, that he entirely overlooks the peculiar nature of Irish exports. Those exports consist almost exclusively of raw, or, to use Adam Smith's word, of *rude* produce; and where this is the case Mr. M'Culloch's principle will not hold without large modifications. Mr. Senior saw this, and, in dealing with Irish Absenteeism he modifies the principle accordingly. In discussing the proximate cause deciding the rate of wages, he lays down as his third proposition, that "It is inconsistent with the prevalent opinion,[320] that the non-residence of landlords, funded proprietors, mortgagees, and other unproductive consumers can be detrimental to the labouring inhabitants of a country *which does not export raw produce.*"

Mr. Senior here affirms Mr. M'Culloch's proposition, quoted above, but with the qualifying clause—"which does not export raw produce." I have italicised this clause because it contains the very exception which makes the general proposition inapplicable to Ireland, and to every country whose chief exports are, like Ireland's, raw produce.

To use the words of Mr. Senior, "If an Irish landlord reside on his estate he requires the services of certain persons, who must be also resident there to minister to his daily wants. He must have servants, gardeners, and, perhaps, gamekeepers. If he build a house, he must employ resident masons and carpenters; part of his furniture he may import, but the greater part of it must be made in his neighbourhood; a portion of his land, or, what comes to the same thing, a portion of his rent, must be employed in producing food, clothing, and shelter for all these persons, and for those who produce that food, clothing, and shelter. If he were to remove to England all these wants would be supplied by Englishmen. The land and capital which was formerly employed in providing the maintenance of Irish labourers, would be employed in producing corn and cattle to be exported to England, to provide the sustenance of English labourers. The whole quantity of commodities appropriated to the use of Irish labourers would be diminished, and that appropriated to the use of English labourers increased."[321] Giving credit for ordinary prudence to the persons employed by resident Irish landlords, they would save a part of their earnings, and the part saved would go to increase the capital of the country; but when the landlords reside in England the moneys so paid away go into the pockets of English servants and mechanics, and their savings are added to the sum of English capital; for it is a fundamental principle of Political Economy that capital and all additions to capital are the result of saving. Writers on Ireland have been long proclaiming with all their might, that the first and greatest want of that country is capital. Half a century ago, when Mr. M'Culloch published his views of Irish Absenteeism, the rents annually paid to our absentee landlords were set down at from four to four and millions of pounds sterling. They have very much increased since, but let us still accept four and a-half millions as the amount. Were the absentee landlords resident, the whole of that rental would not be spent at home, as some of it would go for foreign commodities, such as tea, sugar, wine; but the greater part of it would be spent at home. Now, although the savings of the employees of Irish landlords could not, perhaps, be called large in any one year, yet had those savings gone on from Mr. Prior's time—1729—taking into account the increase of capital by the use of capital,—who can calculate the additions that would have been made to Irish capital, by this means, during so long a period? And as Mr. Mill's first fundamental proposition respecting capital is, that "Industry is limited by capital," who can measure the consequences to Irish industry of the capital lost to it by Absenteeism?

But the soundness of the principle laid down by Mr. M'Culloch as universally received, and which Mr. Senior accepts (with the qualification affecting raw produce) has not passed unchallenged. For greater clearness I shall repeat that principle here. "The gentlemen," says Mr. M'Culloch, "who consume nothing in their families but what is brought from abroad are quite as good, as useful, and as meritorious subjects as they could be if they consume nothing but what is produced at home." And the reason for this is to be found in his Principles of Political Economy where he says that, Foreign commodities are always paid for by British commodities, therefore, the purchase of Foreign commodities encourages British industry as much as the purchase of British commodities" (Principles of Political Economy, p. 152). The important exception to this theorem arising from the *nature* of the commodities exported and imported has been already dealt with. Let us examine the vital principle of the theorem. "The capital," says Adam Smith, "which is employed in purchasing in one part of the country in order to sell in another, the produce of the industry of that country, generally replaces by every such operation two distinct capitals, that had both been employed in the agriculture or manufactures of that country, and thereby enables them to continue that employment. When it sends out from the residence of the merchant a certain value of commodities it generally brings back in return at least an equal value of other commodities. When both are the produce of domestic industry it necessarily replaces by every such operation two distinct capitals which had both been employed in supporting productive labour, and thereby enables them to continue that support. The capital which sends Scotch manufactures to London, and brings back English corn and manufactures to Edinburgh, necessarily replaces, by every such operation, two British capitals, which had both been employed in the agriculture or manufactures of Great Britain.

"The capital employed in purchasing foreign goods for home consumption, when this purchase is made with the produce of domestic industry, replaces too, by every such operation, two distinct capitals; but one of them only is employed in supporting domestic industry. The capital which sends British goods to Portugal, and brings back Portuguese goods to Great Britain, replaces, by every such operation, only one British capital. The other is a Portuguese one. Though the returns, therefore, of the foreign trade of consumption should be as quick as those of the home trade, the capital employed in it will give but one half of the encouragement to the industry or productive labour of the country.

"But the returns of the foreign trade of consumption are very seldom so quick as those of the home trade. The returns of the home trade generally come in before the end of the year, and sometimes three or four times in the year. The returns of the foreign trade of consumption seldom come in before the end of the year, and sometimes not till after two or three years. A capital, therefore, employed in the home trade, will sometimes make twelve operations, or be sent out and returned twelve times, before a capital employed in the foreign trade of consumption has made one. If the capitals are equal, therefore, the one will give four and twenty times more encouragement and support to the industry of the country than the other."[322]

If this position of Adam Smith's be tenable, it cannot be true, that the purchase of foreign commodities encourages British industry as much as the purchase of British commodities. In order to have a clear idea of his reasoning it will be useful to repeat some of the leading principles which regulate and explain the nature of capital. 1. Capital is usually defined to be the *accumulated stock of the produce of labour.* A definition which, if not completely satisfactory, is sufficiently correct for our present purpose. 2. *Capital is essential to production.* 3. *Capital employed in production is wholly consumed in the process of production.* "Capital," as Mill, and in fact as every political economist says, "is all consumed; though not by the capitalist. Part is exchanged for tools or machinery, which are worn out by use; part for seed or materials, which are destroyed as such, by by being sown or wrought up, and destroyed altogether by the consumption of the ultimate product. The remainder is paid to labourers, who consume it for their daily wants; or if they, in their turn, save any part, this also is not generally speaking, hoarded, but (through savings banks, benefit clubs, or some other channel) re-employed as capital, and consumed."[323] These principles open the way to the understanding of what Adam Smith means by the *replacing of capital.*

Capital is consumed in production, and must be replaced. How is it replaced? By the new product. *It reappears in the new product;* in the production of which it was consumed. Moreover it reappears with a profit to the capitalist, who has employed it for the purposes of production. Let us hear well in mind that the capital consumed in production is consumed, not by the capitalist himself, but in the purchase of various things necessary for production, and in wages. All this capital which is employed and consumed in production, is *the net spendable income of the producing nation.* And it is spent in food, raiment, lodging, and other necessaries; and of course in luxuries too; and when it is spent, or "consumed," as the word is, the nation, so far from being the poorer, has grown richer; because the capital consumed has reappeared, or, as Adam Smith says, *has been replaced* by the new product, and, in the usual course, with an increase in the form of profit.

It is plain, then, according to this reasoning, that for every portion of capital consumed in production, a new capital re-appears. If two capitals are consumed in production, two new capitals reappear in their place: if three are consumed, three reappear; and so on. Let us now go back to Adam Smith's words quoted above: "The capital which sends British goods to Portugal, and brings back Portuguese goods to Great Britain, replaces, by every such operation, only one British capital. The other is a Portuguese one. Though the returns, therefore, of the foreign trade of consumption should be as quick as those of the home trade, the capital employed in it will give but *one half* of the encouragement to the industry or productive labour of the country." Applying this principle to the subject in hand, we find that Absenteeism inflicts an injury upon Ireland, in addition to, and quite distinct from the one, which results from the *nature* of the commodities sent by Ireland to England. An Irish absentee in London buys British commodities with Irish commodities. In doing so, *he replaces* two capitals, one British and one Irish; but if he resides in Ireland, and buys Irish commodities with Irish commodities, *he replaces two Irish capitals* instead of one, as happens, when he resides in England; and thus gives double the encouragement to Irish industry which he would give to it if he resided in England.

"The entire price or gross value of every *home-made* article constitutes net revenue, net income to British subjects. Not a portion of the value, but the *whole value*, is resolvable into net income and revenue maintaining British families, and creating and sustaining British markets. Purchase British articles with British articles, and you create *two* such aggregate values, and two such markets for British industry. Whereas, on the contrary, the entire value of every foreign article imported is net income to the foreigner and sustains foreign markets. Purchase foreign articles with British articles, and you only create *one* value for your own benefit instead of creating *two*, and only *one* market for British industry instead of *two*. You lose the acquisition of the entire value on one side, which you might have had, as well as on the other, and you lose a market for British industry to the full extent of that gross value."[324]

If the principle laid down by Adam Smith were unsound, that the man who buys British commodities with British commodities replaces two British capitals, whilst he who buys foreign commodities with British commodities replaces but one British capital, Mr. M'Culloch had an inviting opportunity of exposing its unsoundness in the edition of *The Wealth of Nations* edited by him; and in fact he has written an elaborate note on the passage, but, as it seems to me, without proving the doctrine which it enunciates to be incorrect. Here is the portion of Mr. M'Culloch's footnote which deals with the subject: "Dr. Smith does not say that the importation of foreign commodities has any tendency to force capital abroad; and unless it did this, it is plain that his statement with respect to the effect of changing a home for a foreign trade of consumption, is quite inconsistent with the fundamental principle he has elsewhere established, that industry is always in proportion to the amount of capital." From this, his opening sentence, it would seem that Mr. M'Culloch mistook the force and tendancy of Adam Smith's reasoning, who does not, in the passage annotated by Mr. M'Culloch, advocate the change of a foreign for a home trade of consumption. He only goes to prove that a home trade is more profitable to a nation than a foreign one, in as much as *it replaces two home capitals*, whilst the foreign trade replaces but *one*. For a country with vast manufactories, like Great Britain, the home trade would not be at all sufficient, but—*as far as it goes*—it is double as advantageous as the foreign trade. Adam Smith seeks to prove no more. But Mr. M'Culloch meets the question more directly as follows: "Suppose, for the sake of illustration, that the case put by Dr. Smith actually occurs—that the Scotch manufactures are sent to Portugal; it is obvious, if the same demand continue in London for these manufactures as before they began to be sent abroad, that additional capital and labourers will be required to furnish commodities for both the London and Portuguese markets. In

529

this case, therefore, instead of the industry of the country sustaining any diminution from the export of Scotch manufactures to a foreign country, it would evidently be augmented, and a new field would be discovered for the profitable employment of stock."

As this reasoning is only a continuation of the misconception of Adam Smith's meaning just noticed, a very few words upon it will suffice. If the same demand continue in London for the Scotch manufactures as before they were sent to Portugal, or elsewhere, the Scotch manufacturers will be only too glad to continue to supply London and Portugal too; and the trade of the nation will be expanded; and the capital of the nation will be augmented by the foreign trade, because by that foreign trade British capital is replaced, and with a profit; but surely this does not in any way disturb the principle that the Scotch manufactures sold in London replace, or re-produce two British capitals, whilst those sold in Portugal replace, or reproduce only one.

From these considerations on Absenteeism, it may, I think, be fairly inferred that popular belief regarding its injurious effects is well founded, although misconceptions may be entertained as to the precise way in which the injury occurs.

FOOTNOTES:

314.   "We started at daybreak for Glenties, thirty miles distant, over the mountains; and after leaving the improved cottages and farms on the Gweedore estate, soon came upon the domain of an absentee proprietor, the extent of which may be judged of by the fact, that our road lay for more than twenty miles through it. This is the poorest parish in Donegal, and no statement can be too strong with respect to the wretched condition, the positive misery and starvation in which the cottiers and small farmers on this immense domain are found."—*James H. Tuke's Report to the Relief Committee of the Society of Friends.* Appendix, p. 149. "We proceeded to Glenties from Dungloe. still on the same property; and throughout our journey met with the most squalid scenes of misery which the imagination can well conceive. Whilst thousands

of acres of reclaimable land lie entirely neglected and uncultivated, there are thousands of men both willing and anxious to obtain work, but unable to procure it."—*Ib.* p. 150.

315.   Note to his Essay on Absenteeism.
316.   From the Report, 814, Sess. 1826. Quoted by Mr. Senior.
317.   Political Economy, 5th Ed., p. 167.
318.   Political Economy. Book 3, c. I.
319.   Treatise on Political Economy, pp. 223-4.
320.   That is the common opinion of Political Economists.
321.   Political Economy, p. 155-6. 5th Ed.
322.   Adam Smith here regards Scotland as an integral part of Great Britain, the same as he would regard Yorkshire or Lancashire. *Wealth of Nations*, Book II., Chap. v.
323.   Principles of Political Economy, Book I, c. v. sect. 5.
324.   "*Sophisms of Freetrade*, and popular Political Economy examined." By a Barrister, *4th. Ed.*

* * * * *

(NOTE B.)—
SMITH O'BRIEN'S REFUSAL TO SERVE ON A COMMITTEE OF THE HOUSE OF COMMONS.

At this period the railway mania was at its full height, and so many Bills for the construction of various lines were before Parliament, that what was called a Committee of Selection was appointed by the House of Commons. This Committee divided those railway Bills into groups, and a Sub-committee was formed to consider and report on each group. Smith O'Brien was named on the Committee whose duty it was to examine group eleven. Mr. Estcourt was its chairman. In order to insure punctual attendance, the House, on the 12th of February, passed resolutions declaring the attendance of members upon such Committees to be compulsory. In due time the Committee on group eleven met, but Mr. O'Brien was absent; which circumstance the chairman reported to the House, as he was bound to do; whereupon the Speaker enquired if Mr. O'Brien were in his place. He was; and rising thanked the Speaker for the opportunity he afforded him (Mr. O'Brien) of explaining, but he had, he said, done so in a correspondence with the chairman of the Committee of Selection; he would withdraw nothing he had written on the subject, and with this observation he bowed to the Speaker and left the House. Mr. Estcourt, as chairman of the Committee on which Mr. O'Brien was appointed to serve, then rose and said it was his painful duty to give a narrative of facts that would explain the matter as far as he was concerned in it. He called attention to the resolutions of the House passed in February, compelling the attendance of members on Committees. Mr. O'Brien, he said, had received notice on the 3rd of April, that his attendance would be required on the 27th, in reply to which he wrote to him (Mr. Estcourt), enclosing a letter which he (Mr. O'Brien) had written the year before, to the effect, that he would not serve upon any Committee for the consideration of private Bills not having reference to Ireland. His words were: "Desiring that none but the representatives of the Irish nation should legislate for Ireland, we have no wish to intermeddle with the affairs of England or Scotland, except so far as they may be connected with the interests of Ireland, or with the general policy of the empire." Having read the above, Mr. Estcourt drew special attention to the next passage: "In obedience to this principle, I have abstained from voting on English or Scotch questions of a local nature; and the same motive now induces me to decline attendance on Committees on any private Bills, except such as relate to Ireland." The answer, Mr. Estcourt said, he had given to this communication was, that the Committee could not recognise such an excuse; he reminded Mr. O'Brien of the resolutions of the 12th of February, but offered to consult for his convenience, inasmuch as important Irish business was before the House, by postponing, if possible, his attendance to a later period; but that unless he had heard from him (Mr. O'Brien), assenting to this, he must abide the coming vote of the House on Wednesday. Mr. O'Brien did reply, telling Mr. Estcourt that his former communication contained his final determination; adding, that the matter was not one of private convenience but of public principle.

This statement Mr. Estcourt followed up by a motion, "That William Smith O'Brien, Esq., having disobeyed the order of the House, by refusing to attend the Committee to which the railway group eleven has been referred, has been guilty of a contempt of this House."

On this resolution having been put, O'Connell rose and asked the House to pause before it passed it. In the first place, he said, the House should consider, how far the Act of Union with Ireland gave the power to the members of that House, to enforce the process of contempt and committal against the representatives of Ireland; there was no common law jurisdiction for it, and before 1800 there could be no jurisdiction at all, for both that House and the Parliament of Great Britain disclaimed, in 1783, any species of interference with the representatives of Ireland. The jurisdiction, then, of this House could not stand on common law, nor upon the Act of Union, because that Act gave no jurisdiction. In the second place, as to the Committee of Selection, the question was, by the law and usage of Parliament, could they delegate to a committee the power to make regulations punishable by "Contempt," by placing the party in custody, whereas the House had not the jurisdiction by common law to compel the attendance of members. He took it, the House had no such common law power, because by the Sixth of Henry VIII. it was enacted, that the members of that House should attend the House. Now if the common law jurisdiction existed, this statute would have been wholly unnecessary.

The Attorney-General, Sir William Follett, replied, that all the members of the House had consented to the resolutions of the 12th of February, thereby making them binding upon themselves; and that as Mr. O'Brien might have objected then, but did not, he was of course bound by them; and as to the Act of Union, he considered there was no force in the argument drawn from it, because the third article of that Act had made one Parliament of the two, enacting "that the said United Kingdom be represented in one and the same Parliament, to be styled the Parliament of the United Kingdom of Great Britain and Ireland."

Sir Robert Peel, addressing himself to the most practical point of the discussion, said the question was—"Have we or have we not the power to require the attendance of members on public committees?" He apprehended there could be no distinction between service on Committees and service in the House; and if the Act of Union did not give the power, it was from a belief that such a power was inherent in Parliament. The great man, he said, who drew up those Acts of Union for Ireland and Scotland did not take a statutable sanction, for they all rested on higher grounds.

Sir Thomas Wilde, in giving his view of the case, made a distinction with regard to the common law; saying, that if there was no authority under the common law of the land to compel attendance on committees, there was under the common law of Parliament; a law not so old as the common law of the land, but as old as was necessary. Complimenting O'Connell as a lawyer, he believed, he said, the opinion he had given was not the result of his legal knowledge, but of a laudable desire to release his friend from a difficulty. The House, he said, could send the public to Committees, why not a member? Had they more power over the public than the members of their own House? The question was not whether neglecting to attend a Committee was contempt of the House or not; the question was, whether disobedience to the order of the House did or did not constitute a contempt of the authority of the house.

The resolution having been put, was carried by 133 to 13.

It was then moved that Mr. W.S. O'Brien be given up to the Sergeant-at-Arms. Mr. Ward moved the postponement of the motion to Thursday, the 30th of April; the Premier agreed, and it was accordingly postponed. Smith O'Brien, remaining fixed in his determination, was on that day taken into custody by Sir Wm. Gossett, the Sergeant-at-Arms, and lodged in prison. After being twenty-five days there, Mr. Frederick Shaw made a motion for his release, without, he said, having consulted him, and in fact believing such motion to be contrary to his wishes. It was made on the ground that he had been sufficiently punished by twenty-five days' imprisonment. It was carried *nem con*, that he be released, "on paying his fees."

Although several of the leading Irish Liberal members sustained Smith O'Brien on this occasion, they did not approve of his persisting in his refusal to serve on the Committee, as there was no principle vindicated by his persistence or his imprisonment; his first refusal and the discussion upon it having effected all that could be usefully done in the case.

Whilst Smith O'Brien was yet in prison, the following case was submitted to Mr. Anstey on his behalf:

"1. Whether there is any, and what inherent power or privilege in the House of Commons to imprison its members for constructive contempt of its authority?

"2. Whether there is any and what prescriptive power or privilege in said House to imprison its members for such contempt?

"3. Whether the refusal to serve on the Committee in question can be construed into a contempt of the authority of the house?

"4. Whether, assuming the commitment or detainer to have been unlawful, Mr. Smith O'Brien has any and what legal remedy, and against whom?

"5. Whether the House of Commons has any, and what right, to insist on his paying into the fee fund of the House any, and what fees—either by way of preliminary condition to his discharge out of the custody of the Sergeant-at-Arms or otherwise?"

Mr. Anstey's opinion was in the following terms:

"I am of opinion that the commitment and imprisonment of Mr. Smith O'Brien, by order of the House of Commons for the constructive contempt set forth in the vote and proceedings of the House, and the other papers which have been laid before me, are, *in every respect, illegal.* The House, in my opinion, has no power to enforce its orders by any such penalty, except under the authority of the statute or common law, and no such authority can be shown to justify the commitment and imprisonment complained of. I am further of opinion that, even supposing the House to possess such authority, still the informality of the proceedings in the present case has been such as to vitiate them *ab initio*, and to render null and void everything that has been done under the colour of such authority."

Mr. Anstey further maintained that the Speaker's Warrant, under which Smith O'Brien was arrested, was informal and invalid, that the House had no general authority of commitment for non-attendance on "calls"—that such authority for not attending *select* committees was never claimed until the previous session; that "the Committee to which Railway Group No. 11 had been referred" was unduly appointed under the Standing Orders, and that Mr. O'Brien had his right of action against the Speaker and the Sergeant-at-Arms.

* * * * *

(NOTE C.)—
TREASURY MINUTE, *dated August 31st, 1846.*

My Lords have before them the Act 10 Vict., cap. 107,—"To facilitate the employment of the labouring poor for a limited period in distressed districts in Ireland," and proceed to consider the revised instructions which the provisions of this Act and the experience which has been acquired from the operations for the relief of the people suffering from the failure of the potato crop in Ireland, since the month of November last, render it desirable should be issued to the Board of Works, and to Commissary-General Sir R. Routh, who is in charge of the duties lately executed by the Relief Commission.

"No authority can, from the present date, be given for the execution of any new works under the 9th Vict., cap. 1; and such works as may hereafter be required for the relief of distress must be presented and sanctioned according to the provisions of the 10th Vict., cap. 107."

The Board of Works were instructed by the Treasury Minute, dated the 21st ultimo, to bring to an early close all the works under the 9th Vict., cap. 2, which were not required for the relief of urgent distress; and the Board were informed, that if the parties interested desired that works so discontinued should afterwards be recommenced and completed, it was open to them to take the usual steps to provide for that object, either by obtaining loans secured by grand jury presentment, or by other means.

Their Lordships desire that the Board of Works will report to what extent works have been discontinued under these instructions, on the ground of their not being really required for the purpose of giving relief, and that it may be understood, in accordance with the passage above adverted to in the Minute of the 21st July, that if it should become necessary to recommence any such works, the renewal of them must be provided for either in the manner above referred to, or under the 10th Vict., cap. 107.

With a view to give every practicable assistance to the presentment sessions, the Board of Works should be prepared with plans and estimates of those works in each district in which relief is likely to be required, on which the destitute poor might with the greatest public advantage be employed; and an officer of the Board should be in attendance at the sessions, to furnish every explanation that may be called for.

In order to prevent labourers from being induced to leave their proper employments and to congregate on the relief works, in the hope of getting regularly paid money wages in return for a smaller quantum of work than they have been accustomed to give, the following rules ought, in their Lordships' opinion, to be strictly observed:—

No person should be employed on any relief works who can obtain employment on other public works, or in farming or other private operations in the neighbourhood.

The wages given to persons employed on relief works should, in every case, be at least 2d. a day less than the average rate of wages in the district.

And the persons employed on relief works should, to the utmost possible extent, be paid in proportion to the work actually done by them.

Their Lordships suggest for the consideration of the Lord Lieutenant, that it may be advisable that in every case in which it may be determined to assemble extraordinary sessions, for tin presentment of works under the 10th Vict, cap. 107, instructions should also be issued to the lieutenant of the county, to reassemble the relief committees of the districts in which such works are proposed to be carried on, making such changes in the individuals composing the committees as circumstances may require; or, if no relief committees have yet been organized in the districts in question, to appoint new committees in accordance with the rules prescribed by the relief commission.

Their Lordships also suggest that, in order to obviate inconveniences which have been experienced during the late relief operations, the following alterations should be made in the instructions under which the local relief committees have hitherto acted:—

First, with regard to the assistance given by the relief committees in the proper appropriation of the relief provided under the 10th Viet. cap. 107, by means of public works:—

That tickets should not hereafter be issued by the relief committees entitling persons to employment on such public works. That, instead thereof, the relief committees should furnish (according to a form to be supplied to them for that purpose) the officers in charge of the works on the part of the Board of Works, with lists of persons requiring relief, noting them in the order in which they are considered to be entitled to priority, either on account of their large families or from any other cause; that the committees should revise these lists from time to time, as occasion may require, and that the officers of the Board of Works, from the information contained in these lists, or acquired by them from other sources, should themselves furnish tickets entitling persons to employment on the relief works, for certain limited periods, according to the circumstances of each case.

Secondly, as regards the functions performed by the relief committees, independently of the relief works carried on under the provisions of Acts of Parliament.

Their lordships consider that donations in aid of private subscriptions may be made, when necessary, as heretofore, from the public funds placed for that purpose at the disposal of the Lord Lieutenant; and that these donations may continue to be, as a general rule, in the proportion of from one-third to one-half of the amount of the private subscriptions, according to the extent of the destitution and the means of the subscribers.

But their lordships are of opinion, that, in consideration of the assistance so to be given from the public purse, the proceedings of the relief committees in the appropriation of the funds administered by them should be subjected to any degree of control on the part of the Government that may be considered desirable; for which purpose their accounts and correspondence should, at all times, be open to the inspection of Government officers appointed for the purpose, and any further explanations that may be required on any particular point should be immediately furnished.

In order to keep in check, as far as possible, the social evils incident to an extensive system of relief, it is indispensably necessary that the relief committees should not sell the meal or other food provided by them, except in small quantities to persons who are known to have no other means of procuring food; that the price at which the meal is sold should, as nearly as possible, be the same as the market prices which prevail in the neighbourhood; that the committees should not give a higher rate of wages, nor exact a smaller quantum of work, in any works carried on by them from funds at their own disposal, than is the case in respect to the works carried on under the superintendence of the Board of Works, and that works should be carried on by them only to the extent to which private employment is proved not to be available.

The serious attention of every person who will have to take a part in the measures of relief rendered necessary by the new and more complete failure of the potato crop should be particularly called to this important fact, that the limitations and precautions which have been prescribed to the Government boards and officers in carrying out the relief operations, with the object of rendering the necessary interference with the labour and provision markets productive of the smallest possible disturbance of the ordinary course of trade and industry, will be rendered nugatory if the same prudence and reserve are not practised by the relief committees in the administration of the funds placed at their disposal by private or public benevolence; and their Lordships therefore feel it to be their duty earnestly to request that every person concerned will, to the extent of the influence possessed by him, endeavour to secure such a restriction of the measures of relief to cases of real destitution, and such a just consideration for the interests of merchants and dealers, in the free exercise of whose callings the public welfare is so deeply concerned, that instead of the habitual dependence upon charitable aid which might otherwise be apprehended from the extensive measures of relief in progress, every description of trade and industry may be stimulated by them, and the bonds of society may become more firmly knit, by the benevolent and intelligent cooperation of the different orders and ranks of which it is composed, to avert a common calamity, and to prepare for recommencing the ordinary occupations of social life with advantages which are at present only imperfectly enjoyed in some parts of Ireland.

The limited grant fund, provided by the 10th Vic., cap. 109, entitled, "an Act to authorise a further issue of money in aid of public works of acknowledged utility in poor districts in Ireland," is, according to the terms of the Act, applicable only to the case of unimproved districts, like parts of the Counties Kerry, Galway, Mayo, and Donegal, where, although roads and other works would be productive of more than usual public advantage, the districts are too poor to bear the whole expense of them; and the Act therefore directs that in cases in which the repayment of loans to the amount of at least a moiety of the estimated expense of such works shall have been secured, and such further contributions shall have been made as the Commissioners of Her Majesty's Treasury shall think fit to require from the individuals principally interested in the projected works, such aid shall be afforded from this fund in the shape of grants, as the occasion may appear to require.

The applications which may be received for grants under this Act will have to be carefully examined and inquired into by the Commissioners of Public Works, who will recommend for sanction those works which appear to them to combine the greatest permanent utility with the relief of urgent distress, taking care that the proprietors specially interested are required to contribute in addition to their share of the general assessment for the repayment of half the expense of the works, sums proportioned in some degree to the special benefits they will derive from them.

My Lords have considered with the careful attention which the importance of the subject demands the measures proper to be taken, with a view to continue the late commissariat operations to the extent which may be absolutely necessary for the purpose of providing supplies of food for sale in districts to which the ordinary operations of the provision trade cannot be expected to extend, the strictest regard being at the same time paid to the pledge which has been given, not to interfere in any case in which there is a reasonable expectation that the market will be supplied by mercantile enterprise; and they will proceed to state the course which appears to them to be the best adapted to secure the important object in view.

Their Lordships have already given directions that no portion of the stock of meal remaining in store in the different depôts should be sold merely for the sake of disposing of it, of which depôts they will relieve Commissary-General Coffin, who will remain on full pay, with a view to his being employed hereafter, as the occasion may require.

It has been fully established by the experience of the late operations, that the ports on the northern, eastern, and southern coasts, from Londonderry to Cork, and those parts of the interior which are ordinarily supplied from them, may safely be left to the foresight and enterprise of private merchants; and it will only be necessary to the government, so far as this part of Ireland is concerned, to take effectual precautions that the supplies introduced by private traders from abroad are properly protected, both while they are in transit and when they are stored for future consumption; and for this purpose their Lordships rely upon the Lord Lieutenant making every necessary arrangement in communication with the Commander of the Forces in Ireland, and the Inspector-General of the Constabulary Force.

Acting on this principle, their Lordships have directed that the supplies of food now in store should be concentrated without delay at the following depôts:—

In the interior—Longford, Banagher.

On the coast—Limerick, Galway, Westport, Sligo.

And Commissary-General Hewetson has been instructed to take immediate steps for the transfer of the quantity remaining in store in the depôt at Cork to Limerick, in the charge.

Subordinate depôts will be established, under the charge of the constabulary, at other places on the western coast, as the necessity for taking such a step may become apparent.

Their Lordships desire that it may be fully understood that even at those places at which government depôts will be established for the sale of food, *the depôts will not be opened while food can be obtained by the people from private dealers at reasonable prices*; and that even when the depôts are opened, *the meal will, if possible, be sold at such prices as will allow of the private trader selling at the same price with a reasonable profit.*

The Relief Commission ceased on the 15th ultimo, since which period Commissary-General Sir Randolph Routh has continued to transact such business as required immediate attention; and, considering the experience which has been acquired by that officer, and his well-proved ability for the task, their Lordships are of opinion that the duties confided to the Relief Commission during the late operations may with great public advantage be entrusted to Sir Randolph Routh, acting under the authority of the Lord Lieutenant, and in constant communication with this Board.

Their Lordships have taken steps to procure the early arrival in this country, from the stations where they are employed abroad, of a sufficient number of well qualified commissariat officers, not only to take charge of the depôts which it has been determined to retain, but also, under the orders of Sir Randolph Routh, to communicate with the local relief committees, and to afford, through him, to Her Majesty's Government, correct information as to the state of the districts in which they will be stationed.

Measures have also been taken for strengthening the Board of Works, to enable it to meet the coming emergency, on which subject a separate communication will this day be made to the Board of Works, and his Excellency the Lord Lieutenant.

Transmit a copy of this Minute to Mr. Redington, and request that he will move the Lord Lieutenant, if he shall concur therein, to give the necessary directions in regard to such of the arrangements as more immediately depend upon his Excellency for carrying them into effect.

Also transmit a copy to the Commissioners of Public Works, and to Commissary-General Sir Randolph Routh, for their information and guidance.

* * * * *

(NOTE D.)—
THE "LABOUCHERE LETTER," AUTHORIZING REPRODUCTIVE EMPLOYMENT.

Dublin Castle, *5th October, 1846.*

"Sir—I am directed by the Lord Lieutenant to inform you that His Excellency has had under his consideration the various representations which have been made to him of the operation of the Poor employment Act, and of the difficulty of finding, in the greater number of baronies, public works upon which it would be expedient or beneficial to expend money to the extent requisite for affording employment to the people during the existence of the present distress; and with a view of obviating the bad effects of a great expenditure of money in the execution of works comparatively unproductive, he desires that the Commissioners of Public Works will direct the officers acting under them, in the respective counties, to consider and report upon such works of a reproductive character and permanent utility as may be presented, in the manner hereinafter mentioned, at any Sessions held under the above Act; and His Excellency will be prepared to sanction and approve of such of those works as may be recommended by the Board, and so presented, in the same manner as if they had been strictly 'public works,' and presented as such in the manner required by the Act.

"1. The Presentment Sessions will estimate the sum which it may be necessary to raise off the barony for the purpose of affording employment.

"2. They will also ascertain the proportion of such assessment, which, according to the last poor law valuation may be chargeable upon each electoral division of an union or portion of an electoral division (if the whole shall not be included) in the barony; and they will obtain for this purpose, from the clerk of each poor law union, a copy of such valuation.

"3. They will present for such useful and profitable works to be executed in each electoral division, to the amount of its proportion of the assessment ascertained as above.

"In the case of drainage, however, and subsoiling, so far as it shall be connected with drainage, an undertaking shall be given in writing, and transmitted with the presentments by the person or persons whose lands are proposed to be drained (being 'proprietor' in the terms of the Act 5 and 6 Vic., chap. 89), stating that the money so to be expended shall be a charge exclusively on the lands so to be improved, and be levied from the same, according to an award made by the Commissioners, as under the last mentioned Act and its amendments.

"His Excellency wishes it to be further understood that, in case these regulations are not acted upon, and the portions of the assessment which would be leviable from each electoral division, are not presented to be expended on some work, within such division, the proceedings at such Sessions must be considered with strict reference to the provisions of the 9th and 10th Victoria, cap. 107.

"His Excellency considering also that many baronies have already held Sessions under that Act, to which baronies the opportunity of making applications in the manner now prescribed has not been afforded, it is his desire that all works already sanctioned in these baronies, or applied for, and which it may become requisite to sanction in order to afford continued employment, shall be proceeded with until other Sessions may be conveniently held in such baronies.

"His Excellency, in taking upon himself the responsibility, under the urgent circumstances of the case, of inviting the magistrates and cess-payers to provide employment for the people by the execution of useful and reproductive works, confidently trusts, with their assistance and the blessing of the Almighty on their united exertions, that the calamity with which it has pleased Providence to afflict Ireland may yet in its results become conducive to the production of a greater abundance of human food from the soil, and to the future permanent improvement of the country, I have the honour to be, sir, your obedient servant.

"H. LABOUCHERE.
The Chairman of the Board of Public Works."

* * * * *

END.